THE LIFE OF THE WORLD TO COME

Resurrection, Seeing God, and the Christian Hope

Isaac Augustine Morales, OP

Baker Academic
a division of Baker Publishing Group
Grand Rapids, Michigan

Published by Baker Academic
a division of Baker Publishing Group
Grand Rapids, Michigan
BakerAcademic.com

Printed in the United States of America

Library of Congress Cataloging-in-Publication Data

Names: Morales, Isaac Augustine, 1976– author
Title: The life of the world to come : resurrection, seeing God, and the Christian hope / Isaac Augustine Morales, OP.
Description: Grand Rapids, Michigan : Baker Academic, a division of Baker Publishing Group, [2026] | Includes bibliographical references and index.
Identifiers: LCCN 2026021052 | ISBN 9781540966650 paperback | ISBN 9781493453467 ebook | ISBN 9781493453474 pdf
Subjects: LCSH: Resurrection—History of doctrines | Catholic Church—Doctrines—History
Classification: LCC BT873 .M66 2026
LC record available at https://lccn.loc.gov/2026021052

Nihil obstat:
Rev. Carleton Parker Jones, OP
Censor Deputatus
July 30, 2025

Imprimi potest:
Very Rev. Allen B. Moran, OP
Prior Provincial
August 1, 2025

Approbatio:
Most Reverend Bruce A. Lewandowski, CSsR
Bishop of Providence
August 18, 2025

Baker Publishing Group publications use paper produced from sustainable forestry practices and postconsumer waste whenever possible.

26 27 28 29 30 31 32 7 6 5 4 3 2 1

"This book is characterized by remarkable intellectual breadth. Isaac Morales writes, naturally, as a Dominican, thinking his own Roman Catholic theology in dialogue with Irenaeus, Thomas, and especially Augustine. But above all, Morales is an interpreter of Scripture; hence these pages are full of masterful philology, historical criticism, and biblical theology. Whether you are Catholic like Morales, Protestant like me, or otherwise, you will find here one of the very best discussions of eschatology from any living scholar."

—**Matthew V. Novenson**, Princeton Theological Seminary

"What are we hoping for? What does it mean to say that we will see God? How should we understand the resurrection of the dead? These are the questions Isaac Augustine Morales addresses in this successful synthesis of biblical, patristic, and medieval theology, in which he shows how Irenaeus, Augustine, and Aquinas integrated the hope for resurrection with the beatific vision. Engaging and clearly written, Morales's study is a model of biblical theology that enriches both biblical and theological studies of the resurrection."

—**Frank J. Matera**, The Catholic University of America (emeritus)

"It is a rare scholar who can combine a responsible reading of Scripture's literal sense with careful attention to how those same Scriptures have been received and molded in the Church's theological tradition. In this exemplary book, Morales avails himself of both Scripture and tradition to unpack the way in which the beatific vision will be realized through the resurrected bodies of the redeemed. Though the former has been thought by some to be limited to the realm of the spirit or intellect alone, Morales shows us the crucial role that the resurrection of Christ and the redeemed will play."

—**Gary A. Anderson**, University of Notre Dame (emeritus)

"Isaac Morales has given us a wonderful model of a close reading of the Bible that uses both the tools of modern critical scholarship and the riches of the Christian tradition. What is more, this book is not a mere intellectual exercise but is written to bring into clearer focus the Christian hope for life everlasting. Morales demonstrates the harmony between eschatological themes of reign, rest, worship, vision, and resurrection, which will no doubt prompt further consideration by scholars and believers alike."

—**Elizabeth Klein**, Augustine Institute

"An intellectually stimulating and edifying account of the coherence of humanity's supreme good consisting in both the bodily resurrection and the vision of God. Wide-ranging in canonical scope, careful in exegetical argument, and illuminating in its drawing upon church tradition, this is theological exegesis at its finest!"

—**Joshua W. Jipp**, University of Notre Dame

"Isaac Morales's *The Life of the World to Come* is a lucid and compelling presentation of the case, biblical and traditional, for holding the promise of bodily resurrection together with that of beatific vision. Only when these are kept together, and neither one is permitted to absorb or dilute the other, is the fullness of the Christian promise preserved. An especially compelling aspect of Morales's work is his treatment of worship as a category that permits us to see why and how resurrection and vision require one another."

—**Paul Griffiths**, theologian and author of *Israel: A Christian Grammar*

For
Judith Beall,
Barbara Bolger,
Richard Hays,
and Pamela Mattox,
in memoriam

It is, after all, the one true and only happy life, namely, that, immortal and incorruptible in body and in spirit, we contemplate the delight of the Lord for eternity.

—St. Augustine, *Letter to Proba*

Contents

Preface

Like my previous book, *The Bible and Baptism*, the current study gestated for about ten years. It began as a paper for an eschatology course taught by Michael Root at the Catholic University of America in the fall of 2015. I'm grateful to Michael for giving me the opportunity to begin thinking through a question that had puzzled me for some time: How do the resurrection of the body and the beatific vision fit together, so to speak? What does each contribute to our ultimate beatitude? (The question was first planted by Richard Hays in a lecture on 1 Cor. 15 in a course I took many years ago as a third-year undergraduate. Hays challenged my simplistic understanding of the afterlife. For this challenge, and for much else besides, I will always be grateful to my late doctoral adviser.) Soon after, an edited version of the essay appeared as an article in *Pro Ecclesia*,[1] and during the academic year 2017–18 I expanded it into a thesis as part of the requirements for the Licentiate in Sacred Theology at the Pontifical Faculty of the Immaculate Conception. Thomas Joseph White, OP, who supervised the thesis, kindly encouraged me to continue to develop and ultimately publish the argument. At that point, however, the project went on the back burner, as I resumed a teaching career that had been interrupted by joining the Order of Preachers in 2012 and turned my attention to the baptism book. The past few years have given me the opportunity to return to the project, with particular intensity during a sabbatical over the academic year 2024–25. I trust that this study is a much better work for the time it has spent simmering.

Though I am, by training, a New Testament scholar, this book is not a traditional work of New Testament scholarship. Rather, this study explores two mysteries of the faith—the vision of God and the resurrection of the body—through a reading of the Scriptures in conversation with both contemporary

1. I. Morales, "With My Body I Thee Worship."

biblical scholarship and some of the great interpreters of the Christian tradition. Because this is a work of theology, and I write as a believer primarily (though not exclusively) for believers, I frequently use the first-person pronoun without apology. I feel no compulsion—nor do I see any good reason—to perpetuate the pretense of scholarly neutrality.[2]

Augustine of Hippo suggests that giving thanks to God for his generosity and mercy will be one of our primary activities in the next life.[3] It is with great pleasure that I now thank those the Lord has put in my life who have contributed to this project in various ways. Thanks are due, first, to numerous friends and colleagues who either read and commented on drafts of chapters or discussed different aspects of my argument with me. In particular, I would like to thank Gary Anderson, Lewis Ayres, Michael Barber, Rick Barry, Markus Bockmuehl, Justin Bolger, OP, Andrew Davison, Colum Dever, John Anthony Dunne, Simon Gaine, OP, Andrew Geist, Andrew Hofer, OP, Sam Johnson, Liz Klein, Stephen Long, David Moffitt, Augustine Reisenauer, OP, John Sehorn, Thomas Joseph White, OP, and Logan Williams. Travis Lacy and Sister Agnes Maria of St. John, OP, generously read the entire manuscript and offered invaluable feedback. Once again, it has been a joy to work with the staff at Baker Academic. Thanks especially to Jim Kinney and Bryan Dyer for their enthusiastic support of my work and to Tim West, whose keen editorial eye made numerous improvements to both the prose and the style of the finished product. All errors in judgment with respect to the argument, of course, remain mine. I am also grateful to Tom Wright for sharing with me the manuscript of his book *God's Homecoming* before it went to press. My criticisms should not take away from the fact that we agree on much more than we disagree, and I am indebted to him, in addition to Richard Hays, for impressing upon me early on in my studies the importance of the resurrection. The bulk of this book was drafted during a wonderful sabbatical stay at Blackfriars in Oxford. The warm welcome and hospitality my Dominican brothers extended to me during that time exemplified the psalmist's vision of fraternal charity (Ps. 133:1)—thank you! Thanks also to Providence College for the sabbatical that gave me the time I needed to complete this project.

Portions of chapters 1–3 of this book have been adapted from my article "Genesis, the Threefold End of Human Beings, and Biblical Eschatology."[4] Chapters 11 and 12, as well as the epilogue, have been adapted from my unpublished STL thesis, "The Life of the World to Come."

2. For a deft critique of this all-too-common fiction, see Ratzinger, "Biblical Interpretation in Crisis."

3. *Civ*. 22.30.

4. Isaac Augustine Morales, "Genesis, the Threefold End of Human Beings, and Biblical Eschatology," *Journal of Theological Interpretation* 13, no. 2 (2019): 200–218, doi: 10.5325/jtheointe.13.2.0200. Copyright © 2019 The Pennsylvania State University Press. Used by permission of The Pennsylvania State University Press.

Unless otherwise noted, biblical quotations are taken from the NRSVue, and words or phrases in italics indicate my emphasis. With respect to translations of the works of Augustine and Aquinas, I have consistently modified biblical quotations by putting them in quotation marks rather than in italics and/or bold type. I have also removed the in-text biblical citations.

As I was writing this manuscript, three dear friends passed away from cancer within the span of about three weeks. About six months later, shortly after I submitted the manuscript to Baker, another cherished friend unexpectedly passed away. I dedicate this book to their memory, with the prayer that their loved ones and I will see them again in the life of the world to come.

Isaac Augustine Morales, OP
Feast of St. Teresa of Ávila, 2025

Abbreviations

General

cf.	*confer*, compare
chap(s).	chapter(s)
e.g.	*exempli gratia*, for example
ESV	English Standard Version
JPS	Jewish Publication Society
lit.	literally
LXX	Septuagint
MT	Masoretic Text
NASB	New American Standard Bible
NETS	New English Translation of the Septuagint
NRSVue	New Revised Standard Version, Updated Edition
NT	New Testament
OT	Old Testament

Ancient and Medieval Sources

I Ad Cor.	Thomas Aquinas, *Super I Epistolam ad Corinthios lectura* (*Commentary on the First Letter of Saint Paul to the Corinthians*)
I Ad Thess.	Thomas Aquinas, *Super I Epistolam ad Thessalonicenses lectura* (*Commentary on the First Letter of Saint Paul to the Thessalonians*)
Abr.	Philo, *De Abrahamo* (*On the Life of Abraham*)
Ad Heb.	Thomas Aquinas, *Super Epistolam ad Hebraeos lectura* (*Commentary on the Letter of Saint Paul to the Hebrews*)
Ad Rom.	Thomas Aquinas, *Super Epistolam ad Romanos lectura* (*Commentary on the Letter of Saint Paul to the Romans*)
ANF	*Ante-Nicene Fathers*
Civ.	Augustine, *De civitate Dei* (*City of God*)
Doctr. Chr.	Augustine, *De doctrina christiana* (*On Christian Doctrine*)
Enarrat. Ps.	Augustine, *Enarrationes in Psalmos* (*Expositions of the Psalms*)
Ep.	Augustine, *Epistulae* (*Letters*)

Epid.	Irenaeus, *Epideixis tou apostolikou kērygmatos* (*Demonstration of the Apostolic Preaching*)
Eth. Nic.	Aristotle, *Ethica nicomachea* (*Nicomachean Ethics*)
Fug.	Philo, *De fuga et inventione* (*On Flight and Finding*)
Gen. Litt.	Augustine, *De Genesi ad litteram* (*The Literal Meaning of Genesis*)
Haer.	Irenaeus of Lyons, *Adversus haereses* (*Against Heresies*)
NPNF^2	*Nicene and Post-Nicene Fathers*, Second Series
Retract.	Augustine, *Retractationum* (*Revisions*)
SCG	Thomas Aquinas, *Summa Contra Gentiles*
Scriptum	Thomas Aquinas, *Scriptum super Sententiis* (*Commentary on the Sentences*)
Serm.	Augustine, *Sermones* (*Sermons*)
Smyrn.	Ignatius of Antioch, *Letter to the Smyrnaeans*
Solil.	Augustine, *Soliloquiorum* (*Soliloquies*)
ST	Thomas Aquinas, *Summa Theologiae*
Sup. Io.	Thomas Aquinas, *Super Evangelium Ioannis lectura* (*Commentary on the Gospel According to John*)
Sup. Mt.	Thomas Aquinas, *Super Evangelium Matthaei lectura* (*Commentary on the Gospel According to Matthew*)
Sup. Ps.	Thomas Aquinas, *Super Psalmos* (*Commentary on the Psalms*)
Trin.	Augustine, *De Trinitate* (*On the Trinity*)

Journals and Series

AB	Anchor Bible
ABD	*Anchor Bible Dictionary*. Edited by David Noel Freedman. 6 vols. Doubleday, 1992
AugStud	*Augustinian Studies*
BAC	The Bible in Ancient Christianity
BCOTWP	Baker Commentary on the Old Testament: Wisdom and Psalms
BNTC	Black's New Testament Commentaries
BR	*Biblical Research*
BSac	*Bibliotheca Sacra*
BTS	Biblical Tools and Studies
CBQ	*Catholic Biblical Quarterly*
CBTS	Catholic Biblical Theology of the Sacraments
CCSS	Catholic Commentary on Sacred Scripture
CTJ	*Calvin Theological Journal*
CTQ	*Concordia Theological Quarterly*
DRev	*Downside Review*
EKKNT	Evangelisch-katholischer Kommentar zum Neuen Testament
ExAud	*Ex Auditu*
FC	Fathers of the Church
HTR	*Harvard Theological Review*
ICC	International Critical Commentary
IJST	*International Journal of Systematic Theology*
JBL	*Journal of Biblical Literature*

JETS	*Journal of the Evangelical Theological Society*
JR	*Journal of Religion*
JSNT	*Journal for the Study of the New Testament*
JSOT	*Journal for the Study of the Old Testament*
JSQ	*Jewish Studies Quarterly*
JTI	*Journal of Theological Interpretation*
JTISupp	Journal of Theological Interpretation Supplements
JTS	*Journal of Theological Studies*
LHBOTS	The Library of Hebrew Bible/Old Testament Studies
NBf	*New Blackfriars*
NICNT	New International Commentary on the New Testament
NIGTC	New International Greek Testament Commentary
NovT	*Novum Testamentum*
NSBT	New Studies in Biblical Theology
NTL	New Testament Library
NTS	*New Testament Studies*
OECS	Oxford Early Christian Studies
OTL	Old Testament Library
PIBA	*Proceedings of the Irish Biblical Association*
PNTC	The Pillar New Testament Commentary
ProEccl	*Pro Ecclesia*
RelS	*Religious Studies*
ResQ	*Restoration Quarterly*
RTAM	*Recherches de théologie ancienne et médiévale*
SC	Sources Chrétiennes
SCA	Studies on the Children of Abraham
SJT	*Scottish Journal of Theology*
SMC	*Studies in Medieval Culture*
SP	Sacra Pagina
STAC	Studien und Texte zu Antike und Christentum
STDJ	Studies on the Texts of the Desert of Judah
SVTQ	*St. Vladimir's Theological Quarterly*
THKNT	Theologischer Handkommentar zum Neuen Testament
TJ	*Trinity Journal*
TS	*Theological Studies*
TynBul	*Tyndale Bulletin*
TZ	*Theologische Zeitschrift*
VC	*Vigiliae Christianae*
VCSupp	Vigiliae Christianae, Supplements
WBC	Word Biblical Commentary
WSA	The Works of Saint Augustine: A Translation for the 21st Century
WSTA	Latin/English Edition of the Works of St. Thomas Aquinas
WTJ	*Westminster Theological Journal*
WUNT	Wissenschaftliche Untersuchungen zum Neuen Testament
ZAW	*Zeitschrift für die alttestamentliche Wissenschaft*
ZNW	*Zeitschrift für die neutestamentliche Wissenschaft*

Introduction

The Vision of God and the Resurrection of the Body

What is the nature of the Christian hope? Reflecting on Scripture, the Western Christian tradition has answered this question by holding out two promises: the vision of God and the resurrection of the body.[1] One can see this twofold hope reflected, for example, in Eucharistic Prayer II of the Roman Missal, in which the celebrant prays at one point, "Remember also our brothers and sisters who have fallen asleep *in the hope of the resurrection*, and all who have died in your mercy: *welcome them into the light of your face*." Each part of this hope corresponds to an important aspect of human nature. The hope for the vision of God points to the human desire for knowledge and for love, reflecting the view of the great spiritual writers of the Christian tradition that nothing finite can satisfy that desire. The resurrection of the body underscores the goodness of embodied existence. The human being is not, as some philosophers throughout history have suggested, a ghost in a machine. Our bodies form an integral part of who we are, so much so that any hope that means "escape" from the body is not a hope for us *as human beings*.[2]

Vision and resurrection recur again and again in reflections on the Christian hope. How the two relate to one another, however, is not always obvious. The goal of this book is to offer a proposal for how these two promises might be brought together.

1. By and large, the Eastern Christian tradition denies the possibility of seeing the divine essence. See Meyendorff, *Byzantine Theology*, 133; Lossky, *The Vision of God*. This does not mean that Easterners deny *any* vision of God, but rather only a direct vision of God's essence.

2. See especially chap. 9 on Irenaeus and chap. 11 on Thomas Aquinas below.

The Need for an Integrated Approach

Recent studies of the Christian hope have tended to focus on either vision or resurrection. Hans Boersma's *Seeing God* focuses almost exclusively on the vision of God.[3] Seeking to redress the neglect of this dimension in some quarters, Boersma rightly reminds believers that we are made for more than just an earthly end. God has created us for himself, and true human fulfillment can be found only in him. While Boersma occasionally gives a nod to the resurrection, in seeking to correct a deficiency in some recent works on eschatology, he fails to give due attention to the bodily character of the human end. In addition, as I will argue below, there are some significant problems with Boersma's theophanic interpretation of the beatific vision. Superficially, his position would seem to underscore the importance of the resurrection, in that he presents the beatific vision as always mediated through the resurrected flesh of Christ. The saints, he suggests, will see God by gazing upon the risen Christ with their own bodily eyes.[4] Ironically, however, such an interpretation results in a static conception of the beatific vision, a charge that is sometimes laid at the feet of the tradition represented by Thomas Aquinas. If our vision of God depends on seeing Jesus's resurrected flesh, then this vision does not leave room for much else besides.[5] Samuel Parkison's recent work on the beatific vision avoids some of the problems in Boersma's account and also rightly affirms the importance of the resurrection and embodiment for Christian salvation.[6] Nevertheless, he too offers no explanation of *how* the beatific vision and the resurrection of the flesh might be integrated.

On the other hand, works by N. T. Wright and J. Richard Middleton focus on resurrection almost to the exclusion of the vision of God.[7] Understandably concerned about a dualistic denial of the goodness of the body and of God's creation, Wright and Middleton, each in his own way, present biblical visions of the end that incorporate not only bodily existence but also the renewal of the whole creation. Both scholars bring out beautiful and important aspects of the biblical depiction of the Christian hope. They rightly recognize the perennial temptation to dualism,[8] a temptation that has haunted the church

3. H. Boersma, *Seeing God*. Around ten pages (420–28) are devoted to the resurrection, and his theophanic interpretation of the beatific vision would seem to require the resurrection, but he makes no attempt to show how these two aspects of the Christian hope relate to one another. The brief discussion of the resurrection in *Seeing God* fails to explain how the beatific vision and the resurrection might be integrated, instead arguing for an immaterial understanding of the resurrection based on the writings of Gregory of Nyssa.

4. See, e.g., H. Boersma, "Thomas Aquinas on the Beatific Vision."

5. See chap. 7 below for further engagement with Hans Boersma's position.

6. Parkison, *To Gaze upon God*, especially 58–59, on the importance of the body.

7. See N. T. Wright, *Surprised by Hope*; Wright, *God's Homecoming*; Middleton, *A New Heaven and a New Earth*.

8. By "dualism" I mean those forms of religious expression that have denigrated the material/physical world in some way.

from the very beginning. Although official church teaching has never presented the Christian hope as the floating off of the disembodied soul into an airy heaven, the writings of some Christians throughout history might give that impression. Moreover, one has only to survey the average (poorly catechized) contemporary Christian to discover such a conception of the afterlife. This very real problem notwithstanding, the answer is not to jettison an important part of Scripture's testimony to the Christian hope. Although Wright acknowledges the hope for seeing God, he downplays it, and Middleton seems to dismiss it altogether.[9] As I intend to show in part 2 of this work, one can do so only by ignoring significant strands of Scripture, especially in the OT.

In order to offer a robust, genuinely biblical eschatology, we need to incorporate both the bodily dimension of Christian hope and the desire, expressed beautifully and ardently in several of the psalms (among other biblical texts), to see God's face.

A Biblical Vision

The present work seeks to offer a compelling integration of the bodily resurrection and the beatific vision. My argument proceeds in four parts, each focused in different ways on the interpretation of Scripture.

Part 1 takes as its starting point a dictum frequently attributed to the German OT scholar Hermann Gunkel, according to which "The end resembles the beginning."[10] Biblical portrayals of the end, in both the Old and the New Testaments, draw on imagery from the early chapters of Genesis. Ezekiel's famous account of the new temple (Ezek. 40–48), for example, shares a number of characteristics with the early chapters of Genesis. Similarly, the final visions of the book of Revelation (Rev. 21–22) draw on several images from Genesis 1–3. Given this correspondence between the beginning and the end, it is worth considering what the opening chapters of Genesis suggest about the human vocation. Reading these chapters carefully, one can discern a threefold human vocation. Explicitly, God creates human beings to rule creation (Gen. 1:26, 28). In addition to this explicit task, however, Genesis also implicitly describes two other roles for human beings. We are created to worship God

9. Despite Wright's criticisms of Boersma, the two also share the idea that the vision of God is located exclusively in seeing the resurrected flesh of Christ. See N. T. Wright, *God's Homecoming*, 293. In *A New Heaven and a New Earth*, Middleton does not address the question of the vision of God. In a subsequent essay ("A New Earth Perspective," 91–92), he is ambivalent regarding whether and how the redeemed will see God. His emphasis on the divine presence (*A New Heaven and a New Earth*, 46–49, 166–72) is compatible with the notion of beatific vision, even if he does not articulate it in such terms and seems to misconstrue how the tradition understands the beatific vision.

10. On the actual relationship between this saying and Gunkel, see 3n1 below.

and to participate in God's rest.[11] One of the weaknesses of Wright's and Middleton's approaches is a lopsided emphasis on the royal element of the human vocation. Although both scholars acknowledge a priestly dimension to the early chapters of Genesis, it plays a relatively minor role in their eschatology, being subsumed under the royal dimension, and neither of them adequately incorporates the theme of rest so prominent throughout the OT.[12] The first three chapters of this study, then, will elucidate this threefold vocation both in Genesis and as it unfolds throughout Scripture with a view to its significance for the Christian hope.

Part 2 explores the complex biblical testimony regarding the vision of God. Throughout Scripture one finds expressions of fear at having seen God (e.g., Judg. 13:22); a fervent desire to see God (e.g., Ps. 42:1–2), but also denials that anyone can see God (e.g., 1 Tim. 6:16); and, finally, promises that the saints will see God's face (e.g., Rev. 22:4). Chapter 4 seeks to sort out these and other elements of the biblical texts that speak of seeing God, arguing that, taken as a whole, the Scriptures offer a face-to-face vision of God as an important element of the Christian hope. Chapters 5–7 then consider the ways Irenaeus, Augustine, and Aquinas interpret this hope. Each of these figures makes distinctive contributions to an understanding of the vision of God, but they are united in understanding this vision as an essential element of Scripture's promises.

Part 3 turns to the other foundational element of the Christian hope—namely, the resurrection. Rather than offer an exhaustive account of the biblical texts regarding resurrection (which would require a book in itself), chapter 8 will focus on a few features of the resurrection hope. We will begin by examining some OT accounts of raising the dead as well as expressions of hope for an enduring resurrection. We will then consider the significance of Jesus's resurrection appearances in the Gospels, before exploring three elements of the resurrection hope in the NT. At several points in Paul's letters, he presents Christ's death and resurrection as the pattern of the Christian hope. In 1 Corinthians 15 he discusses the characteristics of the resurrected

11. I recognize that, technically speaking, Gen. 2:1–3 does not speak explicitly of God "resting," but rather of "ceasing" from his work. Nevertheless, in canonical context, this passage can be read in light of the broader Israelite hope for rest. See chap. 2 below.

12. N. T. Wright's more recent *History and Eschatology* and *God's Homecoming* do a better job of acknowledging the centrality of worship. He also underscores the importance of the Sabbath in *History and Eschatology* (155–85), even acknowledging that human beings "are called to share [the] divine Sabbath" (171). Sabbath rest does not, however, play a major part in *God's Homecoming*. The chapter below on rest suggests that this theme runs even deeper throughout Scripture than Wright recognizes. Here we would do well to heed Brevard Childs's salutary reminder to continue to listen to the discrete witness of the OT. See Childs, *Biblical Theology of the Old and New Testaments*, 78, as well as the development of this approach in Anderson, *That I May Dwell Among Them*, 184–209. The same, I will suggest in chap. 4, is true with respect to the biblical hope of seeing God.

body. Finally, John 6 draws a close connection between the Eucharist and the hope of the resurrection. The reason for focusing on these three aspects of the NT is that they feature prominently in the writings of Irenaeus, Augustine, and Aquinas on the resurrection, which form the subjects of chapters 9–11. Irenaeus draws a close connection between the Eucharist and the resurrection; Augustine discusses the nature of the "spiritual body" in ways that anticipate—by many centuries—recent debates regarding that term; and one of Aquinas's primary arguments for the resurrection comes from Paul's letters—namely, the idea that Christ's death and resurrection is the pattern of the Christian hope.

In part 4 we return to the categories of worship, dominion, and rest.[13] In this chapter I offer a proposal for how to integrate the experience of seeing God with the resurrection of the body. The key, I suggest, lies in worship. Drawing on C. S. Lewis's *Reflections on the Psalms*, as well as on Augustine, I argue that the ultimate purpose of the resurrection is to enable us to respond appropriately to the vision of God through bodily worship. Lewis observes that certain human experiences find their consummation in praise.[14] When one sees a beautiful sunset or hears an awe-inspiring symphony, one naturally bursts into praise. In fact, unless a person does so, the experience remains, in a sense, incomplete. If this is true for mundane experiences like symphonies and sunsets, how much more so for the vision of God, whom Augustine describes as perfect Beauty itself! The other two categories, dominion and rest, can be incorporated into worship more easily than worship can be incorporated into dominion, particularly given the close relationship between rest and worship throughout Scripture (a point argued in chap. 2).

Why These Three Interpreters?

One might reasonably ask why I have chosen to enlist Irenaeus, Augustine, and Aquinas, as opposed to other figures from the tradition. Writing as a Catholic, I might point to their status as doctors of the Church, which gives them a particular authority. Two objections could be raised to such a justification, however. First, the Catholic Church has recognized around forty saints as doctors of the Church. The selection of these three on the basis of this status alone would be arbitrary. Second, and more importantly, most non-Catholics do not recognize this authority, and I do not write this work only for Catholics.

There are better reasons for choosing these three figures. First, each of them, in his own time and context, combated dualism in one of its manifold

13. And so, the end resembles the beginning.
14. Lewis, *Reflections on the Psalms*, 95.

forms. For Irenaeus, it was the group he dubbed the "Gnostics"; Augustine battled with his Manichaean past for the rest of his life after his conversion; and Aquinas belonged to a religious order founded to combat the Cathars, who denied the goodness of the body. Second, despite their avowed opposition to dualism, two of these figures (Augustine and Aquinas) are sometimes accused of falling into and even perpetuating a dualistic understanding of the Christian hope. One goal of this work, then, is to defend these great Christian thinkers by showing their commitment to a fully embodied understanding of salvation. Finally, as I will show especially in parts 2 and 3, each of these three figures, to varying degrees, has already proposed ways to integrate the resurrection and the vision of God. There is no need to reinvent the wheel. Another aim of this study, then, is to show that resources for answering its central question have been there all along.

Two additional points are worth making. First, I do not appeal to these theologians as authorities alongside that of Scripture. Rather, each of these figures offers exemplary ways of reading Scripture with respect to the Christian hope. Second, and conversely, the purpose of chapters 4 and 8 is not to present a "correct" interpretation of Scripture by which we can evaluate Irenaeus, Augustine, and Aquinas. Rather, in these chapters I will gather the important data regarding both seeing God and bodily resurrection to show how prominent both aspects of the Christian hope are throughout Scripture. Ultimately, then, this is a book about Scripture and the hope it offers to those who accept its authority.[15]

An Augustinian Proviso

As will become evident over the course of this study, Augustine plays a leading role in my account of the life of the world to come. For that reason, it is fitting at the outset to imitate the great bishop of Hippo's humility when addressing these questions. Augustine often expresses caution when it comes to speculation about the next life. In *Sermon* 362, for example, he notes that it is easier to say what there will not be in the next life than what there will be, because we have not yet experienced it.[16] Given the necessarily tentative nature of our speculation, then, I make my own Augustine's invitation to his readers in his masterpiece on the Trinity: "Accordingly, dear reader, whenever you are as certain about something as I am go forward with me; whenever

15. I am grateful to Sam Johnson, whose insightful questions prompted me to articulate my approach in this way.

16. *Serm.* 362.28. For a contemporary caution regarding what we can and cannot know about the eschaton drawing on the character of the biblical images used to describe it, see Wolfe, *The Theological Imagination*, 127–32. For a defense of speculation about the last things, see Thiel, *Icons of Hope*, 25–28.

you hesitate equally, seek with me; whenever you notice that you have gone wrong come back to me; or that I have, call me back to you. In this way let us set out along the way of charity together, making for him of whom it is said, 'Seek his face always.'"[17]

17. *Trin.* 1.3.5 (modified).

PART 1

"IN THE IMAGE OF GOD HE CREATED THEM"

The Threefold Human Vocation and the Human End

ONE

Dominion

According to a saying commonly attributed to the German OT scholar Hermann Gunkel, *Endzeit gleicht Urzeit*—loosely translated, "The end resembles the beginning."[1] The closing chapters of the book of Revelation exemplify this principle. There the seer draws on imagery from the opening chapters of Genesis, speaking of the "river of the water of life" (Rev. 22:1) and making multiple references to the "tree of life" (Rev. 22:2, 14; cf. Gen. 2:9–10). By these allusions, Revelation suggests that the appointed end of the cosmos will resemble its beginning. If this is true of the general conditions of the cosmos, the writings of the NT suggest that the same can be said of the human vocation. Texts that speak of the Christian hope draw on at least three different but interrelated ends for the human being, each of them featured in the early chapters of Genesis: dominion, rest, and worship. In this chapter I will focus on the first aspect of the human vocation, dominion.

Some contemporary scholars have suggested that dominion or royal status defines what it means to be made in the image of God.[2] While there is certainly a connection between dominion and being made in the image, the two are not identical. After examining the command to rule in Genesis 1, then, it would be helpful to explore the nature of the image. Rather than *defining* what it means to be made in the image of God, I will argue that dominion

1. The exact form of this saying, found with slight variation in many scholarly appeals to Gunkel's work (some scholars use the phrase "Endzeit *gleich* Urzeit," using the adjectival/adverbial rather than the verbal form), does not actually appear in Gunkel, *Schöpfung und Chaos in Endzeit und Urzeit*, though the idea clearly stems from his work. For a recent discussion of the *Urzeit-Endzeit* schema in the Second Temple period, see Doering, "*Urzeit-Endzeit* in the Dead Sea Scrolls and Pseudepigrapha."

2. See, e.g., Middleton, *The Liberating Image*, 88–90. More recently, Middleton has recognized a cultic dimension in addition to the royal dimension. See Middleton, "Image of God."

is a *corollary* or *consequence* of being made in God's image. The "image" language of Genesis points not to royal status, but rather to a filial relationship. Royal rule follows from this relationship on at least two counts. First, in the ancient Near East, being the son of a god frequently went hand in hand with dominion. Second, the one in whose image human beings are made—the God of Israel—is described as Israel's king throughout the OT, especially in the Psalter. To be made in his image, then, entails a royal function. Several eschatological texts in the NT are attuned to this function, connecting the hope for the resurrection with the task of ruling.

"Let Them Have Dominion"

One of the first things God says about human beings when he creates them in Genesis 1 concerns their vocation to rule creation. On the sixth day, God says, "Let us make humans in our image, according to our likeness; and *let them have dominion* over the fish of the sea and over the birds of the air and over the cattle and over all the wild animals of the earth and over every creeping thing that creeps upon the earth" (Gen. 1:26). From the first moment of their creation, God assigns human beings the task of exercising dominion over the rest of the earthly created realm. The extent of human jurisdiction includes most of those things created on the first six days: the earth (day 3), the fish of the sea (day 5), the birds of the air (day 5), the cattle (day 6), and the creeping things (day 6). The only created things exempted from this human rule are the seas themselves (day 2, though dominion over the "fish of the sea" might imply a corresponding authority over the sea itself) and the light (both the initial light of day 1 and the lights in the firmament of the heavens of day 4). The omission of these elements may signal that at least some realms remain the domain of God alone. Regardless, by their governance over their fellow creatures, human beings are called to reflect God's own sovereignty over creation. Once God has created the first human beings, he reiterates his purpose in creating them with a command: "God blessed them, and God said to them, 'Be fruitful and multiply and fill the earth and subdue it and *have dominion* over the fish of the sea and over the birds of the air and over every living thing that moves upon the earth'" (Gen. 1:28). From the very beginning, then, the human vocation entails sovereignty over the rest of living creation.[3]

In his illuminating study of the *imago Dei*, J. Richard Middleton argues that the notion of human rule over creation is closely connected to the creation

3. Middleton (*The Liberating Image*, 51) notes that the Hebrew root for dominion (*rdh*), while not exclusively associated with kingship, frequently appears in this connection in the OT (1 Kings 4:24; Pss. 72:8; 110:2; Isa. 14:6; Ezek. 34:4). M. Smith (*The Priestly Vision of Genesis 1*, 101), without denying the royal connotation of *rdh*, suggests that the Hebrew root *kbsh* (rendered "subdue") may have priestly connotations.

of human beings in God's image.[4] The shape of the text itself points to this connection. The first announcement of the creation of human beings in God's image is followed immediately by the statement that they will have dominion over the rest of creation. Although many translations render God's intention to create human beings in a paratactic structure ("Let us make humans . . . *and* let them have dominion"), some scholars have suggested that the syntax of the sentence actually indicates purpose.[5] On this reading, a better translation would be, "Let us make humans . . . *so that* they might have dominion." While Middleton goes too far in taking the purpose of dominion as the exhaustive meaning of the *imago*, he is nevertheless correct to note the close connection between the image and dominion, even if the latter is not the primary or exhaustive meaning of the former.[6] It is significant that the actual creation of human beings in God's image in Genesis 1:27 is surrounded by the purpose clause of 1:26 and the command to have dominion in 1:28.[7]

In addition to the structure of the text itself, the ancient Near Eastern context of the creation account suggests a link between image and rule. In a number of texts from the ancient Near East, "image" language forms an important part of royal ideology. In a variety of writings ranging from the seventeenth century BC to the second century BC, the pharaoh is often described as the "image" of one or more of the Egyptian gods.[8] As Middleton notes, the "image" language frequently refers to the pharaoh's authority to rule over Egypt.[9] Though fewer in number, ancient Mesopotamian texts describing the king as the image of a god also exist.[10] Seen against this backdrop, it is plausible to suppose that the "image" language in Genesis 1 also has royal connotations, particularly given that other texts in the OT seem to reflect this interpretation. Psalm 8, whose inscription designates it as a "Psalm of David," describes David's rule in language reminiscent of Genesis 1. In the minds of at least some ancient Israelites, then, there was some connection between the *imago Dei* and royal status.

Most modern scholars, with good reason, treat Genesis 1:1–2:3 and Genesis 2:4–25 as two distinct creation accounts arising at different periods in Israel's history. Despite this difference in historical context, the canonical shape of the two accounts exhibits some thematic continuities. With respect to the

4. Middleton, *The Liberating Image*. For a thoughtful critique of some of the excesses of Middleton's theological claims, see Peterson, *The Imago Dei as Human Identity*, 37–42.

5. Middleton, *The Liberating Image*, 52–53. See also Hart, "Genesis 1:1–2:3 as Prologue," 319–20; Clines, "The Image of God in Man," 96.

6. See again Peterson, *The Imago Dei as Human Identity*, 37–42, as well as the discussion below.

7. See Middleton, *The Liberating Image*, 50.

8. Middleton, *The Liberating Image*, 108–11.

9. Middleton, *The Liberating Image*, 109–10.

10. Middleton counts six and discusses them at some length. See Middleton, *The Liberating Image*, 111–22, as well as the discussion below.

question of governing creation, the account of the naming of the animals (Gen. 2:18–20) seems to express in narrative form the dominion God gives human beings in the first creation account.[11]

This emphasis on the royal vocation of the human race helps explain the OT's ambivalence toward the institution of kingship, which may stem in part from the notion that requesting a king was seen by some as a departure from God's intention for Israel. According to Genesis 1, all human beings are made in God's image and so have the vocation to rule creation. While most scholars consider Genesis 1 to be one of the later texts of the OT, there are other hints at the notion of a more universal kingship in Israel. When the people of Israel first arrive at Sinai after the exodus from Egypt, the Lord says to Moses, "Now, therefore, if you obey my voice and keep my covenant, you shall be my treasured possession out of all the peoples. Indeed, the whole earth is mine, but you shall be for me a *priestly kingdom* and a holy nation" (Exod. 19:5–6a). According to Exodus, it seems the Israelites were all to exercise both a royal and a priestly function.[12] Deuteronomy likewise suggests that the Israelites will govern other nations (Deut. 15:6). One could say that, according to the Pentateuch, after the fall the vocation originally given to the whole human race was meant to be fulfilled by Israel.

A few passages in the NT take up this notion of a royal priesthood and apply it to believers (1 Pet. 2:9; Rev. 5:10). Before we consider this appropriation more closely, however, it is worth lingering over the relationship between creation in God's image and the royal vocation. While it is true that there is a connection, it is not one of identity. Rather, the royal vocation stems from the filial relationship that constitutes one of the primary meanings of being made in God's image.

Made in the Image of God

Few biblical ideas have generated as much theological reflection as the *imago Dei*, particularly when it comes to anthropology. Christian interpreters from Irenaeus to Karl Barth have approached the text from numerous angles, resulting in an overwhelming number of proposals for what it means to be made "in the image of God."[13] To adjudicate between all these proposals lies far

11. See Clines, "The Image of God in Man," 98n189; Sawyer, "The Image of God," 65.

12. While the phrase "priestly kingdom" by itself need not imply a royal vocation for all the people, the designation of Israel in Exod. 4:22 as God's "firstborn son" (sometimes a royal title; see, e.g., Ps. 89:27) supports such a reading. It is also worth noting that at least two NT texts (1 Pet. 2:9; Rev. 5:10) interpret Exod. 19:6 in this way. We will return to the priestly function in chap. 3.

13. For two brief discussions of historical and contemporary understandings of the *imago*, see Middleton, *The Liberating Image*, 17–29; Clines, "The Image of God in Man," 54–61. For a fuller (but still brief) treatment, see Peppiatt, *The Imago Dei*.

beyond the scope of this chapter. Instead, I will examine two aspects of the text highlighted by modern interpreters but also found in some premodern readings. I will use these aspects to determine the significance of the *imago Dei* for the human vocation, both in this life and in the next.

The sharpest divide between modern and premodern readings of the phrase *imago Dei* concerns whether the image should be interpreted in a functional sense or in an ontological sense, with most modern interpreters favoring a functional reading and most premodern interpreters seeing the *imago* in ontological terms.[14] The latter typically focus on the powers of the soul such as intellect, memory, and will. The former, by contrast, tend to emphasize the royal dimension of the *imago* and point to human beings as representative rulers participating in God's governance of creation.[15] Some premodern interpreters, however, integrate these two aspects into a unified understanding of the *imago*. Gregory of Nyssa, for example, speaks of the image as entailing both the rational powers and the role of kingship. In fact, he grounds the kingly dimension of the image precisely in the rational powers:

> For the soul immediately shows its *royal and exalted character*, far removed as it is from the lowliness of private station, in that it owns no lord, and is self-governed, swayed autocratically by its own will; for *to whom else does this belong than to a king*? And further, besides these facts, the fact that it is *the image of that Nature which rules over all* means nothing else than this, that *our nature was created to be royal from the first*. For as, in human beings' ordinary use, those who make images of princes both mold the figure of their form, and represent along with this the royal rank by the vesture of purple, and even the likeness is commonly spoken of as "a king," so the human nature also, *as it was made to rule the rest*, was, *by its likeness to the King of all*, made as it were *a living image*, partaking with the archetype both in rank and in name.[16]

Several aspects of Gregory's discussion of the image merit comment. First, it is worth noting that he is aware of the original notion of an image as a statue or figure of some sort made to represent the king ("those who make images of princes . . . mold the figure of their form"). Second, and perhaps more importantly, he draws from this phenomenon a conclusion strikingly similar to that of many modern interpreters—namely, that the making of human beings in God's image entails a royal function ("our nature was created to be royal from the first"). Finally, and in contrast to modern interpreters, Gregory

14. For a concise discussion, see Peterson, *The Imago Dei as Human Identity*, 23–52. In addition to ontological and functional interpretations, he also considers a relational interpretation.

15. Another common interpretation reads the "image" language in light of the images in ancient temples, suggesting to some that the *imago Dei* reflects an anthropomorphic view of God. Human beings, on this reading, resemble God physically. See the survey in Curtis, "Man as the Image of God," 40–44.

16. Gregory of Nyssa, *On the Making of Man* 4.1 (modified and emphasis added).

takes the further step of grounding the royal function in an ontological claim. The soul's power to govern itself is what makes fulfilling its kingly role possible.[17] In this regard, it is worth noting that the opening chapters of Genesis suggest a distinction between human beings and the other animals. In Genesis 1:26–28, God speaks to the first human beings in a way that he does not to the animals. In addition to commanding them to be fruitful and multiply, a command given to other creatures (Gen. 1:22), he also assigns them the task of dominion (Gen. 1:26–28).[18]

There is another aspect of the notion of the *imago Dei* that implicitly contains both the royal and the rational dimensions of human existence. Reading Genesis 1:26–27 in light of the genealogy in Genesis 5:1–3 suggests that the categories of "image" and "likeness" make the most sense as familial or filial language.[19] That is, by describing humans as being made in the image and likeness of God, Genesis presents them as children of God. Such an understanding has several implications. First, it means that human beings, as children of God, have a responsibility to obey and honor him.[20] Second, it means that, being children of the great King (Ps. 48:2), human beings also are called to a royal role.[21] Finally, the family resemblance implied by this reading—particularly if it is not seen in overly physical terms—would suggest a similarity with respect to the intellectual powers, as many interpreters, both Christian and Jewish, have proposed over the centuries.[22]

Understandably, Genesis 1:26–27 has stood at the center of theological discussion of the *imago Dei*. But it is not the only text in Genesis that uses the language of "image" and "likeness." Just a few chapters later, the narrator once again mentions the creation of human beings in God's likeness, then proceeds to apply the language of "image" and "likeness" to the generation of another human being. The list of Adam's descendants in Genesis 5 begins with a reminder of humankind's special creation: "When God created humans, he made them in the likeness of God. Male and female he created them, and he blessed them and named them 'humans' when they were created" (Gen.

17. For a contemporary articulation of a similar point from the perspective of analytic theology, see Farris, "An Immaterial Substance View: *Imago Dei* in Creation and Redemption." Farris puts the point succinctly on 111: "Functionality presupposes substantiality." As a medieval would put it, *agere sequitur esse*.

18. I owe this point to my colleague Stephen Long.

19. Crouch, "Genesis 1:26–7." See also McDowell, "'In the Image of God He Created Them'"; McDowell, *The Image of God in the Garden of Eden*; Ortlund, "Image of Adam, Son of God." Firmage ("Genesis 1 and the Priestly Agenda," 101n12, 111) discusses this idea in the context of a priestly interpretation of the image.

20. This is the aspect that Crouch ("Genesis 1:26–7," 12–15) emphasizes.

21. Crouch ("Genesis 1:26–7," 12) acknowledges this dimension of sonship but does not develop it at any length. The reference to Ps. 48 is my own.

22. Crouch does not consider this possibility in her otherwise insightful study, though she does deny that the resemblance between God and humans should be understood as physical.

5:1b–2, modified). Immediately after these verses, Genesis applies the same language to the generation of Adam's son Seth: "When Adam had lived one hundred thirty years, *he became the father of a son in his likeness, according to his image*, and named him Seth" (Gen. 5:3). The use of the same language in such close proximity can hardly be coincidental. Given the repetition of creation in God's image, the narrator draws the reader's attention to the similarity between God's creation of humans and Adam's begetting of Seth.

On the basis of cognate uses of "image" and "likeness" language in the ancient Near East, some have suggested that the text betrays an anthropomorphic image of God. Human beings resemble God physically, just as Seth resembles Adam physically.[23] Such a reading, however, is unsatisfactory. According to traditional source criticism, Genesis 1 and 5 both come from the priestly source, which is known to avoid anthropomorphisms.[24] Something else must lie behind the comparison between God and Adam in Genesis 5.

C. L. Crouch suggests that the application of "image" and "likeness" language serves to draw an analogy between Adam's relationship to Seth and God's relationship to human beings. Genesis implies that, by begetting Seth, Adam passes on his image and likeness to him. Coming immediately as this statement does after the repetition of God's creation of human beings in his likeness, Crouch argues, "The obvious conclusion is that as Seth is to Adam, so Adam—that is, humanity—is to God."[25] Although many modern interpreters have pressed the physical dimension of "image" language in interpreting the *imago Dei*, Crouch suggests that the resemblance need not be one of physical appearance. Rather, the language of physical resemblance is used "to activate the metaphor" of the parent-child relationship but need not refer to a literal resemblance. Drawing on metaphor theory, Crouch suggests that "the physical resemblance, once it has been used as a trigger for the metaphor's source domain (the parent-child relationship), does not need to be mapped onto the target domain (the God-human relationship)."[26] There are good reasons to reject a physical interpretation of the image. As Hans Wildberger notes, interpreting the image on the basis of physical appearance makes it difficult to explain why Genesis 9:6 justifies capital punishment based on the creation of human beings in God's image.[27] A physical resemblance

23. See again the survey of Curtis in n. 15 above.

24. The second creation account (Gen. 2:4–3:24), by contrast, presents an anthropomorphic God: He forms the first man from the dust like a statue and breathes life into him; he goes for a stroll in the garden.

25. Crouch, "Genesis 1:26–7," 11.

26. Crouch, "Genesis 1:26–7," 11. I would prefer the language of "analogy" to "metaphor," but the basic point remains the same. In both metaphor and analogy there are similarities and differences. The key differences in this case are the lack of physical resemblance and the lack of physical/biological generation.

27. For this and the following points, see Wildberger, "Das Abbild Gottes," 247–49.

alone hardly seems adequate to demand such a punishment for the offense of murder. Wildberger adds two other difficulties for interpreting the image in terms of physical appearance. First, as with capital punishment, a physical resemblance to God hardly helps to account for the dominion of human beings over the rest of creation, which is closely related to their creation in God's image. It seems better to ground humankind's dominion in the traditional understanding of human nature, including intellect and will. Second, although the OT frequently uses anthropomorphisms with reference to God, nowhere does it clearly refer to God having a body.[28] Interpreting the *imago* in filial terms better explains its connection with both capital punishment and governance. To take the latter point first, as I will argue below, the notion of kingship is closely associated with divine filiation. With respect to capital punishment, kinship between God and human beings better accounts for associating the death penalty with the status of human beings as God's image.

Another aspect of Genesis 5:1–3 supports the interpretation of the *imago* in terms of a father-son relationship. The parallels between God's creation of humankind and Adam's begetting of Seth are not limited to the language of "likeness." As Gavin Ortlund argues, the description of the creation of Adam/humankind in Genesis 5:1b–2 shares another structural similarity with the account of Adam begetting his son Seth.[29] After recounting God's creation of Adam/humankind, the narrator notes that God *names* Adam/humankind (Gen. 5:2). Similarly, when Adam begets a son, he *names* him "Seth" (Gen. 5:3). It would be helpful to consider the two descriptions side by side:

Genesis 5:1b–2 (modified)	**Genesis 5:3**
When God created humans,	When Adam had lived a hundred and thirty years,
he made them in the likeness of God. Male and female he created them, and he blessed them	he became the father of a son[a] in his likeness, according to his image,
and named them "humans" when they were created.[b]	and named him Seth.

a. The Hebrew text does not include the word "son," which must be supplied to make sense of the sentence in English.

b. The NRSVue obscures the parallel between God and Adam by saying that God "called them humans," rather than "named them 'humans.'" In both verses the Hebrew expression is *wayyiqra'*.

The repetition of the phrase "male and female" and of the language of blessing evokes the creation of human beings in Genesis 1:26–28, further underscoring the connection between the two passages.[30] This seems to be the narrator's way of pointing to the conception and birth of Seth as an

28. For a good critique of recent attempts to understand Israel's God in corporeal fashion, see Moberly, "Anatomizing God?"

29. Ortlund, "Image of Adam, Son of God," 679–80.

30. Ortlund, "Image of Adam, Son of God," 680.

interpretive key to understanding what it means to be made in the image and likeness of God, particularly given that these two passages are the only two places in Genesis where the combination of "image" and "likeness" appears.[31]

In addition to the structural parallels within Genesis itself, an understanding of "image" language as a parent-child relationship also fits the book's ancient Near Eastern context. As several scholars have noted, a number of ancient Near Eastern texts speak of a human being as made in the image of a god. Significantly, many of these texts connect "image" language with the idea of sonship. Several ancient Egyptian descriptions of the pharaoh, for example, describe him using language relating to image, creation, and begetting.[32] So, for example, one text speaks of the king as "the shining *image* of the lord of all and a *creation* of the god of Heliopolis. . . . *He has begotten him* in order to create a shining seed on earth, for salvation for men, as his *living image*." "Image" language reflects both the pharaoh's creation and his being begotten by the god of Heliopolis. In another text, the god Amon addresses Amenophis III as "my *living image*, *creation* of my members, whom *Mut bare to me*." Once again, image, creation, and birth go together. One last text does not use the language of creation, but it does associate "image" language with sonship. Amon-Re says to Amenophis III, "You are my *beloved son*, who came forth from my members, my *image*, whom I have put on earth. I have given to you to rule the earth in peace."

One text from ancient Assyria also brings together the language of "image" and "sonship" with the status of the king. The author of a letter to Esarhaddon writes, "The father of the king, my lord, was the very image of Bel, and the king, my lord, is likewise the very image of Bel."[33] Here one sees the constellation of kingship, image, and the father-son relationship. Moreover, the word rendered "image" in this letter (*tsalmu*) is cognate with the Hebrew word for "image" (*tselem*). The connection between kingship and divine sonship is not quite as clear in this text as it is in the Egyptian texts, but there is nevertheless a loose connection between the three ideas of kingship, filiation, and divine image.

On both internal literary and historical grounds, then, the language of "image" has a close association with sonship in the ancient Near Eastern context reflected in Genesis and picked up in later biblical tradition.[34]

31. Ortlund, "Image of Adam, Son of God," 680.

32. The following three examples are taken from Clines, "The Image of God in Man," 84–85, with the italics in the texts added. For a brief discussion of the phenomenon of the pharaoh as the son of a god, see Morenz, *Egyptian Religion*, 33–36.

33. For the text, see Parpola, *Letters from Assyrian and Babylonian Scholars*, 181.

34. Clines ("The Image of God in Man," 84–85) does not make much of the filial dimension of these passages, but rather of the royal dimension of being the son of a god. One NT example of this association appears in Colossians, which refers to Christ as "the image of the

Filial Relationship, Royal Vocation

If, then, the "image" language of Genesis 1:26–27 refers to a kind of begetting, what consequences follow from this filial relationship? Crouch surveys a number of OT texts that speak of God with paternal or maternal imagery, both to bolster the idea of the image relating to divine parenthood and to flesh out some of its significance. Several passages commonly dated to the exilic and postexilic periods describe God as both creator and divine parent, suggesting that the two ideas are intimately related. Moreover, these texts fill out some of the consequences that follow from God's role as parent to his children, Israel.

A theme that appears frequently in these texts is the duty of the Israelites to reverence God as a child ought to reverence a parent.[35] So, for example, in the book of Malachi God addresses the people, "A son honors his father and a servant his master. If then I am a father, where is the honor due me? And if I am a master, where is the respect due me?" (Mal. 1:6a). In the wisdom tradition of Israel, the book of Proverbs underscores God's role as disciplinarian:

> My child, do not despise the LORD's discipline
> or be weary of his reproof,
> for the LORD reproves the one he loves,
> as a father the son in whom he delights. (Prov. 3:11–12)[36]

Isaiah shifts to maternal imagery in order to describe God's never-ending love for his people and his desire to show them compassion:

> But Zion said, "The LORD has forsaken me;
> my LORD has forgotten me."
> Can a woman forget her nursing child
> or show no compassion for the child of her womb?
> Even these might forget,
> yet I will not forget you. (Isa. 49:14–15)

These texts illuminate what it means for human beings to be made in God's image—God cares for them in many of the ways a father and a mother care for their children, and human beings owe God their love and respect.

There is another aspect of the filial dimension of the *imago* that Crouch mentions but does not develop. The *imago* relates closely to the notion of

---

invisible God" and "the firstborn of all creation" (Col. 1:15) in the context of a reference to the Son's kingdom (1:13).

35. I owe the following examples to Crouch, "Genesis 1:26–7," 14–15. For a more recent discussion of the portrayal of God as Father in Scripture, see W. Wright, *The Lord's Prayer*, 38–45.

36. Crouch ("Genesis 1:26–7," 14) mistakenly cites the verse as coming from Prov. 2.

royal rule.[37] This is not to say, as many modern scholars have argued, that "image" language is fundamentally identical with kingship. Rather, such language points first to sonship. The royal prerogative comes from human beings' status as children of God. In this respect, my argument resembles Gregory of Nyssa's suggestion that the royal vocation of human beings stems from and can be seen in their self-governance by virtue of reason and will.[38] The difference is that I would root the royal function in sonship rather than in the human intellectual powers on their own. These two approaches are not incompatible, however, since the intellectual powers of human beings also relate to being God's children. Parents pass on traits to their children, and arguably the most important trait God passes on to human beings is the ability to know and to love.

The idea of being God's son is applied to a number of figures in the OT. With respect to the question of royal rule, two in particular stand out. First, in the story of the exodus, God refers to the people of Israel as his (collective) "son." Instructing Moses, the Lord tells him, "Then you shall say to Pharaoh, 'Thus says the LORD: Israel is my firstborn son. I said to you, "Let my son go that he may serve me." But you refused to let him go; now I will kill your firstborn son'" (Exod. 4:22–23). The designation of Israel as God's "firstborn son" suggests more than an ordinary father-son relationship. In ancient Israel, David and his descendants are also referred to as God's firstborn (Ps. 89:27). The use of the adjective "firstborn," then, may subtly point to Israel's royal status, a status confirmed later in Exodus. When the people arrive at Mount Sinai, God instructs Moses to say to the people, "But you shall be for me a priestly kingdom [or 'a kingdom of priests'] and a holy nation" (Exod. 19:6a). Israel, God's "firstborn son," was called to be a royal people, fulfilling the role given to the first human beings at creation.

As already noted, the other important use of the idea of divine sonship appears in a variety of texts relating to the Davidic covenant.[39] Most famously, the establishment of David's dynasty in 2 Samuel 7 includes a promise of divine sonship for David's descendants. Through Nathan the prophet, God promises David concerning the latter's son, "I will be a father to him, and he shall be a son to me" (2 Sam. 7:14a). This association between divine sonship and kingship appears frequently throughout the OT, particularly in the Psalter. Psalm 2, which many see as forming together with Psalm 1 an introduction to the Psalter, develops this theme. The psalmist, speaking of God's promises to him, sings,

37. Crouch, "Genesis 1:26–7," 12.

38. See the discussion of Gregory on pp. 7–8 above.

39. The actual phrase "son of God" appears at times in connection with David, but the idea is more widespread and articulated in different ways, such as in the promises God makes to David in 2 Sam. 7.

I will tell of the decree of the LORD:
He said to me, "You are my son;
today I have begotten you.
Ask of me, and I will make the nations your heritage
and the ends of the earth your possession." (Ps. 2:7–8)

In this psalm we see the same idea as in 2 Samuel 7, but here it is expanded. The sonship of the Lord's "anointed" (Ps. 2:2) makes him king not simply over Israel but to the "ends of the earth," with the nations as his heritage.

This same idea appears in Psalm 89, a text that laments the apparent failure of God's promises to David. The first part of the psalm sings God's praises for his abundant gifts to David. As already noted, among these gifts is the designation of David and his sons as "the firstborn, the highest of the kings of the earth" (Ps. 89:27). This appellation appears in the context of the psalmist's account of the dynasty God established for David. Like Psalm 2, Psalm 89 speaks both of David's royal status and of his being anointed by God:

Then you spoke in a vision to your faithful one and said,
"I have set the crown on one who is mighty;
I have exalted one chosen from the people.
I have found my servant David;
with my holy oil I have anointed him." (Ps. 89:19–20)

In reply David will cry, "You are my Father, my God, and the Rock of my salvation!" (Ps. 89:26). Once again, rule and sonship go together.

One important psalm—particularly with respect to royal imagery as it relates to the *imago* of Genesis 1—is Psalm 8, mentioned briefly above. Although the psalm does not use "son of God" language or imagery, it bears the common title "A Psalm of David." Moreover, the psalmist meditates on the place of human beings in the universe with language that clearly resembles the first creation account of Genesis. Staring at the vast expanse of the heavens, the psalmist wonders at God's care for human beings, asking a well-known question, "What is man that you are mindful of him, and the son of man that you care for him?" (Ps. 8:4 ESV).[40] Despite the (relative) insignificance of human beings, the psalmist goes on to note, they have been given the dignity of ruling creation:

You have given them dominion over the works of your hands;
you have put all things under their feet,
all sheep and oxen,
and also the beasts of the field,

40. The inclusive translation of the NRSVue obscures the singularity of the figure in 8:5 (MT), who is most likely meant to be understood as the Davidic king.

the birds of the air, and the fish of the sea,
whatever passes along the paths of the seas. (Ps. 8:6–8)

Many have recognized the close connection between these verses and Genesis.[41] These similarities suggest that at the heart of humanity's vocation is a royal status.

The opening of the psalm, however, subtly suggests that this royal dignity has a deeper foundation. The psalm begins by addressing God, "O Lord, our Sovereign, how majestic is your name in all the earth!" (Ps. 8:1). The word rendered by the NRSVue as "Sovereign," *'adon*, is the same word frequently used in the OT to refer to the king.[42] The psalm begins, then, with the primacy of God's rule over all the earth. The same line appears at the end of the psalm, framing the meditation on human rule over the earth. The subtle implication is that the royal vocation of human beings derives from God's own sovereignty. A consideration of God's role as king in the OT, as well as the relation between his kingship and the Davidic dynasty, confirms this suggestion.

Made in the Image of the King

In Gregory of Nyssa's discussion of the royal character of the human soul, he makes much of the one in whose image human beings are made: "The fact that it is the image of that Nature which rules over all means nothing else than this, that our nature was created to be royal from the first."[43] The image of God as king is a common one throughout the writings of the OT. All three of its major corpora—the Pentateuch, the Writings, and the Prophets—describe God as king, though the theme is particularly prominent in the Psalter as well as the Prophets.[44] Much has been written and could be said about God's kingship, but I will focus first on its ubiquity in the OT and then on the universality of God's reign. The purpose of this survey is to flesh out one aspect of what it means to be made in the image of God—namely, royal status.

The kingship of the Lord appears in a number of passages throughout the Pentateuch and the Deuteronomistic history. Three poetic texts in the Pentateuch attest to this theme, whether ascribing to God the title "king" or describing him as reigning.[45] The Song of the Sea (Exod. 15:1–18) ends with

41. Humbert (*Études*, 170) describes the psalm as a veritable commentary on Gen. 1:26ff. ("un véritable commentaire de Gen. 1,26 suiv").

42. See, e.g., 1 Sam. 24:9, 11 [MT]; 26:15–19; 29:8; 2 Sam. 3:21; 4:8; 14:12–22; 1 Kings 1:18, 20–21, 24, 27.

43. Gregory of Nyssa, *On the Making of Man* 4.1.

44. The texts do this either by describing God with the noun "king" or by making him the subject of verbs such as to reign or to rule, as the texts discussed here show.

45. Selman, "The Kingdom of God in the Old Testament," 181.

an affirmation of his unending reign: "The Lord will reign forever and ever" (Exod. 15:18). The crossing of the Red Sea illustrates his victory over Pharaoh, as the Song of Miriam celebrates (Exod. 15:21), implicitly highlighting the superiority of the Lord's reign over that of Pharaoh. The second oracle of Balaam in the book of Numbers more explicitly ascribes to the Lord the title of "king." Significantly, it does so in the context of recounting what the Lord has done for his people, specifically bringing Israel out of Egypt:

> He has not beheld misfortune in Jacob,
> nor has he seen trouble in Israel.
> The Lord their God is with them,
> acclaimed as a king among them.
> God, who brings them out of Egypt,
> is like the horns of a wild ox for them. (Num. 23:21–22)

Moses's final blessing of the people Israel offers one last reference to God's kingship in the Pentateuch, associating it both with the Lord's acts on behalf of his people (Deut. 33:2–3) and the giving of the Law (33:4): "There arose a king in Jeshurun when the leaders of the people assembled, the united tribes of Israel" (Deut. 33:5).

A few texts describing Israel's history prior to and leading up to the establishment of the monarchy emphasize God's royal authority over Israel. The book of Judges has a complex understanding of kingship. On the one hand, the last five chapters of the book are framed by the refrain, "In those days there was no king in Israel; all the people did what was right in their own eyes" (Judg. 17:6; 21:25). The narrator describes the nefarious deeds of some of the Israelites—the robbery of Micah and the abuse and murder of a certain Levite's concubine—in association with the Israelites' lack of a king to illustrate the point (Judg. 18:1; 19:1). This seems to imply that at least some of Israel's woes stem from their having no king. On the other hand, part of the point of God raising up judges was that they were not to have a king. As Gideon insists when the people try to make him king, "I will not rule over you, and my son will not rule over you; the Lord will rule over you" (Judg. 8:23). This ambivalence about a human king carries over into the account of the establishment of the monarchy. When the people ask Samuel for a king, the Lord tells him to acquiesce, describing it as a rejection of his own kingship: "And the Lord said to Samuel, 'Listen to the voice of the people in all that they say to you, for they have not rejected you, but they have rejected me from being king over them'" (1 Sam. 8:7; cf. 12:12).

Despite the apparent rejection of God as king in 1 Samuel, the notion of God's kingship continues throughout the OT. Later texts even assimilate the Davidic kingdom into the Lord's kingship. This is particularly prominent in 1–2 Chronicles.[46] The Chronicler's version of the promises God makes to David situates the Davidic dynasty within the kingship of the Lord. Much like the account in 2 Samuel 7, the Lord assures David, "When your days are fulfilled to go to be with your ancestors, I will raise up your offspring after you, one of your own sons, and I will establish his kingdom. He shall build a house for me, and I will establish his throne forever" (1 Chron. 17:11–12). Two verses later, however, the language shifts, connecting the kingship of David's son with the Lord's own kingship: "But I will confirm him in my house and in *my kingdom* forever, and his throne shall be established forever" (1 Chron. 17:14). This emphasis on the Lord's kingdom is part of a running theme throughout the Chronicler's narrative.

In the preceding chapter, as the Levites minister before the ark of the covenant, they sing excerpts from various psalms, including Psalm 96, which includes the line, "Let the heavens be glad, and let the earth rejoice, and let them say among the nations, 'The LORD is king!'" (1 Chron. 16:31; cf. Ps. 96:10). In David's designation of Solomon as the one to build the temple, David proclaims, "And of all my sons, for the LORD has given me many, he has chosen my son Solomon to sit upon the throne of the kingdom of the LORD over Israel" (1 Chron. 28:5). In the subsequent chapter, David again ascribes the kingship to the Lord: "Yours, O LORD, are the greatness, the power, the glory, the victory, and the majesty, for *all that is in the heavens and on the earth is yours; yours is the kingdom, O LORD*, and you are exalted as head above all" (1 Chron. 29:11). One of the later references to the Lord's reign emphasizes the all-encompassing nature of his power. At the beginning of Jehoshaphat's prayer for victory, he acclaims, "O LORD, God of our ancestors, are you not God in heaven? Do you not rule over all the kingdoms of the nations? In your hand are power and might, so that no one is able to withstand you" (2 Chron. 20:5). The Lord's power thus extends to the ends of the earth, not just to Israel.

The universality of the Lord's reign also appears in the Psalter.[47] One of the clearest examples can be seen in Psalm 47, which rejoices over God's aid to the Israelites against their enemies. The psalmist repeatedly refers to the Lord as a king whose reign extends over all the earth (Ps. 47:2, 7) and who rules the nations (47:8). Though less explicit with respect to the nations, Psalm 93 likewise depicts the Lord as one whose reign extends throughout the earth, particularly by virtue of his role in its creation:

> The LORD is king, he is robed in majesty;
> the LORD is robed; he is girded with strength.

46. For an extended discussion of these and other passages, see Selman, "The Kingdom of God in the Old Testament," 163–71.

47. See Selman, "The Kingdom of God in the Old Testament," 177–78.

He has established the world; it shall never be moved;
  your throne is established from of old;
  you are from everlasting. (Ps. 93:1–2; cf. 98:4–6)

Other psalms assert the Lord's superiority to and authority over foreign gods (Pss. 95:3; 97:1, 7) and over all peoples (99:1–2). This note also appears in some of the prophetic writings, usually in conjunction with God's judgment of the nations (see, e.g., Jer. 10:7–10; 48:15; 51:57).[48]

One other important feature of God's kingship in the Psalter is the way several of the psalms connect it to God's creative activity.[49] In Psalm 74, for example, the psalmist refers to God as "my king" (74:12) and describes his command over a variety of natural phenomena:

Yours is the day, yours also the night;
  you established the luminaries and the sun.
You have fixed all the bounds of the earth;
  you made summer and winter. (Ps. 74:16–17)

Psalm 24, which ends by referring to the Lord as the "King of glory" (Ps. 24:7–10), begins by acknowledging his dominion over the whole earth:

The earth is the Lord's and all that is in it,
  the world, and those who live in it,
for he has founded it on the seas
  and established it on the rivers. (Ps. 24:1–2)

Psalm 95 likewise expounds on the Lord's control over the earth, the mountains, and the seas (Ps. 95:3–5). Finally, Psalm 145, the last psalm explicitly connected with David in the Psalter, praises the Lord as the king who wisely and mercifully governs creation.

This widespread OT understanding of God as king of creation, as well as the association of divine sonship with the Davidic dynasty, has important implications for understanding the *imago Dei* of Genesis 1. If, as argued above, the "image" and "likeness" language of Genesis 1:27 signals human beings' filial relationship to God, and if the idea of God as king lies in the background of the text, then it makes sense that a royal vocation follows from being made in God's image. This vocation does not define what it means to be made in God's image; rather, it is a consequence of the filial relationship that "image" language signifies.[50] It is hardly surprising, then, that in the

48. Selman, "The Kingdom of God in the Old Testament," 177.
49. G. Smith, "The Concept of God/the Gods as King," 34.
50. See Crouch, "Genesis 1:26–7," 9; Westermann, *Genesis 1–11*, 154–55. Clines ("The Image of God in Man," 96) acknowledges that dominion is a consequence of being God's image

context surrounding the creation of human beings in God's image and likeness, Genesis describes the purpose for which God makes human beings as involving royal tasks.

The ascription of kingship to both the people of Israel (Exod. 19:6; cf. 4:22) and the Davidic king (1 Chron. 17:11–14) contributes to one aspect of the NT vision of the end. For many of the NT writers, Davidic kingship finds its fulfillment in Jesus, the Messiah.[51] But just as God shares his governance of the universe with human beings (Gen. 1:26–28), so Jesus invites his followers to participate in his rule.

Resurrection and Kingship

Numerous texts in the Old and the New Testaments link resurrection—both that of Christ and that of believers—with royal rule.[52] In the remainder of this chapter, we will focus on a few NT texts that illustrate this connection.[53]

The NT frequently describes Jesus's resurrection with royal imagery, suggesting that the resurrection is connected to his enthronement. I will focus on three passages: the final resurrection appearance of Matthew 28, Peter's speech in Acts 2, and the opening of Romans.

In recounting the appearance of the risen Jesus to the disciples at the end of his Gospel, Matthew subtly alludes to Daniel's vision of the "one like a son of man" in Daniel 7.[54] Jesus tells his disciples, "All authority in heaven and on earth has been given to me" (Matt. 28:18), and commands them to make disciples of "all nations" (28:19). Both images, that of authority and that of the nations, evoke the heavenly vision of Daniel 7. There Daniel writes,

> As I watched in the night visions,
> I saw one like a human being
> coming with the clouds of heaven.
> And he came to the Ancient One
> and was presented before him.

---

but suggests that it is so closely connected that "it loses the character of a mere derivative and virtually becomes a constitutive part of the image itself."

51. On this theme, see Jipp, *The Messianic Theology of the New Testament*.

52. This is the primary focus of Middleton's eschatology. See Middleton, *A New Heaven and a New Earth*, especially 131–54. As I will argue, this aspect of the biblical witness is an important part of the eschatological hope, but not the only part.

53. On the OT passages that speak to this theme, see Middleton, *A New Heaven and a New Earth*, 139–45. For Middleton's discussion of the NT passages, see 145–54. My consideration of the NT evidence focuses on some of the texts Middleton considers, as well as others he does not discuss.

54. Jesus's preferred self-designation throughout the Gospels is "Son of Man," and other passages in Matthew allude to the glory of Dan. 7. See, e.g., Matt. 25:31–46.

> To him was given *dominion*
>   and glory and *kingship*,
> that *all peoples*, nations, and languages
>   should serve him.
> His *dominion* is an everlasting *dominion*
>   that shall not pass away,
> and his *kingship* is one
>   that shall never be destroyed. (Dan. 7:13–14)

Though the lexical overlap between the two passages is not extensive, two elements of Daniel's vision serve as important background for Matthew's interpretation of Jesus's resurrection. First, the LXX renders the Aramaic root *shltn* ("dominion" in the NRSVue) as *exousia*, the same word Matthew uses to describe the authority Jesus receives. Second, the "one like a human being" in Daniel is given authority over "all nations [*panta ta ethnē*]," the same phrase in Jesus's command to the disciples to go out and make disciples. In addition to the "authority" given to the "one like a human being," he is also said to have a kingdom/kingship that will not be taken away. By his allusion to this vision, then, Matthew implicitly associates Jesus's resurrection with his enthronement.

One of the clearest connections between Christ's resurrection and his enthronement appears in Peter's first speech in the Acts of the Apostles. Consider a few details of the sermon. First, Peter explicitly mentions the resurrection twice, announcing to those gathered in Jerusalem: "But God raised him up, having released him from the agony of death, because it was impossible for him to be held in its power" (Acts 2:24); "This Jesus God raised up, and of that all of us are witnesses" (2:32). Second, toward the end of the speech he cites Psalm 110:1, one of the enthronement psalms that speaks of the king taking his throne (Acts 2:34–35). Finally, he applies the psalm to Christ, implicitly linking the resurrection (and the ascension—see 2:34) with Jesus's royal enthronement: "Therefore let the entire house of Israel know with certainty that God has made him both Lord and Messiah, this Jesus whom you crucified" (2:36). The resurrection confirms and leads to Jesus's reign, which begins with the ascension.

We find a similar connection in the opening chapter of Romans. There Paul describes his gospel as a message of Christ's royal enthronement: "the gospel concerning his Son, who was descended from David according to the flesh and was declared to be Son of God with power according to the spirit of holiness *by resurrection from the dead*, Jesus Christ our Lord" (Rom. 1:3–4). The reference to Jesus's descent from David underscores his royal lineage, but his acknowledgment as "Son of God in power" comes about through the resurrection. Here, as in several of the OT texts considered above, there is a close link between divine sonship and royal authority, and for Paul both relate to Jesus's resurrection from the dead. In light of the purpose for which God creates human beings in Genesis 1, it is possible to understand the resurrection as fulfilling—or at least as establishing the conditions to fulfill—this aspect of the human vocation.

Given the close connection between Christ's resurrection and his royal authority, and given that in many NT texts regarding the Christian hope, Christ's resurrection functions as the paradigm for the resurrection of believers, it is fitting that several NT texts also connect the resurrection of believers with obtaining royal authority.[55] In Matthew, Christ promises the Twelve a share in his reign: "Jesus said to them, 'Truly I tell you, at the renewal of all things [*palingenesia*], when the Son of Man is seated on the throne of his glory, you who have followed me will also sit on twelve thrones, judging the twelve tribes of Israel'" (Matt. 19:28). Like the final resurrection appearance, this passage also evokes Daniel 7 with the phrases "the Son of Man" and "the throne of his glory," implying that the Twelve will share in Christ's own royal authority. Similarly, 2 Timothy connects resurrection with reign: "The saying is sure: If we have died with him, we will also live with him; if we endure, we will also reign with him" (2 Tim. 2:11–12a). The parallelism between the phrases "live with him" (which likely refers to resurrection) and "reign with him" once again invests the resurrection with a royal dimension. Finally, in the letters to the seven churches in the book of Revelation, the risen Christ makes various promises "to everyone who conquers." Along with several promises concerning the resurrection (Rev. 2:7, 11; 3:5), two of these letters speak of reigning as the reward for conquering. In the letter to the church in Thyatira, Christ says, "To everyone who conquers and continues to do my works to the end, *I will give authority over the nations, to rule them with an iron scepter*, as when clay pots are shattered—even as I also received authority from my Father" (Rev. 2:26–28a). Similarly, in the letter to the church in Laodicea, Christ promises, "To the one who conquers *I will give a place with me on my throne*, just as I myself conquered and sat down with my Father on his throne" (3:21). Eschatological texts in the NT thus repeatedly portray the Christian hope in a way that recapitulates the royal vocation of human beings described in Genesis 1.

A Royal Eschatological Hope

Let us return to the principle ascribed to Gunkel, "The end resembles the beginning." In the beginning, God created human beings so that they might have dominion over creation, participating in his own royal authority. Many

55. Middleton discusses some of the following texts in *A New Heaven and a New Earth*, 145–54. On the resurrection as the pattern of Christian hope, see pp. 152–56 below.

texts in the NT allude to this original purpose in their descriptions of the Christian hope for the resurrection, suggesting that this royal vocation will be fulfilled at the eschaton. We will return to the question of what this vocation might look like in a later chapter. For now, note that dominion serves as an important aspect of the eschatological hope. It is not, however, the only aspect of that hope. At least two other elements of the creation accounts—rest and worship—also feature in the hope described in the NT. The following two chapters will explore these aspects of the human vocation.

TWO

Rest

At the end of *City of God*, Augustine famously describes the life of the blessed as a "Sabbath" and an "eternal rest" marked by peace, joy, and stillness.[1] Although some contemporary eschatologies affirm the importance of rest, whether explicitly or implicitly, the theme has not featured as prominently as it might either in biblical scholarship or in theologies of the end.[2] Around the middle of the twentieth century, Gerhard von Rad lamented the general neglect of the theme of rest in biblical theology, despite its prominence throughout the OT.[3] In 2017 Kevin Cathcart suggested that the situation had remained largely the same over subsequent decades.[4] Although some work has been done to explore the importance of rest, two recent biblical eschatologies seem to confirm Cathcart's assessment.[5] J. Richard Middleton's biblical eschatology, *A New Heaven and a New Earth*, for example, effectively ignores the theme of rest throughout the Scriptures.[6] N. T. Wright's *Surprised by Hope* fares a little better, acknowledging that "rest" is the language Scripture uses

1. Augustine, *Civ.* 22.30.

2. Rest plays a role, for example, in Griffiths, *Decreation*, 215–40; O'Callaghan, *Christ Our Hope*, 153–59.

3. Von Rad, "There Remains Still a Rest," 94.

4. Cathcart, "The Idea of 'Rest' in the Old Testament."

5. For a treatment of the theme published shortly before Cathcart's essay, see Haydock, *Old Testament Theology and the Rest of God*; with regard to the NT, see also Laansma, *"I Will Give You Rest."*

6. Middleton, *A New Heaven and a New Earth*. This is one of the main weaknesses of Middleton's fascinating contribution to biblical eschatology. Middleton privileges the royal imagery too exclusively, ignoring or downplaying other aspects of the creation account and how they figure into the eschatological promises of the NT. In particular, he says nothing about rest (the term does not even appear in the subject index), and he makes little of the worship imagery that plays a crucial role in the book of Revelation.

to speak of the dead as they anticipate the resurrection. Nevertheless, Wright strangely contrasts rest with resurrection.[7]

The neglect of rest in the works of scholars like Middleton and Wright may stem from the infrequent appearance of that theme in the NT. Hebrews 3–4 is the only extended exposition of the idea. Nevertheless, rest features prominently throughout the OT. Indeed, the OT suggests that rest is an important part of what it means to be human. It also lies at the heart of Israel's hope. To neglect its importance, then, is to miss a crucial aspect of the OT. The present chapter will explore the various facets of rest in the OT before teasing out the way some of the NT writers take up the notion in relation to the Christian hope. We will begin with a discussion of the Sabbath, both as the culmination of the first creation account and as it is described in the two versions of the Sabbath commandment in Exodus and Deuteronomy, as well as the description of the Sabbath law in Exodus 31. From there we will consider two different dimensions of rest in the OT: liberation from enemies and relief from toil.[8] Rounding out the discussion of the OT, we will return to the idea of God's own rest. In several OT texts, God's "rest" signifies his dwelling with his people in the sanctuary. We will then turn our attention to three NT texts that speak of rest: Matthew 11; Hebrews 3–4; and Revelation 14. The combined witness of the Old and New Testaments suggests that rest forms an essential aspect of the Christian hope. Moreover, rest serves as a bridge between the royal vocation and the priestly vocation, being closely associated with the establishment of the sanctuary, which is often the work of a royal figure.

"Six Days Shall You Labor"

Although Genesis 1 describes the creation of human beings on the sixth day, and on that day God gives human beings the command to have dominion over creation, the first creation story does not end there. The account climaxes with the seventh day described in Genesis 2:1–3 when God takes his rest.[9] Four features of this text set it apart from the rest of the creation narrative. First, unlike the first six days of creation, the seventh day does not end with

7. N. T. Wright, *Surprised by Hope*, 22–23. Like Middleton, Wright's book completely ignores Heb. 3–4, though he redresses this neglect in *History and Eschatology*, 162–85.

8. For this taxonomy, see Lee, "Rest and Victory in Revelation 14.13."

9. L. Michael Morales (*The Tabernacle Prefigured*, 94) helpfully distinguishes between "the crown of creation (humanity)" and its purpose or goal. In this chapter I approach the question of the Sabbath from a synchronic, canonical perspective, rather than a diachronic, historical perspective. This is not to deny the value of the latter approach. Nevertheless, as Levenson notes (*Israel's Day of Light and Joy*, 78), for certain purposes a synchronic approach is "positively required" by the biblical text as we have it. For a fascinating discussion of the history behind the Sabbath commandments, see Levenson's study, especially 1–94.

the formula "And there was evening and there was morning."[10] Second, God does not create on the seventh day as he does on the preceding six days, when God repeatedly creates with a word of command. As with the phrase "And there was evening and there was morning," the seventh day breaks up the pattern, although the Hebrew text suggests that God completed creation on the seventh day.[11] According to Abraham Heschel, the ancient rabbis, faced with a text stating that God finished his work on the seventh day, concluded that on it God created *menukhah* (rest)—that is, the Sabbath.[12] This rest was not merely a relief from labor, but rather a positive good that completed creation: "To the biblical mind *menuha* [rest] is the same as happiness and stillness, as peace and harmony."[13] Third, again unlike the preceding six days, the Genesis account mentions not just once but twice that it is the seventh day. Finally, Genesis also distinguishes the seventh day from the other six days by noting that God pronounces this day "holy."

These features underscore the significance of the seventh day in the first creation story. According to some interpreters, the importance of this day extends beyond creation itself. Pointing once again to the absence of the refrain "And there was evening and there was morning," Nicholas Haydock suggests that the seventh day has something of the character of eternity.[14] Whether or not this is an accurate reading of Genesis itself, ancient interpreters, both Jewish and Christian, understood the Sabbath as pointing to—and even in some sense participating in—eternity.[15] Some ancient Jewish interpreters even connected the Sabbath not only with the world to come but also with the notion of reigning. As Heschel notes, "[The Sabbath] is a time in which 'there is neither eating nor drinking nor worldly transactions; but the righteous sit enthroned, their crowns on their heads, and enjoy the luster of the Shechinah.'"[16] For others the Sabbath was not just a foretaste of eternity but its "fountainhead."[17]

10. Haydock, *Old Testament Theology and the Rest of God*, 2.

11. The question of whether God created anything on the seventh day has vexed interpreters since antiquity. Although the Hebrew text suggests that God finished the work of creation on the seventh day, which seems to imply some work on that day, some ancient Greek and Syriac translations substitute "sixth" for "seventh" to avoid the impression that God worked on the Sabbath. For a brief discussion of the issues involved, see M. Smith, *The Priestly Vision of Genesis 1*, 106–7.

12. Heschel, *The Sabbath*, 22–23, 54.

13. Heschel, *The Sabbath*, 23. In an endnote Heschel points to Deut. 12:9, which correlates "rest" with the inheritance of the land.

14. Haydock, *Old Testament Theology and the Rest of God*, 3: "On this matter, there is a natural overlap between the seventh day and the hoped for eschatological rest to come."

15. For the ancient Jewish understanding of the Sabbath in these terms see Heschel, *The Sabbath*, 73–76. In *City of God*, Augustine characterizes the life of the world to come as an eternal Sabbath. See *Civ*. 22.30.

16. Heschel, *The Sabbath*, 74, citing Abot de-Rabbi Nathan chap. 1.

17. Heschel, *The Sabbath*, 74.

Although the first creation account does not explicitly suggest that human beings will participate in God's Sabbath rest, the text seems to imply such a participation. The account of the creation of human beings in 1:26–27 and the description of God hallowing the Sabbath in 2:2–3 share a number of poetic features that link them together.[18] These parallels, combined with humanity's creation in the divine image, suggest to some interpreters an implicit expectation that human beings are created in order to observe the Sabbath.[19]

The book of Exodus explicitly interprets the Sabbath commandment in terms of imitating God:

> Remember the Sabbath day and keep it holy. Six days you shall labor and do all your work. But the seventh day is a Sabbath to the LORD your God; you shall not do any work—you, your son or your daughter, your male or female slave, your livestock, or the alien resident in your towns. *For in six days the LORD made heaven and earth, the sea, and all that is in them, but rested the seventh day*; therefore the LORD blessed the Sabbath day and consecrated it. (Exod. 20:8–11)

The purpose of the Sabbath commandment in Exodus, then, is to draw Israel into a rest analogous to God's own. What remains implicit in the creation account becomes explicit in the commandment. This calling suggests that, like the first human beings, Israel was created not simply for labor, but also to participate in God's own rest.[20]

The first explicit command to observe the Sabbath appears in the text just considered, Exodus 20. The importance of the Sabbath is evident from the frequency and placement of commands relating to its observance. The first implicit reference to the Sabbath commandment appears shortly after the crossing of the Red Sea. When the Lord provides the Israelites with daily food, he orders them to collect twice as much on the sixth day so that they can rest on the seventh day (Exod. 16:5, 26), a day he describes as "a day of solemn rest, a holy Sabbath to the LORD" (16:23).[21] The book returns to the commandment yet again in the midst of the description of the tabernacle

18. See L. M. Morales, *The Tabernacle Prefigured*, 95–96, who builds on Cassuto, *Genesis I*, 57.

19. L. M. Morales, *The Tabernacle Prefigured*, 95–96; Cassuto, *Genesis I*, 64–65; Firmage, "Genesis 1 and the Priestly Agenda," 110; M. Smith, *The Priestly Vision of Genesis 1*, 104–6. Such an expectation remains implicit, however. Levenson (*Israel's Day of Light and Joy*, 95) rightly notes that the first reference to the Sabbath in the Pentateuchal narrative does not occur until Exod. 16.

20. Not all interpreters agree on this point. Von Rad ("There Remains Still a Rest," 101), for example, denies any connection between God's rest and the rest spoken of in Deuteronomy, Chronicles, and the Psalms. See also Laansma, *"I Will Give You Rest,"* 64–65.

21. Levenson (*Israel's Day of Light and Joy*, 65) notes, "As the storyline of the Pentateuch would have it, the sabbatical commandment was announced even before Israel arrived at Sinai/Horeb, as part of the narrative about the manna, the miraculous food with which God sustained them during their wanderings in the wilderness (Exod 16:21–30)."

(Exod. 31) in the last major section of the book. This passage underscores both the importance of the Sabbath and its connection to God's own observance of the Sabbath.

A few comments are in order regarding this discussion of the Sabbath. First, Exodus 31 draws a connection between the Lord and the people with respect to Sabbath observance. The Lord says to Moses, "You yourself are to speak to the Israelites, 'You shall keep *my* Sabbaths, for this is a sign between me and you throughout your generations, given in order that you may know that I, the Lord, sanctify you'" (Exod. 31:13). This initial command speaks of Sabbaths (plural), but as the passage continues the language shifts to a singular Sabbath, drawing a connection between Israelite observance and the Lord's own Sabbath. Toward the end of the passage the Lord says, "Therefore the Israelites shall keep the Sabbath, observing the Sabbath throughout their generations, as a perpetual covenant. It is a sign forever between me and the Israelites that in six days the Lord made heaven and earth, and on the seventh day he rested and was refreshed" (31:16–17). Once again, what remains implicit in the first creation account of Genesis here becomes explicit. The Israelites are called to participate in the Lord's own Sabbath. The Sabbath is also connected with life, or at least with the possibility of forfeiting life. Twice the Lord warns Moses that anyone who disregards or "profanes" the Sabbath will be put to death (31:14–15). By implication, then, the Sabbath is a source of life. It is easy to see how later interpreters would associate the Sabbath with eternity and life.[22]

Before we move on to the Deuteronomic version of the Sabbath commandment, it is worth noting the close connection between the Sabbath and the tabernacle. As Brevard Childs notes, references to the Sabbath punctuate both the end of the first account of the tabernacle and the beginning of the second account of its building (Exod. 35:1–3).[23] In both instances, the references to the Sabbath underscore the importance of rest from toil. This suggests that rest and worship go together.[24]

The Sabbath commandment in Deuteronomy gives a different rationale for the observance, but also suggests that Israel's ultimate vocation is rest, not labor.[25] The Deuteronomic form of the commandment links Sabbath observance with God's act of redeeming Israel from their toil in Egypt:

22. See, e.g., Augustine, *Civ.* 22.30; Mekilta to Exodus 31:17; Mishnah Tamid.

23. Childs, *Exodus*, 541.

24. As Childs (*Exodus*, 541) puts it, "Therefore, the observance of the sabbath and the building of the tabernacle are two sides of the same reality. Just as the sabbath is a surety of Israel's sanctity (31.13), so the meeting of God with his people in the tabernacle serves the selfsame end (29.43)."

25. On the relationship between the two versions of the Sabbath commandment, see Levenson, *Israel's Day of Light and Joy*, 80–94.

> Observe the Sabbath day and keep it holy, as the LORD your God commanded you. Six days you shall labor and do all your work. But the seventh day is a Sabbath to the LORD your God; you shall not do any work—you, or your son or your daughter. . . . *Remember that you were a slave in the land of Egypt, and the LORD your God brought you out from there with a mighty hand and an outstretched arm*; therefore the LORD your God commanded you to keep the Sabbath day. (Deut. 5:12–15)

These verses reflect themes in the early chapters of Exodus, which portray God's redemptive activity as a response to Israel's groaning in slavery (see Exod. 2:23–24). The people's slavery to Pharaoh is the plight that drives the first part of the book (Exod. 1–15); in the initial demand that Moses makes to Pharaoh, however, he simply asks for a respite for the people: "Thus says the LORD, the God of Israel: Let my people go, so that *they may celebrate a festival to me in the wilderness*" (Exod. 5:1b). God's purpose in redeeming Israel thus includes giving the people rest from their labors, a rest that takes the form of offering sacrifice to the Lord (cf. Exod. 3:18; 5:3, 8, 17).[26]

Perhaps the clearest indication of Israel's hope of participating in God's rest appears in Psalm 95. The psalm itself does not explicitly connect the Lord's rest with the Sabbath, but it is an obvious connection for the writer of Hebrews to draw (Heb. 4:4–5).[27] Whether intentionally or not, the psalm also reflects the two different themes associated with the two versions of the Sabbath commandment: creation and the exodus. The first seven verses focus primarily on the Lord's status as creator, noting his dominion over earth, mountains, sea, and dry land (Ps. 95:4–5), before shifting to the imagery of the Lord as shepherd. With this shift the psalmist recalls an episode from Israel's time in the wilderness, the people's contention and grumbling at the waters of Meribah and Massah (Ps. 95:8–9). The psalm ends on a cautionary note, recalling the punishment the wilderness generation received: "Therefore in my anger I swore, 'They shall not enter my rest'" (Ps. 95:11). Some interpreters have seen eschatological overtones in the psalm, suggesting that entering God's rest is the eschatological reward the psalmist's listeners risk losing.[28] Others argue, rather, that this psalm provides the seedbed of later eschatological hopes.[29]

26. Thus, already one sees a close connection between rest and worship, a point to which we will return. Middleton's *A New Heaven and a New Earth* pays no attention to this important theme in Exodus, or anywhere else in the OT.

27. For more on the passage from Hebrews, see pp. 39–42 below.

28. Kaiser, "The Promise Theme and the Theology of Rest."

29. Sigmund Mowinckel writes of this psalm: "Eschatology arose when everything *that one originally expected as the immediate consequences, to be actualized in the course of the year, of the annual enthronement of YHWH experienced in the cult were shifted into an indefinite future*, as something that will come 'one day' when YHWH will ultimately ascend to his throne for the last time, conquer his enemies, hold court, bring great good fortune for his people, fulfill all their expectations and hopes and, then, dwell among them forever as the

Regardless of whether the psalm originally described eschatological hopes, the letter to the Hebrews appropriates the psalm in this way.[30]

"That We Would Be Saved from Our Enemies"

Although the Sabbath commandments are the most obvious and prominent expressions of Israel's delight in rest, the hope for rest appears frequently throughout the OT. In the canticle of Zechariah, traditionally known as the *Benedictus*, Zechariah rejoices in the expectation of Christ's birth, seeing in this birth the hope "that we would be saved from our enemies and from the hand of all who hate us" (Luke 1:71). The OT repeatedly expresses this hope for Israel's relief from their enemies in terms of rest. Significantly, the promise or establishment of rest appears at climactic points in the people's history (e.g., Josh. 11:23; 21:44; 2 Sam. 7:10).[31]

As Cathcart notes, one of the most important passages for the discussion of rest in the OT is Deuteronomy 12:8–11. This text contains a high concentration of terminology relating to the concept of rest, although it uses a variety of Hebrew words to refer to that rest.[32] As such, it brings together many (though not all) of the aspects of rest in the OT both linguistically and thematically. The whole chapter focuses on the establishment of a site for the worship of the Lord in the form of offering sacrifices (12:11), and the other elements of rest relate to that theme.

One such element is relief from enemies. As in several OT texts, this relief is a precondition for proper worship.[33] Thus, Moses says to the people, "When you cross over the Jordan and live in the land that the Lord your God is allotting to you, and *when he gives you rest from your enemies all around* so that you live in safety, then you shall bring everything that I command you to the place that the Lord your God will choose as a dwelling for his name" (Deut. 12:10–11a). Possessing the land is not an end in itself. Rather, its purpose is to serve as a place for God to dwell in the midst of his people and for the people to have a place to bring gifts and sacrifices to the Lord (12:11b).[34]

source of life and light" (Mowinckel, *Psalms Studies*, 401; emphasis original). In this light, it is no surprise that Hebrews interprets Ps. 95 eschatologically, whether or not it originally had an eschatological character.

30. See the discussion on pp. 39–42 below.

31. I am grateful to Neil Martin for this point.

32. See Cathcart, "The Idea of 'Rest' in the Old Testament," 7–8; see also the discussion of G. Robinson, "The Idea of Rest."

33. This should come as no surprise, given the whole thrust of Exodus, in which relief from the Egyptians is ordered to worship and the offering of sacrifice.

34. See Braun, "Solomon, the Chosen Temple Builder," 583: "For Deuteronomy the concept of rest was integrally bound up with the unification of the cult at one central sanctuary, which meant the Jerusalem temple, desired by David and built by Solomon."

Relief from Israel's enemies is ordered to worship. This connection between relief from enemies and the establishment of a sanctuary is a recurring motif in the historical books of the OT.

Rest from enemies and possession of the land feature at important points in the book of Joshua. Toward the beginning of the book, Joshua exhorts the two and a half tribes that have settled beyond the Jordan to help their fellow Israelites in the conquest of the land, appealing to the hope for rest. First, he reminds these tribes that the Lord has already given them a place of rest (Josh. 1:13). He then urges them to help the other tribes "*until the* L*ORD* *gives rest to your kindred as well as to you*, and they also take possession of the land that the LORD your God is giving them" (1:15a). According to the idealized description of the conquest, the Israelites achieve this rest by around the middle of the book: "So Joshua took the whole land, according to all that the LORD had spoken to Moses, and Joshua gave it for an inheritance to Israel according to their tribal allotments. *And the land had rest from war*" (11:23). Roddy Braun astutely connects this verse with another summary statement at the beginning of Joshua 18.[35] Following a description of the allotment of the land, the narrator notes, "Then the whole congregation of the Israelites assembled at Shiloh and set up the tent of meeting there. The land lay subdued before them" (18:1). The establishment of the Israelite worship space follows and depends upon the possession of the land.

The rest described in Joshua is idealized and temporary, as subsequent historical books indicate. The book of Judges describes the early history in the land as anything but restful for the Israelites, and the time of the kings can likewise be characterized as a cycle of alternating rest and warfare. In the description of this cycle, one sees, again, a close connection between rest and worship. Moreover, there seems to be ambiguity regarding whether and to what extent the Israelites enjoyed rest. The account of the establishment of the Davidic covenant in 2 Samuel 7 reflects this ambiguity, as well as the close connection between rest and establishing a place of worship. The chapter begins by suggesting that David is enjoying rest from his enemies (2 Sam. 7:1). Later in the chapter, however, the text implies that this rest is incomplete: "And I will appoint a place for my people Israel and will plant them, so that they may live in their own place and be disturbed no more, and evildoers shall afflict them no more, as formerly, from the time that I appointed judges over my people Israel, *and I will give you rest from all your enemies*. Moreover, the LORD declares to you that the LORD will make you a house" (2 Sam. 7:10–11). Even though David is already enjoying rest from his enemies, the Lord promises to give him rest. In this life, it seems, rest follows a cyclical pattern.

35. Braun, "Solomon, the Chosen Temple Builder," 584.

The cyclical nature of rest appears frequently in the historical books. Several passages seem to suggest that Israel's rest is reversible.[36] Perhaps more importantly, however, the Davidic covenant illustrates a recurring theme throughout the historical books: Rest has a purpose. It is not simply rest *from* something (namely, one's enemies), but rather rest *for* the sake of offering sacrifice.[37] The Lord's promises to David in 2 Samuel 7 are prompted by his desire to build a house—that is, a permanent temple for the Lord. Although the Lord rejects David's offer, he promises David that his son will build a temple. The rest from Israel's enemies that the Lord gives the people thus precedes and makes possible the building of the temple.

This connection between liturgy and rest from enemies appears once again in the description of Solomon's intention to build the temple. Solomon's words even suggest that this rest makes his building project possible. Speaking to Hiram, king of Tyre, Solomon asserts that David could not build a temple for the Lord because of the continual warfare in which he was engaged (1 Kings 5:3). In Solomon's day, by contrast, the Lord has granted him rest from his enemies (5:4) and because of this he decides to build a house for the Lord to fulfill the promise the Lord had made to David (5:5). Once again, we see a close association between rest from Israel's enemies and the establishment of the temple. This connection also appears implicitly in the dedication ceremony for the temple. Solomon's blessing of the people begins with an acknowledgment that the Lord has given his people rest: "Blessed be the Lord, *who has given rest to his people Israel* according to all that he promised; not one word has failed of all his good promise that he spoke through his servant Moses" (8:56). As Wolfgang Roth notes, although the rest of Solomon's blessing does not refer to the temple, it does emphasize God's nearness to his people (see, e.g., 8:57).[38] Rest and the dwelling of God in Israel's midst go hand in hand.

"On It God Rested"

In addition to the theme of relief from Israel's enemies, the rest motif also refers to relief from toil or labor.[39] From a canonical perspective, this kind of rest finds its basis in the Sabbath, both the description of God's rest on the

36. See Roth, "The Deuteronomic Rest Theology," 8. Roth cites Josh. 23:11–13 as an example of the reversibility of Israel's rest. For a similar point, see von Rad, "There Remains Still a Rest," 97.

37. See Roth, "The Deuteronomic Rest Theology," 10: "In other words, the divine gift of rest is not so much 'rest from . . .' as it is 'rest for . . . .'" Along similar lines, see N. T. Wright, *History and Eschatology*, 164–65.

38. Roth, "The Deuteronomic Rest Theology," 11–12.

39. For a brief discussion of these two traditions of rest, particularly with respect to the NT, see Lee, "Rest and Victory in Revelation 14.13," 345–50.

seventh day and the two versions of the Sabbath commandment. Genesis 2 describes the completion of God's work of creation, symbolized by the rest he takes on the seventh day. The two Sabbath commandments likewise reflect this hope for rest from toil. As noted above, the Exodus version of the commandment connects the practice of the Sabbath with God's rest. Human beings are made not only for labor but also to rest as God rests. The Deuteronomic version of the commandment makes this even clearer, connecting the Sabbath with Israel's liberation from Egypt. Observance of the Sabbath serves as a reminder that the Israelites are no longer slaves.

Walter Brueggemann has argued that weariness can extend beyond labor to include things like exile and the chaos that follows from exile.[40] Against this backdrop, rest refers not to sleep or repose, but rather to proper order and well-being.[41] This aspect of rest features in a particular way in the prophetic literature of the OT, especially (though not exclusively) in Isaiah. There we see rest closely associated with God's rule, whether *simpliciter* or as exercised through earthly kings.

Isaiah 14 contains a taunt against the king of Babylon, promising that the Lord will give his people rest. Although this passage is directed to one of Israel's enemies, in contrast to the passages considered above the focus falls not on relief from warfare, but rather from oppression and toil. The text begins with an implicit promise of rest that will lead the Israelites to mock the king of Babylon: "When the LORD has given you rest from your pain and turmoil and the hard service [Hebrew *'abodah*, Greek *douleias*] with which you were made to serve, you will take up this taunt against the king of Babylon" (Isa. 14:3–4a). The "hard service" under which the Israelites have toiled and from which the Lord promises to give them relief recalls their slavery in Egypt (cf. Exod. 2:23; 5:9).[42] As at the exodus, the Lord frees his people once again from their oppressors, who weighed them down with labor. Brueggemann notes that the taunt underscores the "rest and quiet" that characterizes living under the Lord's rule, in contrast to the chaos and destruction that follows from Babylon's rule.[43] This connection between divine rule and rest likewise resembles one of the main themes in Exodus. Immediately after the crossing of the Red Sea, the Song of the Sea ends on the note of the Lord's reign (Exod. 15:18), and toward the end of the chapter the Lord enjoins the Israelites to follow his commandments (15:26). Genuine rest thus stems, in part, from obeying the Lord.

40. See Brueggemann, "Weariness, Exile, and Chaos."

41. Cathcart ("The Idea of 'Rest' in the Old Testament," 22) comes to a similar conclusion: "In the Old Testament 'weariness' refers to misery and trouble, 'rest' means peace and well-being."

42. See also Laansma, *"I Will Give You Rest,"* 53.

43. Brueggemann, "Weariness, Exile, and Chaos," 23.

Elsewhere in Isaiah, the Lord's ordering of Israel is exercised through earthly rulers. Isaiah 32 begins with a reference to such rule and the relief that it brings:

> See, a king will reign in righteousness,
> and princes will rule with justice.
> Each will be like a hiding place from the wind,
> a covert from the tempest,
> like streams of water in a dry place,
> like the shade of a great rock in a weary land. (Isa. 32:1–2)

Once again, the explicit language of "rest" does not appear in this passage, but the theme of relief from weariness is very much present. Rest language does appear later in the chapter in a passage that is likely connected to the earlier promise of a king and princes. The prophet speaks of a time when the Lord (so it is implied) sends a spirit upon the people (32:15). With this outpouring will come conditions similar to those ascribed to the time when the king and the princes govern (32:1). The key words "justice" and "righteousness," which characterize the reign of the king and the princes, reappear in 32:16.[44] This righteousness results in peace, quiet, and trust (32:17) and brings the people to "quiet resting places" (32:18). As is often the case in the OT, the rest envisioned does not mean simply lounging about. Rather, this rest is compatible with agricultural labor, as the oracle ends with the following pronouncement: "Happy will you be who sow beside every stream, who let the ox and the donkey range freely" (32:20). This work differs, however, from the servile labor that characterized Israel's time in Egypt.[45] It is not burdensome, but rather free.

Earlier in Isaiah, the prophet concentrates the promise of rest in a hoped-for king. Isaiah 11, one of the most famous oracles in the book, describes a coming spirit-anointed ruler who is from the line of Jesse and will bring about Edenic conditions (Isa. 11:1–9). The subsequent oracle elaborates on what this king will bring about: "On that day the root of Jesse shall stand as a signal to the peoples; the nations shall inquire of him, and his dwelling [*menukhah*] shall be glorious" (11:10). The word rendered "dwelling" here could also be translated as "rest" or "resting place."[46] The Davidic king will enjoy a glorious rest. The connotation of rest seems important, given what follows in the oracle. The prophet goes on to describe how the Lord will bring

44. Brueggemann (*Isaiah 1–39*, 258) notes this shared language but suggests that perhaps in the latter oracle (32:15–20) God displaces the Davidic king.

45. For a similar point with respect to other OT passages, see Laansma, *"I Will Give You Rest,"* 25.

46. The LXX renders it *anapausis*, "rest."

back a remnant of Israel from exile (11:11–12), and this return is to resemble the exodus from Egypt. The prophet writes,

> And the Lord will utterly dry up
> the tongue of the sea of Egypt
> and will wave his hand over the River
> with his scorching wind
> and will split it into seven channels
> and make a way to cross on foot;
> so there shall be a highway from Assyria
> for the remnant that is left of his people,
> as there was for Israel
> when they came up from the land of Egypt. (Isa. 11:15–16)

Just as the Lord once rescued the Israelites from their toil and oppression in Egypt, he promises to do so once again, bringing them (implicitly) into the glorious rest of the Davidic heir.

The importance of rest can be seen not only in expressions of hope, such as the ones just considered, but also in Israel's laments over its loss at times of exile. One can see this most clearly in the opening chapter of Lamentations. This moving expression of grief over the devastation of Jerusalem notes the people's hard labor:

> Judah has gone into exile with suffering
> and hard servitude [Hebrew *'abodah*, Greek *douleias*];
> she lives now among the nations;
> she *finds no resting place* [Hebrew *manoakh*, Greek *anapausin*];
> her pursuers have all overtaken her
> in the midst of her distress. (Lam. 1:3)

Like Isaiah 14, Lamentations associates the desire for rest with the "hard servitude" under which the exiles suffer. Their situation once again resembles the situation of the Israelites in Egypt. This servile labor is not the only point of contact between Lamentations and the situation at the exodus. In addition to the oppression the people suffer, the writer also laments what this means for the temple:

> The roads to Zion mourn,
> for no one comes to the festivals;
> all her gates are desolate;
> her priests groan;
> her young girls grieve,
> and her lot is bitter. (Lam. 1:4)

As noted above, one primary purpose of the exodus was worship. God's first demand to Pharaoh is to let the Israelites hold a festival to the Lord in the wilderness (Exod. 5:1), and the whole thrust of Exodus points to the importance of worship, as seen in the description of the tabernacle.[47] Similarly, in Lamentations the people's service is certainly bad, but it is made even worse by the suspension of liturgical feasts.

"This Is My Resting Place Forever"

In addition to relief from enemies and from toil or oppression, the OT theme of rest can also have a liturgical connotation. Before turning to the NT, it is worth considering this aspect of rest a little more closely. Recall that relief from enemies often leads to the establishment of a worship site, suggesting that the latter is an important purpose of the former. This notion features prominently in Chronicles, as well as in Psalm 132, which the Chronicler quotes loosely at the end of Solomon's prayer before the dedication of the temple.

Several times in Chronicles the writer associates rest with the establishment of the temple. In 1 Chronicles 22 David explains why Solomon is the one to build the temple. A word from the Lord explains that David is disqualified from the task because he was a man of war (1 Chron. 22:8). Nevertheless, the Lord also promises that David's son will build a house for the name of the Lord. Solomon meets the qualification to erect the temple because, in contrast to his father David, he is "a man of rest [Hebrew *'ish menukhah*; Greek *anēr anapauseōs*]" (1 Chron. 22:9a). This "rest" comes as a gift from the Lord: "I will give him rest from all his enemies on every side; indeed, his name shall be Solomon, and I will give peace and quiet to Israel in his days" (1 Chron. 22:9b). Rest, then, is a prerequisite for building a residence for the Lord. This emphasis on rest is fitting, given that the word also can indicate God's dwelling among his people.

In the next chapter, David draws a subtle connection between rest for the people and the Lord's residence in their midst. Here, rest indicates not a complete cessation of work, but rather a shift from one kind of activity to another. Both activities, however, relate to Israel's worship. So, David says to the Levites, "The Lord, the God of Israel, has given rest to his people, and he resides in Jerusalem forever. And so the Levites no longer need to carry the tabernacle or any of the things for its service" (1 Chron. 23:25–26). Once again, Israel's rest precedes the Lord's residence in Jerusalem. This rest, the text suggests, includes no longer physically carrying the tabernacle and its vessels from place to place. This does not mean, however, that there will be no

47. The MT uses different words for "festival" in each text (*khagag* in Exodus, *mo'ed* in Lamentations), but in Greek both texts use a word related to *heortē*.

activity for the Levites. On the contrary, the Levites' task now consists solely in assisting the priests in the "service [Hebrew *'abodah*; Greek *leitourgein*] of the house of the LORD" (1 Chron. 23:28). True rest, the Chronicler suggests, is ordered to and found in worship. The purpose of rest is to make possible communion between the people and the Lord.

A few chapters later, David gives voice to his frustrated desire to build a temple, once again using the language of "rest":

> Then King David rose to his feet and said, "Hear me, my brothers and my people. I had planned to build a *house of rest* [*bet menukhah*; *oikon anapauseōs*] for the ark of the covenant of the LORD, for the footstool of our God, and I made preparations for building. But God said to me, 'You shall not build a house for my name, for you are a warrior and have shed blood.'" (1 Chron. 28:2–3)

Once again, the Chronicler notes that David's excessive bloodshed prevents him from building the temple. Unlike his son Solomon, David is not a "man of rest" and therefore is not allowed to build a "house of rest" for the Lord. There seems to be a connection between the cessation of warfare and God's taking up his dwelling among his people. For this reason, it seems, the one to build the temple must also be characterized by rest.

The theme of rest appears once more in Solomon's prayer at the dedication of the temple. At the end of this prayer Solomon says,

> Now rise up, O LORD God, and go to your resting place,
> you and the ark of your might.
> Let your priests, O LORD God, be clothed with salvation,
> and let your faithful rejoice in your goodness.
> O LORD God, do not reject your anointed one.
> Remember your steadfast love for your servant David. (2 Chron. 6:41–42)

Interpreters have noted the similarity between this prayer and two other texts from the OT, Numbers 10:35–36 and Psalm 132.[48] Both texts, like Solomon's prayer, refer to the "rest" of the ark of the covenant. In the Numbers passage, the rest seems to be a recurring, temporary interlude during Israel's wanderings in the wilderness. Psalm 132, by contrast, seems to envision a more permanent place of rest located in Zion.

In the first part of Psalm 132, the psalmist recounts David's many efforts on behalf of the Lord, searching for "a dwelling place for the Mighty One of Jacob" (Ps. 132:5b). This dwelling place, a kind of sanctuary, seems to be interchangeable with the place of the Lord's rest. A few verses later, the

48. See Laansma, *"I Will Give You Rest,"* 38–39, and the literature cited there.

psalmist implores, "Rise up, O Lord, and go to your resting place, you and the ark of your might" (132:8). The second part of the psalm summarizes the Lord's response to the prayer in the first part. The Lord first reaffirms the oath he swore to David, an oath that includes conditions regarding the faithfulness of David's descendants. The Lord's reply then shifts to the theme of the sanctuary:

> For the Lord has chosen Zion;
>   he has desired it for his habitation:
> "This is my resting place forever;
>   here I will reside, for I have desired it." (Ps. 132:13–14)

The Lord "rests" on Mount Zion, establishing his dwelling with Israel there.[49]

Old Testament Rest: A Summary

Before turning to the NT, it is worth summarizing a few key aspects of rest in the OT. The pervasiveness of the theme indicates its importance for the ancient Israelites, and, therefore, its significance for any theology that takes the Scriptures seriously. We have considered three different aspects of rest in the OT. First, rest frequently refers to relief from warfare. Rest in this sense is almost synonymous with peace. Second, rest also often concerns relief from oppression and toil, what Brueggemann calls "weariness." One can see this most clearly in the two versions of the Sabbath commandment, especially the Deuteronomic version, which contrasts rest with the Israelites' condition of enslavement in Egypt. Third, and perhaps most importantly, rest is closely associated with the temple. Both the notion of Israel finding a place to dwell and of the Lord finding a resting place come together in the notion of worship. In fact, often relief from warfare and relief from oppression are ordered to worship.[50] Deuteronomy 12, for example, closely connects Israel's relief from her enemies with the establishment of a centralized place of worship where the Lord will dwell in the midst of his people. Lamentations grieves over the people's oppression, longing for the renewal of Israel's festivals. Rest in the OT sense, then, does not simply mean taking a day off. Rather, rest is ordered to and finds its fulfillment in worship of the God of Israel. With this OT vision in mind, we turn now to the NT texts regarding rest.

49. On the connection between "resting place" and the temple, see also Isa. 66:1.

50. All three of these themes come together in the paean to Simon in 1 Macc. 14:4–15, culminating in his making the sanctuary glorious, though the text uses a different word for rest (*hēsychasen*).

"I Will Give You Rest"

Given the pervasiveness of the theme of rest in the Old Testament, we would do well to consider carefully its relatively few appearances in the New. Even though it occurs infrequently, each instance is charged with significance. Rest features prominently in three NT passages: the rest saying of Matthew 11, the exhortation of Hebrews 3–4, and one of the visions of Revelation 14.

Toward the end of Matthew 11, Jesus offers his listeners "rest": "Come to me, all you who are weary and are carrying heavy burdens, and I will give you rest [*anapausō hymas*]" (Matt. 11:28). Several features of this text reflect the OT tradition of rest. Immediately preceding the saying, Jesus speaks about how he, as the Son, reveals the Father to "infants" (11:25). The notion of divine filiation would likely evoke Matthew's presentation of Jesus as the "Son of David," one of the evangelist's favorite Christological titles.[51] Several texts in the OT identify David or one of his descendants as a "son of God."[52] One of the most important is 2 Samuel 7, where the Lord promises David regarding his descendant: "I will be a father to him, and he shall be a son to me" (2 Sam. 7:14a). This promise appears in the context of an offer of rest, as well. Two aspects of the theme, one explicit and one implicit, bear mentioning. Earlier in the passage the Lord promises to give David "rest" from his enemies (7:11). As noted earlier, this is a recurring aspect of rest in the OT tradition. Perhaps just as importantly, this famous passage also includes the promise that David's descendant will build a house for the name of the Lord (7:13), a house that is sometimes called the Lord's "resting place" (e.g., Ps. 132:14; 2 Chron. 6:41).

Jesus's saying taps into this tradition, but with two important twists. First, rather than *receiving* rest, as David does, Jesus *offers* rest to those who come to him.[53] Even though he is the Son of David, he nevertheless also plays the role of the Lord in giving rest to the weary. Second, and related to this point, in the subsequent passage, one of two Sabbath controversies that follow Jesus's offer of rest, he tells the Pharisees, "Something greater than the temple is here" (Matt. 12:6). What is it that is greater than the temple? The answer implicit in Matthew is Jesus himself. Elsewhere in the Gospel, Matthew applies to Jesus the notion of the divine presence. Early on, the evangelist translates the title "Emmanuel" from Isaiah 7:14 for his audience, "God is with us" (Matt. 1:23). Two other times in Matthew, Jesus appeals to this notion of being present among his disciples. First, in his teaching on fraternal correction, he

51. On the use of this title in Matthew, see Zacharias, *Matthew's Presentation of the Son of David*. The title "Son of David" appears with reference to Jesus eight times in the Gospel (Matt. 1:1; 9:27; 12:23; 15:22; 20:30–31; 21:9, 15; cf. 22:42, which implies Jesus's status as the Son of David).

52. See, e.g., Pss. 2:7; 89:26–27; 1 Chron. 17:13.

53. Laansma, *"I Will Give You Rest,"* 248–50.

tells the disciples, "For where two or three are gathered in my name, I am there among them" (18:20). At the end of the Gospel, Jesus famously promises to be with his disciples until the end of the age (28:20). In both texts, Jesus associates his presence with the name (18:20; 28:19).[54] This emphasis on the name indirectly relates to rest. Recall that in Deuteronomy 12 the Lord promises to give the people rest once they enter the land (Deut. 12:10). This rest, however, has a further purpose: to establish a place where the Lord will make *his name* dwell (12:11).

This combination of themes—divine filiation, rest, Sabbath, and temple—in Jesus's saying in Matthew 11 can hardly be coincidental. Matthew taps into OT rest traditions as a way of summing up what Jesus offers.[55] The salvation he brings fulfills the ancient Israelite hope for rest, both in the sense of relief from toil and in the sense of God dwelling with his people. As the Son of David, Jesus builds the temple.[56] As the Lord of the Sabbath (Matt. 12:8), he dwells in the temple and invites his followers to enter into his rest. Much like the OT motif of rest, Jesus's offer of rest in the present is proleptic, anticipating the fullness of rest to come in the eschaton—he does, after all, still speak of a yoke and a burden that his disciples must carry, even if these are "easy" and "light" (Matt. 11:29–30). The fullness of rest awaits an even fuller consummation. This fullness features prominently in the letter to the Hebrews.

"Let Us Therefore Make Every Effort to Enter That Rest"

The most extended meditation on rest in the NT appears in the letter to the Hebrews. Hebrews 3:7–4:13 exposits Psalm 95:7–11 at some length, focusing on the motif of "rest" and connecting it explicitly to the Sabbath.[57] The passage begins by exhorting the audience to obedience, warning them of the possibility of falling away from the living God (Heb. 3:12). One can see the eschatological nature of the text by the exhortation to faithfulness "to the end": "For we are partakers in Christ, if only we hold fast the beginning of our conviction firm *to the end*" (3:14, my translation). The disobedient Israelite generation that came out from Egypt failed to enter into God's rest, never entering the promised land (3:18).[58] For the audience of Hebrews, the hope

54. There are good reasons to equate Jesus's name, to which he refers in 18:20, with the proto-trinitarian name of 28:19. See Gieschen, "The Divine Name as a Characteristic of Divine Identity," 78–79.

55. For a brief exposition of this background, see Laansma, *"I Will Give You Rest,"* 224–32.

56. On this theme, see Barber, *The Historical Jesus and the Temple*.

57. For a helpful discussion of why the author of Hebrews applies Ps. 95 to his audience, attentive to the dynamics of the psalm itself, see France, "The Writer of Hebrews as a Biblical Expositor," 269–71.

58. Thiessen ("Hebrews and the End of the Exodus") makes a strong case that the author of Hebrews interprets all of Israel's history as a time in the wilderness.

of entering into God's rest remains, but only if they stay faithful to the end: "Therefore, while the promise of entering into his rest is still open, let us take care that none of you should seem to have failed to reach it" (Heb. 4:1).

Hebrews goes on to connect this eschatological rest with the Sabbath rest of the first creation account: "For somewhere it speaks about the seventh day as follows, 'And God rested on the seventh day from all his works'" (Heb. 4:4).[59] By reading the Genesis citation in concert with Psalm 95, the author argues that God's Sabbath rest was intended not just for himself, but for all God's people. To enter into that rest, the people of God must not disobey as the wilderness generation did. The "today" of the psalm suggests to the author of Hebrews that the possibility of entering God's rest continues for each generation, particularly because, according to Hebrews, Joshua did not give the people rest: "For if Joshua had given them rest, God would not speak later about another day" (Heb. 4:8).[60] The promise of rest continues throughout Israel's history and into the time of the audience: "So then, a Sabbath rest still remains for the people of God, for those who enter God's rest also rest from their labors as God did from his" (Heb. 4:9–10). What remains implicit in the first creation account—that human beings are called to enter into God's rest—becomes explicit in Hebrews.

We can offer a more precise account of the nature of the rest in Hebrews by attending to the immediate context of the passage, as well as the broader context of the book. Hebrews 3 begins by contrasting Jesus's role as high priest with Moses's role as a servant "faithful in all God's house" (Heb. 3:2, 5). This phrase ("faithful in all God's house") comes from Numbers 12:7, the story of the conflict between Moses and his siblings. In context, the "house" in question is the tabernacle or the tent of meeting.[61] Whereas Moses serves in the tent of meeting, Jesus is the high priest (Heb. 3:1), a term that reappears in Hebrews 4:14–15, thus forming an *inclusio* around chapters 3 and 4.[62] This *inclusio*, as well as the repetition of the exhortation to "hold firm" in 3:6 and 14, suggests that the chapters form one unit. Additionally, the "therefore [*dio*]" of 3:7 implies that the writer's exposition of Psalm 95 is connected to 3:1–6.

59. Both R. T. France and Peter Enns note that the phrase "my [= God's] rest" in the psalm is what leads the writer of Hebrews to connect the rest of Ps. 95 to God's Sabbath rest in Gen. 2. See France, "The Writer of Hebrews as a Biblical Expositor," 271; Enns, "Creation and Re-Creation," 278–79.

60. See Thiessen, "Hebrews and the End of the Exodus," 355–56, 360.

61. D. Kim, "Jewish and Christian Theology from the Hebrew Bible," 33. Although the OT frequently uses the word "house" with respect to the temple (e.g., 2 Sam. 7:13; 1 Chron. 22:9–10; 28:2), occasionally it can refer to the tabernacle. LXX Ps. 41:5, for example, speaks of "a place of a marvelous tent [*skēnēs*]" in parallel with "the house of God [*tou oikou tou theou*]." Note also how 1 Samuel refers to the tabernacle as the "house of the Lord" (1:7, 24; 3:15).

62. For an analysis of the structure of these chapters, see D. Kim, "Jewish and Christian Theology from the Hebrew Bible," 34.

One difficulty in reading these chapters as a unit concerns the author's apparently abrupt shift from speaking about a house to speaking about rest. Daniel Kim argues that one can account for this shift by reading the text in light of the targums.[63] The targum of Psalm 95 renders verse 11, "concerning whom I swore in *the strength of* my anger that they should not come into *the rest of the house of my sanctuary*" (Tg. Ps. 95:11, emphasis original).[64] The targumist combines the idea of "rest" with the image of a sanctuary, specifically a house, thus producing "one complex idea."[65] If such an understanding was in the air at the time of the writing of Hebrews, then it would explain how the author can move seamlessly from speaking about a house sanctuary (3:1–6) to speaking about rest (3:7–4:11) and back to the image of Jesus as high priest (4:14–15). As is well known, the targums are notoriously difficult to date. Nevertheless, even if this particular interpretation was not available to the author of Hebrews, the OT frequently associates the notion of rest with God's dwelling in the sanctuary.[66] Seen in this light, the rest of which Hebrews speaks refers to dwelling with God in the heavenly sanctuary. This becomes clearer if we consider the connection between the promise of rest and the exhortation in Hebrews 11–12.

The word "rest" appears nowhere in Hebrews outside chapters 3 and 4, but the author links this rest with the "promise [*epangelia*]" in 4:1. Hebrews 11 repeatedly speaks of the promise (11:9, 11, 13, 17, 33, 39).[67] Although the writer refers to some of the heroes obtaining "promises" (11:33), he is nevertheless clear that none of them obtained *the* promise (11:13, 39). Hebrews 12 describes this promise in liturgical terms. Reminding the audience that they are on the cusp of Mount Zion (Heb. 12:22), he urges them not to refuse the Lord (12:25) but to offer him "acceptable worship" (12:28).[68] Like the word "house," Zion might seem far removed from the notion of rest. As we have seen, however, at times the OT associates Zion with God's resting place (see,

63. D. Kim, "Jewish and Christian Theology from the Hebrew Bible," 36–39. For readers unfamiliar with the term, the targums are early Jewish translations of the Scriptures into Aramaic. For a brief overview, see Alexander, "Targum, Targumim."

64. Translation taken from Cathcart et al., *The Aramaic Bible: The Targum of Psalms*, 179.

65. D. Kim, "Jewish and Christian Theology from the Hebrew Bible," 37.

66. See, e.g., Num. 10:35–36; Ps. 132:8, 14–15. LXX Num. 10:35 uses the word *katapausis* for the place of God's rest, the same word that appears in LXX Ps. 95:11 and throughout Heb. 3:11–4:11. D. Kim ("Jewish and Christian Theology from the Hebrew Bible," 39–41) points to texts from 2 Chronicles, but these seem less likely as background to Hebrews, since they refer to the temple rather than to the tabernacle. As Thiessen ("Hebrews and the End of the Exodus," 368n61) rightly notes, none of the Greek words for "temple" appear anywhere in Hebrews. Earlier (359) Thiessen suggests that for Hebrews God's "rest" is the earthly Zion or the heavenly Zion (or both).

67. Thiessen ("Hebrews and the End of the Exodus," 360) suggests that Heb. 11 expands the argument of chaps. 3–4. See also France, "The Writer of Hebrews as a Biblical Expositor," 271.

68. For the idea that the audience has approached but not yet entered Zion, see Koester, *Hebrews*, 544.

e.g., Ps. 132:13–14; cf. 76:2).[69] God's rest, then, is not simply relief from one's toil (though it includes that—see Heb. 4:10). God's rest is rooted in worship, and the audience of Hebrews can begin to experience that rest by engaging in acceptable worship.

"See, the Tabernacle of God Is with Human Beings"

The last book of the NT also draws on the theme of rest, contrasting the fate of those who persecute the church with the fate of those who remain faithful to the end. The seer's vision of the three angels in Revelation 14:6–13 warns that the worshipers of the beast will have no rest (14:11), whereas the saints who endure until the end will receive rest (14:13).

Chee-Chiew Lee suggests that these statements draw on the OT themes of rest from toil and relief from one's enemies.[70] In context, the former is the more obvious sense of rest. According to the vision, the Spirit promises, "[Those who die in the Lord] will rest from their labors, for their deeds follow them" (Rev. 14:13b). As Lee rightly notes, the combination of labor, deeds, and endurance (14:12) recalls the letters to the churches of Ephesus and Thyatira in the early chapters of Revelation (2:1–2, 19).[71] Those who persevere to the end will receive an eschatological rest from their toil.

The broader context of the message of the three angels in Revelation 14 also suggests a reading of "rest" as relief from enemies.[72] The chapter preceding this promise of rest describes a battle between the dragon and its beasts, on the one hand, and the saints, on the other (13:7). At the heart of this battle is the question of worship. When the first beast arises, "all the inhabitants of the world will worship it" (13:8a). The second beast is given power to force people to worship the first beast (13:12). Given this military context, as well as the widespread OT association of rest with the cessation of battle and relief from enemies, the rest promised to the faithful has the connotation of an end to their military strife.

As I have argued, both these OT themes often relate to a third element of rest—namely, worship. The ultimate purpose of the exodus is to allow Israel to worship the Lord (Exod. 3:18); the Lord gives David rest from his enemies with an eye to the building of the temple, a resting place for the Lord (2 Sam. 7:11–16; 1 Chron. 22:17–19; 2 Chron. 6:41). It is unsurprising, then, that at the heart of the battle between the beasts and the faithful is the question of worship. Refusal to worship the beast can result in death for those who remain faithful to the Lord (Rev. 13:15). The rest the faithful ultimately receive, then,

69. Thiessen, "Hebrews and the End of the Exodus," 368.
70. Lee, "Rest and Victory in Revelation 14.13."
71. Lee, "Rest and Victory in Revelation 14.13," 353–54.
72. Lee, "Rest and Victory in Revelation 14.13," 354–57.

is ordered to worship. One day, in the words of Zechariah, the faithful will be free "to serve [the Lord] without fear" (Luke 1:74).[73]

The final visions of Revelation underscore the importance of worship in a way that implicitly relates to the theme of rest.[74] The book climaxes with a vision of a new heaven and a new earth (Rev. 21:1), and at the heart of this vision is the announcement of God's presence among his people: "And I heard a great voice from the throne saying, 'See, the tabernacle of God is with human beings, and he will dwell [lit., "tabernacle"] with them, and they will be his people, and God himself will be with them'" (Rev. 21:3, my translation). The tabernacle language, appearing twice in this verse, would evoke the notion of the sanctuary as God's resting place. At the same time, the vision of Revelation 22 also implicitly recalls the early chapters of Genesis, as is often noted.[75] The presence of a river, garden imagery, and the tree of life recall the Edenic conditions of creation at the beginning. In light of these connections, the promise of God dwelling with his people relates to his Sabbath rest. The temple imagery suffusing these final chapters also suggests that the rest offered to the faithful, much like many of the rest promises in the OT, is ordered ultimately to worship. It is only in worshiping God and the Lamb that the faithful will find their true rest.

"Our Heart Is Restless Until It Rests in You"

Rest is not the most prominent feature of the NT, either generally speaking or with respect to eschatology. Nevertheless, the relative paucity of references to rest ought not to mislead us into seeing it as an unimportant aspect of biblical eschatology. The ubiquity of the theme in the OT underscores how crucial it is to Israel's hope, and therefore also to any eschatology that is truly biblical. In a few key places, the NT brings together the various strands of this theme, underscoring the hope for relief from toil and from enemies that will lead to the ultimate rest found in worship of God and the Lamb. To that theme we now turn.

73. The word for "serve" (*latreuein*) has liturgical connotations.

74. Lee, "Rest and Victory in Revelation 14.13," 357.

75. See, e.g., Beale, *Revelation*, 1107–11; Aune, *Revelation 1–5*, 152–54; Caird, *Revelation*, 280.

THREE

Worship

So far, we have considered the human vocation to exercise dominion over the created world and to enter into God's rest. The early chapters of Genesis implicitly suggest a third element in the human vocation: worship. Alongside dominion and rest, worship lies at the heart of human identity. Human beings are created for worship and find their fulfillment in the communion with God established by it, which in Scripture takes shape in the temple and the priesthood. To make this case, I will first examine the roles of temple and priesthood in the creation accounts of Genesis and in Exodus. I will then show that some of the prophetic books envision a hope for a new temple and a new priesthood. From there we will move to the NT, where both Jesus (in himself) and the church (by participation) are characterized as a new temple and a new priesthood. Finally, I will show how the final visions of Revelation depict the end in terms of an eschatological temple and priesthood.

Created for Worship: Temple and Priesthood in Genesis 1–3

For some time, scholars have noted parallels between the first creation account (Gen. 1:1–2:3) and the creation of the tabernacle and the temple.[1] One of the most obvious features of this account is the significance of the number seven. Creation takes place over the course of seven days, and Genesis 2:1–3 repeats the phrase "the seventh day" three times. As Umberto Cassuto notes,

1. Among the many who have seen these parallels, see Levenson, *Sinai and Zion*, 142–45; Weinfeld, "Sabbath, Temple, and the Enthronement of the Lord," 503; Anderson, *That I May Dwell Among Them*, 21–30. For a brief defense of taking Gen. 2:4 as part of the following passage rather than what precedes it, see Levenson, *Israel's Day of Light and Joy*, 243–44n91.

the heptadic structures of this account are even more apparent in Hebrew.[2] The first verse of the book, for example, consists of seven words in Hebrew, and the second contains fourteen. Several of the most significant words in the passage ("God," "earth," "heavens") occur in multiples of seven, and the phrases "and it was so" and "God saw that it was good" also appear seven times.

The importance of the number seven becomes clear when one compares the creation account with the OT descriptions of the tabernacle and the temple.[3] The instructions for building the tabernacle are characterized by a series of sevens. Moses's encounter with God on Mount Sinai follows a six-plus-one structure reminiscent of Genesis 1. Moreover, when God gives Moses the instructions for building the tabernacle, he does so in a series of seven speeches punctuated by the phrase, "The LORD said to Moses" (Exod. 25:1; 30:11, 17, 22, 34; 31:1, 12).[4] The final speech (31:12–17) focuses on the Sabbath, using the term five times and connecting it explicitly to the six days of creation: "It is a sign for ever between me and the Israelites that in six days the LORD made heaven and earth, and on the seventh day he rested, and was refreshed" (Exod. 31:17).[5] The culmination of the tabernacle instructions with the Sabbath commandment implies that God's rest in Genesis 2:1–3 is connected with the institutions of temple and worship.

The building of the tabernacle and its furnishings likewise follows a sevenfold structure. As Gary Anderson notes, both the preparation of the priests' vestments and the construction of the tabernacle are punctuated by the refrain "as the LORD had commanded Moses," approving the execution of the Lord's instructions.[6] Moreover, the description of the building of the tabernacle ends with the phrase "So Moses finished the work" (Exod. 40:33), echoing the completion of creation (Gen. 2:2: "On the sixth day God finished the

2. Cassuto, *Genesis I*, 13–15; see also Levenson, *Creation and the Persistence of Evil*, 66–68; Morrow, "Creation as Temple-Building," 1–4; Anderson, *That I May Dwell Among Them*, 25–28. For a critique of some of Cassuto's examples that nevertheless affirms the importance of the heptads throughout this text, see Levenson, *Israel's Day of Light and Joy*, 122–24.

3. See, among others, Levenson, *Sinai and Zion*, 143–44; Weinfeld, "Sabbath, Temple, and the Enthronement of the Lord," 503–7; Kearney, "Creation and Liturgy"; Anderson, *That I May Dwell Among Them*, 28–33.

4. Kearney ("Creation and Liturgy") also suggests parallels between the days of creation and specific parts of the tabernacle and the account of its building, but see the criticisms of Levenson, *Israel's Day of Light and Joy*, 117–18. The NRSVue obscures the sevenfold commandment by translating the same Hebrew expression in some verses as "The LORD said" and in others as "The LORD spoke."

5. Middleton, *The Liberating Image*, 84–85. It is remarkable that Middleton notes the importance of the Sabbath here, and yet it plays practically no role in his account of the human vocation, either here or in his later work. On the similarities between Exod. 31:12–17 and Gen. 2:1–3, see Levenson, *Israel's Day of Light and Joy*, 118–21, who rightly notes that not every use of the term "Sabbath" in the text refers to the seventh day.

6. Anderson, *That I May Dwell Among Them*, 33.

work that he had done").[7] The descent of the glory cloud into the tabernacle following the completion of the work thus parallels God's rest on the seventh day. Again, as Anderson notes, "Just as Genesis 1 ends by sanctifying a moment in time by describing the deity at rest, so Exodus 40 ends with God sanctifying a place through anointing (vv. 9–11) and indwelling (vv. 34–35)."[8]

The seven days of creation also parallel Solomon's construction and dedication of the temple in 1 Kings 6–8. Jon Levenson points out several features of the latter account that also reflect the significance of the number seven, even if the verbal similarities are not as pronounced as in the tabernacle account.[9] Solomon completes the building project in seven years (1 Kings 6:38), corresponding to the seven days it takes God to complete creation.[10] Moreover, the dedication of the temple takes place during the feast of tabernacles, which lasts seven days and is celebrated in the seventh month. Finally, Solomon's speech at the dedication consists of seven petitions for the people (1 Kings 8:31–53).[11]

In addition to the structure of creation and its parallels with the tabernacle and the temple, the account of the creation of human beings on the sixth day also invites a cultic interpretation. Several scholars have noted that the Hebrew word typically translated as "image" (*tselem*) appears elsewhere in the OT with respect to pagan idols (see Num. 33:52; Amos 5:26; 2 Kings 11:18; Ezek. 7:20; 23:14).[12] Given this connotation of the language of "image," some see in Genesis 1:26–27 an implicit rationale for the prohibition of idols in ancient Israel.[13] God already has an image, the living human being. For this reason, it makes no sense to create lifeless idols.[14] If this interpretation of the *imago Dei* is correct, then one could see the creation of the human being as the creation and placement of the cult statue in the temple of creation. Moreover, as Mark Smith argues, there is likely a connection between the divine

7. See M. Smith, *The Priestly Vision of Genesis 1*, 75–76.

8. Anderson, *That I May Dwell Among Them*, 32. John Walton notes that in the ancient Near East, temples explicitly functioned as a resting place for the gods. See Walton, "Genesis 1:1–2:3 and the Ancient Near East," 60–61.

9. Levenson, *Sinai and Zion*, 143–44.

10. Levenson also notes (*Sinai and Zion*, 143) that, according to Lev. 25:3–7, the seventh year in a cycle also is called a "Sabbath," thus connecting the two accounts more closely.

11. Levenson, *Sinai and Zion*, 144.

12. Provan, "To Highlight All Our Idols," 25; Fletcher-Louis, "God's Image," 83; for a discussion of this idea in its ancient Near Eastern context, see Kutsko, *Between Heaven and Earth*, 58–63.

13. Fletcher-Louis, "God's Image," 83; Mauser, "God in Human Form," 91.

14. Mauser, "God in Human Form," 91: "In polytheistic cults images of the gods abound in temples and in shrines. But the one God of Israelite faith also has an image. It is not found in statues of metal, stone, or wood. In fact, it is no product of human ingenuity and industry at all. The real image of the one, true God is the living human being itself." See also M. Smith, *The Priestly Vision of Genesis 1*, 101: "Humanity is not only the representation of God on earth; the human person is the living representation pointing to a living and real God, perhaps unlike the lifeless images of other deities made by human hands."

blessing God bestows and the priestly role for which human beings are created.[15] Throughout the first creation account, God blesses: He blesses both animals and human beings with fertility (Gen. 1:22, 28), and he blesses the seventh day (Gen. 2:3). Elsewhere in the Pentateuch and throughout the OT, priests mediate God's blessing to the people. Aaron and his sons are instructed to bestow a priestly blessing (Num. 6:22–26), Melchizedek blesses Abram (Gen. 14:19), and the high priest Simon blesses the people (Sir. 50:20–21).[16] If, as some have suggested, "image" language also has connotations of kinship, then one could see implicit in the creation of human beings a priestly calling.[17]

As with the royal imagery that unifies Genesis 1–3, so the cultic imagery of the first creation account carries over into the second.[18] As Gordon Wenham has shown, Genesis 2–3 also reflects certain aspects of the Jewish temple.[19] Wenham argues that the garden should be seen as "an archetypal or ideal sanctuary."[20] Genesis 3:8 describes God "walking back and forth" (*hithallek*) in the garden. In three other places in the OT (Lev. 26:12; Deut. 23:15 [MT]; 2 Sam. 7:6–7) the same verb is used to describe God's presence in the tabernacle.[21] Moreover, the placement of the cherubim at the gates of Eden evokes the temple. God stations the cherubim east of the garden to prevent Adam and Eve from approaching the tree of life (Gen. 3:24). The furnishings of both the tabernacle (Exod. 25:18–22) and the temple (1 Kings 6:23–28) included cherubim made of gold.[22] References to gold and onyx stones (Gen. 2:11–12) also suggest a cultic setting, as many of the furnishings of the tabernacle and the temple were covered in gold, and onyx stones were used for the priestly vestments (Exod. 25:7; 28:9; cf. 1 Chron. 29:2). The fact that a river flows out from Eden to water the garden (Gen. 2:10) may also reflect the temple vision of Ezekiel 47.[23]

Most important for my purposes is the way that Genesis describes Adam's task in the garden. Genesis 2:15 notes that God put the man in the garden "to

15. M. Smith, *The Priestly Vision of Genesis 1*, 102–4.

16. M. Smith, *The Priestly Vision of Genesis 1*, 103–4.

17. For the kinship connotations of "image" language, note the parallels between Gen. 1:26–28 and 5:2–3, and see the discussion in chap. 1 above. Firmage ("Genesis 1 and the Priestly Agenda," 111) connects the kinship aspects of "image" language with the ability to generate new images of oneself. This reading need not exclude notions of priestly likeness to God.

18. This is not to deny that these two accounts come from different sources. Rather, it is to suggest that the final redactor has integrated the accounts in a variety of ways. On the thematic connection between the two Genesis accounts with respect to the idea of the image, see Sawyer, "The Image of God," though I do not follow his positive appraisal of the serpent's role in the story.

19. Wenham, "Sanctuary Symbolism." The understanding of Eden as a garden sanctuary has roots in ancient Judaism and Christianity. See Anderson, *The Genesis of Perfection*, 43–62.

20. Wenham, "Sanctuary Symbolism," 400.

21. Wenham, "Sanctuary Symbolism," 400–401.

22. Wenham, "Sanctuary Symbolism," 401.

23. Wenham, "Sanctuary Symbolism," 402. See the rest of Wenham's essay for further discussion of these and other cultic images in the description of the garden of Eden.

till it and keep it." G. K. Beale notes that, although the Hebrew verb *'abad* when used on its own can have agricultural connotations ("to cultivate"), often when the root appears either as a verb or as a noun in tandem with the verb *shamar* ("to keep") it refers to temple service (Num. 3:7–8; 8:25–26; 18:5–6; 1 Chron. 23:32; Ezek. 44:14).[24] Additionally, as Michael Morales points out, God's act of clothing Adam and Eve (Gen. 3:21) uses language similar to Moses's act of clothing Aaron and his sons in the rite of ordination (Lev. 8:13).[25] Given the cultic imagery found in the description of Eden, Adam's primary task seems to be a priestly one, ministering in the archetypal sanctuary of Eden.[26]

Redeemed for Worship: Temple and Priesthood in Exodus

Temple and priesthood also feature prominently in Exodus.[27] Since we have already noted the parallels between creation and the construction of the tabernacle, I will focus here on the book's structure and its implications for Israel's vocation. The arc of the story underscores the cultic goal of God's redemption of Israel. Although people often interpret the exodus primarily as a story of (political) liberation, it has a twofold purpose reflected in the structure of the book.[28] The first half of the Lord's demand to Pharaoh ("Let my people go") is fulfilled in roughly the first half of the book (Exod. 1–18); the second half of the demand ("so that they may serve me") takes up roughly the second half of the book (Exod. 19–40). This twofold demand explains why so much of the book concerns the regulations for building the tabernacle and for serving God there (Exod. 25–40). Joseph Ratzinger puts it well: "Israel departs, not in order to be a people like all the others; it departs in order to

24. Beale, *The Temple and the Church's Mission*, 66–67; see also Wenham, "Sanctuary Symbolism," 401; Morrow, "Creation as Temple-Building," 12. L. M. Morales (*The Tabernacle Prefigured*, 99) suggests that these terms might more aptly be rendered "to worship and obey."

25. L. M. Morales, *The Tabernacle Prefigured*, 99–100. The fact that this takes place after Adam and Eve's transgression might imply that they did not thereby forfeit their priestly vocation.

26. Middleton notes this cultic imagery, especially in Gen. 1, but in his earlier work he does not make much of the priestly dimension of creation in the image of God, even going so far as to suggest that the notion of priestly service is absent from the Genesis theology of the *imago*. Thus, he writes (*The Liberating Image*, 209), "In connection with the priestly, cultic dimension of the *imago Dei*, it is further noteworthy that language of human service is entirely absent from Genesis 1." While it is true that Gen. 1 does not contain the language of human service, Gen. 2 clearly does, and in a configuration that appears elsewhere in cultic contexts. For a more recent acknowledgment of the importance of cultic language with respect to the image, see Middleton, "Image of God."

27. More accurately, Exodus speaks of the tabernacle. Here I use the word "temple" simply to refer to Israel's place of worship.

28. This dual purpose is briefly but insightfully explored in Ratzinger, *The Spirit of the Liturgy*, 13–23.

serve God."[29] Exodus highlights this particular vocation at the very beginning of the people's encounter with God at the foot of Mount Sinai: "Now, therefore, if you obey my voice and keep my covenant, you shall be my treasured possession out of all the peoples. Indeed, the whole earth is mine, but you shall be for me *a priestly kingdom* and a holy nation" (Exod. 19:5–6a). Like Adam in the early chapters of Genesis, the people of Israel are called to serve the Lord as priests. In Israel, moreover, the roles of ruler and priest are joined, as they are for Adam.

This liturgical end does not appear out of nowhere. On the contrary, the Lord signals it from his first meeting with Moses at Mount Horeb. The initial message the Lord sends to Pharaoh through Moses is not simply "Let my people go," but rather "Let us now go a three days' journey into the wilderness, *so that we may sacrifice to the Lord our God*" (Exod. 3:18).[30] Although God's ultimate intention is to free the Israelites from Egyptian slavery (Exod. 3:8), the initial demand to Pharaoh (reiterated in similar words in Exod. 5:1) indicates that their liberation has a higher end. For much of the story of the ten plagues, this end remains in the forefront, as God repeatedly tells Pharaoh, "Let my people go, *so that they may serve me*" (Exod. 7:16; 8:1, 20; 9:1, 13; 10:3).[31] This twofold demand implies that the Israelites' full liberation will come about only through proper worship of their God. Seen in this light, the instructions regarding the tabernacle are not a lengthy add-on to the story, but rather its culmination. Some scholars have even suggested that the establishment of the cult represents the completion of creation.[32]

Prophetic Hopes for a New Temple and a New Priesthood

Given the significance of the priestly vocation in Genesis and Exodus, it should not surprise us to see prophetic expressions of hope include the desire for a new temple and a new priesthood.[33] An oracle preserved in the books of Isaiah

29. Ratzinger, *The Spirit of the Liturgy*, 16.

30. God repeats this command in Exod. 4:23 using the same language of "service" (*'abad*) that appears in Gen. 2:15: "Let my son go that he may serve me" (Exod 4:23a). The noun form *'abodah* is also at times used with respect to servile labor (e.g., Gen. 29:27) and at other times to describe the liturgical service performed in the tabernacle and the temple (e.g., Num. 3:8; 4:23).

31. The NRSVue has corrected the NRSV's "Let my people go, so that they may worship me." The older translation, though accurately conveying the meaning, obscures the contest between God and Pharaoh that serves as a leitmotif, playing on the different connotations of the Hebrew word *'abad*.

32. Kearney ("Creation and Liturgy," 381) speaks of the building of the tabernacle as a "new creation." See also the more recent discussion in Anderson, *That I May Dwell Among Them*, 21–25.

33. It is likely that the first creation account is one of the later texts of the OT. Nevertheless, the second account also has priestly and temple imagery. Moreover, if, as many argue, the first

and Micah illustrates the hope for a new temple that appears frequently in the prophets. Speaking of the latter days, the oracle envisions a pilgrimage to the temple on Mount Zion:[34]

> In days to come
>   the mountain of the LORD's house
> shall be established as the highest of the mountains
>   and shall be raised above the hills;
> all the nations shall stream to it.
>   Many peoples shall come and say,
> "Come, let us go up to the mountain of the LORD,
>   to the house of the God of Jacob,
> that he may teach us his ways
>   and that we may walk in his paths."
> For out of Zion shall go forth instruction
>   and the word of the LORD from Jerusalem.
> He shall judge between the nations,
>   and shall arbitrate for many peoples;
> they shall beat their swords into plowshares
>   and their spears into pruning hooks;
> nation shall not lift up sword against nation;
>   neither shall they learn war any more. (Isa. 2:2–4; cf. Mic. 4:1–3)[35]

The establishment of Mount Zion as the highest mountain will have several important consequences.[36] Implicitly, it will result in people—in fact, many peoples—acknowledging the Lord as the true God. It will also bring an end to war. Perhaps most importantly, this latter-day pilgrimage will bring about communion between the Lord and those who stream to his temple.[37] He will teach them his ways and they will walk in his paths (2:3). This emphasis on God's holy mountain is a recurring theme throughout Isaiah.[38]

One of the most famous oracles associated with Israel's longing for a messianic figure culminates in an expression of hope oriented toward the

creation account is one of the last texts of the OT, one could see it as an interpretive key to the whole, underscoring the importance of temple and priesthood.

34. On the eschatological character of the passage, see Wildberger, *Isaiah 1–12*, 88; Blenkinsopp, *Isaiah 1–39*, 190.

35. For a brief discussion of some of the theories regarding the origins of this passage, see Childs, *Isaiah*, 29.

36. Childs (*Isaiah*, 29–30) interprets this idea as pointing to "a new creation, but one that bears the marks of God's original intention of primordial harmony of the universe."

37. On the technical meaning of the verb "go up" (*'alah*) as referring to pilgrimage, see Wildberger, *Isaiah 1–12*, 90. On 92, he notes that the people "hurry toward Jerusalem . . . because they seek an encounter with the God who had made his glory known in Israel."

38. Interestingly, references to the "holy mountain" are absent in Isa. 40–55 (the section of the book commonly called "Deutero-Isaiah") but dot the first and third sections of the canonical book (though see Isa. 40:9).

mountain of the Lord. Isaiah 11 begins with a description of the hoped-for king from Jesse's line, upon whom the Spirit of the Lord will come to rest (Isa. 11:1–3). This expected ruler will bring about justice for Israel, especially for the poor (11:4). The prophet goes on to describe the Eden-like conditions that will accompany his reign, as animals normally at odds with one another will lie down in peace (11:6).[39] Toward the end of the oracle the prophet reveals both the setting of this vision and its full fruition: "They will not hurt or destroy on all my holy mountain, for the earth will be full of the knowledge of the Lord as the waters cover the sea" (11:9). Israel's hopes as expressed in this oracle are centered on God's holy mountain, and they will include knowledge of the Lord.[40]

Another oracle concerning Israel's hope for redemption underscores the importance of worship as part of God's plan for his people. Isaiah 27, the conclusion of a unit that extends from chapters 24 to 27, again envisions the fulfillment of Israel's hope taking place on the holy mountain. The oracle is preceded by the promise that the Lord will conquer the mythical creature Leviathan, a symbol of evil and chaos (Isa. 27:1).[41] The prophet proceeds to describe the Lord's care for Israel, comparing Israel to a vineyard and the Lord to the vineyard's keeper (27:2–5).[42] The Lord promises to protect Israel and to plant them again (27:6). In the process, Israel's sins will be atoned for:

> Therefore by this the guilt of Jacob will be expiated,
>   and this will be the full fruit of the removal of his sin:
> when he makes all the stones of the altars
>   like chalkstones crushed to pieces;
>   no sacred poles or incense altars will remain standing. (Isa. 27:9)

At the heart of Israel's redemption is the abandonment, even the destruction, of the people's idolatrous practices, symbolized by the "sacred poles" and "incense altars." The oracle culminates once again in an expression of hope centered on God's holy mountain. In contrast to the idolatrous worship that will be removed, Israel will at last worship the Lord appropriately: "And on that day a great trumpet will be blown, and those who were lost in the land of Assyria and those who were driven out of the land of Egypt will come

39. For a critique of a return-to-Eden reading of the text, see Childs, *Isaiah*, 103–4, who argues that the text points forward to the eschatological new creation.

40. Wildberger (*Isaiah 1–12*, 481) correctly writes, "One must assume that the holy mountain of Yahweh refers to Zion/Jerusalem (cf. Pss. 2:6; 3:5; 48:2; 99:9)."

41. Commentators tend to treat this verse as distinct from 27:2–13 or even connected to the preceding oracle. See Blenkinsopp, *Isaiah 1–39*, 368; Wildberger, *Isaiah 13–27*, 575. Childs (*Isaiah*, 196) writes, "Verse 1 is a discrete unit, both in form and content, and separated from what precedes and follows."

42. On the relation between this passage and Isa. 5:1–7, see Wildberger, *Isaiah 13–27*, 584–85; Blenkinsopp, *Isaiah 1–39*, 374.

and worship the LORD on the holy mountain at Jerusalem" (27:13).[43] Proper worship, then, is an essential aspect of Israel's hope.

The mountain vision of Isaiah 2 speaks not just of Israel, but of all the nations streaming to the mountain of the Lord (Isa. 2:2), a theme the last part of the canonical book of Isaiah develops.[44] Not only will foreigners come to the Lord's temple on his holy mountain—they will even minister there. Isaiah 56 begins with an exhortation to right conduct in light of the impending salvation that the Lord promises (Isa. 56:1).[45] The prophet then describes a vision focused on the Sabbath that includes foreigners and eunuchs among those who benefit from the Lord's blessings and salvation (56:3).[46] Both foreigners and eunuchs will be remembered in the temple. The Lord promises to give eunuchs "an everlasting name" (v. 5), and foreigners will be allowed to minister to him (v. 6). As in the oracles of Isaiah 11 and 27, this vision culminates in a pilgrimage to the temple:

> These I will bring to my holy mountain,
> and make them joyful in my house of prayer;
> their burnt offerings and their sacrifices
> will be accepted on my altar,
> for my house shall be called a house of prayer
> for all peoples. (Isa. 56:7)[47]

The last verse of the oracle clarifies that this pilgrimage is not at the expense of Israel, but rather in addition to the redemption of the people:

> Thus says the Lord GOD,
> who gathers the outcasts of Israel:
> I will gather others to them
> besides those already gathered. (Isa. 56:8)

Israel's redemption thus signals hope for the nations.

A few points are worth making about this oracle. First, once again we see the significance of the holy mountain, the place of God's dwelling in Israel's midst. Second, the oracle speaks explicitly about offering sacrifices. Worship forms an integral part of hope for Israel and for the world. Given the way the opening chapters of Genesis describe creation as a temple, this makes

43. On the "holy mountain" as a reference to the temple, see Wildberger, *Isaiah 13–27*, 600.

44. For the connection between these two oracles, see Childs, *Isaiah*, 458. Blenkinsopp (*Isaiah 56–66*, 131–32) suggests that Isa. 56:1–8 forms a bookend with 66:15–24.

45. Blenkinsopp, *Isaiah 56–66*, 132–33.

46. On the connection between this Sabbath injunction and Exod. 31:12–17, see Blenkinsopp, *Isaiah 56–66*, 135.

47. As Blenkinsopp (*Isaiah 56–66*, 140) notes, the focus shifts from the city Jerusalem in Isa. 49–55 to the temple in 56–66.

sense. One day human beings will fulfill the purpose for which they were made, offering God proper worship. Finally, in offering this proper worship, human beings will find joy. Making sacrifice will not be a burden, but rather the fulfillment of their desires.

The subsequent chapter of Isaiah returns to the recurring problem of idolatry, as the prophet castigates the Israelites for straying after other gods. Both in the valley (Isa. 57:6) and "upon a high and lofty mountain" (57:7), the people offer grain offerings and other sacrifices to false gods.[48] These sins, the prophet warns, will ultimately result in disaster. When the people are in distress, the Lord will leave them to the help offered by their idols (57:13a). By contrast, the Lord offers hope to the faithful: "But whoever takes refuge in me shall possess the land and inherit my holy mountain" (57:13b). There is a clear contrast between the mountain on which the Israelites practice idolatry and the holy mountain promised as an inheritance to those who remain loyal to the Lord. This emphasis on the holy mountain once again underscores proper worship's central role in Israel's hope.

The final chapter of Isaiah introduces a new element to the picture of Israel's hope, both with respect to the nature of the temple and with respect to the sacrifices to be offered to the Lord. At the beginning of Isaiah 66 the Lord seems to deny the validity of the temple, noting that no house can contain him (Isa. 66:1–2).[49] Moreover, the Lord seems also to reject the standard offerings of the temple—namely, oxen, lambs, grain, and frankincense (66:3). This does not mean, however, that no offerings will be made. On the contrary, the book ends with a promise of beholding the glory of the Lord and of offering worship. The Lord promises to gather the nations to see his glory, as well as to send out Israelites to the nations, declaring the Lord's glory among them (66:18–19).[50] The oracle culminates with a pilgrimage from among the nations to the Lord's holy mountain (66:20) in which the people streaming to Jerusalem become both a sacrifice and priests (vv. 20–21). The end toward which all this is ordered is an eternal act of worship:

48. Childs (*Isaiah*, 467) sees the language of "a high and lofty mountain" as a perversion of the oracle of Isa. 2:2. Blenkinsopp (*Isaiah 56–66*, 159) connects it with the references to the temple in 56:7; 57:13; 65:11, 25; 66:20.

49. The Lord's words in this oracle loosely resemble a part of Solomon's prayer at the dedication of the temple, where he acknowledges the inadequacy of the temple as a house for the Lord (1 Kings 8:27). As Levenson (*Israel's Day of Light and Joy*, 112–13) notes regarding this passage, "The Temple restored and the world renewed are not, at least in origin, two separate visions of the ultimate future. They are, rather, inextricably linked and founded in the same idea: the Temple is a microcosm, and the world is—in its ideal state—a Temple." Blenkinsopp (*Isaiah 56–66*, 294) wisely cautions against playing these verses off against the temple given the many positive statements throughout Isa. 56–66 about the Lord's holy mountain and the house of the Lord.

50. Blenkinsopp (*Isaiah 56–66*, 313) notes the continuity between Isa. 66:18–19 and other oracles with a universalistic tendency, such as 2:2–4; 19:24–25; 25:6–8.

> For as the new heavens and the new earth,
> which I will make,
> shall remain before me, says the LORD,
> so shall your descendants and your name remain.
> From new moon to new moon
> and from Sabbath to Sabbath,
> all flesh shall come to worship before me,
> says the LORD. (Isa. 66:22–23)

The new creation God promises is ultimately ordered to worship.

A similar vision appears in the book of Ezekiel, but before we turn to that text, it is worth briefly considering one last passage from Isaiah.[51] One of the most beautiful oracles in the book expresses the hope that one day the Lord will conquer death. Although the prophet does not use the phrase "holy mountain," the vision takes place on "this mountain" (Isa. 25:6), referring to Mount Zion (24:23).[52] There the prophet speaks of the Lord's reign on Zion, as well as the revelation of his glory. On that same mountain, the Lord will prepare a banquet "for all peoples" (25:6), celebrating his reign. This festal meal is accompanied by the Lord's victory over death:

> And he will destroy on this mountain
> the shroud that is cast over all peoples,
> the covering that is spread over all nations;
> he will swallow up death forever.
> Then the Lord GOD will wipe away the tears from all faces,
> and the disgrace of his people he will take away from all the earth,
> for the LORD has spoken. (Isa. 25:7–8)[53]

Significantly, the hope for immortality is closely bound up with worship and experiencing God's presence.[54] The Lord is the source of life, and it is his presence and his power that conquer death. A similar connection between God's presence and new life appears in the prophet Ezekiel.

One of the central themes of Ezekiel is the departure of God's visible presence, described as his "glory," from the temple, as well as its hoped-for return. Early in the book the prophet is commissioned to pronounce judgment on Israel for its repeated acts of idolatry. In a vision, he sees, first, the various

51. Ezekiel differs from Isaiah, however, with respect to its view of the gentiles and the temple. See the discussion in Sankamo, "Rival Visions of the Eschatological Temple of Jerusalem," 85–92.

52. Childs, *Isaiah*, 184; Blenkinsopp, *Isaiah 1–39*, 358.

53. Cf. Isa. 26:19. I have focused on Isa. 25 because of its liturgical context. The imagery of a "shroud" or "covering" most likely refers to mourning. See Childs, *Isaiah*, 184–85; Blenkinsopp, *Isaiah 1–39*, 359; Wildberger, *Isaiah 13–27*, 532.

54. On this point more generally, see Levenson, *Resurrection and the Restoration of Israel*, 82–107.

abominations that the Israelites were performing in the temple (Ezek. 8) and then the departure of God's glory from the temple, driven out by Israel's abominations (Ezek. 10). The departure of God's glory, however, is presented as temporary, and the book holds out hope that one day this glory will return to Israel, filling a new and glorious temple.

Ezekiel devotes a full nine chapters (Ezek. 40–48) to describing the new temple, indicating its importance for OT hope.[55] The first three chapters of this section (Ezek. 40–42) begin a detailed account of the various parts of the new temple, an account that resumes in Ezekiel 43:13. Embedded within this description appears the most important feature of the vision, the return of God's glory (43:1–12).[56] The prophet recounts this return by referring back to the earlier visions of judgment, when the Lord abandoned the temple, thereby indicating its impending destruction: "The vision I saw was like the vision that I had seen when he came to destroy the city and like the vision that I had seen by the River Chebar, and I fell upon my face" (43:3). Ezekiel had witnessed the glory of the Lord depart by the east gate of the temple (10:19; 11:23); now he sees it return by the same way (43:1–2, 4). The glory of the Lord then takes up its residence in the temple, promising to continue to abide with Israel: "He said to me: 'Mortal, this is the place of my throne and the place for the soles of my feet, where I will reside among the people of Israel forever'" (43:7a). The temple plays a crucial role in the vision because it signifies and mediates the Lord's presence among the people.

One other feature of this vision bears comment, one of the most famous images in Ezekiel. Toward the end of the book, the prophet sees water flowing out "from below the entryway of the temple" (Ezek. 47:1). The water gradually grows into a great river that gives life, restoring the conditions of creation. On either side of the river, the prophet sees trees, evoking the garden of Eden.[57] The waters, moreover, are filled with "every living creature that swarms" (47:9; cf. Gen. 1:20–21) and fish (cf. Gen. 1:26, 28), and on either side of the river are found "all kinds of trees for food" (Ezek. 47:12; cf. Gen. 2:9). Here we see a clear confluence between the temple and creation reminiscent of the opening chapters of Genesis. The building of the new temple will bring with it a return to the conditions of paradise, where God dwelt in the midst of his people (Ezek. 43:7). There he will provide for their needs (47:12). According to the early chapters of Genesis, God created human beings, at least in part,

55. This hope does not appear out of nowhere. At several points throughout the book, other oracles describe a return of the Lord to dwell among his people. See, e.g., Ezek. 20:40–44; 37:26–27. On the connection between Ezekiel's vision and immortality, see Levenson, *Resurrection and the Restoration of Israel*, 88–90.

56. Blenkinsopp (*Ezekiel*, 210) describes this section as the "climactic point of the vision narrative." See also Zimmerli, *Ezekiel*, 2:412.

57. On this point, see Levenson, *Theology of the Program of Restoration*, 30–32; Zimmerli, *Ezekiel*, 2:514–16; Eichrodt, *Ezekiel*, 583–85.

for the sake of worship. Old Testament visions of hope for the end entail the fulfillment of this purpose. This priestly understanding of the human vocation carries over with some modifications into the NT.

The New Temple and the New Priesthood in Person

As with the vocation to rule and to rest, the NT interprets the vocation to worship both with respect to Christ and with respect to the church. Visions of a new temple—albeit one with different contours—appear at least as frequently in the New Testament as in the Old, if not more so. For the sake of space, I will focus on three ways the NT develops this theme. First, and most importantly, Jesus is presented as the new temple and the new priest, fulfilling especially the hopes described in Ezekiel. Second, the NT ascribes to the church the roles of new temple and new priesthood, thus fulfilling both Israel's vocation at the exodus (Exod. 19:6) and the expectation of a new temple. Finally, the vision of the end found in the book of Revelation emphasizes both temple and priestly worship as the goal of all creation. It is important to begin with Jesus as the new temple and the new priest because he is the primary fulfillment of these themes. The church shares in them by participation.

The NT frequently draws comparisons between Jesus and the temple (see, e.g., Matt. 12:6; Mark 14:58), but the most thoroughgoing presentation of Jesus as the new temple appears in the Gospel of John.[58] From the very beginning, John subtly prompts his readers to understand Jesus as a new temple. One of the most significant verses in John's Gospel, John 1:14, draws on cultic imagery to describe the event of the Word becoming flesh. Most English translations obscure the significance of the verb, rendering the first part of the verse, "And the Word became flesh and dwelt among us" or "lived among us." The verb commonly translated "dwelt" or "lived" (*eskēnōsen*), however, might more evocatively be rendered "pitched his tent" or "tabernacled." This verb is related to the Greek word used with reference to the tabernacle, the portable worship space described in the latter half of Exodus.[59] In taking on flesh and blood, the Word makes of that body a new place for God to dwell in the midst of his people.

The cultic connotation of this verb is confirmed by the second half of the verse: "And we have seen his glory [*tēn doxan autou*], the glory as of a father's

58. On the temple theme in Matthew, see Barber, *The Historical Jesus and the Temple*; in Mark, see Gray, *The Temple in the Gospel of Mark*. Numerous studies have examined this theme in John. For a survey and analysis of literature from 1996 to 2016, see Mzebetshana and Asumang, "Temple Christology in the Gospel According to John."

59. Hoskyns (*The Fourth Gospel*, 147) notes, "The allusion to nomadic life contained in the word *tabernacled* renders it a natural and effective symbol for the transitory character of human life lived in the body as in a tent (Wisd. ix. 15; 2 Cor. v. 1; 2 Pet. i. 14)."

only son, full of grace and truth" (John 1:14b). Like the verb "to tabernacle," the language of "glory" also finds its home in Israel's cultic life. The account of the building of the tabernacle culminates with the cloud covering the tent and the "glory of the Lord [*kabod adonai*; LXX *doxēs kyriou*]" filling it (Exod. 40:34–35), and one of the most important aspects of Ezekiel's visions is the departure of the glory from the temple (Ezek. 10:18) and its return (43:5).[60] From the very beginning, then, John presents Jesus as a new sanctuary. This theme reappears in John's account of Jesus overturning the tables in the temple, where the evangelist uses the language of "temple" rather than "tabernacle."

As is well known, John places this event toward the beginning of his Gospel, whereas the Synoptic accounts place it toward the end of Jesus's ministry. It seems likely that John's ordering of events serves to emphasize the temple theme.[61] After Jesus drives out the sheep and the cattle, the Jewish leaders ask him for a sign to justify his actions. Jesus replies, "Destroy this temple [*naon*], and in three days I will raise it up" (John 2:19). Although the Jews do not understand the meaning of Jesus's saying, the evangelist clarifies for the reader, "But he was speaking of the temple [*naou*] of his body" (2:21). What remains implicit in the prologue becomes explicit in the evangelist's account of one of Jesus's first public acts: Jesus's body is a new temple.

One of the most pervasive temple themes in John, appearing at least three times, is the motif of living water. This image plays a significant role in Ezekiel, as well as in other prophetic texts of the OT.[62] John develops the theme, applying it both to Jesus and to those who believe in him.

The first occurrence of the image is found in Jesus's conversation with the Samaritan woman at the well. This conversation includes numerous themes, but at the center of the dialogue, both literally and figuratively, lies the question of the proper mode and place of worship.[63] The words "worship [*proskyneō*]" or "worshiper [*proskynētēs*]" occur ten times in the span of John 4:20–25. This emphasis on worship underscores the centrality of the temple in the passage. Seen from this perspective, the earlier part of the conversation between Jesus and the woman takes on new meaning. The initial dialogue culminates in Jesus's offer of living water: "The water that I will give will become in them a spring of water gushing up to eternal life" (John 4:14b). Several OT texts describe water as a source of life, but the most elaborate appears in Ezekiel 47.[64]

60. Both verses in Ezekiel use the same language as Exodus. See also 1 Kings 8:11. For additional references to the glory and its association with the temple, see Hoskyns, *The Fourth Gospel*, 148–49.

61. See, e.g., Schnackenburg, *The Gospel According to St. John*, 1:356–57.

62. Ezek. 47:1–12; Zech. 14; Joel 3–4 (MT). For a discussion of this imagery and its significance for baptism, see I. Morales, *The Bible and Baptism*, 18–19.

63. See Coloe, *God Dwells with Us*, 87, 99–105.

64. Schnackenburg fails to make this connection. He does, however, propose several other OT passages that likely underlie Jesus's promise of quenching thirst, including Sir. 24:21; Isa. 55:1–3;

Jesus offers the very life-giving water envisioned by the prophet. The symbolism of Jesus's position in the chapter further supports such a reading. Although translations typically suggest that Jesus was sitting "beside" the well, Mary Coloe notes that the Greek literally has him sitting "upon [*epi*]" the well in John 4:6, most likely referring to the rock that covered the well most of the time.[65] Jesus, the new temple, thus sits over a source of water and offers himself as the true source of living and life-giving water, a water that gushes up to eternal life.

This water imagery reappears in John 7 as Jesus teaches during the festival of tabernacles. On the last day of the feast, the evangelist tells us, Jesus makes a promise similar to the one he makes to the Samaritan woman in John 4: "Whoever believes in me, as the Scripture has said, 'Out of his heart will flow rivers of living water'" (John 7:38, my translation). Scholars have long debated how to interpret the personal pronoun "his" in the Scripture quotation. Does it refer to Jesus or to the one who believes in Jesus? In other words, does the promised water flow out of Jesus's own heart or out of the heart of whoever believes in him? Good arguments can be made for either interpretation.[66] Considering the broader context of the Gospel, perhaps it is best to take the ambiguity as intentional. In his conversation with the Samaritan woman, Jesus promises that the water he gives will well up within the believer (4:14). Toward the end of the Gospel, in the third and final instance of this water theme, water flows from the side of Christ as he hangs upon the cross (19:34). Given this Gospel's understanding of Jesus as the new temple, implied in the prologue and explicitly stated in John 2, it seems likely that the imagery of water flowing from Christ's pierced side alludes to the prophetic hope of water flowing from the temple.[67] John thus seems to affirm both that Jesus is the source of living water and that this water will eventually flow from whoever believes in him. In other words, for John, Jesus is the primary referent of the new temple, but those who believe in him are implicitly drawn in to become a part of this new temple.[68]

In addition to the temple motif, the NT also presents Jesus as a priest, most obviously and most explicitly in the letter to the Hebrews. Jesus's priesthood

---

58:11; 59:10; Jer. 31:25. For a fuller list and discussion, see Schnackenburg, *The Gospel According to St. John*, 1:429–32.

65. Coloe, *God Dwells with Us*, 95.

66. For a brief discussion of the question, see Coloe, *God Dwells with Us*, 125–28, and the literature cited there.

67. Barrett (*John*, 557) sees Zech. 13:1 as the "probable allusion," particularly given the citation of Zech. 12:10 a few verses later in John 19:37; F. Martin and W. Wright (*John*, 326–27) also point to Zech. 13:1 but add that this text belongs to a broader prophetic tradition associating water with salvation (e.g., Joel 4:18 [MT]; Ezek. 47).

68. For a temple ecclesiology in John, see Coloe, *Dwelling in the Household of God*; Schneiders, *Jesus Risen in Our Midst*, 99–118. Such an understanding is also implicit in Kysar, "'As You Sent Me,'" 375, insofar as he describes the church in John's Gospel as the place where God's glory dwells.

is one of the dominant themes in Hebrews.[69] A detailed examination of this motif is far beyond the scope of this chapter.[70] Instead, I would like to highlight three features of Jesus's priesthood in Hebrews: his offering of sacrifice, his entry into the sanctuary, and his ongoing priestly identity and activity. The first two aspects have analogs in the Levitical priesthood, though in each case with a new dimension in Jesus. The third aspect offers a sharp contrast with the Levitical priesthood.

According to Hebrews, sacrifice is essential to the priesthood—offering sacrifice simply is what priests, especially the high priest, do (Heb. 5:1, 3; 8:3). This understanding flows naturally from the Hebrew idiom for the rite of ordination, which literally refers to "filling the hand." So, for example, Exodus 28:41, which is commonly translated in part "you shall anoint them and ordain them," more literally says in Hebrew "you shall anoint them and *fill their hand* [*mille'ta et-yadam*]."[71] The priests' hands are filled in the rite with the sacrifice to be offered to God (see Lev. 8:27–28; 9:17).[72] In this respect, Jesus's priesthood generically resembles the Levitical priesthood—he, too, offers sacrifice. His priesthood differs in two ways, however—namely, in the substance of the sacrifice he offers and in the frequency with which he offers it.

With respect to the substance, instead of the blood of bulls and goats, Jesus offers his own body in obedience to God's will (Heb. 10:5–10). In his sacrifice, he gives in return to the Father from the gift he himself receives:

> Consequently, when Christ came into the world, he said,
>
> "Sacrifices and offerings you have not desired,
> but a body you have prepared for me;
> in burnt offerings and sin offerings
> you have taken no pleasure.
> Then I said, 'See, I have come to do your will, O God.'" (Heb. 10:5–7a)

In this act we see the logic of sacrifice, which entails making an offering to God from the gifts we have received.[73]

69. For a caution against making priesthood the sole or foundational Christological theme of the text, see Jipp, *The Messianic Theology of the New Testament*, 257–59.

70. For a study of the theme, see Mason, *"You Are a Priest Forever."*

71. So also Exod. 29:9, 29, 33, 35; Lev. 8:33; 16:32; 21:10; Num. 3:3. The LXX of Exod. 28:41 retains the idiom, using the verb *empimplēmi*, but in the rest of the verses cited shifts to the verb *teleioō*.

72. Leithart, *The Priesthood of the Plebs*, 74–77. Leithart correctly notes that, in addition to receiving the offering, the priests participate in the sacrificial meal, thus enjoying table fellowship with God. There is an analog to this OT ritual in the contemporary rite of priestly ordination of the Roman Catholic Church. At one point in the rite, the ordaining bishop ceremonially hands the paten and the chalice to the one being ordained, symbolizing both the sacrifice to be offered and participation in the sacred meal.

73. Such an understanding of sacrifice seems to underlie Paul's exhortation, "I appeal to you therefore, brothers and sisters, on the basis of God's mercy, to present your bodies

With respect to the timing of Jesus's offering, Hebrews notes that the Levitical priests offered sacrifices repeatedly, year after year (Heb. 7:27; 10:1–3, 11). By contrast, Jesus offers a once-for-all, ongoing sacrifice. Although interpreters frequently interpret this sacrifice as Jesus's death on the cross, the logic of the atonement ritual, on which the author draws to explicate Jesus's sacrifice, suggests that his offering is complete only when he presents himself to the Father in the heavenly sanctuary.[74]

This leads to the second point of comparison between Jesus's priesthood and the Levitical priesthood: the location of the offering. In ancient Israel the high priest would complete the sacrifice by bringing the blood into the inner sanctuary of the earthly tabernacle once a year on the Day of Atonement (Heb. 9:1–7). Jesus, too, brings his sacrifice into a sanctuary, but he does so once for all, and he offers it in the heavenly sanctuary, on which the earthly sanctuary is modeled (Heb. 8:1–6; 9:11–15).[75] In referring to the heavenly sanctuary, Hebrews expands on an idea found in Exodus, according to which God shows Moses the pattern on which the earthly tabernacle was to be modeled (see Exod. 25:9, 40). In contrast to the Levitical priests, Jesus enters the heavenly sanctuary.

Finally, Jesus's priesthood differs markedly from the Levitical priesthood with respect to its origin and endurance. As Hebrews notes, the Levitical priesthood is based on genealogical descent (Heb. 7:5). Moreover, because of their mortality, individual priests could hold the office only for a time (7:23). By contrast, Jesus's priesthood stems not from genealogical descent, but rather from his resurrection, by which he now has an indestructible life (7:15–16).[76] And because he has this indestructible life, he is able to serve as a priest forever, constantly interceding for his people (7:20–28).

In Jesus the new temple and the new priest, we see the perfect fulfillment of one of God's purposes for human beings. The NT extends these roles by participation to the Christian people, both now and in the eschaton.

The New Temple and the New Priesthood in Community

Two images dominate Paul's understanding of the church in 1 Corinthians: the temple and the body of Christ.[77] Twice in the first half of the letter,

---

as a living sacrifice, holy and acceptable to God, which is your reasonable act of worship" (Rom. 12:1).

74. For a detailed defense of this reading, see the pioneering work of Moffitt, *Atonement and the Logic of Resurrection* and *Rethinking the Atonement*.

75. For further discussion, see Moffitt, *Rethinking the Atonement*, 117–34.

76. See the discussion in Moffitt, *Atonement and the Logic of Resurrection*, 198–208.

77. In this regard, there are interesting parallels between this letter and John's Gospel. I do not mean to suggest that Paul depends on John (or vice versa), which is very much a minority position (though see, recently, Gorman, *Paul and John in Harmony*). Rather, I simply note the

Paul reminds the Corinthians that they are God's temple. The first reminder appears in 1 Corinthians 3 in the context of a warning about the day of judgment. Some have suggested that Paul here alludes to the book of Malachi, and with good reason.[78] Paul's warning has significant verbal overlap with Malachi 3, speaking of a "day" of fiery judgment involving silver and gold and the purification of a temple (1 Cor. 3:12–13, 16–17; cf. Mal. 3:1–3). Most importantly for my purposes, Paul underscores the indwelling presence of God's Spirit among the Corinthians, one of the clearest signs of their status as God's temple (1 Cor. 3:16).

Paul draws on the image of the church as temple once more in 1 Corinthians 6, again in the context of a warning. Rebuking the Corinthians for thinking that they are free to do whatever they want (1 Cor. 6:12), Paul reminds them, first, of their union with Christ. The Corinthians, through their baptism, have become "members of Christ."[79] As such, they must refrain from going to prostitutes, thereby joining Christ to a prostitute (6:15–16). Rounding out his exhortation, he reminds the Corinthians that they are temples of the Holy Spirit and urges them, "Glorify God in your body" (6:19–20). The church's status as temple thus involves both the Spirit dwelling within them and a duty to worship God by their everyday acts.

Ephesians likewise uses the image of the church as temple, employing it as in 1 Corinthians 3. In 1 Corinthians, Paul addresses divisions based on allegiance to different church leaders (1 Cor. 3:4–5); Ephesians 2 speaks to the Jew-gentile divide. Like 1 Corinthians, Ephesians blends the imagery of "body" and "temple," with both images undergirding the letter's call to unity. Paul explains how Christ has put an end to the hostility between Jew and gentile, "abolishing the law with its commandments and ordinances, that he might create in himself one new humanity in place of the two, thus making peace, and might reconcile both to God in one body through the cross, thus putting to death that hostility through it" (Eph. 2:15–16). Later in the same passage, he shifts to temple imagery: "In him the whole structure is joined together and grows into a holy temple in the Lord, in whom you also are built together spiritually into a dwelling place for God" (2:21–22). As in 1 Corinthians, in Ephesians the church is portrayed as a temple, and specifically the place where God dwells in the midst of his people.

Finally, although 1 Peter does not use the technical language for "temple" (none of the Greek words for "temple" appear in the text), the letter

parallel use of similar themes. On the considerable overlap between body and temple imagery in the NT, see Macaskill, *Union with Christ*, 146–71.

78. Ciampa and Rosner, *First Corinthians*, 153–54; Proctor, "Fire in God's House"; Beale, *The Temple and the Church's Mission*, 250–51; Schrage (*Der erste Brief an die Korinther*, 1:301–2) points to Malachi, among other prophetic texts.

79. On the connection between baptism and union with Christ in 1 Cor. 6, see I. Morales, "Washed, Sanctified, Justified."

nevertheless describes the church both as a temple (implicitly) and as a priesthood (explicitly). Like 1 Corinthians and Ephesians, 1 Peter draws a close connection between Christ and his people, particularly with respect to their status as a temple: "Come to him, a living stone, though rejected by mortals yet chosen and precious in God's sight, and like living stones let yourselves be built into a spiritual house, to be a holy priesthood, to offer spiritual sacrifices acceptable to God through Jesus Christ" (1 Pet. 2:4–5). Christ is the "cornerstone" of the temple (2:6, citing Isa. 28:16), into which Christians are incorporated. Whereas Ephesians emphasizes the church's status as God's dwelling place (Eph. 2:22), 1 Peter, drawing on the exodus tradition (1 Pet. 2:9; cf. Exod. 19:6), highlights the priestly vocation to offer sacrifices to God (1 Pet. 2:5). Already in this life, in the church, the human vocation to worship God finds its initial fulfillment.

An Eschatological Temple and Priesthood

From the beginning, God creates human beings to offer worship. The prophets attest to Israel's hope for a new temple after the first temple's destruction, and the NT proclaims this hope fulfilled proleptically in Christ and in the church. Given this trajectory, it is fitting that the last book of the Bible describes the human end in largely cultic terms. Liturgical symbolism pervades the entire book, from the lampstands of the first chapter (Rev. 1:12) to the references and exhortations to worship in the last chapter (22:3, 9). Readings, hymns, and incense punctuate the book, underscoring the liturgical nature of the end it describes. A full discussion of this symbolism lies outside the scope of this chapter. Instead, I would like to highlight a few images in the culminating vision of the book.

Revelation 21 begins with a description—filled with liturgical imagery—of a new heaven and a new earth. Describing the descent of Jerusalem (the "holy city"), the author recounts what God tells him:

> See, the home [*skēnē*, lit., "tabernacle"] of God is among mortals.
> He will dwell [*skēnōsei*] with them;
> they will be his peoples,
> and God himself will be with them and be their God. (Rev. 21:3)

The language of God's dwelling evokes both the tabernacle and the temple, the two places where God dwelt in Israel's midst (see Exod. 40:34–38; 1 Kings 8:10–11). The description of the holy city also reflects Ezekiel's vision of the new temple in several ways. The introduction to this account (Rev. 21:10: "And in the spirit he carried me away to a great, high mountain") reflects the vision of Ezekiel 40:1–2 and 43:5.[80] Moreover, the fact that the city descends upon a high mountain most likely alludes to this vision, which also takes place on "a very high mountain" (Ezek. 40:2).[81] Revelation depicts the city as having "the glory of God and a radiance like a very rare jewel" (Rev. 21:11). Ezekiel likewise speaks of the temple as shining and filled with the glory of God (Ezek. 43:2, 4–5).[82] Finally, the twelve gates of the city (Rev. 21:12) reflect the twelve gates of the city in Ezekiel 48:31–34.[83]

This temple, however, is not without human ministers. Returning to an image introduced early in the book (Rev. 5:10), Revelation describes the activity of the redeemed in priestly terms. The inhabitants of the city will bear the name of God on their foreheads (22:4b), likely an allusion to the way the high priest bore the name of the Lord on a signet fastened to the forehead (see Exod. 28:36–38).[84] In that role the saints will also see the face of God and the Lamb directly (Rev. 22:4a).[85] Intriguingly, the temple in which the saints minister and see the face of God is nothing other than God and the Lamb: "I saw no temple in the city, for its temple is the Lord God the Almighty and the Lamb" (21:22). In other words, this vision will no longer be mediated—it will be a direct, face-to-face vision (cf. 1 Cor. 13:12) of God and the Lamb.[86]

Here, at the end of part 1, it is worth summarizing the biblical portrayal of the human vocation and its significance for the Christian hope. Each of the themes considered in these chapters (dominion, rest, and worship) features prominently not only in Genesis but also throughout much of Scripture to describe both temporal and eschatological hopes. The command to have dominion over creation of Genesis 1:26–28 carries through Israel's vocation to be a kingdom of priests (Exod. 19:6) to Jesus's status as the messianic Son of David, confirmed by his resurrection from the dead (Rom. 1:3–4). Jesus does not receive this role at the expense of others, however, but gives his disciples a share in it, a share that is closely bound up with the resurrection (2 Tim. 2:11–12a). The desire for rest that features so prominently throughout the OT has implicit roots in the seventh day of creation and addresses the various trials of life in this world, particularly toil and warfare. It points to the hope for stillness and peace. Rest also serves as a bridge between dominion and the third aspect of the human vocation: worship. One of the Lord's promises to David in 2 Samuel 7 is rest, a rest that has as its further end the building of a

80. Beale, *Revelation*, 1065.

81. Beale, *Revelation*, 1065. Levenson (*Theology of the Program of Restoration*, 25) identifies the high mountain of Ezek. 40:2 with Mount Zion.

82. Beale, *Revelation*, 1066.

83. Beale, *Revelation*, 1068. For a fuller discussion of these and other indications of the temple-like structure of the city in Rev. 21, see Beale, *Revelation*, 1065–71.

84. Williamson, *Revelation*, 360; see also Beale, *Revelation*, 1116.

85. See chap. 4 for arguments in favor of this interpretation of the object of vision.

86. I will discuss the significance of this shift in chap. 4.

house for God's name. God created the world as a temple and human beings to be his priests, offering him worship in the cosmic temple. This priestly vocation has, as its purpose, communion with God, expressed in one of the final scenes of Revelation as face-to-face vision. Thus, we see in the eschatological fulfillment of this threefold human vocation the two predominant strands of the Western Christian tradition, (what later theologians would call) the beatific vision and the resurrection. In the next two parts of this study, we will examine what Scripture has to say about these two hopes, aided by three of the great biblical interpreters of the Christian tradition. In the final part of the study, we will bring these two strands together, interpreting them through the lens of the threefold human vocation.

PART 2

"SEEING GOD IS THE LIFE OF THE HUMAN BEING"

The Beatific Vision in Scripture and Tradition

FOUR

Seeing God in Scripture

The figure of Moses exemplifies the tension that characterizes the biblical testimony regarding the vision of God. In the book of Exodus, in the midst of the golden calf incident, Moses makes the bold request, "Please show me your glory" (Exod. 33:18). The Lord gives Moses an enigmatic reply, saying in part, "You cannot see my face, for no one shall see me and live" (Exod. 33:20). To complicate things even more, earlier in the same chapter we read, "Thus the LORD used to speak to Moses face to face, as one speaks to a friend" (33:11a).[1] The Scriptures are thus ambiguous, to put it mildly, with regard to whether or how human beings can see God. Beneath this ambiguity, however, lies an implicit human desire for this vision. The Christian tradition has taken this desire seriously, frequently speaking of ultimate human happiness as precisely the vision of God.[2] Before considering a few representatives of this tradition, I would like to explore the multifaceted biblical account of seeing God. The desire to see God and its fulfillment, whether partial or complete, find a number of expressions throughout the Scriptures. Taken as a whole, the testimony of Scripture holds out the promise that this desire is not destined to futility. One day we will see God face to face, finding in that vision our true fulfillment.

To reach this conclusion, we must first consider the different ways Scripture speaks about the phenomenon of seeing God. We will begin by exploring the mysterious biblical encounters between human beings and the God of

1. See also Num. 12:8a and Deut. 34:10.

2. As Paul Griffiths notes, "This final and unsurpassable good is depicted with different emphases by different strands in the tradition's fabric, but common to most of them is the scriptural trope of vision." See Griffiths, *Decreation*, 217–18. For a recent, though selective, study of the history of this belief, see H. Boersma, *Seeing God*.

Israel, encounters that simultaneously attest to the possibility of seeing God in some fashion and the danger of such vision. From there we will consider the frequently expressed hope of gazing on the beauty—or the face—of the Lord. For the ancient Israelites, this hope found at least partial fulfillment in the vision of the temple, and so we will next look at some of the ways the temple was associated with the vision of God. The Gospel of John presents Jesus as a new temple. Given the OT traditions about the temple as the place where one sees God, this has important implications for John's understanding of this hope. Christ's flesh must play some role in the way Christians think about the vision of God. Important as the incarnation is, though, it does not exhaust the ways the NT speaks about this vision, either in the Johannine tradition or in other NT texts. In the Beatitudes, Christ himself promises a vision of God for "the pure in heart" (Matt. 5:8). Paul holds out hope for a similar vision (1 Cor. 13:12), as does the first letter of John (1 John 3:2), and the book of Revelation closes by promising a face-to-face vision of God (Rev. 22:4). All these texts, then, contribute either explicitly or implicitly to the Christian hope for the beatific vision.

The Peril of Seeing God's Face

Numerous texts in the OT suggest that seeing God can be dangerous. One could call it a recurring motif, sometimes expressed with the language of seeing God "face to face" and at other times simply as seeing God. Regardless of the expression used, in each case the person who has an encounter with God registers surprise at having survived the experience unharmed. The earliest example in the narrative of Scripture appears in Genesis 16. Hagar, having run away from her abusive mistress, Sarai, encounters the angel of the Lord (Gen. 16:7–13). He commands Hagar to return to her mistress, but not without promising her fruitfulness and describing her son's future life (16:10–12). At the end of their encounter, Hagar marvels: "So she called the name of the Lord who spoke to her, 'You are a God of seeing,' for she said, 'Truly here I have seen him who looks after me'" (16:13 ESV). The second half of this verse presents notorious difficulties, as can be seen by the variety of translations.[3]

3. To give just three examples besides the ESV, the NRSV renders the phrase, "Have I seen God and remained alive after seeing him?" This translation, however, is based on an emendation proposed by Julius Wellhausen and has no basis in the textual tradition. See the discussion in Westermann, *Genesis 12–36*, 246–48. The NASB has, "Have I even seen *Him* here *and lived* after He saw me?" The italics, as is common in the NASB, indicate words that do not appear in the original language but are added to make sense of the verse. Likely the additions are based, as in the NRSV, on Wellhausen's emendation. The JPS Torah translates the phrase, "Have I even here seen Him that seeth me?" Chavel ("The Face of God," 3) proposes, "I still see even after looking" and suggests that the danger could involve either death or blindness, as in Gen. 19:11 and 2 Kings 6:18.

Whatever the correct interpretation of the phrase, Hagar expresses wonder at an encounter with God that emphasizes some kind of seeing.[4]

The patriarch Jacob likewise marvels after his wrestling match with the mysterious figure at the River Jabbok.[5] Having sent his family and all his possessions ahead of him, Jacob suddenly finds himself in a contest with a man who appears out of nowhere (Gen. 32:24).[6] As the bout comes to an end near the break of day, the man injures Jacob permanently, but Jacob refuses to let him go until he gives him a blessing. Once the man obliges and leaves, Jacob recognizes the true identity of his opponent and, like Hagar before him, says in awe, "For I have seen God face to face, yet my life is preserved" (32:30b). Once again, Jacob's statement presumes that seeing God involves danger, in this case death.

Encounters with the living God are not limited to these one-on-one instances. Exodus describes a scene in which several people look upon God and yet live. At Mount Sinai, during the covenant-making ceremony, Moses brings with him Aaron, Nadab, and Abihu, together with seventy elders of Israel. After the sacrifice and ritual of sprinkling the blood on the altar and on the people (Exod. 24:5–6), Moses takes the men up the mountain for a feast. The narrator notes twice that the men see God: "And *they saw the God of Israel*. Under his feet there was something like a pavement of sapphire stone, like the very heaven for clearness. *God did not lay his hand on the chief men of the Israelites*; *they beheld God*, and they ate and drank" (24:10–11). As with Jacob, the narrative strikes a note of surprise that God does nothing to the men who see him.

This motif occurs twice in the book of Judges, first with Gideon, then with Samson's parents. Unlike the examples in the Pentateuch, both instances of seeing God in Judges are followed by an explanation—or at least a reassurance—that the vision will not result in death.[7] The angel of the Lord appears to Gideon and commissions him to rescue his people Israel (Judg. 6:11–27).[8] When Gideon asks for a sign to confirm that he will have support in his task, the Lord consumes the offering that Gideon brings and disappears.

4. It is interesting to note that Hagar marvels at having seen God, given that nothing else in the passage necessarily indicates that she in fact saw the angel of the Lord. The angel of the Lord finds her (16:7) and speaks to her (16:8–12), but nowhere does the passage use the language of appearance. It is possible, then, that seeing here may have the sense of being in God's presence.

5. On this story, see Wessner, "Toward a Literary Understanding of 'Face to Face' (פָּנִים אֶל־פָּנִים) in Genesis 32:23–32."

6. Given the physical nature of the encounter, this passage suggests more clearly than the story of Hagar that Jacob's experience includes a visual element.

7. These two episodes also differ from the Hagar story: In both cases, the narrator speaks of the angel of the Lord "appearing" to Gideon and to Samson's parents (Judg. 6:12; 13:3, 10). Both stories seem to imply some kind of visionary experience.

8. One should note that the narrator moves back and forth between calling Gideon's visitor "the angel of the LORD" (Judg. 6:11–12, 20–22) and "the LORD" (6:14, 16, 23). This ambiguity has

Like Jacob, Gideon expects this encounter to result in death and so asks for help: "And Gideon said, 'Help me, Lord GOD! For I have seen the angel of the LORD face to face'" (6:22b). Unlike Jacob, however, Gideon receives explicit reassurance from the Lord: "But the LORD said to him, 'Peace be to you; do not fear; you shall not die'" (6:23). Manoah and his wife have a similar encounter with the angel of the Lord, who again promises a redeemer to rescue Israel from their enemies (Judg. 13). Like Gideon, they ask for a sign from the angel to confirm his message. When they bring him an offering, he consumes it (13:15–20). Upon realizing that they have seen the angel of the Lord, Manoah expresses the familiar fear that they will die: "And Manoah said to his wife, 'We shall surely die, for we have seen God'" (13:22). This time it is not the Lord, but rather Manoah's wife who sensibly reassures her husband: "But his wife said to him, 'If the LORD had meant to kill us, he would not have accepted a burnt offering and a grain offering at our hands or shown us all these things or announced to us such things as these'" (13:23). The fact that they do not die on the spot—and that God has further plans for them—suggests to this wise woman that they will not be punished for seeing God.

It has been common, going back to the early centuries of the church, to see beneath these stories a principle that seeing God in this life will result in death. Interpreters often support this reading by appealing to the Lord's response to Moses's request in Exodus 33. When he asks to see the Lord's glory, Moses receives this response: "And he said, 'I will make all my goodness pass before you and will proclaim before you the name, "The LORD," and I will be gracious to whom I will be gracious and will show mercy on whom I will show mercy. But,' he said, 'you cannot see my face, for no one shall see me and live'" (Exod. 33:19–20). Taking the Lord's words as an absolute principle, interpreters label the stories recounted above as exceptions to the rule.[9] There are significant problems with such an interpretation, however, as Simeon Chavel has argued.[10]

First, and most obviously, each of the figures discussed above is said to have "seen" God, and yet none of them dies on the spot. In addition to those figures, there are several other occasions in the OT that speak nonchalantly of someone seeing God, without even a hint of these figures risking mortal danger. At least three times in the Pentateuch, Moses is said to have a face-to-face relationship with God. The first of these occurs, significantly, in the same chapter as the alleged principle forbidding humans to look on God's face. Describing Moses's practice of setting up a tent outside the camp where

been the subject of much scholarly debate. For a concise discussion of the phenomenon and some of the interpretive possibilities for understanding it, see Newsom, "Angels (Old Testament)."

9. According to Chavel ("The Face of God," 5), scholars "nearly unanimously" interpret the Lord's saying as suggesting that there is some physical quality of the Lord's countenance that results in death to those who behold it.

10. Chavel, "The Face of God," to which I am indebted for much of the following. I am grateful to my colleague Andrew Geist for drawing my attention to this essay.

he would speak with the Lord, the narrator writes, "Thus the LORD used to speak to Moses face to face, as one speaks to a friend" (Exod. 33:11).[11] Some might argue that the situation changes with Moses's request on Mount Sinai, but the Pentateuch affirms twice more *after* Sinai that Moses spoke to the Lord face to face. In Numbers 12, when Aaron and Miriam grumble against Moses, the Lord replies to them,

> Hear my words:
>
> When there are prophets among you,
> I the LORD make myself known to them in visions;
> I speak to them in dreams.
> Not so with my servant Moses;
> he is faithful in all my house.
> *With him I speak face to face* [literally "mouth to mouth," *peh 'el-peh*]—*clearly, not in riddles,*
> *and he beholds the form of the* LORD.
>
> Why then were you not afraid to speak against my servant Moses? (Num. 12:6–8)

Moses has a privileged position among the prophets of Israel, continuing to speak to the Lord as to a friend. This privilege remained part of Israel's memory. In one of the last verses of the Pentateuch, Deuteronomy says of Moses, "Never since has there arisen a prophet in Israel like Moses, whom the LORD knew face to face [*panim 'el-panim*; LXX *prosōpon kata prosōpon*]" (Deut. 34:10).[12] These three statements suggest that perhaps the Lord's response in Exodus 33:20 should not be taken as an absolute principle, a point to which I will return.[13]

In addition to Moses, it is common for the OT to speak of the prophets beholding God without fear of death.[14] When Isaiah sees the Lord sitting on his throne in the temple, for example, he fears not simply because he has seen the Lord, but because he is "a man of unclean lips" living "among a people of unclean lips" (Isa. 6:5). The danger stems not simply from seeing God, but rather from Isaiah's (and the people's) state of impurity.[15] Other factors may also contribute to the prophet's fear. Significantly, in the vision the

11. On this passage, see Wessner, "Toward a Literary Understanding of Moses and the Lord 'Face to Face'"; Parkison, *To Gaze upon God*, 29–31.

12. In Hebrew, the phrase is identical to the description in Exod. 33:11; the Greek of Exodus uses a different, though synonymous, expression (*enōpios enōpiō*).

13. Chavel ("The Face of God," 6) comments, "All these passages must modulate the absolute theological significance flatly granted to Exod 33:20." Cf. Wilson, "'Face to Face' with God," 112n23.

14. See the discussion of Chavel, "The Face of God," 32–40.

15. Chavel, "The Face of God," 33, 39. *Pace* Tournay (*Seeing and Hearing God*, 113), it is not merely that Isaiah has seen the Lord, but rather the condition of Isaiah and of the people that evokes the prophet's fear.

seraphim are said to cover their faces (Isa. 6:2), perhaps out of reverence.[16] The important point, however, is that it is not simply "seeing" God (however we understand this experience) that frightens Isaiah.

A second difficulty with interpreting the face of the Lord as inherently death-dealing is that the OT frequently affirms quite the opposite. Rather than being a source of death, the face of the Lord is often portrayed as a source of blessing and life.[17] One thinks, for example, of the priestly blessing in Numbers: "The Lord bless you and keep you; the Lord make his face to shine upon you and be gracious to you; the Lord lift up his countenance upon you and give you peace" (Num. 6:24–26). While it is true that this blessing does not speak of looking upon the face of the Lord, it nevertheless associates the Lord's face with blessing and peace, not death. A similar idea appears in the psalms, which often express a desire for the Lord's face to shine upon the psalmist or on the people as a whole. In Psalm 80, this desire appears as a sort of refrain, with the shining of the Lord's face upon the people bringing salvation (Ps. 80:3, 7, 19).[18] These examples do not seem to refer to an actual vision of God's face. Rather, they use the image of the Lord's face to describe the way he blesses his people. Although these texts do not recount visionary experiences, they nevertheless suggest that, far from being a source of death, the face of the Lord confers blessing, life, and salvation.[19]

If the vision of God's face does not instantaneously cause death, then what is one to make of the traditions that express the fear of dying for looking upon God? Chavel argues that, contrary to the nearly unanimous scholarly opinion that the Lord's face inherently brings death to those who see it, the danger of seeing the Lord lies in an "etiquette of eye-contact" drawn from the world of human interaction, particularly with respect to royalty.[20] Two examples from the OT illustrate the principle. In the book of Exodus, after the ninth plague and Moses's demand that Pharaoh allow the Israelites to take all their property

16. I am grateful to David Moffitt for pointing this out to me.

17. Chavel ("The Face of God," 7–9) astutely contrasts this portrayal of the face of the Lord with Greek traditions about Medusa, the beholding of whose countenance would instantly turn the beholder to stone. The notion that a god's face can bestow blessing also appears in other ancient Near Eastern texts. See Wilson, "'Face to Face' with God," 108–9. One should note, however, that many of the texts that speak of the Lord's face in this way do not necessarily envision a face-to-face encounter, as discussed below.

18. Interestingly, the LXX speaks not of the Lord's face shining, but rather asks the Lord, "Show your face [*epiphanon ton prosōpon sou*], and we shall be saved" (Ps. 79:4, 8, 20 [LXX], my translation). For similar examples asking the Lord to show his face or to let it shine, see, e.g., Pss. 4:6; 31:16; 67:1; 119:135. For a brief discussion of the way early translators treat the theme of seeing God, see Hanson, "The Treatment in the LXX of the Theme of Seeing God."

19. Wilson ("'Face to Face' with God," 114) comes to a similar conclusion with respect to the various OT narratives describing face-to-face encounters with God discussed above. As I will suggest below, a similar idea seems to be at work in 1 John 3:2. Seeing God causes the one who sees to become like him—that is, to become immortal.

20. Chavel, "The Face of God," 7–23 passim.

with them into the wilderness, Pharaoh threatens Moses, "Take care that you do not see my face again, for on the day you see my face you shall die" (Exod. 10:28b). There is no quality in Pharaoh's face that will cause Moses's death. Rather, Pharaoh threatens Moses with the death penalty if he seeks an audience again.[21] A similar phenomenon can be seen in the case of David's son Absalom, banished from the king's presence for murdering his brother Amnon. When Absalom returns to Jerusalem from his exile in Geshur, David forbids his son from coming into his presence: "And the king said, 'Let him return to his house, but my face he will not see.' And Absalom returned to his house, but the king's face he did not see" (2 Sam. 14:24, my translation).[22] A little later in the chapter, Absalom insists on seeing the king, even if it means death: "And now, I will see the king's face, and if there is guilt in me, let him kill me" (14:32b, my translation). As with Pharaoh, there is nothing about David's countenance that will automatically kill Absalom. Rather, by presumptuously seeking an audience with the king, Absalom runs the risk of the death penalty.[23]

This phenomenon helps explain several features of the accounts of people seeing God: the fear of those who see God, the fact that they do not die on the spot, and the Lord's refusal to show Moses his face in Exodus 33:20. All those who marvel at having seen God and not died seem to have been aware of the etiquette involved in seeing a king, whether earthly or heavenly. Those who see God risk death not because the Lord's face is intrinsically death-dealing, but rather because to look upon the Lord presumptuously can merit a death sentence.[24] None of these figures (Jacob, Gideon, and the rest), however, seek out an audience with God. Rather, he appears to them of his own volition. This might explain why their encounters do not result in death. This etiquette also might clarify the Lord's response to Moses's request in Exodus 33. As Chavel puts it, "The problem in the case of Moses may very well inhere in his having requested the view. To initiate a request retains, indeed, presupposes a sense of self. It admits some hint of audacity, an over-stepping of bounds." A little later Chavel suggests that one might render the Lord's response, "You cannot *simply* look upon my face, for man cannot *simply* look upon me and live."[25] Seeing the face of God is a gift that comes about on God's initiative,

21. The LXX makes this clear by rendering the second part of Pharaoh's warning, "Now on whatever day you should appear to me, you shall die!" (Exod. 10:28b [NETS]).

22. The NRSVue, rendering the idiom more colloquially ("he is not to come into my presence"), obscures the reference to David's "face," although it captures the meaning of the idiom.

23. For further analysis of these and other human examples, see Chavel, "The Face of God," 10–11. In addition to Pharaoh and David, Chavel notes the case of Joseph and his brothers, which uses the same expression several times (Gen. 43:3, 5; 44:23, 26).

24. As I will suggest below, a similar phenomenon seems to be at work with respect to the ark of the covenant.

25. Chavel, "The Face of God," 41–42 (emphasis original). Along similar lines, see Wessner, "Toward a Literary Understanding of Moses and the Lord 'Face to Face,'" 114, 116; Wilson, "'Face to Face' with God," 112n23.

not something that human beings can presume to obtain for themselves. The Lord reiterates in Exodus 33:23b, "My face shall not be seen," but this statement seems to apply to this particular episode, especially when read in light of the later statements affirming Moses's face-to-face friendship with God (Num. 12:8; Deut. 34:10).

With this distinction in mind, one can make better sense of another puzzling aspect of the encounters discussed at the beginning of this section. Not only do they not result in death; often they result in some kind of blessing for the one who sees God.[26] Hagar is strengthened to return to Abram and Sarai, enduring the hardships involved; Jacob receives the courage to face his brother Esau; Gideon, fearful when he first realizes that he has seen God, receives peace. Although he is still fearful of his task (Judg. 6:27), he nevertheless accomplishes it. Seeing God in the proper circumstances thus results in a blessing. These encounters, however, are a far cry from what the Christian tradition would eventually refer to as the "beatific vision." From a Christian canonical perspective, it is difficult to affirm that any of these OT figures—even Moses—saw the divine essence. The Johannine writings affirm more than once that no one has ever seen God (see John 1:18; 1 John 4:12; cf. 1 Tim. 6:16). As the Christian tradition affirms, these "visions" of God were mediated, probably by some outward manifestation.[27] Nevertheless, one can see how these stories might contribute to a deeper understanding of the beatific vision. As the mediated vision of God led to blessings for those who encountered him in the old covenant, so the direct vision of God will one day lead to fullness of blessing for those who gaze on him for all eternity. Some of these stories also attest to the human desire to see God's face, a desire that appears frequently in the Psalter.[28]

The Desire to See God's Face

The book of Psalms deserves special consideration because of its emphasis on the importance of God's face. Two kinds of expressions are particularly important in this regard. First, the psalmists frequently lament the hiddenness of God's face or ask the Lord not to hide his face from them. Second, several

26. For further analysis of the following episodes, see Wilson, "'Face to Face' with God," 110–14, on which I rely for these examples.

27. The most difficult case to account for in the figures we have considered is Moses, but even this can be explained if one considers the context of Num. 12:8. The Lord contrasts his communication with other prophets "in visions" and "in dreams" with the manner in which he speaks to Moses "mouth to mouth." The "face-to-face" relationship Moses enjoys could be interpreted as one of deeper intimacy with the Lord without necessarily suggesting that he saw the divine essence.

28. As Parkison (*To Gaze upon God*, 25–26) puts it, "These episodes intrinsically maintain a hint of longing and intrigue."

psalms also express a desire to see God's face. This desire should come as no surprise, given the close association already noted between God's face, blessing, and life. While the desires expressed in the Psalter, like the visions of the figures discussed in the previous section, are not a full-blown expression of the beatific vision, they nevertheless serve as important precursors to the later Christian understanding of this hope.

Numerous psalms express dismay at the hiddenness of God's face, usually in times of distress.[29] This hiding is usually associated with death and despair.[30] Psalm 13 begins with the plea, "How long, O LORD? Will you forget me forever? How long will you hide your face from me?" (Ps. 13:1). The hiddenness of God's face, the source of blessing (Num. 6:24–26), results in pain and sorrow (Ps. 13:2). The picture in Psalm 30 is even more stark. There, the hiddenness of God's face leads not only to dismay but also to the fear of death, of descending to "the Pit" (Ps. 30:7–9). Similarly, Psalm 44 associates the Lord's hiding with the danger of death:

> Why do you hide your face?
> Why do you forget our affliction and oppression?
> For we sink down to the dust;
> our bodies cling to the ground. (Ps. 44:24–25)

Psalm 88, arguably the darkest poem in the Psalter, associates the hiding of God's face with the terror of death (Ps. 88:3–6, 15 [MT]). Finally, Psalm 143 seems to draw a causal connection between God hiding his face and death:

> Answer me quickly, O LORD;
> my spirit fails.
> Do not hide your face from me,
> or I shall be like those who go down to the Pit. (Ps. 143:7)

Just as the shining of God's face results in blessing and life, the hiding of his face can bring about death, or at least conditions equivalent to death.[31] None of these texts necessarily speaks to the desire to see God's face. Rather, they seem to describe God as turning away from the psalmist, often expressed in the language of "forgetting," which means withdrawing help or protection.

29. For a good discussion of the hiding of God's face both in the Psalms and elsewhere in the OT, see Balentine, *The Hidden God*, 46–79.

30. Balentine (*The Hidden God*, 56–63) shows that the effect of God hiding his face is separation from God, though this can be expressed in a variety of ways. I mention here only a few representative examples. For a full discussion, see Balentine's treatment of these and other texts.

31. Although Irenaeus does not appeal to any of these psalms, they seem to offer biblical support for his claim, "Seeing God is the life of the human being" (Irenaeus, *Haer.* 4.20.7 [my translation]). See the following chapter for a discussion of Irenaeus's understanding of the vision of God.

Again, though, one can see how this understanding might contribute to the more explicit articulations of the desire to see God's face.

In parallel with this association between the hiddenness of God's face and deathlike conditions, several psalms link the deep desire to see God's face with joy and life.[32] Psalm 11 describes how the Lord tests the righteous and the wicked (11:5), appointing recompense to each. The reward of the righteous, on which note the psalm ends, is the vision of God's face: "For the LORD is righteous; he loves righteous deeds; the upright shall behold his face" (11:7). Psalm 17 ends on a similar note, expressing hope that the psalmist will see the Lord's face: "As for me, I shall behold your face [*panekha*] in righteousness; when I awake I shall be satisfied, beholding your likeness" (17:15). The most extended expression of this hope of seeing God's face appears in Psalm 27, another song of confidence in God akin to Psalm 11. Here the psalmist describes his prayer:

> One thing I asked of the LORD;
> this I seek:
> to live in the house of the LORD
> all the days of my life,
> to behold the beauty of the LORD,
> and to inquire in his temple. (Ps. 27:4)[33]

A few verses later, the psalmist reiterates this desire, "'Come,' my heart says, 'seek his face!' Your face, LORD, do I seek. Do not hide your face from me" (Ps. 27:8–9a). Like Psalms 11 and 17, Psalm 27 also ends on a note of confidence in attaining the psalmist's desire: "I believe that I shall see the goodness of the LORD in the land of the living" (27:13). One of the most moving expressions of the desire to see God appears in Psalm 42, which begins,

> As a deer longs for flowing streams,
> so my soul longs for you, O God.
> My soul thirsts for God,
> for the living God.
> When shall I come and behold
> the face of God? (Ps. 42:1–2)

32. On this motif in the psalms, see M. Smith, "'Seeing God' in the Psalms"; Tournay, *Seeing and Hearing God*, 119–30.

33. The parallelism between beholding the beauty of the Lord and inquiring in the temple may suggest that it is by visiting the temple that the psalmist will see the Lord's beauty. On this theme see Anderson, *That I May Dwell Among Them*, and the discussion below. Parkison (*To Gaze upon God*, 180) provocatively describes this verse as "the entire biblical psalter in one verse."

Rather than describing the benefits attached to this vision of God, the psalm focuses on the plight of the psalmist brought about by being far from God's face. Among the psalmist's trials are tears (42:3), distress of soul (42:4–7), and the mockery of adversaries (42:10). Despite these trials, the psalmist continues to trust in the Lord, repeating the refrain,

> Why are you cast down, O my soul,
> and why are you disquieted within me?
> Hope in God, for I shall again praise him,
> my help and my God. (Ps. 42:5–6a, 11; 43:5)[34]

At the heart of the psalmist's hope is the expectation of praising God once again. As Psalm 43 makes clear, this hope is bound up with a return to the temple (43:3–4). This emphasis on returning to the temple suggests a connection between temple worship and seeing God's face, a point to which I will return. Finally, although Psalm 63 does not refer to the Lord's face, it does express a desire to see God. The psalm begins with language resembling Psalm 42:

> O God, you are my God; I seek you;
> my soul thirsts for you;
> my flesh faints for you,
> as in a dry and weary land where there is no water. (Ps. 63:1)

The remedy for this deep thirst is a vision of God: "So I have looked upon you in the sanctuary, beholding your power and glory" (63:2). As the rest of the psalm makes clear, this vision is bound up with worship (63:3–8).

None of these psalms, whether those that speak of God's hiddenness or those that speak of seeing his face, refers to the beatific vision as later Christian tradition would come to understand it.[35] As already noted, the psalms that speak of God's hiddenness most likely do not even suggest a desire for an actual vision of God. Nevertheless, two points are worth making with respect to this theme. First, these psalms attest to an inchoate desire to see God in some way, even if not to a robust hope for the beatific vision. One can easily see how texts like these would provide fodder for later discussions of this vision. Second, several of these psalms closely associate the vision of God with temple worship. Mark Smith offers an intriguing explanation for this association: "'Seeing God' thus represents the culminating experience of the temple. Going to the temple re-presented the experience of paradise with the elements of cherubim, palm trees, gold, water, abundant food, etc.,

34. Scholars agree that Pss. 42 and 43 are closely related, perhaps even originally comprising a single psalm. See, e.g., Goldingay, *Psalms 42–89*, 29.

35. See again M. Smith, "'Seeing God' in the Psalms."

and this included the divine presence."[36] There may be, however, even more to this connection than Smith suggests. Some OT texts imply that seeing the temple and its furnishings was in fact how ancient Israelites could see God.

The Temple and the Vision of God

According to Exodus 23:17 and Deuteronomy 16:16, the men of ancient Israel were commanded to "appear before" the Lord God three times each year. At least that is how most modern translations render the commandment. Since the nineteenth century, however, scholars have argued that these verses may in fact command that the men should "see" the Lord God three times in the year.[37] Given the aniconic nature of ancient Israelite religion, such a command would seem impossible to obey. The Israelites were expressly forbidden from making images of their God (see Exod. 20:4; Deut. 5:8). Does the God of Israel demand the impossible?

Gary Anderson offers a compelling solution to this puzzle, based on ancient Israelite understandings of the temple, the tabernacle, and the sacred furnishings of both sanctuaries.[38] In brief, because the temple and its furnishings were suffused with the presence of God, by their association with the Lord they were considered to participate in the being of God.[39] Thus, to look upon them was to look upon the Lord himself.

One of the central pieces of Anderson's argument lies in the characteristics of the ark of the covenant.[40] In speaking about the ark, the OT draws several connections between this object and God. First, just as human beings are not to take the initiative in beholding the face of God, so also there is a peril associated with seeing the ark.[41] One can see this (and perhaps the reason behind it) in the instructions for taking down the tabernacle for transportation in Numbers 4. In the instructions given to the Kohathites (one of the Levitical families) regarding their duty to carry the ark, the Lord commands Moses and Aaron, "When

36. M. Smith, "'Seeing God' in the Psalms," 181.

37. For a concise explanation of the features of the Hebrew that support such an interpretation, see Anderson, "Towards a Theology of the Tabernacle and Its Furniture," 162–64, and the literature cited there.

38. Anderson has written extensively on this topic since at least 2008. In addition to the article cited in the previous footnote, see "To See Where God Dwells" and his recent full-length treatment, *That I May Dwell Among Them*. To avoid cumbersomeness, hereafter I will refer either to the tabernacle or to the temple, together with its furnishings, but in most cases the point applies to either tabernacle or temple.

39. Anderson, *That I May Dwell Among Them*, 55–56.

40. For a full discussion, see Anderson, *That I May Dwell Among Them*, 50–61.

41. Chavel ("The Face of God," 2) also notes this connection. Later (25–26) he points out that the Samaritan Torah preserves a variant in Exod. 23:17 and 34:23, where the commandment that the Israelite men should come to Jerusalem to see the Lord says instead that they should come to see the ark.

Aaron and his sons have finished covering the sanctuary and all the furnishings of the sanctuary, as the camp sets out, after that the Kohathites shall come to carry these, but they must not touch the holy things, or they will die" (Num. 4:15). A few verses later, a second warning is given: "But the Kohathites must not go in *to look on the holy things even for a moment*, or they will die" (4:20). Looking on the ark and the other temple furnishings, like looking on the face of God, runs the risk of death.[42] Noting these parallels, Anderson concludes that, in some mysterious way, "the [tabernacle] furniture participates in the being of God."[43] First and Second Samuel likewise attest to this understanding of the ark's holiness. In 1 Samuel 6, when the Israelites have recovered the ark from the Philistines, some of the laypeople foolishly look into the ark with disastrous results, as some of them are struck down (1 Sam. 6:19).[44]

In addition to noting the danger of looking into the ark illicitly, Scripture also identifies the ark with God's presence.[45] A famous text from Numbers 10 associates the movement of the ark with the movement of the Lord himself: "Whenever the ark set out, Moses would say, 'Arise, O Lord, let your enemies be scattered and your foes flee before you.' And whenever it came to rest, he would say, 'Return, O Lord, to the ten thousand thousands of Israel'" (Num. 10:35–36; cf. Ps. 132:8). Similarly, in 1 Samuel 4 the Israelites bring the ark to their camp to accompany them into battle against the Philistines, seeing in the ark God's tangible presence among them (1 Sam. 4:3). Finally, when David goes into exile to escape his son Absalom, he refuses to take the ark with him but expresses hope that he will return to the city and see the ark (2 Sam. 15:25–26).[46]

At least one text extends the presence of God beyond the temple and its furnishings to the entire city.[47] Psalm 48, a hymn of praise to the Lord for his steadfast love and for his dwelling place on Zion, suggests that God's presence saturates not only the temple but the whole city, or at least the city of Zion.[48] Thus, the psalmist urges his listeners,

> Walk about Zion; go all around it;
> count its towers;
> consider well its ramparts;
> go through its citadels,

42. See the discussion of this danger on pp. 68–74.
43. Anderson, *That I May Dwell Among Them*, 56.
44. The NRSVue obscures the meaning, but it is clear in Hebrew that the people look into the ark. The text suggests that the Lord strikes down the people *because* they look into the ark, which indicates that simply looking into the ark would not *automatically* result in death.
45. Anderson, *That I May Dwell Among Them*, 56–61.
46. Anderson, "Towards a Theology of the Tabernacle and Its Furniture," 165–66.
47. Anderson, "Towards a Theology of the Tabernacle and Its Furniture," 167–68.
48. In the OT, "Zion" can refer to Jerusalem as a whole or to different parts of the city. See Mare, "Zion."

that you may tell the next generation
that this is God,
our God forever and ever.
He will be our guide forever. (Ps. 48:12–14)

The psalm effectively equates the city with God, such that inspecting its various features amounts to beholding God.

This understanding of the temple and its furnishings as participating in God's presence helps explain the expectation of seeing God expressed in the psalms. It is not only, as Smith suggests, that going to the temple meant returning to Eden, though that probably factors into the psalmist's delight. In addition, going to the temple and gazing upon the temple furnishings meant gazing upon the Lord.

Before we turn to the NT, however, two difficulties need to be resolved. First, looking at the ark could result in death, even for those charged with the responsibility of transporting it. How, then, could Israelites fulfill their desire to see God when gazing at the ark meant almost certain death? Second, most of the temple furnishings resided within parts of the temple restricted to priests, and the ark in the holy of holies, where only the high priest was allowed to enter once a year. How, then, could the Israelites satisfy their duty to see God?

The first question can be resolved somewhat quickly in light of Chavel's analysis of the etiquette of eye contact. Setting eyes on the ark would not, in itself, necessarily result in death. Rather, what seems to be forbidden is *illicitly* gazing upon this sacred object. Just as no human being was able to initiate an audience with the Lord, so no human being had the right to gaze upon the ark except under conditions specified by the one whose presence made the ark holy.

With respect to the second question, one possible solution, suggested by later Jewish texts, is that on the major festivals the priests would bring out some of the temple furnishings so that the people could look upon them.[49] In this way the males among the Israelites could fulfill their duty to "see the Lord God" three times a year (Exod. 23:17; Deut. 16:16). Another, perhaps simpler, solution is to take seriously the perspective of Psalm 48. Simply by approaching the temple, the Israelites were able to see God and so to fulfill their obligation.

The New Temple and the Vision of God

As noted in chapter 3, the Gospel of John presents Jesus as a new temple. There is no need to rehearse the details of this temple Christology again.

49. For a fuller discussion, see Anderson, *That I May Dwell Among Them*, 61–67, and, in much greater detail, Anderson, "Towards a Theology of the Tabernacle and Its Furniture," 168–83.

Rather, I would simply like to note how it relates to the ancient Israelite understanding of seeing God in the temple.

While the prologue of John reaches its climax with the affirmation that "the Word became flesh and tabernacled among us" (John 1:14, my translation), it ends with a denial and an affirmation: "No one has ever seen God. It is the only Son, himself God, who is close to the Father's heart, who has made him known" (1:18). The first half of this verse, the denial that anyone has ever seen God, might seem to imply that John rejects the validity of the theophanies discussed above. While such an interpretation is possible, it seems better to look for other explanations, not least because the evangelist so often appeals to Scripture to testify to Jesus.[50] One likely explanation is that John fits into a tradition that qualified the theophanies of the OT.[51] Other Jewish writers of the time, interpreting texts such as Exodus 24:9–10, suggest that these visions were indirect.[52] The denial of John 1:18 must not, however, be read on its own, but rather in conjunction with the affirmation in the second half of the verse. John is concerned not only with denying the fullness of previous encounters with God but also with presenting Jesus as the one through whom people now have access to the Father.[53] The Gospel frequently describes this access in terms of vision, and that vision often draws on Israel's traditions of tabernacle and temple.

The high point of the prologue describes the incarnation with language evocative of the tabernacle narrative in Exodus 25–40, especially the filling of the tabernacle with the glory of the Lord in Exodus 40:34: "The Word became flesh and tabernacled among us, and we have seen his glory, glory as of the only Son from the Father, full of grace and truth" (John 1:14, my translation). John portrays Jesus as the new tabernacle, the new dwelling of God among human beings, where God's glory is revealed. Moses famously asks to see that glory, and the Lord rejects the request, or at least qualifies it (Exod. 33:18–20). The incarnation of the Son reveals the Father's glory to all those who believe in the Son's name (John 1:12) and does so in the tabernacle of the Son's flesh.

Toward the end of John 1 the evangelist again subtly alludes to temple traditions in conjunction with a promise of vision. In Jesus's first encounter with Nathanael, having impressed the skeptic from Bethsaida with supernatural knowledge about him (John 1:47–49), Jesus tells him that he will see greater things yet (1:50). Those greater things concern Jesus himself: "And he said to him, 'Very truly, I tell you, you will see heaven opened and the angels of God ascending and descending upon the Son of Man'" (1:51). This cryptic

50. Irwin, "Divine Visibility in the Gospel of John," 428.

51. Thompson, *John*, 35–36.

52. See, e.g., Philo, *Fug.* 208–13.

53. For a good discussion of this theme and its connection to Jesus's "hour," see Filtvedt, "The Transcendence and Visibility of the Father in the Gospel of John."

saying alludes to the famous episode of Jacob's ladder in Genesis 28. There in a dream the patriarch sees angels ascending and descending on a ladder that joins heaven and earth (Gen. 28:12). Upon waking, Jacob interprets the vision, describing the place as "the house of God" and "the gate of heaven" (28:17). Using his favorite self-designation ("the Son of Man"), Jesus identifies himself as the new meeting place between heaven and earth.[54] Nathanael, then, will see the temple that joins heaven and earth in Christ's flesh, and in this way he will also see God.[55]

Another subtle allusion to seeing the temple appears in John's passion narrative. In a scene unique to this Gospel, the Roman soldier pierces Jesus's side, and out flow blood and water (John 19:34). Based on the identification of Jesus's body with the temple in John 2:21, this scene most likely alludes to the prophetic vision of the new temple in Ezekiel 47.[56] Ezekiel saw water flowing from the new temple (Ezek. 47:1–12), and now water flows from the temple of Jesus's body. Immediately following this description of Jesus's pierced side, the evangelist underscores the importance of vision in two ways. First, he affirms that he himself "saw this" (John 19:35). Second, he interprets the event in light of an oracle from Zechariah: "And again another passage of scripture says, 'They will look on the one whom they have pierced'" (19:37, citing Zech. 12:10).[57] Those standing by, whether they recognize it or not, behold the new temple of God's presence.

One final instance of beholding the temple takes place in the resurrection accounts of John 20. Earlier in the Gospel, Jesus tells the Jews that he will raise up the temple of his body in three days (John 2:19–21); toward the end of the Gospel, he fulfills this saying. The simple fact of the resurrection would be enough to confirm his words, but one detail of this appearance subtly alludes to the lifting up of the temple on the cross in John 19.[58] Jesus not only appears to the disciples; he shows them his side (John 20:20, 27). The obvious reason for this act is to confirm that he is in fact the same one whose side had been pierced while he hung on the cross two days earlier. More subtly, however, this display

54. For different proposals regarding which element of the Jacob story Jesus identifies himself with, see Thompson, *John*, 53–54; R. Brown, *The Gospel According to John*, 1:89–91.

55. This understanding of the incarnation appears in the writings of Athanasius. See his *Letter to Adelphius* and the discussion of that letter in Anderson, "Towards a Theology of the Tabernacle and Its Furniture," 188–92. Anderson notes how certain aspects of the early Christological controversies led to this temple theology eventually being transferred from Christ to Mary.

56. See the discussion of these texts in chap. 3 above.

57. See Filtvedt, "The Transcendence and Visibility of the Father in the Gospel of John," 114–15. Filtvedt interprets this vision in light of the ongoing theme of seeing Jesus the human being and the king (John 19:5, 14). This is not incompatible with seeing temple imagery, however, because it is precisely as the Word made flesh that Jesus is the new temple.

58. I owe this point to Schneiders, *Jesus Risen in Our Midst*, 108, who writes, "The significance of Jesus showing his open side (not his feet as in Luke) lies in the relation of temple, water, and Spirit in the Fourth Gospel."

underscores the identification of Jesus's body as the new temple.[59] Jesus's open side recalls the water that flowed from the new temple on the cross, and that will now come to flow from those who believe in Jesus (cf. John 4:13–14; 7:37–39).

Although seeing the new temple of Jesus's body is an important theme in John, it is only one aspect of the Gospel's understanding of the vision of God. Believers can see God in Jesus's body, just as the ancient Israelites saw God in the temple and its furnishings. But Jesus also promises the disciples another kind of vision, a vision of the Father. Toward the beginning of the farewell discourse, Jesus tells Thomas, "If you know me, you will know my Father also. From now on you do know him and have seen him" (John 14:7). It is a striking statement, particularly in light of the denial in John 1:18a, "No one has ever seen God." Space does not permit a full treatment of the question. Suffice it to say that John 1:18 must be read as a whole—no one has seen God, but, as the Gospel continues, "It is the only Son, himself God, who is close to the Father's heart, who has made him known" (1:18b).[60] This is the import of Jesus's response to Philip's request that Jesus show them the Father: "Jesus said to him, 'Have I been with you all this time, Philip, and you still do not know me? Whoever has seen me has seen the Father. How can you say, "Show us the Father"?'" (14:9).[61] For John, the disciples see God in the temple of Jesus's body. But in seeing that temple, they also see the Father.[62]

Does this vision of the Father completely fulfill the human desire to see God expressed in the OT? Perhaps it would be best to give the traditional theological answer, "Yes and no." On the one hand, Jesus fully reveals the Father, making him known to his disciples. On the other hand, other texts in the NT (including the Johannine tradition) also hold out hope for an eschatological vision that includes both the incarnate flesh of the risen Lord and the triune God.

The Eschatological Vision of God

In addition to the Johannine idea that the Word made flesh reveals the Father, such that those who see the Son see the Father, the NT also speaks of a hope

59. For an insightful interpretation of these two episodes, see Schneiders, *Jesus Risen in Our Midst*, 99–118. Mollat (*Études johanniques*, 153) notes another way in which Jesus's act of showing the disciples his side points to his body as the new temple. In John 2:18 the Jews ask Jesus what sign he will "show" (*deiknyeis*) them to justify his actions. In John 20:20 Jesus "shows" (*edeixen*) the disciples his side, the very sign of his status as the new temple (2:19).

60. For a good discussion of the way that Jesus reveals the Father, see again Filtvedt, "The Transcendence and Visibility of the Father in the Gospel of John."

61. N. T. Wright (*God's Homecoming*, 293) suggests that the desire to see God in any other way than through the incarnate flesh of Christ "misses the point." Careful attention to 1 John, I will argue below, suggests otherwise.

62. As we will see in the next chapter, this aspect of John's theology plays a crucial role for Irenaeus.

for a direct vision of God. Like the Gospel of John, some of these verses also play on the motif of Moses's face-to-face relationship with God (Num. 12:8). All these texts, either directly or indirectly, contribute to the Western tradition of the beatific vision.

One of the most important texts for this tradition is the sixth beatitude, "Blessed are the pure in heart, for they will see God" (Matt. 5:8). The conciseness of this saying makes it difficult to know what exactly is being promised, but a few points are worth making.[63] First, certain aspects of the Beatitudes as a whole suggest that Jesus speaks of a promise to be fulfilled in the future. Some of the other beatitudes, such as the promise of comfort to those who mourn or of the earth to the meek (Matt. 5:4–5), make most sense as a future reward. In addition, some interpreters argue that the rewards attached to each beatitude are simply different ways of explicating the primary reward mentioned in the first and eighth beatitudes—namely, the "kingdom of heaven."[64] Insofar as the kingdom is at least in part not yet here but an eschatological promise, each of the rewards of the Beatitudes points forward to the full in-breaking of the kingdom.[65] Second, some have suggested that the beatitude refers to Jesus, whom Matthew refers to as "God with us" (Matt. 1:23), but this seems unlikely for two reasons.[66] Although good arguments have been made that Matthew portrays Jesus as divine, throughout the Gospel the word "God [*theos*]" always refers to the Father.[67] Moreover, in the one other text referring to the vision of God in Matthew, Jesus speaks of how the angels of the little ones "continually see the face of my Father in heaven" (Matt. 18:10).[68] This beatitude, then, seems to point forward to an unmediated vision of the Father to be given when the kingdom comes in its fullness.

A similar hope appears in 1 Corinthians 13. Toward the end of Paul's famous hymn on love, he riffs on the Moses traditions to express an expectation of seeing God: "For now we see through a mirror in a riddle, but then face to face. Now I know only in part; then I will know fully, even as I have been fully

63. For an overview of the different ways interpreters over the centuries have understood the vision, see Allison, *Studies in Matthew*, 43–63.

64. See Davies and Allison, *Matthew*, 446.

65. On the difficulty of parsing out the present and the future with respect to the Beatitudes, see France, *Matthew*, 164.

66. For a discussion of both ancient and modern interpreters who favor such an interpretation, along with criticisms of this reading as the evangelist's intended meaning, see Allison, *Studies in Matthew*, 48–51.

67. For arguments that Matthew presents Jesus as divine, see Leim, *Matthew's Theological Grammar*; Leim, "Worshiping the Father, Worshiping the Son"; Moffitt, "God Attested by Men."

68. Allison, *Studies in Matthew*, 51. While Matt. 18:10 does not speak directly about the beatific vision, it does suggest that, for Matthew, seeing God does not refer to seeing the human Jesus. The object of the angels' vision is the Father in heaven.

known" (1 Cor. 13:12, modified).[69] The phrase "in a riddle [*en ainigmati*]," contrasted with face-to-face vision, alludes to an OT passage. The juxtaposition of these two ways of seeing evokes the Lord's response to the complaints of Aaron and Miriam in Numbers 12, where the Lord highlights the difference between Moses and other prophets. Ordinary prophets receive communication in a vision or a dream (Num. 12:6); not so with Moses: "Mouth to mouth I will speak to him, in visible form and not through riddles [*ou di' ainigmatōn*]. And he has seen the glory of the Lord" (Num. 12:8 NETS). Seeing through "riddles" seems to imply a mediated communication, in contrast with the direct communication Moses receives (cf. Deut. 34:10). Similarly, Paul contrasts the present, indirect vision and knowledge of God with a future direct vision.[70] Two points are worth making with respect to Paul's language of "knowledge." First, Numbers 12:6 uses similar language to speak of God's communication to ordinary prophets: "If there is a prophet among you for the Lord, I will be known [*gnōsthēsomai*] to him in a vision and I will speak to him in sleep" (LXX, my translation). In the current time of prophecy (1 Cor. 13:9), Paul suggests, believers know only in part.[71] When that time comes to an end (13:10), believers will see "face to face" and will "know" (13:12). Speaking in the first person, he continues, "Then I will know [*epignōsomai*] even as I am known [*epegnōsthēn*]" (13:12b).[72] A few chapters earlier Paul also speaks of knowledge in the context of an exhortation to love (1 Cor. 8:1–3). The love of God, Paul instructs the Corinthians, leads to knowledge, though not the kind that the Corinthians are obsessed with: "But anyone who loves God *is known* [*egnōstai*] *by him*" (1 Cor. 8:3).[73] Love and knowledge, particularly the knowledge of God, are intertwined, and Paul describes that knowledge in terms of vision, expressing hope for an unmediated vision of God.[74]

69. For a recent discussion of the imagery in this verse, see Hollander, "Seeing God 'in a Riddle' or 'Face to Face.'"

70. It was common in the ancient world to speak interchangeably of vision and knowledge. See Hollander, "Seeing God 'in a Riddle' or 'Face to Face,'" 396–97.

71. First Corinthians 13:8 suggests that Paul is contrasting the present time in which the spiritual gifts are operative with the future time when they will give way to face-to-face vision. D. Smith ("Reflecting Ancient Ethics") argues that the passage concerns moral growth rather than hope for a future face-to-face vision of God. Without denying the possibility that there may be a moral dimension to this passage, it seems to me, based on Paul's allusion to the gifts coming to an end, that he is contrasting the present age with the age to come. On the temporary nature of the gifts in contrast to love's enduring existence, see Fee, *First Corinthians*, 643–44, 649. Augustine also sees prophecy in this life as "childhood" in comparison to the vision of the world to come, which represents maturity. See *Civ*. 22.29.

72. It is worth noting that Deuteronomy speaks of the Lord "knowing [*yeda'o*; LXX *egnō*]" Moses face to face (Deut. 34:10).

73. On the connection between 1 Cor. 8 and 1 Cor. 13, see also Collins, *First Corinthians*, 487. Cf. Gal. 4:9.

74. This connection between knowledge and vision probably explains why interpreters in the tradition also appeal to John 17:3 ("And this is eternal life, that they may know you, the

Love and vision come together once again in 1 John, another important text for the tradition of the beatific vision.[75] Chapter 3 begins with words of wonder at the Father's love: "See what love the Father has given us, that we should be called children of God, and that is what we are" (1 John 3:1a).[76] Like 1 Corinthians 13, the subsequent verse of 1 John contrasts the present with the future: "Beloved, we are God's children now; what we will be has not yet been revealed" (1 John 3:2a). The second half of the verse describes the Christian eschatological hope: "What we do know is this: when he [or "it"] is revealed, we will be like him, for we will see him as he is" (3:2b). Interpreters are divided on the question of who or what is to be revealed and who is the object of vision in the second half of the verse.[77] Although the language of being "revealed" is sometimes associated with Christ in 1 John (1:2; 3:5, 8), there are good reasons to understand the verb as referring back to "what we will be." In 1 John 2:28, where the same verb appears ("abide in him, so that when he is revealed"), the subject is naturally the "him" of "abide in him" in the first half of the verse.[78] By analogy, in 3:2 one should take "what we will be" as the subject of both occurrences of the verb "to be revealed." When our future state is revealed, the author continues, "We will be like him, for we will see him as he is" (3:2b). The Christian hope according to 1 John is twofold, involving both a transformation and a vision of the Father. In support of such a reading, it is worth noting that the qualification of the vision by the phrase "as he is [*kathōs estin*]" makes more sense with reference to the Father, particularly if read in light of the denial in 1 John 4:12 that anyone has seen God.[79] First John holds out hope that one day the

only true God, and Jesus Christ, whom you have sent") in discussing the beatific vision. See Aquinas, *ST* I, q. 12, a. 4.

75. As we will see, this verse plays a crucial role for Aquinas. Although Irenaeus does not cite this text in *Against Heresies*, the idea of transformative vision is present throughout his work as well.

76. The idea of being called "children of God" is quite close to the beatitude for the peacemakers ("they will be called sons of God," Matt. 5:9, my translation; although the NRSVue renders the expression "children of God," the Greek text refers to "sons" [*huioi*]), which immediately follows the beatitude regarding the pure in heart and the vision of God. This similarity is also noted by R. Brown, *The Epistles of John*, 425n17.

77. For arguments in favor of seeing Christ as both the subject of the verb "is revealed" and the object of vision, see Marshall, *The Epistles of John*, 172–73; Kruse, *The Letters of John*, 116; Painter, *1, 2, and 3 John*, 220–21. Strecker (*The Johannine Letters*, 88–89) does not give a clear answer to either question, suggesting (89n22) that "there is no alternative between God and Christ in 1 John" when it comes to statements about being revealed. R. Brown (*The Epistles of John*, 394), whom I follow, argues that the verb "is revealed" points back to the phrase "what we will be" of 3:2a (i.e., "What we will be has not yet been revealed").

78. Most commentators interpret this "him" as referring to Christ, particularly in light of the language of "coming [*parousia*]" at the end of 2:28. Gaine (*Did the Saviour See the Father?*, 28) argues to the contrary that in 2:28 it is the Father who is revealed.

79. I owe this point to Gaine, *Did the Saviour See the Father?*, 31.

human desire to see God, expressed in a variety of ways in the OT, will be fulfilled.[80] This vision ought not to be restricted to seeing the glorified flesh of the incarnate Son—after all, the letter opening emphasizes seeing "with our eyes" (1 John 1:1). In addition to bodily fellowship with the risen Son, 3:2 and 4:12 seem to hold out hope for a vision of the Father, made possible by the Son.

One final NT text attests to this expectation of seeing God face to face. In the final visions of the book of Revelation, the seer speaks of the servants of God and the Lamb seeing God's face (Rev. 22:4). Significantly, this vision takes place in the context of worship. The previous chapter describes the New Jerusalem coming down from heaven (21:9–17). In the course of this description, the author notes, "I saw no temple in the city, for its temple is the Lord God the Almighty and the Lamb" (21:22). In the OT the temple served as a medium through which the people could see God, as it participated in God's presence.[81] In the new heavens and the new earth, there will be no need for this mediation: God and the Lamb will be the new temple. In this temple one of the activities of the saints will be to worship God and the Lamb on their throne (Rev. 22:3).[82] In this act of worship, the seer writes, the servants of God "will see his face" (22:4).[83] The desire that characterizes so much of Israel's hope will at last come to fruition, as believers will have an unmediated personal encounter with the God of Israel.[84]

The desire to see God is not based on a few prooftexts—it is deeply embedded in the Scriptures, expressed in a variety of texts and genres.[85] Over

80. Cf. R. Brown, *The Epistles of John*, 395. As Brown notes later in the commentary (425), the association of a future vision of God with the fulfillment of all happiness was known among some contemporary Jewish writers. See, e.g., Philo, *Abr.* 12.57–59. For other contemporary or near contemporary Jewish texts to similar effect, see Strecker, *The Johannine Letters*, 90n31.

81. See pp. 78–80 above.

82. The text says literally, "and his servants will worship him." Because the first part of the verse refers to both God and the Lamb, the object of worship is unclear. It seems best, with Beale (*Revelation*, 1113), to take the pronoun to refer to both God and the Lamb, who are so closely associated that they share one throne. See also Koester, *Revelation*, 835: "In the city, God and the Lamb rule as one and are worshiped as one (22:3)." As Gaine rightly notes (*Did the Saviour See the Father?*, 26), "The beatific vision of 'his face', as it is presented in the Apocalypse, is thus a gaze that takes in *both* the Father and the incarnate Son, something more than simply seeing the Father in seeing his incarnate Son, as had been granted during Christ's earthly life (cf. Jn 14.9)" (emphasis original).

83. As in the preceding verse, the pronoun "his" should be taken to refer to both God and the Lamb. This vision, as in 1 John, corresponds to Jewish hopes of seeing God. See Beale, *Revelation*, 1113–14. For additional Jewish and Greco-Roman sources regarding the vision of God, see Aune, *Revelation 17–22*, 1179–80.

84. We will return to this passage and its cultic themes in chap. 12.

85. It is thus inaccurate to characterize the hope for the beatific vision as a "philosophically inspired dream," as N. T. Wright (*God's Homecoming*, 293) does. It may be true that vision plays a relatively minor role in the NT (*God's Homecoming*, 192). Nevertheless, as with the desire for rest, with respect to this vision one sees how important it is to pay attention to both Testaments.

the centuries, Christians in the West have reflected on these texts, deriving from them a deeper understanding of the biblical promises of seeing God's face. In the following chapters we will consider how three important thinkers interpret this desire for face-to-face vision as a crucial aspect of the Christian hope.

FIVE

Irenaeus, Seeing God, and the Life of the Human Being

One of the most famous lines in Irenaeus of Lyons's great work *Against Heresies* frequently appears only in part and out of context. Many authors cite the beautiful phrase *Gloria enim Dei vivens homo*: "For the glory of God is the living human being." Less often does one see the second half of the sentence, *vita autem hominis visio Dei*: "and seeing God is the life of the human being."[1] This twofold saying eloquently captures Irenaeus's understanding of the Christian hope, encompassing both resurrected life and the vision of God. In chapter 9, I will argue that, for Irenaeus, the idea of *vivens homo* necessarily includes fleshly—that is, physical—existence. That fleshly existence, however, depends on the vision of God, which bestows on human beings the incorruptibility necessary to overcome death definitively. In this chapter we will focus on Irenaeus's understanding of that vision, noting its threefold nature and its contribution to human fulfillment.

Two features characterize Irenaeus's discussion of the vision of God. First, Irenaeus roots this hope in the Scriptures of both the Old and the New Testaments. This should come as no surprise, given that *Against Heresies* directly targets the Gnostics, who pitted the God of the OT against the God of the NT.[2] Second, Irenaeus presents the human vision of God as a progression

1. Irenaeus, *Haer.* 4.20.7 (my translation). Throughout this study, unless otherwise noted, translations of *Against Heresies* are taken from the *ANF* with occasional modification. Daley ("A Hope for Worms," 145n34) notes the common tendency to quote this passage in part and so to distort its meaning. See also Donovan, "Alive to the Glory of God," 283. Hereafter parenthetical in-text citations come from *Against Heresies*.

2. Some recent scholarship has questioned the appropriateness of the traditional term "Gnostic" to describe Irenaeus's opponents. Among other reasons, scholars note that certain early

that takes place in stages. As is well known, Irenaeus's answer to the Gnostics involves, among other things, an account of the divine pedagogy whereby God instructs human beings progressively.[3] We should expect no less when it comes to the fulfillment of the human desire to see God. The three stages of vision correspond to the time of the OT prophets, the current age (which began with the incarnation), and the time of the end, when believers will enjoy the full vision of God the Father.[4] Irenaeus's articulation of the vision of God is thus necessarily trinitarian and directed ultimately to the Father, the vision of whom will bestow incorruptibility of both flesh and soul to those who attain it.

Seeing the Invisible God

Irenaeus's most extended discussion of the vision of God appears in *Against Heresies* 4.20.[5] In this chapter he is at pains to affirm two seemingly incompatible claims: Human beings cannot see God, and yet God can make himself known to human beings. The former statement Irenaeus attributes to God's "greatness" or "grandeur," the latter to God's love.[6] So, at the beginning of this section of the work, he writes, "As regards His greatness [*secundum magnitudinem*], therefore, it is not possible to know God, for it is impossible

---

Christians (e.g., Clement of Alexandria) also referred to themselves as "Gnostics," as well as the fact that the term comes from Irenaeus, who uses it for polemical purposes in a way that may distort differences among the various groups he (together with other early Christians) calls "Gnostic." Despite its limitations, I have chosen to retain this term for the sake of convenience. For a brief discussion of the question, see Steenberg, *Irenaeus on Creation*, 11–15, who also at times retains the term "Gnostics" for lack of a suitable alternative. For an extensive critique of the category of Gnosticism, see Williams, *Rethinking "Gnosticism."* For a more recent, appreciative criticism of Williams maintaining the usefulness of "Gnostics" and "Gnosticism" as a social category, see Brakke, *The Gnostics*, especially 21–28. Whatever the merits of the various criticisms of "Gnosticism" as a historical category, its usefulness as a theological category, as well as Irenaeus's evaluation of a specifically Valentinian variety of this phenomenon, has been skillfully defended by O'Regan, *Gnostic Return*, especially 143–67.

3. For a brief discussion of Irenaeus's understanding of pedagogy with respect to the vision of God, see H. Boersma, *Seeing God*, 401–4. Although in some ways insightful, in my view Boersma's treatment has at least two weaknesses. First, although he rightly notes the earthiness of Irenaeus's language, he makes little to nothing of the way the bishop connects the vision of God with the resurrection. Second, he passes too quickly over the importance of the "paternal vision" as the goal of this pedagogy. More helpful is his wise caution regarding how to understand the idea of pedagogy (388).

4. It is important to note, however, that these stages are not, strictly speaking, chronological. As Lanne notes ("La vision de Dieu," 315), God's two "hands" (the Word and the Spirit) are constantly at work in all three stages.

5. For a reading of this and other texts as they relate to the significance of theophanies, see Kloos, *Christ, Creation, and the Vision of God*, 50–57.

6. See the discussion of Andia, *Homo Vivens*, 321–22.

that the Father can be measured" (4.20.1). Irenaeus repeatedly underscores God's transcendence, as well as its corollary, the limits of human knowledge.[7] By their own powers, human beings are incapable of knowing God. Alongside this insistence on divine transcendence, however, Irenaeus equally affirms what later theologians would refer to as God's "condescension" or "accommodation."[8] Human beings receive the ability to know God because of his love: "But as regards His love [*secundum autem dilectionem eius*] (for this it is which leads us to God by His Word), when we obey Him, we do always learn that there is so great a God, and that it is He who by Himself has established, and made, and adorned, and contains all things; and among all things, both ourselves and this our world" (4.20.1, modified).[9] Love is the key to the human vision of God, both its possibility and, as I will argue, its ultimate end.

Toward the end of 4.20, Irenaeus returns to this twofold claim in the context of discussing the complex biblical record regarding Moses's relationship with God. On the one hand, quoting Numbers 12:8, Irenaeus affirms with Scripture that God spoke to Moses as one speaks to a friend (4.20.9).[10] On the other hand, he also quotes the Lord's response to Moses's request to see God's glory in Exodus 33, which reads in part, "But My face you shall not see: for no man sees My face, and shall live" (4.20.9, modified). As many throughout the tradition have done, Irenaeus interprets the statement "My face you shall not see" in absolute terms—at least when it comes to the human ability to see God in this life. He goes on, however, to draw two conclusions from this passage, particularly as interpreted in light of the transfiguration: "Two facts are thus signified: that it is impossible for a human being to see God; and that, through the wisdom of God, the human being shall see Him [*videbit eum homo*] in the last times, in the depth of a rock, that is, in His coming as a human being" (4.20.9, modified). In the Gospel account of the transfiguration, Irenaeus sees the fulfillment of Moses's request: Moses (together with Elijah) speaks "face to face" with the Lord (4.20.9).[11] This appeal to the incarnation to explain how human beings might see God appears frequently in *Against Heresies*. It forms an essential part of his understanding of the vision of God, most likely

7. For a discussion of God's transcendence with respect to other themes in *Against Heresies*, see Gendle, "St. Irenaeus as Mystical Theologian," 188–90.

8. John Chrysostom, for example, speaks of the *synkatabasis* of God. Robert Hill argues that this word should be translated as "considerateness" rather than the etymologically closer "condescension" in order to avoid the pejorative connotation of the latter word, which in no way characterizes Chrysostom's use of the term. See Hill's introduction to St. John Chrysostom, *Homilies on Genesis 1–17*. For an extensive discussion of the phenomenon of accommodation in Jewish and Christian thought, see Benin, *The Footprints of God*.

9. See the brief discussion of Osborn, *Irenaeus of Lyons*, 203–4.

10. Irenaeus suggests that it was in fact the Word who spoke with Moses as with a friend, likely in this way attempting to safeguard the invisibility of the Father.

11. See Lanne, "La vision de Dieu," 318.

under the influence of the Gospel of John.[12] If one were to focus only on this aspect of Irenaeus's account, one might conclude that for him human beings see God in the incarnate Son and only in him. One more passage affirming the tension between the impossibility of humans seeing God and of God's accommodation to human beings shows that, crucial though the incarnation is for the possibility of seeing God, it is nevertheless a step on the way to the third and final stage of the human vision of God.

Near the middle of 4.20, Irenaeus once more emphasizes the inability of human beings to see God by their own powers. In doing so, he lays out the three-stage process of coming to see God. First, he affirms that, according to both the prophets and Jesus, human beings will one day see God. This poses a problem, however, because of God's transcendence: "But in respect to His greatness [*secundum magnitudinem*] and His indescribable glory, 'no human being shall see God and live,' for the Father is incomprehensible" (4.20.5, modified). Human beings are incapable of seeing God because he is beyond their powers. The solution is to be found in God's love for human beings: "But in regard to His love and kindness [*secundum autem dilectionem et humanitatem*], and as to His infinite power, even this He grants to those who love Him, that is, to see God, which thing the prophets also predicted" (4.20.5, modified). Paradoxically, it is God's infinite power, part of his incomprehensibility, that makes it possible for him to capacitate human beings to see him. Irenaeus roots this claim in Luke 18:27 ("For those things that are impossible with human beings, are possible with God," as rendered in *ANF* and modified). The vision of God comes not from human power, but rather from the will of God. He reveals himself to human beings when he will and as he will (4.20.5).[13] Having safeguarded the transcendence of God and acknowledged the limitations of human knowledge, Irenaeus summarizes his understanding of the vision of God, both its stages and its end goal:

> For God is powerful in all things, having been seen at that time indeed, prophetically [*prophetice*] through the Spirit, and seen, too, adoptively [*adoptive*] through the Son; and He shall also be seen paternally [*paternaliter*] in the kingdom of heaven, the Spirit truly preparing human beings in the Son of God, and the Son leading them to the Father, while the Father, too, confers [upon them] incorruption for eternal life, which comes to everyone from the fact of his seeing God. (4.20.5, modified)

12. On Irenaeus as a "Johannine" theologian (including all the NT writings attributed to John), see Mutschler, "John and His Gospel in the Mirror of Irenaeus of Lyons," and his fuller study, *Irenäus als johanneischer Theologe*.

13. Andia (*Homo Vivens*, 322) says with respect to Irenaeus's use of Exod. 33 and Luke 18, "Voir Dieu est impossible aux hommes, se laisser voir par les hommes est possible à Dieu" ("To see God is impossible for human beings, but to let oneself be seen by human beings is possible for God").

This lengthy, complex sentence captures three important features of Irenaeus's understanding of the vision of God. First, this vision occurs in stages—not for every human being, but over the course of human history.[14] Second, these stages have as their goal the vision of the Father. The first stage consists of the obscure vision of the prophets, pointing forward to the fuller vision yet to come. The second stage comes about through the incarnation and involves an "adoptive" vision. Through this adoption, it seems, human beings see God in and through the Son. The Son is not the end point of this vision, however. Irenaeus holds out hope for a third stage that entails a "paternal" vision of God in the kingdom of heaven. Finally, this vision of the Father is what makes possible eternal life, by that very vision equipping those who see God with incorruption.[15]

Keeping in mind the gratuitous nature of the vision of God, let us now consider each of the stages in Irenaeus's schema in more detail.

Prophetic Vision

Irenaeus understands prophecy in terms of prediction: "For prophecy is a prediction of things future, that is, a setting forth beforehand of those things which shall be afterwards" (4.20.5). Although Irenaeus sees the prophets' primary task as the prediction of future things, they fulfill this role in various ways. Prophetic action includes not only words but also visions, manner of life, and acts (4.20.8). In each mode of expression the prophetic activity of the OT concerns God's plan for saving humanity, and an important part of that plan is drawing human beings gradually into the vision of the Father. Although the prophets themselves do not experience the fullness of this vision, through them God prefigures events to come (4.20.12).

Because the words of the prophets foretell a future hope, they have both a Christological and a trinitarian shape. Both kinds of prophecy, the Christological and the trinitarian, have as their end communion with the Father. Prophetic activity is shaped by the Word, both in that the Word gives the prophets the substance of their visions and in that these visions point especially to the incarnation. For Irenaeus, the incarnation points to God's goal of making himself known to human beings and establishing communion with them:

> Wherefore the prophets, receiving the prophetic gift from the same Word, announced His advent according to the flesh, by which the blending and communion of God and man took place according to the good pleasure of the

14. For discussions of these three stages or modes of vision, see Andia, *Homo Vivens*, 323; Donovan, "Alive to the Glory of God," 286–88; Orbe, "Visión del Padre," 201–5.

15. On the connection in Irenaeus's thought between the vision of God and incorruptibility, see Andia, *Homo Vivens*, 321–27.

> Father, *the Word of God foretelling from the beginning that God should be seen by human beings* [*ab initio praenuntiante Verbo Dei quoniam videbitur Deus ab hominibus*], and hold converse with them upon earth, should confer with them, and should be present with His own creation, saving it, and becoming capable of being perceived by it, and "freeing us from the hands of all that hate us," that is, from every spirit of transgression; and causing us "to serve Him in holiness and righteousness all our days," in order that human beings, having embraced the Spirit of God, might pass into the glory of the Father. (4.20.4, modified and emphasis added)

The vision of God is not an afterthought, according to Irenaeus. Rather, it was part of God's plan from the beginning, but it was not something that would occur naturally. Creation needs the presence of God to become capable of perceiving him. This presence takes place in a unique way through the incarnation, by which the Son brings together the divine and the human. Initially, Irenaeus seems to be speaking of the physical vision of the Son.[16] Even this incarnational vision, however, is not an end in itself. Physically seeing the Son is meant to lead human beings to a vision of the Father ("in order that human beings, having embraced the Spirit of God, might pass into the glory of the Father"). Later in the same chapter, Irenaeus reaffirms that the purpose of this prophetic activity is to prepare human beings to enter into God's glory (4.20.8).

Because the vision of God for which Christians hope has a trinitarian contour, the vision of the prophets has trinitarian elements, even if it does not amount to the eschatological vision that forms the substance of Christian hope. The prophets each saw different aspects of the trinitarian mystery:

> For certain of these used to see the prophetic Spirit [*Spiritum propheticum*] and His active influences poured forth for all kinds of gifts; others, again, [beheld] the advent of the Lord [*adventum Domini*], and that dispensation which is from the beginning, by which He accomplished the will of the Father with regard to things both celestial and terrestrial; and others [beheld] paternal glories adapted to the times [*glorias paternas temporibus aptas*], and to those who saw and who heard them then, and to all who were subsequently to hear them. (4.20.6, modified)

The variety of prophetic visions mirrors the three-stage unfolding of human beings' vision of God. Irenaeus once again underscores that the incarnation formed part of God's plan "from the beginning." Implicitly, the Son's advent was prepared for by the activity of the Spirit among the prophets, and it points forward to its ultimate end, the vision of the Father. The prophets receive a

16. This is something of a recurring theme in *Against Heresies*, as we will see presently. Johns ("Seeing Salvation," 271) rightly notes, "It is impossible to overemphasize the significance of the Incarnation in Irenaeus' vision of salvation."

glimpse of that end, but one "adapted to the times," since they were not yet given the full vision of God.[17]

Adoptive Vision

It would be hard to overstate the importance of the incarnation for Irenaeus's schema. The Son plays a crucial two-part role in making God visible. First, by taking on human flesh, the Son makes God accessible to human eyes.[18] Although Irenaeus never quotes John 14:9–10, his understanding of the incarnation and the way it reveals the Father very much fits this Johannine text. Second, the Son also leads believers to a direct vision of the Father, although this latter point is not expressed as clearly as the former.[19]

The incarnation does not appear without precedent. As the texts just considered show, for Irenaeus the prophets were given knowledge of the three-stage process of coming to see God. Although making the Father known is the central purpose of the incarnation, it is not the only one. In Book 3 of *Against Heresies*, Irenaeus writes:

> There is therefore one and the same God, the Father of our Lord, who also promised, through the prophets, that He would send His forerunner; and His salvation—that is, His Word—He caused to be made visible to all flesh, [the Word] Himself being made incarnate, that in all things their King might become manifest. For it is necessary that those [beings] which are judged do see the judge [*iudicantur oportebat videre Iudicem*], and know Him from whom they receive judgment; and it is also proper, that those which follow on to glory should know Him who bestows upon them the gift of glory [*eum qui munus gloriae eis donat*]. (3.9.1)

Irenaeus insists that the incarnation was part of the Father's plan and that he made it known in advance through the prophets. The incarnation makes the king visible to "all flesh" for two reasons. First, because the Son will one day judge the world, it is important for those to be judged to be able to see

17. Cf. Irenaeus, *Haer.* 4.20.10.

18. Barnes suggests ("Irenaeus's Trinitarian Theology," 89), "The reader takes from Irenaeus the impression that God is seen in Jesus with the same kind of vision as that by which I see my wife, that is, the empirical sight of Jesus, seen as everyone is seen." This is certainly one aspect of Irenaeus's understanding, but it is not, I will suggest, the only one. By contrast, Anatolios ("Historical Memory and the Eschatological Vision of God's Glory in Irenaeus," 107) rightly notes that "Irenaeus does not categorically deny human knowledge of God *in se*, but rather strongly affirms such knowledge as long as it is conceived in terms consistent with the God-world distinction."

19. Lanne ("La vision de Dieu," 320) notes that Irenaeus says little about this last stage in the vision of God.

the one passing sentence on them. Second, those who will enter into glory by believing in the Son ought to see their benefactor.

The glory to be bestowed on those who believe comes ultimately from knowing the Father, and this is what Irenaeus more commonly emphasizes. Only through this knowledge, which comes through the "instrumentality" of the Son become flesh, can human beings attain to glory: "And for this purpose did the Father reveal the Son, that through Him [i.e., the Son] He [i.e., the Father] might be manifested to all [*ut per eum omnibus manifestetur*], and might receive those who believe in Him rightly into incorruption and everlasting rest" (4.6.5, modified). The pronouns in this statement are a bit unclear, but the preposition *per* seems to suggest that the Father is made known (*manifestatur*) to all through the Son. We will return to this connection between the vision of the Father and the attainment of incorruption. For now, let us continue to consider the Son's role in revealing the Father. Later in the same paragraph Irenaeus writes, "The Father therefore has revealed Himself to all, by making His Word visible to all; and, conversely, the Word has declared to all the Father and the Son, since He has become visible to all" (4.6.5). By revealing the Father, the Son simultaneously reveals distinction within the inner life of God. In the present life, vision of the Father is always mediated through vision of the Son in the flesh: "And through the Word Himself who had been made visible and palpable, was the Father shown forth, although all did not equally believe in Him; but all saw the Father in the Son [*omnes viderunt in Filio Patrem*]: for the Father is the invisible of the Son, but the Son the visible of the Father" (4.6.6). On the basis of statements like this, it would seem that human vision of God is limited to seeing the Father in the flesh of Christ. Other hints in *Against Heresies*, however, suggest that one day human beings will see the Father face to face.

From Adoptive to Paternal Vision

It seems clear that the Son's primary mission is to make known the Father. For Irenaeus, it is impossible to come to knowledge of the Father apart from the Son.[20] Some passages suggest that this knowledge always maintains the invisibility of God, both in itself and with respect to human vision. To take one example, in Book 4 Irenaeus writes:

> But as He who works all things in all is God, [as to the points] of what nature and how great He is, [God] is invisible and indescribable [*invisibilis et inenarrabilis*] to all things which have been made by Him, but He is by no means unknown: for all things learn through His Word [*omnia enim per Verbum eius discunt*] that there is one God the Father, who contains all things, and who

20. Irenaeus, *Haer.* 4.6.7; 4.7.3.

> grants existence to all, as is written in the Gospel: "No one has seen God at any time, except the only-begotten Son, who is in the bosom of the Father; He has declared [Him]." (4.20.6, modified)

The Father remains "invisible" and "indescribable" because of his greatness, but not unknown thanks to the mediation of the Son.[21] Passages like this might make it seem as though the only way that human beings can see God the Father is in the primary sense in which the Gospel of John speaks of this vision—namely, by seeing the incarnate Son. Other texts, however, suggest that, in the future, the redeemed will attain to a direct vision of the Father, made possible by the Son.

Irenaeus's threefold understanding of the vision of God practically demands such a direct vision of the Father. If believers were to see God only in the incarnate flesh of the Son, then the third stage of the vision of God would be superfluous, adding nothing to the second stage. The very fact that Irenaeus speaks of seeing God "paternally" necessitates an additional vision beyond that made possible through Christ's flesh.[22] Several passages in the work confirm the existence of such a hope in Irenaeus's thought.

Some texts do not speak explicitly of such a vision but imply it. Toward the beginning of his discussion of the vision of God, Irenaeus speaks of a "paternal light" that is bestowed upon the redeemed through Christ. Listing the various benefits given through the incarnation to those who believe, he writes, "and that the paternal light might meet the flesh of our Lord, and come to us from His resplendent flesh, and that thus human beings might attain to incorruptibility, having been invested with the paternal light" (4.20.2, modified).[23] Earlier in the same passage Irenaeus speaks again of seeing the "king," by whom he seems to mean Christ. Nevertheless, the "paternal light" given to Christ and through him to other human beings seems to have another end. A little later, in a passage discussed briefly above, Irenaeus describes the ultimate end of Christ's mission to make it possible for human beings

21. For a good recent discussion of the notions of knowing God according to his greatness as it relates to knowing God according to his love, see Anatolios, "Historical Memory and the Eschatological Vision of God's Glory in Irenaeus," 107–11. Anatolios convincingly argues that, for Irenaeus, knowing God "according to his love" means knowing him through the mediation of Christ.

22. Irenaeus, *Haer.* 4.20.5. It seems incorrect, then, to affirm with Barnes ("Irenaeus's Trinitarian Theology," 90): "The vision of the Father does occur in a true and complete form by sight of the incarnate Word, who dwells in the bosom of the Father and thus is one with the Father and who can reveal him as no theophany ever did." The incarnate Word does indeed play a crucial role in revealing the Father, but this revelation does not end with the vision of Christ's flesh. The vision offered in the incarnate Word is certainly "true," but for Irenaeus, strange as it may sound, it is not "complete."

23. For a good discussion of this image, read in light of its background in the Gospel of John, see Behr, "Flesh Invested with Paternal Light."

to "pass into the glory of the Father" (4.20.4). Once again, the text does not speak explicitly of face-to-face vision, but such a vision seems likely to come about by entering into the Father's glory.

In addition to a "paternal light," Irenaeus also speaks of a "paternal grace," and in this context strongly implies that believers will eventually see the Father. Once more describing the Son's work both before and after the incarnation, he notes that there is a proper ordering to the different gifts given to human beings. At various times throughout history, the Son "did also show to the human race prophetic visions, and diversities of gifts, and His own ministrations, and the glory of the Father, in regular order and connection, at the fitting time for the benefit [of humankind]" (4.20.7, modified). Among the things the Son revealed to human beings Irenaeus includes "the glory of the Father [*Patris glorificationem*]." This revelation is not, however, something accomplished once for all in the past. Irenaeus goes on to suggest that there is still more to come. The Son reveals in different ways according to the suitability of the times. According to this understanding, seeing the Father is not absolutely impossible; it is simply not suited to the present era. Irenaeus gives an intriguing explanation of why that is the case:

> And for this reason did the Word become the dispenser of the paternal grace for the benefit of human beings, for whom He made such great dispensations, revealing God indeed to human beings, but presenting the human being to God, and preserving at the same time the invisibility of the Father, lest the human being should at any time become a despiser of God, and *that he should always possess something towards which he might advance* [*ut semper haberet ad quod proficeret*]; but on the other hand, revealing God to human beings through many dispensations, lest the human being, falling away from God altogether, should cease to exist. (4.20.7, modified and emphasis added)

Two observations are worth making about this passage. First, the invisibility of the Father to human beings seems to be something temporary, limited to this life while human beings can still fall away. Second, Irenaeus implies that at a future time this invisibility will be overcome. In the present the invisibility of the Father is maintained, among other reasons, so that human beings "should always possess something towards which they might advance." This is the context in which Irenaeus's famous dictum (*Gloria enim Dei vivens homo*) appears, and it is followed by a further explication of how the vision of God leads to life: "For if the manifestation of God which is made by means of the creation, affords life to all living in the earth, much more does that revelation of the Father which comes through the Word, give life to those who see God" (4.20.7). Seeing God bestows upon human beings a qualitatively different kind of life than the present one.

That human beings should someday attain the vision of the Father can be seen in other passages. As already noted, Irenaeus's three-stage understanding of the vision of God demands that, eventually, human beings will see the Father. A recurring theme in his discussion of this vision is that it conveys incorruptibility to human beings.[24] This incorruptibility is closely connected to the "paternal" vision that is to be attained only in the next life. In a passage discussed toward the beginning of this chapter, Irenaeus writes, "He shall also be seen paternally in the kingdom of heaven, the Spirit truly preparing human beings in the Son of God, and the Son leading them to the Father, while the Father, too, confers [upon them] incorruption for eternal life, which comes to everyone from the fact of their seeing God" (4.20.5, modified). As important as the vision of the Father in the incarnate Son is, this passage suggests that there is yet one more stage to this vision for believers. They will eventually see him "paternally," being led to that vision by the Son. Irenaeus then explains how this vision leads to incorruptibility, using an analogy with light: "For as those who see the light are within the light, and partake of its brilliancy; even so, those who see God are in God [*sic et qui vident Deum intra Deum sunt*], receiving His splendor. But the splendor of God vivifies [them]; those, therefore, who see God, receive life" (4.20.5, modified).[25] Those who see God participate in his incorruptibility. Irenaeus returns to this theme in the following paragraph, reaffirming, "Human beings therefore shall see God, that they may live, being made immortal by that sight [*per visionem immortales facti*], and attaining even unto God" (4.20.6, modified). The vision of God both bestows life and unites human beings to God.

Toward the end of Book 4, Irenaeus returns to the connection between seeing God and incorruptibility. He presents this vision as the end goal of a life of striving to attain immortality, basing this on Paul's exhortation to run the race in 1 Corinthians 9.[26] This effort makes the prize all the more valuable, because the lack of a good makes its recovery or attainment that much more pleasing. Irenaeus uses two specific qualities to illustrate the point—namely, vision and health: "Moreover, the faculty of seeing would not appear to be so desirable, unless we had known what a loss it were to be devoid of sight; and health, too, is rendered all the more estimable by an acquaintance with disease; light, also, by contrasting it with darkness; and life with death" (4.37.7). Although Irenaeus lists four examples (sight, health, light, and life), he is really speaking about two things, as light makes vision possible and life is the fullness of health. The choice of these two characteristics is significant. They are the two most central objects of the Christian hope, the vision of

24. Again, see the discussion of Andia, *Homo Vivens*, 321–27.

25. Andia (*Homo Vivens*, 324–25) interprets this passage in light of the association between light and life in John 1:4, noting also the participatory nature of Irenaeus's argument. To see light is to participate in its glory; by analogy, to see God is to participate in his splendor.

26. Irenaeus, *Haer*. 4.37.7.

God and immortality, and for Irenaeus the two are closely related. The vision of God is the ultimate end of growth in Christian maturity:

> God thus determined all things beforehand for the perfection of human beings, for their edification, and for the revelation of His dispensations, that goodness might be made apparent, and righteousness perfected, and that the Church might be fashioned after the image of His Son, and that human beings might finally be brought to maturity at some future time, maturing through such things to see and grasp God [*ad videndum et capiendum Deum*]. (4.37.7, modified)

The Christian life is ultimately oriented toward the vision of God. In the following chapter, Irenaeus once again speaks of the process of growing in maturity as leading to the vision of God and, through that vision, to immortality:

> Now it was necessary that the human being should in the first instance be created; and having been created, should receive growth; and having received growth, should be strengthened; and having been strengthened, should abound; and having abounded, should recover [from the disease of sin]; and having recovered, should be glorified; and being glorified, should see his Lord. For God is He who is yet to be seen [*Deus enim est qui habet videri*], and the beholding of God is productive of incorruptibility, but incorruptibility renders one near to God. (4.38.3, modified)[27]

Even though Irenaeus affirms elsewhere that God becomes visible to human beings through the incarnation, there nevertheless remains a further vision to be attained in the future: "God is He who is yet to be seen" (cf. 1 John 4:12). The fullness of vision is yet to come, and with it will come the immortality that will conquer death definitively.

Following the lead of the NT, Irenaeus understands this immortality in terms of bodily resurrection.[28] The vision of God does not produce a disembodied immortality, but rather perfects the whole human being: The *vivens homo* will one day live again in bodily fashion. For Irenaeus, believers experience this immortality in a partial way in the present by the indwelling of the Spirit, which makes believers "spiritual" (5.8.1). He is quick to note, however, that this spiritual existence does not mean sloughing off the flesh: "This, however, does not take place by a casting away of the flesh [*non secundum iacturam carnis*], but by the impartation of the Spirit. For those to whom he was writing were not without flesh [*non enim errant sine carne*], but they were those who had received the Spirit of God, 'by which we cry, Abba, Father'"

27. Osborn's comment on this passage (*Irenaeus of Lyons*, 229) is apt: "Here, for Irenaeus, the glory is to be found, neither in exaltation above creation nor in any form of separation, but in the intimate joining of God with his creature to produce immortality (4.38.3)."

28. For a brief discussion of the relationship between vision and resurrection in Irenaeus, see Arnold, "'To Behold Its Own Delight,'" 35–37.

(5.8.1).[29] The Spirit strengthens the flesh and brings this strengthening to its completion at the resurrection: "If therefore, at the present time, having the pledge, we do cry, 'Abba, Father,' what shall it be when, on rising again, we behold Him face to face [*quid fiet quando resurgentes facie ad faciem videbimus eum*]; when all the members shall burst out into a continuous hymn of triumph, glorifying Him who raised them from the dead, and gave the gift of eternal life?" (5.8.1, modified). For Irenaeus, resurrection and the vision of God are linked. This vision, moreover, will transform those who receive it: "For if the pledge, gathering the human being into itself, does even now cause him to cry, 'Abba, Father,' what shall the complete grace of the Spirit effect, which shall be given to human beings by God? It will render us like unto Him, and accomplish the will of the Father; for it shall make the human being after the image and likeness of God" (5.8.1, modified). Without citing 1 John, Irenaeus offers an account of the effects of the vision of God that closely resembles 1 John 3:2.[30]

Irenaeus connects this vision of God not only with the resurrection but also with the new creation. For him there seems to be a twofold character to seeing God, involving both a direct, face-to-face vision of the Father and a recognition of the Father's glory in and through creation: "It behooves the righteous first to receive the promise of the inheritance which God promised to the fathers, and to reign in it, *when they rise again at the appearance of the Lord* [*ad apparitionem Domini resurgentes*] *in this creation which is renewed* [*renovatur*]" (5.32.1, modified and emphasis added).[31] Eschatological hope thus involves the vision of God, resurrection, and embodied life in a new or "renewed" creation. Irenaeus goes on to explain the logic behind this hope: "For it is just that in that very creation in which they toiled or were afflicted, being proved in every way by suffering, they should receive the reward of their suffering; and that in the creation in which they were slain because of their love of God, in that they should be revived again; and that in the creation in which they endured servitude, in that they should reign" (5.32.1, modified). We will consider more of Irenaeus's arguments for the resurrection in a subsequent chapter. For now, let it suffice to note that, for him, resurrection and the vision of God are complementary aspects of the Christian hope, with the latter often supporting the former. In one of the last passages of the treatise, he affirms once more that the vision of God strengthens the righteous, noting that at the time of the resurrection "the righteous shall reign in the earth, *waxing stronger by the sight of the Lord* [*crescens ex visione Domini*]: and

29. See also *Haer*. 5.8.2.

30. Andia (*Homo Vivens*, 331) rightly notes that, even though Irenaeus never explicitly cites this biblical text, it is implied in his argument.

31. This passage and the next two appear in a section in which Irenaeus defends a chiliastic eschatology, on which see the excursus "Irenaeus's Millenarianism" in chap. 9. The compatibility between resurrection and seeing God does not depend on this chiliasm.

through Him they shall become accustomed to partake in the glory of God the Father" (5.35.1, emphasis added).

Vision and the Fulfillment of Desire

One last aspect of Irenaeus's teaching on the vision of God deserves consideration: its connection with the fulfillment of human desire. This aspect is somewhat muted but nevertheless appears twice in the treatise. It first appears as part of an argument supporting the continuity between the old covenant and the new covenant. The Father who created the universe and gave the Law to Israel will one day make himself known to the righteous. This vision will be a trinitarian one, including not only the Father but also the Son and the Holy Spirit:

> As, therefore, when that which is perfect is come, we shall not see another Father, but Him whom we now desire to see [*non alterum Patrem videbimus, sed hunc quem nun videre concupimus*] (for "blessed are the pure in heart: for they shall see God"); neither shall we look for another Christ and Son of God, but Him who [was born] of the Virgin Mary, who also suffered, in whom too we trust, and whom we love; as Isaiah says: "And they shall say in that day, Behold our Lord God, in whom we have hoped, and we have rejoiced in our salvation"; and Peter says in his Epistle: "Whom, not seeing, you love; in whom, though now you see Him not, you have believed, you shall rejoice with indescribable joy"; neither do we receive another Holy Spirit, besides Him who is with us, and who cries, "Abba, Father"; and we shall make increase in the very same things [as now], and shall make progress, so that no longer through a glass, or by means of enigmas, but face to face, we shall enjoy the gifts of God. (4.9.2, modified)

With this trinitarian, face-to-face vision comes the fulfillment of human desire in inexpressible joy. This understanding is firmly rooted in Scripture, as Irenaeus cites Matthew 5:8, Isaiah 25:9, 1 Peter 1:8, Romans 8:15, and 1 Corinthians 13:12. He appeals to 1 Peter 1 and 1 Corinthians 13 again later in the treatise, once more drawing a connection between the human vision of God and the fulfillment of joy:

> "For now," he says, "we know in part, and we prophesy in part, but then face to face." This is what has been said also by Peter: "Whom, even though you have not seen, you love; in whom now also, not seeing, you believe; and believing, you shall rejoice with an indescribable joy." For our face shall see the face of God [*Faciem enim nostra videbit faciem Dei*] and shall rejoice with an indescribable joy—that is to say, when it shall see its own joy. (5.7.2, modified)[32]

32. There is an ambiguity in this passage regarding whose face the righteous will see. Some manuscripts speak of the face of "the living God [*dei vivi*]" or simply "of God [*dei*]," whereas

For Irenaeus, then, seeing God constitutes not only the life of human beings, but also their ultimate joy.

The Irenaean Roots of a Theological Tradition

The desire to see God, expressed in so many ways throughout the Scriptures, finds an able expositor in Irenaeus. He systematizes and incorporates several strands of the biblical testimony discussed in the previous chapter, while at the same time developing this theme in ways that remain implicit in Scripture. His account brings together the Johannine emphases on the mediation of the incarnate Christ (John 14:9–10) and the hope of seeing God "as he is" (1 John 3:2). Although he does not cite the latter verse explicitly, his affirmation that incorruptibility comes through the vision of the Father reflects a similar theological instinct. Moreover, in line with hopes expressed in the Psalter, he often describes the fulfillment of this desire as a face-to-face vision. Irenaeus also more explicitly teases out the trinitarian nature of the vision of God. This trinitarian shape is reflected both in the developmental process by which humans gradually come to a more direct vision of God and in the character of that vision, which involves what later tradition would come to call all three persons of the Trinity. Most importantly for my purposes, Irenaeus does not simply affirm a hope in both resurrection and the vision of God; he articulates a rationale for how the two are intertwined, a rationale rooted in the fulfillment of human desire and the delight in seeing God's face.

Standing near the fountainhead of the Christian tradition, the great bishop of Lyons lays a solid foundation for reflection on the vision of God. Nevertheless, he also leaves some questions unaddressed. How might one reconcile the many biblical passages suggesting that various OT figures saw God's face with other texts that deny this possibility? What purpose will the resurrected eyes of the saints serve? Will they see God in some way, either directly or indirectly? For answers to these and other questions, we turn to the writings of another great early bishop, Augustine of Hippo.

---

others (as the one followed by the *ANF* edition) speak of the face of "the Lord [*domini*]." If the latter reading is correct, then Irenaeus could be referring to Christ rather than the Father. There are, however, two reasons for seeing the passage as a reference to the Father. First, the language of face-to-face vision makes more sense as a reference to the divine nature. Second, the earlier passage from Book 4 of *Against Heresies*, which also cites or alludes to 1 Peter and 1 Corinthians, speaks unambiguously of a vision of both the Father and the Son (cf. Rev. 22:4).

SIX

Augustine on Seeing the Invisible God

In the year 413, Augustine of Hippo penned a lengthy letter to a woman named Paulina, who had asked him whether human beings can see God with their bodily eyes.[1] About two-thirds of the way through the letter, Augustine raises and succinctly addresses two basic questions: "For, if you ask whether God can be seen, I reply: He can. If you ask how I know this, I reply: Because we read in the scripture, which is completely true, 'Blessed are the clean of heart because they shall see God' and other such passages."[2] From the time of his conversion on, Augustine had a confident hope that one day he would see God face to face. This hope was founded not primarily in some Platonic notion of the Good (though the influence of Plato is undeniable, and at times Augustine's hope might be expressed with such language), but rather in the Scripture, "which is completely true [*veracissima*]."[3] Augustine sees in this vision the purpose for which human beings were created and the only thing

1. Augustine, *Ep*. 147. Within his lifetime this letter came to be known as *On the Vision of God*, as he himself refers to it in the *Retractations*.

2. Augustine, *Ep*. 147.15.37. Among the "other such passages" to which Augustine refers should be included 1 John 3:2 and 1 Cor. 13:12, to which he returns frequently in discussions of seeing God. See also *Ep*. 147.1.3; 147.5.12.

3. For an example of such Platonic descriptions of the Christian hope, see Augustine, *Enarrat. Ps*. 26.2.8, where he refers to "The Good of all good, from which all good derives, the Good to which nothing can be added to explain what goodness is." Augustine does not mean simply moral goodness, as he goes on to refer to the goodness of a field, a house, and a tree, among other things. Throughout this book, when modifying translations, I have relied upon the Latin texts collated in the Corpus Augustinianum Gissense (https://www.augustinus.de/projekte-des-zaf/corpus-aug-gissense/cag-online/cag-online-english).

that can satisfy the deepest longings of the human heart.[4] Over the course of his post-conversion writing career, his understanding of how human beings see God developed, but at least two things remained constant in his thought throughout this period. First, God does not have a body, nor does he exist in a place (*in loco*). Using language likely drawn from the Neoplatonic philosopher Plotinus, Augustine repeatedly insists that God is "everywhere whole [*ubique totus*]."[5] Second, Augustine closely links the vision of God with the resurrection of the body.[6]

In this chapter we will consider some of the key texts and ideas that elucidate Augustine's understanding of the vision of God. We will begin with his treatment of those passages in the OT that seem to suggest that certain figures saw God. From there we will move to the question that prompted his letter to Paulina, whether God can be seen with bodily eyes. As we will see, Augustine changes his position on the question. For much of his episcopal ministry, he insists that God cannot be seen with bodily eyes because God is spirit. Toward the end of his life, however, he tentatively affirms that, after the resurrection, the saints may see God with their resurrected, glorified eyes, though in a way that does not do away with the intellectual vision of God in the mind. We will then briefly consider the timing of this vision. In contrast to the later decree of Pope Benedict XII that those who die in grace may see God even before the resurrection, Augustine asserts that the saints will not see God until the resurrection and the last judgment. Finally, we will examine why Augustine sees the vision of God as the source of human fulfillment. Unsurprisingly, he interprets this vision in terms of a love that leads to joy. Through this survey, I hope to show that, for Augustine, happiness is to be

4. Recent scholarship on Augustine's understanding of seeing God has tended to focus on his innovative interpretation of the OT theophanies. See the two works by Kloos, "Seeing the Invisible God," and, more recently and extensively, *Christ, Creation, and the Vision of God*; Barnes, "The Visible Christ and the Invisible Trinity"; H. Boersma, *Seeing God*, 96–126. For a critical appraisal of Augustine's interpretation from an Eastern Christian perspective, see Bucur, "Christological Exegesis of Theophanies," 118–24, and "Theophanies and Vision of God." Bucur rightly notes that, prior to Augustine, many of the Fathers interpreted the OT theophanies as Christophanies. Whether the alleged losses of Augustine's "revolutionary" interpretation outweigh the gains is debatable, but the question lies beyond my purposes. For an earlier study on mystical vision of God in the present, see Teske, "St. Augustine and the Vision of God."

5. On the importance of this understanding of divine omnipresence for the vision of God, see G. Boersma, "Augustine on the Beatific Vision." For a good definition of God's omnipresence explicated in terms of the Scriptures (Jer. 23:24; Wis. 1:7; 8:1; Ps. 139:7–8), see Augustine, *Ep*. 187.4.14.

6. It is in some ways artificial to treat these two ideas in Augustine's thought separately. Nevertheless, it can be helpful to distinguish different aspects of the same reality, even while recognizing their close connection—as the old scholastic axiom goes, "Distinguish in order to unite." For a recent discussion of this connection, see Reisenauer, *Augustine's Theology of the Resurrection*, 226–37. On the development of Augustine's understanding of the resurrection, see the sources in chap. 10, n. 4, below.

found in the vision of God alone; this vision, however, does not compete with the bodily vision of the resurrected saints, because it is the result of the proper ordering of their loves, which enables the saints to enjoy God and to enjoy everything else in God.

God Appears When He Will

Augustine opens his letter to Paulina with a discussion of the different types of knowing as they relate to the eyes and to the mind.[7] Some things are known experientially by the senses, such as the sun, the moon, and the stars.[8] Others, such as our living, wishing, and seeking, are known experientially by "the gaze of the mind" (147.1.3). Still others—a great many things, in fact, from historical events to the identity of one's parents—are known on the basis of the testimony of others (147.1.4–5). The purpose of this brief discourse on epistemology is to set the terms for considering whether and how human beings can see God. As already noted, Augustine affirms, via the testimony of Scripture (Matt. 5:8), that human beings can see God.[9] Immediately after this statement, he entertains the idea that perhaps he should say "We believe [*credimus*]" rather than "We know [*scimus*]," because we have not actually seen God (147.5.12). Appealing again to the testimony of Scripture, he maintains the legitimacy of affirming this knowledge, because the apostle John himself uses the language of "knowledge" with respect to the expectation of seeing God (147.5.12).[10]

Were those the only texts in Scripture to speak about seeing God, Augustine's job would be simple—indeed, unnecessary. As in so many areas, however, the testimony of Scripture is more complex. On the one hand, some texts seem to suggest that no one has ever seen God (147.5.13).[11] On the other hand, according to the OT, numerous figures, such as Jacob, Moses, and the prophet Isaiah, did see God (147.5.13).[12] What is the interpreter to do with this apparent contradiction?

To address this difficulty, Augustine draws on the work of his spiritual father, Ambrose of Milan. In the latter's commentary on Luke, he makes three

7. On the different types of knowing, see also Augustine, *Gen. Litt.* 12.6.15, and the discussion of this text in Teske, "St. Augustine and the Vision of God," 155–65, as well as the briefer discussion in McGinn, "Visions and Visualizations in the Here and Hereafter," 230–31.

8. Augustine, *Ep.* 147.1.3. Hereafter, parenthetical in-text citations are from this letter.

9. On the trinitarian dimension of Augustine's reading of this verse, see Barnes, "The Visible Christ and the Invisible Trinity," 332–36.

10. Augustine cites 1 John 3:2. Like most premodern interpreters, Augustine takes the author of 1 John to be the apostle John.

11. Here Augustine quotes John 1:18 (or possibly 1 John 4:12). Later in the letter (e.g., 147.16.39), he also quotes 1 Tim. 6:16.

12. Augustine adds to the list Abraham, Isaac, Job, and Micaiah in *Ep.* 147.5.14.

important distinctions: First, God cannot be seen in the same way objects in this world are seen. Rather, he is seen only when and as he wishes to be seen (147.6.18). Second, God appears to whomever he pleases. At the stoning of Stephen, the protomartyr looked into heaven and saw Jesus standing at God's right hand, but those stoning him saw nothing (147.6.18). Finally, and perhaps most importantly, when God appears to those to whom he will, he does so by means of a manifestation, but his hidden nature is not seen:[13]

> But whoever saw God saw God because he appeared to whom he willed, as he willed, and *in that form his will chose, while his nature remained hidden* [*ea specie, quam voluntas elegerit, etiam latente natura*]. For if, when the patriarchs saw God, his nature appeared to them although if he had not willed this it would, of course, not have appeared, how is it that "no one has ever seen God," when his very nature was seen by so many patriarchs when he willed? (147.7.19, modified and emphasis added)[14]

For both Ambrose and Augustine, this distinction is the key to resolving the tension between the appearances to the OT figures and John's statement that "No one has ever seen God" (John 1:18).[15]

The importance of this distinction, however, should not obscure the fact that there is a close connection between the OT theophanies and the vision of God promised to the redeemed. As Augustine argues, these appearances point to a desire in the saints to see God's substance. Moses's request was not to see a manifestation of God's presence, but rather to see God himself:[16]

> But the desire of truly pious persons by which they long and avidly desire to see God does not, I believe, burn to gaze upon that form in which he appears when

13. For the circumstances that contributed to Augustine's interpretation of the theophanies in this way, see Barnes, "The Visible Christ and the Invisible Trinity"; Kloos, *Christ, Creation, and the Vision of God*, 129–64.

14. Later in the letter, Augustine notes that in this form God can be seen even by the wicked like Cain or the devil (147.15.37). In support of God's ability to manifest himself as he will, Augustine offers an analogy with human signs (147.19.47): "If our will, while remaining in itself and hidden without any change in itself, utters words by which it somehow or other reveals itself, how much more easily can almighty God appear, while his nature is hidden and remains immutably [*sua latente atque in se incommutabiliter manente substantia*], in whatever form he wills, to whom he wills! For he created all things from nothing and, while remaining in himself, he renews all things."

15. Note the similar interpretation offered in *Trin.* 2.9.16: "As for us, we say that God has never shown himself to bodily eyes, neither the Father nor the Son nor the Holy Spirit, except through some created bodily substance at the service of his power [*nisi per subiectam suae potestati corpoream creaturam*]." Cf. *Trin.* 2.15.25. On the historical background of the development in Augustine's understanding of the theophanies, see the two works by Kloos, "Seeing the Invisible God" and *Christ, Creation, and the Vision of God*.

16. On the importance of Moses for Augustine's treatment of the vision of God, see H. Boersma, *Seeing God*, 112–17.

> he wills, which is not himself, but to gaze upon *that substance by which he is what he is* [*in eam substantiam, qua ipse est, quod est*]. The saintly Moses, his faithful servant, revealed the flame of this desire of his when he said to God, with whom he was speaking face to face like a friend, "If I have found favor before you, show yourself to me." (147.8.20, emphasis added)

By way of exception to the general rule, Augustine suggests that Moses did in fact see God in this lifetime (147.13.32).[17] Moses's exceptional vision of God points to the hope of all believers, a hope to be fulfilled not in this life but in the next: "God was, therefore, in that form in which he had willed to appear, but he did not appear in his own nature, which Moses longed to see. *That vision is, of course, promised to the saints in the next life* [*in alia vita*]" (147.8.20, emphasis added). In this letter, as in several of his writings up to around the year 415, Augustine affirms that the vision for which the saints hope cannot be attained by bodily eyes, for reasons we will consider shortly.[18]

How, then, will the saints see God? What manner of vision will it be? Following Ambrose, Augustine suggests that it will be a vision of the mind rather than of the eyes, one analogous to the "vision" of angels (147.9.22). Those who are to inherit the kingdom will receive this vision: "But in the age to come all the clean of heart, who are going to receive the kingdom that was prepared for them from the beginning, will see him, and in that kingdom there will be only such people" (147.10.23). In the following chapter, Augustine makes clear that *only* the "clean of heart" will see God (147.11.24). Anyone with an impure heart excludes himself from the vision (147.11.25).[19]

The mode of the beatific vision, then, distinguishes it from the OT theophanies. Whereas God made himself known to the patriarchs and the prophets by an act of his will, making himself visible not by his essence but by an appearance, the beatific vision is not one seen with the eyes (147.11.26).[20] This vision will satisfy the longing to see God's "face" expressed in numerous biblical passages, in both Old and New Testaments. As Ambrose teaches, this sight will not be a matter of any of the senses, but rather a seeing with the heart (147.11.26). Moreover, the vision will be limited to those who rise to the life of the world to come. Although all human beings will be raised on the last day, only those who are pure in heart will see God face to face (147.11.27).

17. Augustine points to Num. 12:8 as evidence that Moses's request was granted, though he emphasizes that this vision was an exception.

18. On the shift in Augustine's thought and its timing, see Reisenauer, *Augustine's Theology of the Resurrection*, 228–30.

19. Elsewhere Augustine appeals to Phil. 2:5–7 to distinguish between the experience of the saved and that of the damned. The saints will see Jesus both in the form of God and in the form of a servant, whereas those who reject God will see him only in the form of a servant. See the discussion in Barnes, "The Visible Christ and the Invisible Trinity," 334–35.

20. It is worth recalling, however, that God's appearance requires more than mere eyesight, but also God's willingness to be seen by certain people.

A Bodily Vision of a Spiritual Reality?

One of the marks of Augustine's humility is that he changed his mind on questions that matter deeply, and he did so publicly in writing. Toward the end of his life, he took it upon himself to revisit his vast collection of works and assess the positions he had once held, explaining what he was aiming at in each writing and correcting himself where he thought it necessary. With respect to the question of seeing God with the eye of the body, Augustine changed his mind later in life: "I wrote a book on seeing God, in which I postponed a more detailed investigation about the spiritual body that will exist in the resurrection of saints, as to whether or how 'God, who is spirit,' may be seen by a body like that. But later, and to my own satisfaction, I resolved that question, which is indeed very difficult, in the last—that is, the twenty-second—book of *The City of God*."[21] It is worth considering this development to see the elements of continuity and of discontinuity in his thought.

In the letter to Paulina, Augustine closely follows Ambrose, as we have seen. He does so not primarily because Ambrose is an authority, but because the early Augustine found his understanding of the question compelling. At the root of their denial of the possibility of seeing God with our bodily eyes lies the nature of God. A nonnegotiable element of the theology of these two bishops is that God does not have a body and does not exist in space.[22] In a phrase to which Augustine returns again and again, Ambrose insists, "Nor is God seen in a location [*nec in loco deus videtur*]."[23] This lack of a "location" means, for Ambrose (and for the early Augustine), that apart from the manifestations that occur by God's will, God cannot be experienced by the bodily senses.[24] Augustine takes the beatitude to indicate not only *how* a person will be able to see God but also "where" God is to be seen—namely, in the heart (147.11.26). The vision of God, then, will not be one of the bodily eyes, but rather one of the "mind" or the "heart" (147.11.28).[25]

21. Augustine, *Retract*. 2.41.68. I owe this reference to Reisenauer, *Augustine's Theology of the Resurrection*, 230.

22. See Augustine, *Ep*. 162. On Augustine's understanding of God's presence, see again G. Boersma, "Augustine on the Beatific Vision."

23. The phrase *in loco* appears some ten times in the letter with reference to God (Augustine, *Ep*. 147.6.18; 11.25, 26, 28; 15.37, 39; 19.46, 47; 21.49; 23.52), once with respect to charity (147.17.44), and once with respect to an indefinite "something" that must also be God (147.11.27). See also *Ep*. 148.3.12.

24. *Ep*. 147.6.18; 11.28; see also *Ep*. 92.

25. In another letter (*Ep*. 92.5), Augustine wryly asks why those insistent on a bodily vision limit such a sensual experience to eyesight: "Next, why do they maintain that this gift was given only to Christ's bodily eyes and not also to the other senses? Will God, then, be a sound so that he can also be heard by his ears? Will he be a scent so that he can be perceived by his sense of smell? Will he be a liquid so that he can be drunk? And a solid mass so that he can be touched?" For a sophisticated contemporary account of the beatific vision sympathetic to extending its effects to all the senses, see Davison, *Astrobiology and Christian Doctrine*, 337–42.

Another way of putting the point is that God does not have a body. Augustine denies that God has a body because the idea is unworthy of him. If God had a body, he would also have parts and, being extended through space, there would be more of him in larger parts of the universe and less of him in smaller parts.[26] In addition to this silly understanding of God, Augustine also appeals to the beatitude in support of the notion that God does not have a body (147.20.48). If the ultimate vision of God can be attained with bodily eyes, so Augustine reasons, then the purification of heart called for by the beatitude would seem superfluous.[27] For the early Augustine—and in this regard, as we will see, his opinion does not change—the heart must be purified because those who attain to the vision of God will see God with the heart.[28] In one of his sermons, he draws an analogy from bodily vision to make the point: Just as unhealthy eyes cannot enjoy a sunrise, so also an impure heart cannot enjoy the vision of God.[29]

The idea that God does not have a body is crucial for Augustine's earlier denial that God will be seen through bodily eyes. The reason for this is that our eyes are suited to seeing objects "in a place [*in loco*]" (147.20.48). Although he is open to persuasion, at the time of his writing to Paulina he does not see how anything "not . . . in a location" could be seen by physical eyes (147.21.49). In contrast to his openness on this question, there are two other ideas on which his mind is settled. The first, as we have already seen, is the idea that God is incorporeal. The second concerns the nature of the eyes after the resurrection. Some who agree with Augustine that God is incorporeal suggest that perhaps the eyes will become spiritual (that is, incorporeal) and therefore have the capacity to see God.[30] Although Augustine finds this idea more tenable than the idea that God has a body, he nevertheless rejects it for the reason that, if the eyes become spirit, then they will no longer be bodily eyes, and so in this case it will not be with bodily eyes that the saints see God (147.21.49).

The tone of Augustine's letter to Paulina seems to have offended one of his brother bishops. In a subsequent letter to his fellow bishop Fortunatianus (not

26. In addition to the texts discussed here, see Book 1 of the *Confessions*. For the way Augustine overcame this stumbling block, see G. Boersma, "Augustine and the Beatific Vision," 19–23. Augustine expounds on this point in *Ep*. 148.1.1–3.

27. See also *Ep*. 92.6: "Our hearts are cleansed by faith for this purpose, for the vision of God is promised to us as a reward of faith. And if that vision will be attained by the eyes of the body, the mind of the saints is trained to no purpose for attaining it; in fact, a mind that thinks so perversely is not trained in itself, but is entirely absorbed in the flesh."

28. Augustine never rejects this aspect of his theology. Rather, he adds to it. Cf. Kloos, *Christ, Creation, and the Vision of God*, 187: "Underpinning Augustine's discussion of the eyes of the spiritual body is his assumption that any such bodily vision of God *complements* the spiritual or intellectual vision of God in eternity" (emphasis original).

29. Augustine, *Serm*. 53.6.

30. Augustine does not name anyone belonging to this group.

the offended party), he apologizes for his tone and elaborates on his reasons for denying a bodily vision of God at the resurrection.[31] There he maintains his denial that God has a body and addresses the question of anthropomorphic language about God. At the beginning of the letter, he summarizes his reasoning: "I added the reason why I said this, namely, so that God himself would not be thought to be bodily and visible in a stretch or area of space. After all, the eye of this body cannot see anything in any other way [*nihil enim videre aliter istius corporis oculus potest*]. And I said it so that the words, 'face to face,' would not be interpreted in the sense that God is limited by the members of a body."[32] Before giving further arguments against God having a body, he appeals to several authorities in support of his position. In addition to Ambrose, he notes, Jerome, Athanasius, and Gregory all affirm that God is invisible and has no body.[33] When the OT figures see God, they do so because God appears by a creaturely manifestation. These manifestations do not constitute a part of the divine essence, but they mediate an understanding of what God is like.

The language of body parts applied to God throughout Scripture, then, must be understood in a spiritual way. Scripture speaks of God's "wings" not because he has actual wings, but to teach us that human beings are not made in the image of God according to "the form and shape of this flesh [*carnis huius formam et figuram*]."[34] The careful reader of Scripture, then, must see in each of these parts a symbol for some characteristic of God: "Just as when we hear 'wings,' we think of his protection, so when we hear 'hands,' we ought also to understand his working. And when we hear 'feet,' we ought to understand his coming, and when we hear 'eyes,' we ought to understand the vision by which he knows. And when we hear 'face,' we ought to understand the knowledge by which he makes himself known."[35] Augustine appeals once more to Jerome to make the point more clearly. Commenting on Psalm 94 (LXX 93), Jerome argues against the anthropomorphites on the basis of verse 9, which reads (in the NRSVue), "He who planted the ear, does he not hear? He who formed the eye, does he not see?" As Jerome notes, the psalmist does not say about God, "He who plants the ear, therefore, does not himself have an ear."[36] The one who creates ears and eyes has the power of those organs without having the organs themselves.

31. *Ep*. 148.1.1.

32. *Ep*. 148.1.1.

33. There is disagreement about which "Gregory" Augustine has in mind here, with some suggesting Gregory of Nazianzus and others Gregory of Elvira.

34. *Ep*. 148.4.13.

35. *Ep*. 148.4.13. For a similar interpretation, see *Serm*. 53.7.

36. *Ep*. 148.4.14. The text Augustine has in mind is Jerome, *Breviarium in Psalmum* 93, which reads *Non dixit: qui plantavit aurem, ergo ipse aurem non habet*. The Latin text is taken from Patrologia Latina 26:1108b.

Despite his early rejection of a bodily vision of God, Augustine was open to persuasion, provided one does not ascribe to God a body or existence "in a location." What keeps Augustine committed to the early rejection of this bodily vision, in addition to his steadfast denial that God has a body, is that he cannot imagine how bodily eyes could see something not in a place.[37] Were he to find a satisfactory explanation of how bodily eyes might experience such a vision, then he would be open to persuasion. Indeed, as he concedes toward the beginning of the letter to Fortunatianus, the idea that eyes might see God's incorporeal substance "not divisible in areas and stretches of space or limited by the lines and bounds of members, but whole everywhere [*ubique totam*]" is not repugnant.[38] Better to ascribe a new power to the body than to demean God by thinking of him in corporeal terms.

To experience such a vision, however, our eyes would need to undergo a dramatic transformation. It will not suffice for our bodily eyes simply to become immortal. They must receive an intellectual quality that equips them to "see" the invisible God.[39] Even granting this possibility in theory, Augustine holds fast to two important ideas with respect to seeing God. First, even if the bodily eyes will be given the ability to see the invisible God, this will not take away from the mind's enjoyment of the vision:

> Such a power of the body will not, I think, take from the mind its vision so that the outer self could then see God but the inner self could not, as if God would be only outside in relation to a human being and not inside within him, since scripture says with perfect clarity, "That God may be all things in all things." Or will he who is whole everywhere [*ubique totus*] without any stretches of space be inside so that he can only be seen outside by the outer self but cannot be seen inside by the inner self?[40]

For God to be "all in all" (1 Cor. 15:28), Augustine argues, he must be known to the inner human being and not just externally.[41] Thus, the body's (theoretical) ability to see God will result from an addition, not a subtraction.[42] Second, the change necessary to make such a vision possible will take place in human beings, not in God. God remains invisible in his nature, even if he grants human beings the ability to see his invisible nature with their bodily eyes.[43]

Toward the end of his life, Augustine changed his mind on this question, tentatively affirming that after the resurrection the saints will see God not

37. *Ep*. 147.21.49. See also *Serm*. 277.14.
38. *Ep*. 148.1.2.
39. *Ep*. 148.1.3.
40. *Ep*. 148.5.17.
41. The importance of 1 Cor. 15:28 for Augustine's thought can be seen in the role it plays both in Book 1 of *On the Trinity* and Book 22 of *City of God*.
42. *Ep*. 148.5.17. See again Kloos, *Christ, Creation, and the Vision of God*, 187.
43. See *Serm*. 277.14–15.

only with their minds but also with their risen and glorified bodily eyes.[44] Before we consider what led him to this conclusion, we should take note of two important points about his earlier position. First, even though Augustine limits the vision of God to the mind, this does not mean that the resurrected eyes of the saints are superfluous, nor does it mean that they will be inactive. As he notes toward the end of his letter to Paulina, the existence of visible, bodily eyes in the resurrection implies that there will be other bodily objects to see.[45] The vision of God, then, is not in competition with other activity on the part of the resurrected saints.[46] Augustine expects the saints to lead an embodied existence in a bodily location of some sort, one that complements the act of seeing God with the intellect. Second, Augustine insists that the eyes of the saints will be bodily, not spiritual in the sense of being immaterial.[47] If they were to become spiritual in that sense, then the question of whether the saints will see God with bodily vision would become moot.

By the time Augustine completed writing *City of God*, he had found arguments to persuade him that the saints will see God not only with the "eyes of the mind" but also with their risen, bodily eyes, although in humility he proposes the position cautiously.[48] In the penultimate chapter of this work, Augustine once more raises the question of whether we will see God with our resurrected eyes, acknowledging from the beginning that it is "no easy question."[49] In this life it is impossible to know with certainty what the experience of the saints will be like. Nevertheless, Augustine offers a speculative answer to the question, reasoning from a story in 2 Kings that perhaps the saints will be able to see God with their bodily eyes. In that story Elisha's servant Gehazi asks Naaman the Syrian for gifts in exchange for the healing Naaman had received, passing off the request as Elisha's own (see 2 Kings 5:20–27). Although Elisha is absent from the encounter between Gehazi and Naaman, he sees the exchange in his spirit and pronounces judgment on Gehazi for his duplicity when he returns. Elisha thus saw a physical event with his spirit. At the same time, Augustine argues,

44. Cavadini ("Ideology and Solidarity in Augustine's *City of God*," 95) rightly notes of this later position, "Augustine is aware that he has pushed the reader to the brink of the imagination."

45. *Ep*. 147.23.54.

46. Cf. Pierce, "Augustine's Eschatological Vision," 229. Relatedly, Augustine speaks elsewhere of the ultimate reward of the saints in a twofold manner: "And the supreme reward is that we should enjoy [God] and that all of us who enjoy him should also enjoy one another in him" (*Doctr. Chr*. 1.32.35). I owe this reference to Miles, "Vision: The Eye of the Body and the Eye of the Mind," 136. Kloos (*Christ, Creation, and the Vision of God*, 191) writes, "Thus, just as the proper ordering of loves does not oppose but unites the love of God and neighbor (cf. *Doc. Chr*. 1.22.21), so the true vision of God unites the whole redeemed creation in God."

47. *Ep*. 147.21.49.

48. Augustine, *Civ*. 22.29. For a recent discussion of this passage, see Reisenauer, *Augustine's Theology of the Resurrection*, 229–35.

49. Augustine, *Civ*. 22.29.

Elisha's bodily eyes were performing their natural function. The resurrected saints, he then speculates, will have a similar experience. Just as Elisha did not need his bodily eyes to see Gehazi's dishonest act, so the saints will not need their bodily eyes to see God—even when their eyes are closed, they will continue to gaze upon God.

But will they be able to see God with their bodily eyes when those eyes are open, as well? Augustine reaffirms the condition he articulates earlier in his letter to Paulina. If the saints are to see God with their bodily eyes, those eyes must change qualitatively. This will be a difference in kind, not degree: "Therefore the power of those eyes will be extraordinary in its potency—not in the sense of being a sharper eyesight than that possessed, they say, by snakes and eagles (for however keen-sighted those animals may be, they can see only material things)—but in the sense of having the ability to see the immaterial."[50] Augustine also continues to hold that such a vision will not be corporeal—when Paul speaks of seeing God "face to face," he does not mean that God has a bodily face (apart, of course, from the incarnate Son). For Augustine, God is "everywhere whole."

Having reaffirmed these conditions, Augustine considers a philosophical argument against the possibility of seeing God with bodily eyes. Some philosophers argue that intelligible things can be seen only with the intellect, whereas sensible things are seen only with the senses. On its surface, the argument seems sound, and if it were an ironclad rule, one could definitively rule out the possibility of seeing God with the bodily eyes. Augustine notes two exceptions, however, that contradict this argument. If it were true that sensible things can be seen only with bodily senses, then God could not see the material world unless he had a body, an idea that (again, with the exception of the incarnation) Augustine finds absurd. Moreover, the story of Elisha suggests that it is possible even for ordinary human beings to see physical events in their spirit without the aid of their bodily organs. If, then, material things can be seen by the spirit, Augustine reasons, why should it not be possible for spiritual things to be seen by material eyes (provided they receive a qualitatively new power)?

On the basis of this reasoning, Augustine concludes, "It is possible, it is indeed most credible [*credibile*], that we shall then see the physical bodies of the new heaven and the new earth in such a fashion as to observe God in utter clarity and distinctness, seeing him present everywhere [*ubique presentem*] and governing the whole material scheme of things."[51] A few points are worth making about this initial expression of Augustine's new position. First, he makes the argument cautiously, calling his understanding "most credible." Because he has not seen the things of which he speaks, he cannot

50. Augustine, *Civ*. 22.29. Cf. *Ep*. 148.1.2.
51. Augustine, *Civ*. 22.29.

say with absolute certainty.[52] Second, this vision of God is not in competition with the observation of the new heaven and the new earth. On the contrary, Augustine suggests that this vision may be seen in and through the new creation. In this regard, the vision of God in the new heaven and the new earth has an analogy with our present earthly existence. We see the lives of others, he notes, through their bodies—indeed, we cannot see their lives apart from their bodies. In a similar way, we will see God through the bodies of the new creation: "In the future life, wherever we turn the spiritual eyes of our bodies we shall discern, by means of our bodies, the incorporeal God directing the whole universe."[53] Augustine is quick to note that his position is difficult to support on the basis of Scripture. Nevertheless, even if one cannot prove his position from Scripture, it does account for much of what the Scriptures have to say about the life of the blessed.

Toward the end of the chapter, Augustine offers one more possible articulation of what that life will be like:

> Perhaps God will be known to us and visible to us in the sense that he will be spiritually perceived by each one of us in each one of us, perceived in one another, perceived by each in himself; he will be seen in the new heaven and the new earth, in the whole creation as it then will be [*videatur in caelo novo et terra nova atque in omni, quae tunc fuerit, creatura*]; he will be seen in every body by means of bodies, wherever the eyes of the spiritual body are directed with their penetrating gaze.[54]

Once again, for Augustine the vision of God and the vision of our bodily eyes overlap, both contributing to the happiness of those who attain to eternal life.

The Timing of the Vision

Given the importance of the resurrection for Augustine, it should come as no surprise that he denies that anyone will experience the fullness of the vision of God until the resurrection, although the point does not necessarily follow. In a few places Augustine suggests that no human being will see God as the angels do until they are reunited with their bodies.[55] In the *Expositions of the*

52. Kloos (*Christ, Creation, and the Vision of God*, 18) calls this position a "possibility," though perhaps it would be more accurate to call it a "probability" for Augustine. Lootens ("Augustine," 64n36) rightly notes, "[Augustine] is clearly speculating on these matters and offers no firm conclusions; he seems willing to hold open this possibility so long as one does not think that God will be seen as a body."

53. Augustine, *Civ*. 22.29.

54. Augustine, *Civ*. 22.29.

55. For this section I am indebted to Reisenauer, *Augustine's Theology of the Resurrection*, 232–36.

Psalms, for example, he asserts that the direct vision of God is reserved for the day of the resurrection.[56] Similarly, in his work on the Trinity, Augustine affirms that the saints will attain face-to-face vision after the resurrection: "But the image which is being renewed in the spirit of the mind in the recognition of God, not outwardly but inwardly from day to day, this image will be perfected *in the vision that will then be face to face after the judgment* [*visione quae tunc erit post iudicium facie ad faciem*], while now it makes progress through a puzzling reflection in a mirror."[57] As the broader context of this passage indicates, the time of judgment corresponds to the time of the resurrection, when the bodies of the saints are raised incorruptible and glorious.

In neither of these texts does Augustine explain why the full vision of God is reserved for the resurrection—he simply asserts it. In one of his commentaries on Genesis, he gives a reason for his position. Toward the end of *The Literal Meaning of Genesis*, Augustine takes up the question of the resurrection. He begins with a difficulty regarding whether disembodied souls can see God face to face: "But if anyone has a problem about what need there is for the spirits of the departed to get their bodies back in the resurrection [*corpora sua in resurrectione recipere*], if that supreme blessedness can be offered them even without their bodies [*sine corporibus*], it is indeed too difficult a question to be completely tied up in this work."[58] Augustine follows this question by affirming once more that the mind, separated from the body, cannot see God face to face. Here he offers two possible reasons (or, more accurately, one reason). It may be due to some "more hidden cause [*latentiore causa*]," which is to say, we do not know. Alternatively, he offers an argument based on human nature: "Or the reason may be that there is ingrained in the soul a kind of natural appetite for governing the body [*naturalis quidam adpetitus corpus administrandi*], and that as long as it does not have a body at its disposal, it is somehow or other held back by this unsatisfied appetite from pressing on with undivided attention to that highest heaven."[59] In other words, the disembodied soul is incomplete and lacks fulfillment until it can govern the flesh that makes up an important part of the human being. Until the soul can fulfill its natural function, it cannot enjoy the fullness of the vision of God.[60]

56. Augustine, *Enarrat. Ps.* 43.5. He reiterates the point two more times in the same paragraph, though he does not explain why the vision should be reserved for the resurrection.

57. Augustine, *Trin.* 14.19.25 (emphasis added). Cf. *Trin.* 2.17.28.

58. Augustine, *Gen. Litt.* 12.35.68. As we will see in the next chapter, precisely this objection is a difficulty for Aquinas's understanding of the vision of God, a question he himself recognizes and addresses.

59. Augustine, *Gen. Litt.* 12.35.68 (modified).

60. Although Aquinas disagrees with Augustine, maintaining that the souls in heaven do enjoy the beatific vision, we will see in chap. 11 that he offers a similar argument for the necessity of the resurrection based on his Aristotelian anthropology.

This does not mean, however, that the souls will be completely frustrated or asleep between death and the resurrection. As Augustine states elsewhere, when the saints die, "Cleansed from all infection of corruption, they are established in tranquil abodes [*in placidis sedibus*] until they get their bodies back—but incorruptible bodies now, which will be their reward, not their burden."[61] As they await the last judgment, then, the souls of those who belong to Christ will enjoy a measure of tranquility.[62] Nevertheless, the fullness of their happiness awaits the resurrection.

As a result of a medieval controversy, Pope Benedict XII weighed in on this question in his papal bull *Benedictus Deus*, promulgated in 1336. This bull rejects the position espoused by Augustine, affirming that the saints enjoy the vision of God even before the bodily resurrection.[63] The document does not cite any biblical texts, but one can conjecture what passages the pope had in mind. In Philippians, Paul speaks of his desire "to depart and be with Christ, for that is far better" (Phil. 1:23). Similarly, in 2 Corinthians Paul writes, "Yes, we do have confidence, and we would rather be away from the body and at home with the Lord" (2 Cor. 5:8). Neither of these texts excludes the hope of the resurrection. On the contrary, both letters strongly affirm such a hope.[64] Nevertheless, they do leave open the possibility that the time between death and resurrection may include the vision of God, given that Paul speaks of such a state as better than the present one and that Scripture supports a spiritual vision of God that does not come through the body.[65]

Even though the Catholic Church eventually rejected Augustine's understanding of the timing of the beatific vision, his theology demonstrates two important aspects of his thought. First, the resurrection of the body forms an essential part of the Christian hope. Second, for Augustine, the resurrection is not only compatible with the vision of God—it is essential to that vision.

"Seek His Face with Ardor"

Important though the resurrection is to Augustine's understanding of the Christian hope, by itself it is not enough to satisfy the longings of the human heart. Our desire finds its fulfillment only in the face-to-face vision of God. This is arguably the most important aspect of Augustine's teaching on the

61. Augustine, *Trin.* 15.24.44 (modified).

62. See the discussion in Daley, *The Hope of the Early Church*, 137–38.

63. The bull does not name Augustine, as the controversy was prompted by sermons preached by Benedict's predecessor, Pope John XXII, who, like Augustine before him, suggested that perhaps the saints would not see God until the last judgment.

64. See the discussion on pp. 154–56 below.

65. For a brief contemporary discussion of this question, which affirms both a postmortem beatific vision and the necessity of the resurrection, see Parkison, *To Gaze upon God*, 58–59.

end.[66] The human desire for perfect love and for perfect goodness will be fulfilled in the direct vision of God promised in Scripture.

Although Augustine's treatise *On the Trinity* is often characterized by difficult abstract thought, its motivation lies not in an empty intellectual pursuit, but rather in the desire of a lover. As Robert Wilken rightly notes, the work is punctuated at important points by the citation of Psalm 105:4 ("Seek his face always"), which serves as a kind of refrain.[67] This work of speculative theology is thus also the pursuit of a lover for his beloved.[68] At the outset, Augustine urges his audience on, quoting the psalm for the first of four times in the work.[69] In the prologue of Book 9, which marks the beginning of a new part of his argument, he returns to the verse, emphasizing the adverb "always": "'Look for God,' it says, 'and your souls shall live'; and in case anyone should be too quick to congratulate himself that he has got there, 'look for his face,' it goes on, 'always' [*Quaerite, inquit, faciem eius semper*]."[70] For Augustine, the search for God's face, as we will see, continues even into the next life.

Augustine quotes this verse two more times in Book 15. In the prologue, he ponders why the psalmist urges his audience to seek the Lord's face "always." Does this mean that God's face will never be found? If so, how can anyone find satisfaction? Augustine clarifies the mystery through a dialectic of seeking and finding rooted in God's incomprehensible nature: "So if he can be found when he is sought, why does it say 'Seek his face always'? Does he perhaps have to be sought even when he has been found? That is indeed how incomprehensible things have to be searched for, in case the man who has been able to find out how incomprehensible what he is looking for is should reckon that he has found nothing."[71] A recurring theme in Augustine's understanding of happiness in the next life is the notion of a never-satisfied satisfaction.[72] The joy of the blessed is found in this tension between seeking and finding: "[The Lord's face] is sought in order to be found all the more delightfully [*dulcius*], and it is found in order to be sought all the more avidly [*avidius*]."[73] For this

66. Daley (*The Hope of the Early Church*, 145) suggests that Augustine sees this direct vision of God "as the very heart of the eternal beatitude of the saints." In his famous letter to Proba, Augustine writes, "It is, after all, the one true and only happy life, namely, that, immortal and incorruptible in body and in spirit, we contemplate the delight of the Lord for eternity" (*Ep.* 130.14.27).

67. Wilken, *The Spirit of Early Christian Thought*, 106–9.

68. Wilken, *The Spirit of Early Christian Thought*, 107–8.

69. Augustine, *Trin.* 1.3.5.

70. Augustine, *Trin.* 9.1.1.

71. Augustine, *Trin.* 15.2.2.

72. For a good discussion of this notion, see Pierce, "Augustine's Eschatological Vision," 234–37. We will return to this idea in the closing chapter.

73. Augustine, *Trin.* 15.2.2. Augustine's point here resembles Irenaeus's explanation of why the Father remains invisible to human beings in this life. As we will see in chap. 12, Augustine extends this balance of striving and satisfaction into the world to come.

reason, in the closing prayer of the treatise Augustine asks the Lord to help him seek his face "with ardor [*ardenter*]."[74]

Augustine's ardor is on full display in the opening book of *On the Trinity*. In the midst of a discussion of the way the Son in his humanity is lower than the Father, Augustine digresses to explain why the vision of God is the ultimate human end. He interprets the statement in 1 Corinthians 15:24 that Christ will hand over the kingdom to the Father in terms of this vision: "The fact is that the 'man Christ Jesus, mediator of God and men,' now reigning for all 'the just' who 'live by faith,' is going to bring them to direct sight of God, to the 'face to face' vision, as the apostle calls it, that is what is meant by 'When he hands the kingdom over to God and the Father,' as though to say 'When he brings believers to a direct contemplation of God and the Father.'"[75] The ultimate end of Christ's work and of the creation of human beings is this face-to-face encounter with God, which will fulfill the deepest human desires. Thus, in the next few paragraphs Augustine rhapsodizes about that vision: "This contemplation is promised us as the end of all activities and the eternal perfection of all joys."[76] He supports this interpretation by citing a series of biblical texts associated with this face-to-face vision of God, among them 1 John 3:2; Exodus 3:14; and John 17:3. Whereas in this life we can be distracted by other things, in the next we will seek nothing else, because that vision will be the source of our joy: "We will not seek anything else when we reach that contemplation of him, which is not yet ours as long as we are rejoicing only in hope."[77] This joy, which we enjoy now "only in hope," will reach its perfection in the trinitarian vision of the next life: "For the fullness of our happiness [*plenum gaudium nostrum*], beyond which there is none else, is this: to enjoy God the three in whose image we were made."[78]

Finally, this vision should be the motivation for everything we do. Once again bringing together a number of biblical texts regarding the vision of God, Augustine describes the search for this vision as the search of a lover:

> For that sight of God in which we shall behold his unchanging substance, invisible to human eyes and promised only to the saints and described by the apostle Paul as "face to face," of which the apostle John says, "We shall be like him, because we shall see him as he is," and of which it is said, "One thing

74. Augustine, *Trin.* 15.28.51.

75. Augustine, *Trin.* 1.8.16. On this interpretation of 1 Cor. 15:28, see again Barnes, "The Visible Christ and the Invisible Trinity," 332–36. Later in that same essay (340), Barnes notes that a similar interpretation is found in Hilary's *De Trinitate*. It is also worth mentioning that Augustine later interprets the kingdom ecclesiologically—that is, as referring to the body of believers Christ brings to the vision of the Father (*Trin.* 1.10.21). I am grateful to Augustine Reisenauer for this suggestion.

76. Augustine, *Trin.* 1.8.17.

77. Augustine, *Trin.* 1.8.17.

78. Augustine, *Trin.* 1.8.18.

> have I begged of the Lord, to behold the delight of the Lord," and of which our Lord himself says, "And I will love him and show myself to him," in order to be "blessed the pure of heart, because they shall see God," and whatever else is said about this sight, which anyone who directs the eyes of love [*oculum amoris*] to seeking it may find scattered plentifully throughout the scriptures; this sight alone is our supreme good, and it is to gain this that we are bidden to do whatever we do rightly.[79]

As a student, Augustine was "enamored with the idea of love [*amare amabam*]" and "in love with loving [*amans amare*]."[80] As a mature bishop, he now directs that love and exhorts his readers to direct their love to the One in Three who *is* Love (1 John 4:8, 16). Finding that Love, which "alone is our supreme good," will satisfy the human heart.

Augustine speaks eloquently of this vision again in his *Expositions of the Psalms*, describing it in terms of both goodness and beauty. In his second sermon on Psalm 37, he interprets the inheritance of which the psalm speaks in verse 18, in light of 1 John 3:2, as a vision: "There is reserved for us some kind of wholly delightful vision [*dulce spectaculum omnino*], the beauty of which can be thought of in some degree, though only through riddling reflections in a dark mirror [*in aenigmate et per speculum*]. In no way can it be described, the ravishing beauty of that joy God keeps for those who fear him, and consummates for those who hope in him."[81] The beauty for which we long cannot be compared with any earthly beauty, although the beautiful things of this world offer intimations of that eternal beauty. He develops the comparison between the beautiful things of creation and God's perfect beauty in a sermon on Psalm 85:

> So he has promised to show himself to us. Think, my brothers and sisters, think what his beauty is like [*qualis est pulchritudo eius*]! All these beautiful things [*omnia ista pulchra*] that you see and love—he made them. If they are beautiful, what of him? If they are great, how great is he? Let us rise up from the things we love here to desire him even more; let us hold them cheap and choose him for our love, and by this love so cleanse our hearts through faith that the vision of God may find our hearts already purified.[82]

Read out of context, Augustine's words might give the impression that we must abandon all earthly things in order to see God. If we recall his treatment of the final vision of God in *City of God*, however, it should be clear

79. Augustine, *Trin.* 1.13.31.

80. Augustine, *Conf.* 3.1.1.

81. Augustine, *Enarrat. Ps.* 36.2.8 (modified). Note the allusion to 1 Cor. 13:12 in the phrase *in aenigmate et per speculum*. Augustine numbers the psalms according to the LXX, so that his Ps. 36 is Ps. 37 in most modern English translations.

82. Augustine, *Enarrat. Ps.* 84.9. Cf. *Serm.* 241.2.

that Augustine is speaking rather of the proper ordering of our loves.[83] At the resurrection, the vision of God will not be in competition with the vision of physical objects—rather, he will be seen in and through those objects, his beauty shining gloriously through them. To attain such a vision, however, it is necessary to purify our hearts, putting God above all else.

One of Augustine's most extended discussions of the vision of God in terms of goodness and love is in his second exposition of Psalm 27. Commenting on the psalmist's desire to dwell in the house of the Lord "all the days of my life," Augustine offers a brief meditation on the nature of happiness. Happiness, he notes, stems from having what one loves, but the only person who can be genuinely happy is "the one who loves what is worthy of love [*amet quod amandum est*]."[84] The psalmist is one who loves worthily. He desires to dwell in God's house in order "to contemplate the Lord's delight." Augustine expands on this verse, initially speaking in the person of the psalmist, "'Now you can see what I love, now you can see why I want to dwell in the Lord's house all my days.' It offers something wonderful, the chance to contemplate the Lord's own joy."[85] Augustine goes on to describe this joy, the object of our contemplation, as "sheer Goodness-Itself [*ipsum bonum*]."[86] Ordinary, temporal goods delight us. How much more, Augustine writes, will the contemplation of goodness itself satisfy us: "Now, brothers and sisters, if the things which are called good delight us, if we are delighted with things not intrinsically good (for no changeable things are intrinsically good), what will the contemplation of the unchangeable good [*contemplatio incommutabilis boni*] be like, the good which is eternal and abides the same for ever?"[87]

The contemplation of this perfect, unchangeable good is what the Scriptures mean when they speak of seeing God's face. This desire to see God is born of love, and for Augustine only those who love rightly understand it: "'To you my heart has spoken: I have sought your face, O Lord, for your face will I seek. Do not turn your face away from me, nor turn away in anger from your servant.' How wonderful that is; nothing more consonant with God's being can be said. Those who love truly experience this [*sentiunt hoc qui vere amant*]."[88] Because this vision is born of love, those who truly love God are willing, if necessary, to sacrifice everything for its sake. Nothing other than God, even if it were to last forever, could satisfy the lover's longing: "'What if he were to make you immortal in the pleasures and the enjoyment of earthly satisfactions?' Such a

83. On the importance of love for the vision of God, as well as the compatibility between love of God and love of neighbor, see Miles, "Vision: The Eye of the Body and the Eye of the Mind," 137–38.

84. Augustine, *Enarrat. Ps.* 26.2.7.

85. Augustine, *Enarrat. Ps.* 26.2.8.

86. Augustine, *Enarrat. Ps.* 26.2.8.

87. Augustine, *Enarrat. Ps.* 26.2.8.

88. Augustine, *Enarrat. Ps.* 26.2.16 (modified).

lover replies, 'That is not what I want. Whatever is not God holds no sweetness for me. Whatever my Lord may want to give me, let him take away the whole lot, if he will give me himself.'"[89] As the great Spanish mystic Teresa of Ávila would put it around one thousand years later, "God alone suffices."[90]

Augustinian Vision

The influence of Platonic thought on Augustine is undeniable. As he himself recounts in the *Confessions*, the Platonists helped him grasp the possibility of immaterial substance.[91] As we have seen, his description of the vision of God often rings with the tones of Plato: the perfect good, the desire for beauty. Nevertheless, though Augustine's language certainly borrows from Plato, his vision of the Christian hope cannot be reduced to Platonism. Rather, he offers a synthesis of Platonic thought and Scripture, at times correcting the former by the latter, but always affirming what is good and true in Platonism in light of the Scriptures. The ardent desire of the psalmist resonates with his own passionate nature and helps him to articulate the desire for the vision of God in terms of love. Just as importantly, Augustine closely associates this vision with the resurrection. Even if those (like me) who accept the authority of the Catholic Church must ultimately reject his insistence that the saints will not enjoy the vision of God until the resurrection, this insistence nevertheless shows how essential the resurrection is to his view of the end. Perhaps more importantly, Augustine offers a sophisticated account of how the resurrection will transform our bodily vision. With their resurrected eyes the saints will have a greater awareness of God's presence in and through the new heaven and the new earth, above all through Jesus and the other saints, such that their bodily vision will in some way complement and correspond to their intellectual vision of God.

Whereas Augustine's Platonic background leads him to describe this vision in terms of beauty and goodness, the rediscovery of Aristotle in the medieval West offered other resources for supporting the biblical hope of seeing God with philosophical analysis. Thomas Aquinas offers such a synthesis in several of his writings on the topic. Moreover, and contrary to common misconceptions, Aquinas also incorporates the bodily vision of the risen Christ into his account of human beatitude. To that account we now turn.

89. Augustine, *Enarrat. Ps.* 26.2.16.

90. For the text of Teresa's famous poem in both Spanish and English, see Teresa of Ávila, *The Collected Works*, 3:386. In his *Explanation of the Ten Commandments* Aquinas similarly affirms, "For God alone suffices to fulfill our desire [*quia solus Deus sufficit ad implendum desiderium nostrum*]" (prologue). Significantly, he does so in the context of citing the opening of Augustine's *Confessions*. This translation is mine from the text found at http://www.corpusthomisticum.org/iopera.html. I am grateful to Andrew Hofer for drawing my attention to this passage.

91. See *Conf.* 7.

SEVEN

Aquinas, Seeing God, and the Fulfillment of All Desire

Thomas Aquinas discusses the vision of God in numerous places throughout his corpus.[1] Common to these various discussions is the idea that the beatific vision is the last end of human beings, that in which we will find our true fulfillment.[2] In explaining why God alone can be the ultimate end of human beings, he develops the tradition represented in the writings of Irenaeus and Augustine, building upon it with philosophical analysis made possible by the medieval rediscovery of the works of Aristotle. Although Thomas insists that this vision is an incorporeal activity of the soul, such activity is compatible with and even informs the bodily activity that the saints will enjoy in the new heavens and the new earth.

Aquinas's most famous dialectical arguments regarding human happiness and the vision of God appear in the *Summa Theologiae* and the *Summa Contra Gentiles*. Before considering those treatments of the question, however, it will be worthwhile to attend to a few of his biblical commentaries. Although he frequently writes in an idiom derived from Aristotelian philosophy (much like Augustine writes in a Platonic style), his hope for the vision of God is rooted not only in philosophical analysis but also (and primarily) in Scripture.

1. For a list of passages, see Root, "The Christological Character of the Beatific Vision," 132n9. In addition to the texts he cites, I would add the biblical commentaries on Matthew and 1 Corinthians discussed below. Hütter (*Bound for Beatitude*, 389–409) offers a clear and succinct summary of Aquinas's understanding of the beatific vision.

2. Gaine ("Thomas Aquinas and John Owen on the Beatific Vision," 433n2) notes that Aquinas speaks of "blessed vision (*visio beata*)" rather than "beatific vision." I use the latter term since it has become standard.

A Précis on Happiness

Continuing a tradition that stretches back at least to Augustine, Thomas reads the Sermon on the Mount through the lens of the Beatitudes.[3] Understood in this way, Jesus's moral teaching does not primarily concern commandments. Rather, the Sermon is a guide to the happy life—a treatise on happiness, with the Beatitudes serving as a précis that lays out the foundational principles.[4] Aquinas divides the Sermon into three parts: In the first section (Matt. 5:1–16), Jesus promises rewards to his listeners; in the second (5:17–7:6), he describes the kind of life that leads to receiving those rewards; in the final section (7:7–29), he shows how to live such a life. Aquinas underscores the necessity of grace to fulfill Jesus's teaching, noting that Jesus says, "Ask, and it will be given to you" (7:7).[5]

When he begins his discussion of the Beatitudes, Aquinas notes four common opinions regarding happiness. Although all people desire happiness, people seek different objects to fulfill that desire. Some seek happiness in external or temporal goods; others seek to fulfill their own will, doing whatever they desire; still others pursue the virtues of the active life; finally, some seek happiness in the virtues of the contemplative life.[6] All these opinions, Thomas suggests, are mistaken in one way or another, as indicated by the Beatitudes.

The first beatitude, addressed to the poor, shows that wealth will not bring a person true happiness.[7] The second, third, and fourth beatitudes, those directed to the merciful, the meek, and those who mourn, all challenge the notion that one can find happiness by doing one's own will.[8] No specific beatitude challenges the virtues of the active life as the source of happiness. Aquinas suggests that those who hold to this idea are less wrong than the others, because these virtues are the way to happiness, but not its substance.[9] As for those who seek happiness in the virtues of the contemplative life, their sole mistake lies in seeking a temporal happiness. Happiness cannot be attained in its fullness in the present life but only at the eschaton. For

3. See Pinckaers, *The Sources of Christian Ethics*, 145–58. Aquinas explicitly acknowledges his debt to Augustine in his discussion of the Beatitudes (*Sup. Mt.* 403).

4. I arrived at this description independent of ten Klooster (*Thomas Aquinas on the Beatitudes*, 74), who similarly calls the preface of Thomas's treatment of the Beatitudes in the Matthew commentary "a small treatise on happiness."

5. *Sup. Mt.* 403. Throughout this chapter, unless otherwise noted, I cite the biblical text as it appears in Aquinas's works, which at times differs from modern translations.

6. *Sup. Mt.* 404.

7. *Sup. Mt.* 405.

8. *Sup. Mt.* 406. Cf. 1 Cor. 10:24. On Thomas's numbering and ordering of the Beatitudes, which differs slightly from modern translations, see ten Klooster, *Thomas Aquinas on the Beatitudes*, 69–70.

9. *Sup. Mt.* 407.

that reason, Jesus says that the pure of heart "*will* see God."[10] For Aquinas, happiness is found in the last two beatitudes, the ones concerning "the pure in heart" and "the peacemakers."[11] The ultimate human end consists both in seeing God and in becoming children of God—it is attained by knowledge and by love.[12]

All the beatitudes follow the pattern of extolling a behavior that is praiseworthy, then promising a corresponding reward.[13] Ultimately these rewards are reduceable to God himself. Thomas cites three biblical texts (Lam. 3:24; Ps. 16:5; Gen. 15:7) in support of this position, the first two of which clearly describe God as a reward.[14] All the things people seek in their pursuit of happiness can be found in God.

In treating the sixth and seventh beatitudes Aquinas reiterates that the ultimate human happiness is twofold, described here as the vision of God and becoming children of God. Happiness consists in knowledge and in love, a love that is twofold—namely, love of God and neighbor. Like Irenaeus and Augustine before him, Thomas recognizes some of the difficulties in Scripture regarding the vision of God—its testimony is mixed.[15] Some texts suggest that no human being has seen or can see God (1 Tim. 6:16; 1 John 4:12). Others hold out hope for a future vision of God (1 Cor. 13:12; 1 John 3:2). Aquinas gives these latter texts primacy and seeks to account for the former texts, drawing on Augustine's treatment of the question.

Although Thomas holds fast to this hope for the vision of God, he agrees with Augustine's earlier position, denying that human beings will see God with their bodily eyes.[16] Like Augustine (and Ambrose) before him, he appeals to the words of the beatitude: It does not say "blessed are those who have clean and pure eyes [*beati qui habent mundos et puros oculos*]."[17] The heart is the spiritual organ by which we will see God.[18] In addition to the beatitude itself, Thomas points to the nature of bodily vision, which is directed to

10. *Sup. Mt.* 408.

11. Aquinas, again following Augustine, counts only seven beatitudes, considering the eighth to be a summary of the ones that precede it.

12. *Sup. Mt.* 408. Thomas cites 1 John 3:1 in support of this twofold understanding of beatitude.

13. *Sup. Mt.* 409.

14. *Sup. Mt.* 412. The choice of Gen. 15:7 seems odd, in that it refers to the land as Abram's reward. One might have expected Aquinas to cite Gen. 15:1 instead, as he does later in the commentary (449), since in his translation God says to Abram, "I God am your reward [*merces*]."

15. As ten Klooster (*Thomas Aquinas on the Beatitudes*, 109) notes, this shorter discussion of the question shares several elements with Thomas's treatment in the John commentary.

16. On the development of Augustine's thought on the question, see chap. 6 above.

17. *Sup. Mt.* 434.

18. Thomas points to Eph. 1:18 in support of the heart having "eyes." This vision extends not only to seeing the divine essence, but also to recognizing Jesus for who he is at his return. Simply having functioning eyes will not suffice to know him as the Son of God. See *Sup. Mt.* 434. I owe this point to ten Klooster, *Thomas Aquinas on the Beatitudes*, 109n176.

physical objects and sees essences only in a secondary way. Unsurprisingly, given that he is drawing on Augustine's *City of God*, Aquinas suggests that in some way we will recognize God even with our bodily eyes in the new creation: "Just as when I see something living, we can say that I see life [*possumus dicere quod video vitam*], insofar as I see certain indications [*quaedam indicia*] by which its life is pointed out to me, so it will be in the divine vision, because *the reflection of God in the new heaven and the new earth and the glorified bodies will be so great that by it we will be said to see God as though with the bodily eyes* [*quasi oculis corporalibus*]."[19] The primary vision of God will be with the eyes of the heart, then, but this does not mean that for Aquinas our resurrected eyes will be inactive or that they will in no way experience God.[20]

What, then, of texts like 1 John 4:12, which seem to suggest that it is impossible to see God? Thomas gives three answers drawn from Augustine.[21] First, no human being can comprehend God—that is, have an exhaustive vision of God. The finite cannot completely encompass the infinite. Second, no human being can see God with bodily eyes.[22] Finally, no human being can see God in this life. Even though the full vision of God is reserved for the next life, however, we can nevertheless have some sense of what it will be like, even now. For Aquinas, in this life we are prepared for that vision by living the Beatitudes. The more our hearts become pure, the better we can see. Thus, the saints see God "more excellently [*excellentius*]" than those who recognize him only by his effects in this world.[23] This vision spills over into love, and the activity praised in the seventh beatitude disposes believers to love of God and neighbor.[24] As important as the sixth beatitude is, the rewards of the Beatitudes culminate in the seventh, because, as Thomas puts it, "it is more to be a son of the king than to see the king."[25] Vision and love thus comprise the complete happiness of human beings, though, as we will see below, the act of knowledge has primacy in attaining this happiness.

19. *Sup. Mt.* 434 (emphasis added). Aquinas seems to endorse Augustine's more moderate interpretation of how the saints might see God indirectly with their resurrected eyes in *City of God* 22.29. See the discussion in chap. 6 above.

20. Even in this life, those who live the beatitudes will be more disposed to see God through his effects. See *Sup. Mt.* 435; ten Klooster, *Thomas Aquinas on the Beatitudes*, 110.

21. *Sup. Mt.* 434.

22. Here Aquinas departs from Augustine's later position, though he does not draw attention to it.

23. *Sup. Mt.* 435.

24. *Sup. Mt.* 436.

25. *Sup. Mt.* 440. As ten Klooster (*Thomas Aquinas on the Beatitudes*, 111) notes, here Aquinas evidences his respect for Scripture in that he does not impose his usual practice of describing vision as the ultimate happiness on the sacred text.

"No One Has Ever Seen God"?

Aquinas addresses the question of seeing God at greater length in his commentary on the Gospel of John. The Gospel's prologue ends with the statement, "No one has ever seen God; the only begotten Son, who is in the Father's bosom, has made him known."[26] Immediately Thomas notes the difficulty with this phrase—namely, that it seems to contradict other texts of Scripture. According to Isaiah 6, the prophet "saw the Lord seated on a high and lofty throne."[27] Moreover, Jesus himself promises that the pure in heart will see God (Matt. 5:8).[28] This tension in Scripture leads Aquinas to a brief discussion of the nature of seeing God.

Thomas begins by entertaining the possibility that John refers simply to the past—although no one has ever seen God, they will see him in the future. This interpretation encounters the difficulty of 1 Timothy 6:16, which describes God as the one "whom no [human being] has seen or can see." In response, someone might suggest that the text speaks only of human beings. Angels, by contrast, may be able to see God (Matt. 18:10). Such a reading does not resolve the problem for Aquinas, however, because elsewhere in Scripture Jesus says that those who rise from the dead will be like the angels (Matt. 22:30). For this reason, Scripture suggests—and in fact explicitly says (1 John 3:2)—that, one day, human beings will see God.[29]

What then, Aquinas asks, is the interpreter to make of John's statement that "no one has ever seen God"? In typical fashion, he makes distinctions, illustrating each of them with examples from Scripture. There are at least three ways in which a person "sees" God. First, some people have seen God with their bodily eyes through a created manifestation. Aquinas cites Abraham's encounter with the three men in Genesis 18 as an example. Second, at times God reveals himself to a person's imagination through a representation. This is how Aquinas interprets Isaiah's temple vision (Isa. 6:1). Such visions occur frequently throughout the Scriptures. Third, a person can "see" God "through an intelligible species abstracted from material things." Simply put, a person can reason from the greatness of the created order to the existence and the greatness of the Creator. Scripture attests to this kind of "vision" (which is really a kind of knowledge), for example, in Wisdom 13:5 and Romans 1:20. To these three kinds of vision Aquinas adds a fourth, a vision that comes from "a certain spiritual light infused by God into spiritual minds during

26. This is my translation of the Latin text found in Aquinas's lectures on John. See *Sup. Io*. 208.

27. *Sup. Io*. 210.

28. *Sup. Io*. 210. Aquinas also cites 2 Sam. 6:2, which describes God as "seated upon the cherubim," implying that one can see God in a particular location.

29. *Sup. Io*. 210.

contemplation."[30] As an example of this kind of vision he cites the story of Jacob wrestling with God in Genesis 32:30, appealing to Gregory the Great for this interpretation.[31]

For all their differences, these four ways of seeing God have a common thread. According to Aquinas, in no instance does a person see the divine essence; all these visions are mediated through some created "appearance [*species*]." By its nature, a created appearance is finite and so cannot fully represent the infinite God. Created media can represent some aspect of God's being, but not his full essence. For that reason, all four kinds of vision amount to "a knowledge that is dark and mirrored [*aenigmatica et specularis*]."[32] In this life, therefore, no mere human being has seen God's essence.

Given this analysis, as well as the testimony of Scripture in 1 Timothy, one might expect Aquinas to deny that any created intellect can see God. As is so often the case, however, Thomas surprises the reader, rejecting this position for three reasons.[33] First, although some passages of Scripture seem to deny the possibility of seeing God, others present this vision as a promise.[34] Second, he cryptically argues, "because the brightness of God is the same as his substance; for he does not give forth light by participating in light, but through himself."[35] Here Aquinas offers no biblical support for this position, but he likely has in mind a text like Psalm 36:9, which states, "For with you is the fountain of life; in your light we see light" (NRSVue), and Revelation 21:23, which he appeals to in support of his idea of the "light of glory."[36] Finally, he suggests that human happiness consists in the vision of the divine essence, offering a philosophical argument for this position, then supporting it with a biblical citation. The human intellect, he suggests, desires to know and understand the causes of all effects. Such knowledge can be had only if the intellect arrives at "the first universal cause of all things."[37] If it is impossible for human beings to see this universal cause, then the human desire for happiness will be forever frustrated. For this reason, he implies, Christ promises the vision of God in the Beatitudes (Matt. 5:8).

Having established to his own satisfaction that human beings will one day see the divine essence, Aquinas makes three notes about this vision.[38] First,

30. *Sup. Io.* 211.

31. Apart from the appeal to Gregory, it is not clear to me why this episode should differ from Abraham's encounter with the three men in Gen. 18.

32. *Sup. Io.* 211.

33. *Sup. Io.* 212.

34. Aquinas cites 1 John 3:2 and John 17:3, the latter text identifying knowledge of God (which for Thomas is often equivalent to vision) with eternal life.

35. *Sup. Io.* 212.

36. Aquinas cites this psalm in a similar argument in *SCG* 3.53.7. See the discussion of this text below.

37. *Sup. Io.* 212.

38. *Sup. Io.* 213.

human beings will not see God with their bodily eyes: "God is spirit" (John 4:24) and bodily eyes have as their function to see bodily things.

Second, Aquinas suggests "that as long as the human intellect is in the body it cannot see God, because it is weighed down by the body so that it cannot attain the summit of contemplation."[39] Here one might wish that Thomas had made more distinctions, as this statement, out of context, could be interpreted to mean that human beings see God only as disembodied souls. There are obvious exceptions in his own thought. As is well known, the clearest exception is Jesus, who, Thomas argues, had the beatific vision throughout his earthly life.[40] With respect to the next life, Aquinas resolutely affirms the resurrection of the body and in no way holds that having a resurrected body will impede the vision of God.[41] The body impedes the contemplation of God in this life through the passions, particularly when they are disordered.[42] So, he notes, "the more a soul is free of passions and is purged from affections for earthly things, the higher it rises in the contemplation of truth and tastes how sweet the Lord is."[43] As long as human beings are attached to earthly goods, they will be distracted from enjoying the Lord's own goodness. This does not mean, however, that one must do away with the passions altogether to see the divine essence. Rather, Aquinas suggests that "so long as a [human being] lives in a body *which is necessarily subject to many passions* [*subiecto ex necessitate passionibus multis*], he cannot see God through his essence."[44] The phrase I have emphasized explains why there are exceptions to Thomas's argument. Jesus could enjoy the beatific vision in this life because his body was not "necessarily subject to many passions."[45] Likewise, in the resurrection, the body will no longer be dominated by the passions and so it will not impede the vision of God.[46]

39. *Sup. Io.* 213.

40. See *ST* III, q. 10. For a recent, robust defense of Aquinas's position, see Gaine, *Did the Saviour See the Father?*

41. On Aquinas's arguments for and understanding of the resurrection, see chap. 11 below.

42. Blond ("The Beatific Vision of St Thomas Aquinas," 202) rightly suggests, "In this respect perhaps it is indeed true that the soul freed from *fallen* matter is indeed closer to God than the soul in this life" (emphasis added).

43. *Sup. Io.* 213. This argument resembles Aristotle's observation that the ongoing care for bodily needs prevents a human being from contemplating the Unmoved Mover continuously. See Aristotle, *Eth. Nic.* 10.8.

44. *Sup. Io.* 213 (emphasis added).

45. See *ST* III, qq. 14–15. This is not to say that Christ did not have the passions; rather, it simply means that his passions were ordered perfectly.

46. In the Matthew commentary (*Sup. Mt.* 438), for example, Aquinas describes peace as including the subjection of the human being's lower powers to the higher powers, suggesting that such a subjection will be perfected in the resurrection. Later, in *Sup. Io.* 213, he asserts, "Therefore, if the human intellect is to see the divine essence it must wholly depart from the body: either by death . . . or by being wholly abstracted from the senses of the body." Again, one wishes the Angelic Doctor had made more distinctions here.

Third and finally, Aquinas argues that no created intellect can "comprehend" the divine essence. Even though the saints see the "whole divine essence [*divina essentia tota*]," they do not see it "wholly [*totaliter*]."[47] This argument resembles the one he makes earlier for why none of the OT figures saw the divine essence. But whereas, earlier, Thomas focuses on the created medium by which those figures encountered God, here he underscores the finite minds with which the saints gaze upon God. Because the human intellect is created, it is also finite and so can know only in a finite way. God, however, is infinite, and for that reason he cannot be fully known by a finite intellect. God alone can know the divine nature—that is, himself—comprehensively.

This argument brings Thomas back at last to the question of how to interpret John's statement, "No one has ever seen God."[48] In light of his considerations in the preceding paragraphs, Aquinas notes, first, that no one has ever seen the divine essence with the bodily eye or with "the eye of the imagination." Second, no one in this life has seen the divine essence.[49] Finally, neither in this life nor in the next has anyone, whether human being or angel, seen God comprehensively.

"Now I Know in Part"

Aquinas discusses the vision of God at least one more time in the biblical commentaries, in his lectures on 1 Corinthians 13.[50] His remarks about the vision appear in lecture 4, where he discusses another of the classic NT texts regarding face-to-face knowledge of God (1 Cor. 13:12); however, it is worth considering lecture 3 as well, because it sheds further light on his eschatology. This lecture, which treats 1 Corinthians 13:8–11, discusses the differences between the present life and the future life with respect to the gifts of the Holy Spirit.

In Paul's famous encomium on love, the apostle writes, "Charity never falls away" (1 Cor. 13:8). The meaning of this phrase, Aquinas suggests, must be understood in its context, which concerns "the cessation of spiritual gifts which pertain to this life through supervening glory."[51] Love never falls away, he argues, because, unlike the other spiritual gifts, charity will continue into the next life. By contrast, the charismatic gifts will cease to have any purpose

47. *Sup. Io.* 213.

48. *Sup. Io.* 214.

49. For Thomas, though he does not mention it here, there is, of course, one exception—namely, Christ. See *ST* III, q. 10.

50. It is important to note that the latter third of this commentary does not come from his own hand, but is a compilation put together by Reginald of Piperno. See Bynum, *The Resurrection of the Body in Western Christianity*, 232–33, and the literature cited there.

51. *I Ad Cor.* 787.

in the state of glory. Prophecy will cease for two reasons. First, prophecy concerns the future, and in the eschaton there will be no future, since it will be the consummation of all things.[52] Second, prophecy involves mediation by visions, but in the next life the saints will enjoy face-to-face vision.[53] Similarly, the gift of tongues will cease, because in the state of glory everyone will understand each other.[54] Significantly, before he makes this argument, Thomas underscores that Paul speaks of the spiritual gift of tongues, not of bodily tongues. The resurrected body, being incorruptible, will have all its members in their integrity, including tongues, which will be used to praise God.[55] The third gift that "will be destroyed" (1 Cor. 13:8), in contrast to charity, is knowledge. Aquinas offers an analysis of knowledge informed by Aristotelian anthropology, suggesting that knowledge informed by phantasms will cease when the soul is separated from the body at death.[56] In summary, Aquinas notes that all three gifts (prophecy, tongues, knowledge) are imperfect and partial, and so will pass away when the perfect arrives.[57] In this life, charity, too, is imperfect, but its imperfection has a different character. Whereas knowledge and prophecy (and tongues) will no longer be necessary in the next life, charity will come to its perfection and continue throughout eternity.[58]

In lecture 4, on 1 Corinthians 13:12–13, Aquinas comes to the topic of face-to-face vision. He identifies this vision as knowledge of God and suggests that the spiritual gifts serve to bring believers to such a vision.[59] In the present we see "through a glass in a dark manner: but then face to face" (1 Cor. 13:12a). The first phrase refers to knowing God by the mediation of created things, whether the natural world or visions and images.[60] Seeing "face to face," by contrast, means a direct, unmediated vision of God. In interpreting this phrase, Aquinas begins by underscoring the metaphorical nature of Paul's language: "God *as God* [*secundum quod Deus*] does not have a face."[61] For this reason, he interprets Paul's phrase with reference to 1 John 3:2. The

52. *I Ad Cor.* 788. This presumes an understanding of prophecy as prediction of future events, rather than critique of the present order. Aquinas's point would stand, however, even on that understanding, because in the state of glory there will be nothing to critique.

53. *I Ad Cor.* 788.

54. *I Ad Cor.* 789. Here Aquinas seems to interpret the gift of tongues in light of the events of Pentecost in Acts 2. His reasoning might more aptly apply to what Paul calls the "interpretation of tongues" (1 Cor. 12:10).

55. *I Ad Cor.* 789. Aquinas cites 1 Cor. 15:52 in support of the hope for incorruptible bodies and Ps. 149:6 regarding the praise of God.

56. *I Ad Cor.* 790–91. This is the least persuasive aspect of Aquinas's reading of this chapter as an interpretation of Paul's thought, but it does not detract from his broader point.

57. *I Ad Cor.* 793.

58. *I Ad Cor.* 795.

59. *I Ad Cor.* 799.

60. *I Ad Cor.* 800–801.

61. *I Ad Cor.* 802 (emphasis added). The qualification "as God" is important, because Aquinas is well aware that the incarnate Son has a human face.

apostle means that the saints will see the divine essence (seeing him "as he is" in the language of 1 John).[62]

For Aquinas, this vision must be direct and cannot be mediated by a created likeness, as some argue.[63] The reason is that a substance's essence cannot be known through a likeness. For example, if we learn about a stone through an image in a book, we may know something about the stone, but we will not know its essence. A thing's essence can be known and understood only through immediate experience. For this reason, one cannot know God directly, as Scripture promises, through a created likeness, because that likeness does not grant access to the divine essence. Seeing a manifestation of his glory, such as brightness, is not the same as seeing God directly.[64] In addition, Thomas notes that if human beings saw God through a created likeness, then their happiness would be found not in God himself, but in something else. In the end, the human desire to know the ultimate cause of all things would be frustrated.[65]

Aquinas rounds out his discussion of this vision with brief comments on the second half of 1 Corinthians 13:12 ("Now I know in part; but then I shall know even as I am known"). Paul moves from the general principle to the particular of his own life, once more underscoring the imperfect and partial knowledge of the present life, which will be replaced with direct knowledge in the next. The "as" of Paul's statement "I shall know even *as* I am known" points to a similarity rather than an identity between the knowledge of the saints and God's own knowledge. As God knows our essence, so, too, the saints will know God's essence, though not in a comprehensive way.[66]

Aquinas's approach to Scripture is obviously shaped by his philosophical principles.[67] Nevertheless, though at times these principles may lead to questionable readings of the text (e.g., interpreting Paul's reference to the gift of knowledge in terms of phantasms), often they help elucidate it. More

62. *I Ad Cor.* 802.

63. *I Ad Cor.* 803. As is not infrequently the case, here Aquinas does not identify the people he is criticizing. Elsewhere, in the *Sentences* commentary, he points to Alfarabi and Avampace, mediated through the writings of Averroes, as proponents of this position. See Krause, *Thomas Aquinas on Seeing God*, 87.

64. This is my summary and paraphrase of Aquinas's reasoning in *I Ad Cor.* 803. Aquinas might have added that vision of God through a created likeness, such as his brightness, would be no different than the vision that some of the OT prophets received (see, e.g., Ezek. 1).

65. *I Ad Cor.* 803.

66. *I Ad Cor.* 804. Aquinas does not use the language of "comprehension," but it seems implicit, particularly in light of his discussion in the John commentary.

67. This is, of course, true of all biblical interpreters. What sets Aquinas apart from many modern exegetes is that he is aware of and open about his presuppositions. For an older analysis of the way philosophical principles shape eighteenth- and nineteenth-century German exegesis, see Lagrange, *The Meaning of Christianity*, and my discussion of that text, "Père Lagrange and the Criticism of Criticism." For another recent call to honesty about philosophical presuppositions in exegesis, see Ratzinger, "Biblical Interpretation in Crisis."

importantly, Aquinas's hope for the vision of God does not stem primarily from his philosophical principles, but rather from Scripture. Seeing the promise of a vision of God in Scripture, as well as in the Christian tradition, he analyzes the texts with the tools of philosophical analysis to supplement and explain why God would make such a promise.

The Fulfillment of All Desire

In the *Summa Contra Gentiles* and the *Summa Theologiae*, Aquinas develops his understanding of the beatific vision at greater length. While his discussion of the vision in these works takes on a more philosophical mode, he never loses sight of the biblical basis for this hope. In question 12 of the *Prima pars*, Thomas appeals to two texts from the Johannine writings to show that this vision of God is possible.[68] In the first article, which asks whether any creature can see God's essence, he cites 1 John 3:2: "We shall see him as he is."[69] Article 4 of the same question asks whether creatures can see God by their own natural powers. Aquinas answers in the negative, arguing that created intellects depend on grace to see God. Nevertheless, with the help of grace human beings can see God, and eternal life consists in this vision, a point he supports with an appeal to John 17:3. In question 3 of the *Prima secundae*, which discusses the nature of happiness, Thomas appeals once again to 1 John 3:2 to show that human happiness consists in the vision of God.[70]

Aquinas supports this biblical foundation with a philosophical analysis of human happiness. In question 2 of the *Prima secundae* he presents a dialectical examination of the various ends human beings seek in order to attain happiness. A consideration of the most common things pursued by human beings in this search—wealth, honor, fame, power, bodily goods, pleasure, or any other good of the soul—leads Thomas to conclude that no created good can lead a person to happiness.[71] In keeping with the testimony of Scripture, only God can fulfill the human desire for happiness, and he does so by granting human beings a vision of the divine essence.[72] Aquinas reaches this conclusion after a consideration of the nature of human happiness that rules out certain aspects of human nature as the locus of happiness. While the senses

68. For readers unfamiliar with the *Summa Theologiae*, the work is divided into three parts, with the second part further subdivided into two parts. These parts are conventionally referred to as the *Prima pars*; the *Prima secundae* and the *Secunda secundae*; and the *Tertia pars*. Each part consists of questions further subdivided into articles. Citations indicate the part with a Roman numeral (I, I-II, II-II, III), followed by the question and the article with Arabic numerals.

69. St. Thomas Aquinas, *ST* I, q. 12, a. 1, sed contra.

70. *ST* I-II, q. 3, a. 8, sed contra.

71. *ST* I-II, q. 2, aa. 1–8. See also the discussion of Levering, *Jesus and the Demise of Death*, 110–11.

72. *ST* I-II, q. 3, a. 8.

can participate in happiness, they do not contribute to the ultimate human end, because that end is the uncreated God, and human beings cannot be joined to God by means of the senses.[73] Similarly, although the will rests in happiness once attained, happiness is not an operation of the will, but of the intellect. The reason for this is that the will, oriented to the end by desire or by delight, can delight only in what is present. But neither desire nor delight can make the thing present, thus the action of the will cannot be what constitutes happiness. The will is necessarily involved in happiness, but it is not the means by which a person attains it. This role is reserved for the intellect, which he discusses in the subsequent articles.[74]

Aquinas discusses the nature of this vision, as well as how one attains it, at greater length in his earlier *Summa Contra Gentiles*. This vision concerns the one uncreated reality that is the divine essence, and so it cannot come about by means of a created species.[75] Rather, the beatific vision must imitate the way God sees himself: "Therefore, if God's essence be seen at all, it must be that the intellect sees it in the divine essence itself [*per ipsammet essentiam divinam intellectus ipsam videat*], so that in that vision the divine essence is both the object and the medium of vision [*divina essentia et quod videtur, et quo videtur*]."[76] From this description it should be clear that, for Thomas, the beatific vision is unlike corporeal vision, a point he shares with Irenaeus and Augustine's earlier position.[77] Rather, God grants human beings this vision by uniting his essence directly with the human intellect; there is no mediation between God and creatures.[78] Thomas sees this hope confirmed by Scripture: "This immediate vision of God is promised to us in Sacred Scripture: 'Now we see in a mirror dimly, but then face to face.'"[79] The language of face-to-face vision is a metaphor, indicating the unmediated nature of the vision, as opposed to a corporeal vision. When we see someone face to face, we see that

73. *ST* I-II, q. 3, a. 3.

74. On the role of the will, see *ST* I-II, q. 3, a. 4; on the nature of the intellect's role, see *ST* I-II, q. 3, aa. 5–7. On this point Aquinas is consistent throughout his writings. It is simply inaccurate to suggest, as Blond does ("The Beatific Vision of St Thomas Aquinas," 187), that in the *Sentences* commentary "the vision is both corporeal and intellectual." Thomas writes, "And because [the human being] possesses the fact of being [a human being] not from the body but rather from the soul, though the body pertains to [the human being's] essence inasmuch as it is perfected by the soul, [the human being's] beatitude consists principally only in an act of the soul" (*Scriptum* 4.49.2.2 ad 6). The beatitude of the soul spills over into the body, but the vision of God is, strictly speaking, incorporeal, as Aquinas makes clear in the corpus of the same article.

75. St. Thomas Aquinas, *SCG* 3.51.2.

76. *SCG* 3.51.2.

77. Again, for the slight shift in Augustine's thought, see chap. 6.

78. *SCG* 3.51.4. As many have noted, this understanding means that "vision" is not something external, but rather involves union with God. See, e.g., Root, "The Christological Character of the Beatific Vision," 142–46.

79. *SCG* 3.51.5, citing 1 Cor. 13:12.

person without an intermediary. So likewise, our ultimate end will entail a direct, unmediated encounter with God.[80]

In this vision the blessed attain perfect happiness, because by it they become like God.[81] As God sees himself by his own essence, so will the redeemed, a promise Thomas finds in Scripture: "God understands his substance by his essence, and this is his bliss. Hence it is said: 'When he appears we shall be like to him, for we shall see him as he is.'"[82] Seeing God as he sees himself, however, is not something any created intellect can achieve by its own natural powers. Rather, it is a grace of God.[83] By that grace God elevates the redeemed, illuminating them with the divine light and giving them a share in the divine nature.[84] The transcendent character of the object of this vision demands the gift of a new capacity beyond the powers of nature: "But increase through intensification of the natural power is insufficient because that vision is not of the same kind as the natural vision of the created intellect." In order to see God, then, the power of the intellect must be given "a new disposition [*novae dispositionis*]."[85]

For Thomas, even though the beatific vision is not corporeal, the use of such language is fitting, because the knowledge of God is analogous to the way we know sensible things. Vision enjoys a preeminent place in human knowledge of the world, and so it is a fitting way to refer to the knowledge of God.[86] Vision is also an apt image because it depends on light. In this regard it illustrates another aspect of the beatific vision. For, Aquinas argues, it is by the "light of glory" that the intellect is strengthened to see God.[87] The imagery of light has a solid foundation in the Scriptures themselves, which frequently refer to God as light—both the light *by which* we see and the light *which* we see, as Thomas interprets Psalm 36: "This is the light of which it is said: 'In your light we will see the light,' namely, the light of the divine substance."[88] Numerous other passages refer to God's light and his glory in connection with both the manner of vision and that which the redeemed see.[89]

According to Thomas, the vision of God is also the source of eternal life, because by it the blessed become like God.[90] This participation stems from

80. *SCG* 3.51.5.
81. *SCG* 3.51.6.
82. *SCG* 3.51.6, citing 1 John 3:2.
83. *SCG* 3.52.1, 6–7.
84. *SCG* 3.53.1–2.
85. *SCG* 3.53.5.
86. *SCG* 3.53.6.
87. *SCG* 3.53.6. On the light of glory, see Waddell, "Aquinas on the Light of Glory."
88. *SCG* 3.53.7. For Aquinas, as for most premodern Western Christians, following the Vulgate, Ps. 36 would be referred to as Ps. 35.
89. *SCG* 3.53.7; Aquinas refers to Rev. 22:5; Isa. 60:19; John 1:9; 1 John 1:5; and Ps. 104:2.
90. *SCG* 3.61.1.

both the mode of the vision and the object of the vision. As Aquinas understands the vision, there is no succession of moments before and after. Rather, the intellect perceives it whole and entire all at once. By definition, such a simultaneous vision is eternal, and since the act of the intellect is "a kind of life [*vita quaedam*]," the vision of God consists in eternal life.[91] Moreover, because the object of the vision is eternal, the vision itself confers a participation in eternity.[92] Thomas sees confirmation of this understanding in Christ's words in John's Gospel, "This is eternal life, that they know thee the only true God."[93]

The eternal life of the beatific vision brings with it the perfect fulfillment of all the lower goods that some human beings mistakenly seek as their final end. Recall that in the *Prima secundae* Thomas rules out wealth, honor, fame, power, bodily goods, pleasure, and any other good of the soul as the ultimate end of the human being. Although striving for these as one's ultimate end is misguided, those who attain the beatific vision also receive the good represented in each of them. Human beings also desire to know the truth and strive after it in various ways, above all through the contemplative life. In the vision of God, the blessed will have immediate access to First Truth (i.e., God as the source of all truth) and—through the knowledge of God's essence—knowledge of all truths.[94] In *SCG*, Thomas describes the attraction to power as a desire to govern lower things. This desire, too, will be fulfilled in the beatific vision, since reason will be perfected and so the lower powers will obey the intellect.[95] Honor and fame, too, will accompany eternal life, because by the beatific vision the blessed are united to God himself and reign with him, giving them true renown.[96] Earthly wealth pales in comparison with "a sufficiency of all goods" that the just will enjoy by virtue of their union with God.[97] Likewise, the pleasure associated with attaining the vision of God far exceeds any earthly pleasures: "The most perfect delight is found in this felicity: as much more perfect than the delight of the sense, which even brute animals can enjoy, as the intellect is superior to sense power."[98] Finally, the desire for self-preservation, common to all creatures, will find its perfect fulfillment in that vision because immortality comes along with it.[99] In short, the vision of God will fulfill every human desire.

91. *SCG* 3.61.2.
92. *SCG* 3.61.3.
93. John 17:3, as cited in *SCG* 3.61.6.
94. *SCG* 3.63.2.
95. *SCG* 3.63.3.
96. *SCG* 3.63.4–5.
97. *SCG* 3.63.6.
98. *SCG* 3.63.7 (Bourke, *On the Truth of the Catholic Faith*, 208).
99. *SCG* 3.63.8.

Seeing God and the Lamb

On the basis of the texts we have considered thus far, one might conclude that Aquinas's understanding of the beatific vision has little place for Jesus's risen and glorified body. Recently, Hans Boersma has accused Thomas's position of a twofold "christological deficit."[100] First, he argues, Aquinas does not adequately emphasize the role Christ—more specifically, Christ's humanity—plays in leading the saints to the beatific vision.[101] Second, and more importantly for Boersma, Aquinas does not locate the vision in Christ's glorified flesh. Boersma advocates a "theophanic" interpretation of the beatific vision, whereby the object of the beatific vision is Christ's glorified body, not an intellectual vision of the divine essence.[102]

Simon Gaine has ably defended Aquinas against these critiques.[103] With respect to the first part of the alleged deficit, Gaine shows that, for Aquinas, Christ not only enables the saints to come to the vision of God; he also plays an ongoing role in that vision. Christ's humanity is the means by which the blessed come to see God by virtue of their participation in Christ's own vision

100. See H. Boersma, "Thomas Aquinas on the Beatific Vision." Boersma's essay is one of a spate of pieces regarding this question that began prior to his own work, but since then his publications have tended to focus on his Christocentric understanding of the beatific vision. For the main contributions to this conversation (in order of publication and in addition to Boersma's essay referred to at the beginning of this note), see McDonald, "Beholding the Glory of God in the Face of Jesus Christ"; Gaine, "Thomas Aquinas and John Owen on the Beatific Vision"; H. Boersma, "The 'Grand Medium'"; Gaine, "The Beatific Vision and the Heavenly Mediation of Christ"; H. Boersma, *Seeing God*; Gaine, "Thomas Aquinas, the Beatific Vision, and the Role of Christ"; Root, "The Christological Character of the Beatific Vision."

101. In his earlier piece ("The 'Grand Medium,'" 187–88), Boersma suggests that Christ plays no role in Aquinas's account of the vision (though even there he acknowledges that these criticisms are "the result of caricatures, misunderstandings, and contemporary cultural predispositions"). As a result of his exchange with Gaine, he has "slightly" revised his assessment, while maintaining that Thomas could have emphasized this aspect of salvation more. See H. Boersma, "Thomas Aquinas on the Beatific Vision," 130.

102. Ormerod ("'And We Shall See Him Face to Face,'" 652–54) and Strand ("Seeing Christ, Seeing the Trinity," 414–18) have recently countered Boersma's accusation of a "christological deficit" in Thomas's account of the beatific vision by suggesting that Boersma's approach suffers from a "trinitarian deficit." On 653, Ormerod notes of Boersma's *Seeing God*, "There are [only] passing references to the Father and the Spirit." Similarly, one should note that there is not a single reference to the Holy Spirit in either of Boersma's contributions to his exchange with Gaine. Although Aquinas does not develop the trinitarian nature of the beatific vision, there are resources within his thought, particularly his understanding of the Trinity, that lend themselves to developing a trinitarian account of this vision. For an attempt to develop such an account with the aid of Bernard Lonergan, see Ormerod, "'And We Shall See Him Face to Face,'" 658–62. Strand ("Seeing Christ, Seeing the Trinity," 418–22) proposes another account, drawing on Karl Rahner and Matthias Scheeben. Both studies are worth engaging, but the question lies beyond the scope of the present work.

103. See the essays referenced in n. 100.

of God.[104] Moreover, Christ's mediation does not end once the saints attain to the vision—an aspect of Christ's priestly activity continues into eternity. Whereas his expiation on behalf of others will be complete, according to Thomas, he will continue to mediate the capacity to see God: "The Saints who will be in heaven will not need any further expiation by the priesthood of Christ, but having been expiated, they will need consummation through Christ Himself, on Whom their glory depends, as is written (Rev. 21:23): 'The glory of God hath enlightened it'—that is, the city of the Saints—'and the Lamb is the lamp thereof.'"[105] As Gaine notes, Aquinas cites Revelation in support of his notion of the "light of glory" whereby the saints are equipped to see God. This light of glory, which is part of Christ's priestly role, never fades away but continually sustains the saints in their vision of God.[106]

With respect to Boersma's second critique, he is right that Aquinas does not locate the beatific vision in the glorified flesh of the risen Lord but in an intellectual vision of the divine essence. Far from being a drawback, however, this is a strength of Aquinas's account. Before explaining some of the advantages of this interpretation, it is important to note that Thomas's understanding of the beatific vision as an act of the intellect seen with the eyes of the mind does not exclude a bodily vision of the risen and glorified Christ. As noted above, the intellectual vision of God does not compete with a vision of bodily things. On the contrary, following Augustine, Thomas suggests that the blessed will in some way see God *in* and *through* the glorified bodies of the new heavens and the new earth.[107] He notes further that, in addition to being seen physically by the saints, Christ's humanity also forms a part of the beatific vision. Thus, in the *Compendium of Theology* he affirms that the knowledge of the saints will include two truths, "namely, the divinity of the Trinity and the humanity of Christ."[108] In his commentary on John, Aquinas again affirms that the beatific vision includes the Son's risen flesh: "In eternal life we will also rejoice in the humanity of Christ."[109] Thomas's account of the beatific vision, then, does not set aside Christ's glorified body.

How, then, does the intellectual vision of the divine essence relate to the bodily vision of the incarnate Son? Gaine argues that the solution is found in

104. *ST* III, q. 9, a. 2, citing Heb. 2:10. See Gaine, "Thomas Aquinas and John Owen on the Beatific Vision," 439.

105. *ST* III, q. 22, a. 5, ad 1 (modified). See the discussion of this text in Gaine, "The Beatific Vision and the Heavenly Mediation of Christ," 5–6.

106. For an insightful discussion of Aquinas's teaching on grace and how it relates to the beatific vision, see Root, "The Christological Character of the Beatific Vision," 140–45.

107. *Sup. Mt.* 434. Aquinas makes this point even more explicitly in *Scriptum* 4.49.2.2. Cf. Gaine, "Thomas Aquinas, the Beatific Vision, and the Role of Christ," 165.

108. *Compendium* 1.2, citing John 17:3. I owe this and the following reference to Gaine, "Thomas Aquinas and John Owen on the Beatific Vision," 436.

109. *Sup. Io.* 2188.

God's knowledge of the divine essence.[110] According to Aquinas, the saints' beatific vision is a participation in God's own knowledge of himself. In that knowledge, God knows everything that he does *ad extra*, including the incarnation and the entire plan of salvation. If the saints participate in that knowledge, then they, too, will know Christ's humanity. Knowledge of the divine essence and knowledge of Christ's humanity, then, do not in any way compete with one another. In fact, for Aquinas, it is crucial that the saints reflect on Christ's saving work so that they can give proper thanks to God.[111] As Gaine summarizes, "To focus on the divine essence is thus to *include* Christ as an object of beatific knowledge, not to exclude him."[112]

In an earlier piece, Gaine enumerates seven advantages of Thomas's approach to the beatific vision as opposed to the theophanic approach.[113] I would like to highlight two. First, Aquinas's account offers a more satisfactory explanation of how the saints will know that the one they see with their glorified bodily eyes is in fact God. Mere physical sight does not suffice to recognize the divinity of Christ. By participating in the divine essence, the saints receive the knowledge necessary to see Christ's true identity.[114] Second, a theophanic approach to the vision of God requires a fixed gaze on Christ's humanity. If Christ's body is the medium of the beatific vision, then the saints will enjoy that vision only as long as their bodily eyes are fixed on him. By contrast, Aquinas's understanding allows the blessed to move their eyes freely for two reasons. First, their intellect will be constantly united to the divine essence and so will not depend on physical sight. Second, even their bodily vision will recognize God active *in* and *through* the new creation, the bodies of the glorified saints, and, above all, the glorified body of Christ.[115] By contrast, the theophanic view favored by Boersma, and by John Owen before him, is limited and static.[116] To summarize the contrast with images from the book of Revelation, the approach favored by Boersma focuses all the attention of the saints on the Lamb, whereas in Aquinas's account the saints will see

110. The following is a summary of Gaine, "Thomas Aquinas, the Beatific Vision, and the Role of Christ," 161–63.

111. *Compendium* 1.2. Cf. Augustine, *Civ.* 22.30.

112. Gaine, "Thomas Aquinas, the Beatific Vision, and the Role of Christ," 163 (emphasis original).

113. Gaine, "Thomas Aquinas and John Owen on the Beatific Vision," 440–45. Gaine proposes these advantages vis-à-vis Owen, but they apply equally to Boersma.

114. Gaine, "Thomas Aquinas and John Owen on the Beatific Vision," 441–42.

115. Gaine, "Thomas Aquinas and John Owen on the Beatific Vision," 444–45.

116. One could also criticize this approach from another angle. Presuming more than a handful of people attain the beatific vision (as one should hope and as the church's calendar of saints suggests), how will they all gaze on Christ's glorified body at once? Will some be seated in the "nosebleed" section of the new heavens and the new earth? If so, will they be given eagle eyes so as to see Christ as more than a mere speck?

God (that is, the divine essence) *and* the Lamb (that is, Christ's risen flesh; see Rev. 22:1–5).[117]

Intellectual Vision and Bodily Resurrection

Aquinas offers a beautiful account of the beatific vision, drawn from Scripture and elucidated with philosophical insights. Knowing from experience that nothing earthly can satisfy our deepest longings, he shows that human desire is fulfilled only by the vision of God. In that vision, all the things we seek in this life, whether bodily goods or honor or fame, will be supplied superabundantly. Occasionally one might wish Thomas had been more careful with his language. He seems at times to imply (against his better instincts) that only disembodied souls can enjoy the beatific vision. As I argue above, however, these moments in his writings rub up against some of his more foundational principles. Considering his work as a whole, the beatific vision does not compete with bodily existence, but rather enhances it, enabling the saints to recognize Christ for who he is and to see God at work in the new heavens and the new earth.

Looking back at the preceding four chapters, a picture emerges of one important aspect of the Christian hope. Despite the many texts noting the danger of seeing God, taken as a whole, Scripture presents the face-to-face vision of God as an integral aspect of the human end, fulfilling the desires frequently expressed in the psalms and implicit in ancient Israel's cultic life. The ancient Israelites approached the temple to see God. In the end, the mediation of the temple will be removed as God and the Lamb take its place, both dwelling with God's people and becoming the object of direct vision (Rev. 21:22; 22:4). Irenaeus systematizes certain aspects of the biblical testimony, highlighting the trinitarian shape of the hope for the vision of God, both in its historical unfolding and in its orientation to the Father. In addition to presenting this vision as the fulfillment of the common human desire for perfect beauty and goodness, Augustine also offers important resources for integrating this vision with the hope for the resurrection. The resurrected eyes of the saints will in some way participate in the knowledge of God, whether by actually seeing the divine essence or by perceiving God's presence in the new heavens and the new earth more clearly. Finally, Aquinas complements the biblical expressions of the desire to see God with a philosophical analysis of why that vision is essential. Moreover, despite the occasional suggestion that only the disembodied soul can enjoy the beatific vision, he nevertheless ultimately affirms the importance of seeing the risen Christ with resurrected

117. Of course, for Aquinas (and for the Christian tradition) the Lamb is also God. Here I use the term to refer to Christ's humanity.

bodily eyes as part of the beatitude of the saints. As with Augustine's account of the resurrected eyes of the saints, Thomas's account of the bodily vision of the risen Christ demands a transformation, one that flows from the beatific vision. Nevertheless, the fact that Aquinas describes the beatific vision as an incorporeal activity of the soul that satisfies every human desire raises the question of why human beings will need a body at all in the world to come. In the next part of this study, I will offer a similar analysis of the Christian hope for the resurrection of the body.

PART 3

"MORE PLEASING IN BEING MORE COMPLETE"

Reasons for the Resurrection

EIGHT

The Resurrection Hope in Scripture

Alongside the Western Christian tradition emphasizing the vision of God, one also finds countless expressions of hope for bodily resurrection. This is the dominant theme in the creeds, which repeatedly speak of the "resurrection of the flesh" or the "resurrection of the body," and also of the great thinkers of the tradition, including those considered in part 2 of this book.[1] This should come as no surprise, given that Irenaeus, Augustine, and Aquinas, each in his own way, argued vigorously for the goodness of the created order and criticized those who would deny the importance of the body for Christian salvation. In this and the following three chapters, I will explicate the importance of the resurrection hope in Scripture and in the thought of Irenaeus, Augustine, and Aquinas. Each of these three figures offers insightful interpretations of this hope as found in Scripture.

In the present chapter, I will paint with broad strokes the nature of that hope as presented in Scripture, as well as the reasons for it. As with the desire for the beatific vision, hope for the resurrection has OT roots. I will thus begin by discussing how some of these texts either foreshadow or express a robust belief in a future resurrection through the categories of victory over death, bodily continuity, and restoration of relationships.[2] Next, I will offer a brief interpretation of the resurrection appearances of Jesus in the Gospels, reading them through these same themes. I will then consider two aspects of Paul's understanding of resurrection hope: the paradigmatic nature of Christ's passion, death, and resurrection, and the characteristics of the resurrected

1. For a list of ancient, medieval, and Reformation creeds that emphasize the resurrection, see Ware, "Paul's Understanding of the Resurrection," 811n8.

2. As discussed below, I borrow these categories from Harris, *Refiguring Resurrection*, 88–108.

body. Finally, I will discuss the way the Gospel of John links hope for the resurrection with the Eucharist. A clear picture will emerge from considering these texts. The Scriptures ground the hope for resurrection in at least two aspects of human nature: First, human beings are composites, consisting of a "due mingling of flesh and soul," to borrow a phrase from Irenaeus.[3] Second, human beings are social creatures. Resurrection is not only about individual hope, but also about the reunion of the redeemed with their loved ones.

The treatment of resurrection in this chapter is in no way meant to be exhaustive. Rather, my goal is to explore some of the primary elements of this normative Christian hope. The selection of texts is motivated by the themes that will feature prominently in the following three chapters on Irenaeus, Augustine, and Aquinas.

Prefiguring Resurrection

It may be true that the explicit articulation of hope for the resurrection did not arise until a few centuries before the time of the NT. This does not mean, however, that this hope arose out of nowhere.[4] Throughout the OT there are scattered hints of this desire for the defeat of death.[5]

Most scholars hold that belief in the resurrection developed late in Israel's history, arising sometime in the second century BC.[6] Daniel 12:2 is considered by many to be the first clear reference to a hope for bodily resurrection; more explicit (and graphic) expressions of this hope appear in the Maccabean literature.[7] One thinks, for example, of the moving story of the woman and her seven sons put to death by Antiochus Epiphanes. Faced with the ultimatum of eating unclean food or death, each of the brothers, as well as their mother, chooses to die rather than disobey God's commandments. Three of the brothers affirm their confidence that the Lord, the "King of the universe" (2 Macc. 7:9), will reward them for their fidelity by giving them back their bodies in the resurrection (7:9, 11, 14). The mother, likewise, urges her sons to persevere in the face of persecution by appealing to this expectation of resurrection:

3. Irenaeus, *Haer.* 4, Pref.4 (my translation).

4. Levenson (*Resurrection and the Restoration of Israel*, passim) makes a strong case that hope for the resurrection is rooted in the ancient Israelite understanding of God's power over life and death.

5. For much of what follows, I am indebted to Harris, *Refiguring Resurrection*.

6. For a provocative but nuanced challenge to this near consensus, see Levenson, *Resurrection and the Restoration of Israel*.

7. For a detailed interpretation of Dan. 12:1–3 read in light of earlier biblical antecedents as well as contemporary or near contemporary texts, see Levenson, *Resurrection and the Restoration of Israel*, 181–200. As important as this text is, in the first part of this chapter I will focus primarily on prefigurations of resurrection to underscore their contribution to an understanding of the resurrection hope.

"I do not know how you came into being in my womb. It was not I who gave you life and breath nor I who set in order the elements within each of you. Therefore the Creator of the world, who shaped the beginning of humankind and devised the origin of all things, in his mercy gives life and breath back to you again, since you now forget yourselves for the sake of his laws" (7:22–23). An important aspect of this scene is the repeated appeal to God's creative power, which grounds the mother's hope to receive her sons back (7:27–29).[8] Equally important is the desire for *bodily* resurrection. Resurrection here does not mean an expectation of an ongoing disembodied existence after death. The Maccabean martyrs trust that God will give them back their hands and their tongues in a new body as a reward for their faithfulness to his law.[9]

First and Second Kings recount three instances of people rising from the dead. For various reasons, many modern scholars have dismissed the significance of these accounts for understanding the resurrection.[10] Some reject the stories as mere legends. Influenced by naturalism, they deny the possibility of the dead coming to life again. But even some who affirm the resurrection of Christ reject the significance of these events (as well as the stories of raising the dead in the Gospels and Acts) because the recipients of these miracles all died again. For these scholars, Jesus's resurrection is utterly unique, without analogy. Steven Harris makes a strong case for reading these stories as prefigurations (or "post-figurations" in the case of the miracles in Acts) of Christ's resurrection. While it is true that the people who were raised from the dead would die again, there are enough similarities between these stories and Christ's own resurrection that they can illuminate the Christian hope.

The three accounts of raising the dead in the OT all appear in 1–2 Kings as part of the Elijah-Elisha cycle. As Harris notes, two of these accounts appear toward the beginning and toward the end of this cycle, forming bookends around the cycle and underscoring the power of the God of Israel over life and death.[11] Even though these miracles were only temporary, they nevertheless attest to God's ability to bring life out of death. Beyond this simple fact, other features of these stories shed important light on the significance

8. This connection between God's creative power and resurrection also appears in the NT. See, e.g., Rom. 4:17.

9. Thiessen (*A Jewish Paul*, 138–39) acknowledges that this resurrection is bodily but entertains the idea that the resurrection might not involve flesh and blood, suggesting that perhaps we should not take the brothers' language in an overly literal fashion. Would they, he asks, get back exactly the tongues and hands that Antiochus had cut off? Levenson's comment (*Resurrection and the Restoration of Israel*, 106–7) regarding Daniel applies equally to the Maccabean literature: "Since this new life is thought to follow upon resurrection, it perforce entails embodiedness: people come back in the flesh. But the flesh in which they come back is necessarily different from the kind they knew in their mortal life, for now they have become immune to death and the bodily infirmities associated with it."

10. This paragraph summarizes Harris, *Refiguring Resurrection*, 3–8.

11. Harris, *Refiguring Resurrection*, 43.

of resurrection, both Christ's resurrection and the Christian hope for a future resurrection.

The first account takes place shortly after the mysterious appearance of Elijah in 1 Kings 17.[12] As is often noted, Elijah arrives on the scene without introduction. His first words refer to the God of Israel as the one who "lives" (1 Kings 17:1), implicitly affirming his power over life. Soon after his introduction, Elijah is sent to a widow in Zarephath, where he steps into a fraught situation. When he asks the widow to give him something to eat, she tells him that she is nearly out of food. Using a similar expression to Elijah's first words, she says, "*As the Lord your God lives*, I have nothing baked, only a handful of meal in a jar and a little oil in a jug; I am now gathering a couple of sticks so that I may go home and prepare it for myself and my son, *that we may eat it and die*" (17:12). The contrast between the living God of Israel and the inevitability of death is strong, but Elijah reassures the widow that the Lord will provide for her (17:13–14). Not long afterward, however, despite the provision of food, the woman's son falls sick and dies (17:17). In response to the woman's distress, Elijah takes her son to an upper room and prays for him. The living God of Israel hears Elijah's prayer and restores the child to life (17:21–23).

As is often the case in the Elijah-Elisha cycle, Elijah's successor, Elisha, performs a similar miracle. Having received a double portion of Elijah's spirit, Elisha's miracle takes on greater proportions.[13] Whereas Elijah was sent to a woman who already had a child, Elisha encounters a childless Shunammite woman. As a reward for her generosity to the prophet, he promises the woman a child, and the promise is fulfilled (2 Kings 4:12–17). Once again, though, after the child has grown, the powers of death invade, killing the child. The woman sends for Elisha, who after a failed attempt to raise the child from a distance (4:29), takes the child to a private room, prays to the Lord, and stretches himself out over the child. In answer to his prayer, the child comes back to life (4:33–35). Elisha returns the child to his mother, who bows to the ground in thanksgiving.[14] Significantly, one of the results of this miracle is that "the flesh of the child became warm" (4:34), as both the Hebrew and the Greek texts note.[15] This raising of the dead very much involves the flesh.

12. The following three paragraphs rely on Harris, *Refiguring Resurrection*, 43–51.

13. For a brilliant reading of this story that points out parallels between the Shunammite woman and the story of Abraham and Isaac as well as the theme of God's victory over death throughout the surrounding context, see Levenson, *Resurrection and the Restoration of Israel*, 124–31. See also Harris, *Refiguring Resurrection*, 46–49.

14. Levenson (*Resurrection and the Restoration of Israel*, 132) draws the following conclusion from this story: "Long before the apocalyptic framework came into existence, the resurrection of the dead was thought possible—not according to nature, of course, but through the miraculous intervention of the living God."

15. I owe this point to Cook, *The Enspirited Body in 1 Corinthians 15*, 35, though he cites only the Greek. The Hebrew reads *wayyaham besar hayyaled*; the Greek reads *kai diethermathē hē sarx tou paidariou*.

The final resurrection story in the Elijah-Elisha cycle has a less personal dimension to it and is described in the brief span of two verses (2 Kings 13:20–21). The account is astonishing, not least because the miracle is brought about by simple contact with the bones of Elisha. Some see in this second instance of a resurrection the "double portion" that Elisha asked of Elijah (2 Kings 2:9).[16] One might also see the double portion in the fact that Elisha's mediation of miracles continues even after his death. The story makes explicit what the earlier stories of resurrection implicitly affirm: The power over life and death belongs to the Lord, not to his prophets, who serve as intermediaries. This strange miracle concludes the Elijah-Elisha cycle, enclosing this section with bookends that highlight the victory of life over death.

Much could be said about these three miracles and their significance for the Christian hope, even if they only point forward to that hope in a figural way. Harris draws out five important elements in these stories, of which I would like to highlight three.[17] First, each of these stories exemplifies the Lord's victory over death. The God of Israel, frequently designated as "the living God" in the OT, has power over life and death.[18] He can sustain life, as he does for the widow of Zarephath and her son, and he can restore life, as he does for the widow and for the Shunammite woman, as well as the anonymous man in 2 Kings 13. Second, this victory over death involves bodily continuity. Life is restored to the corpses of the dead, who return to a bodily existence. Resurrection is not simply about a continued spiritual existence after death. Finally, and closely related to the first two points, this victory over death through bodily existence leads to restored relationships: Mothers receive back their sons (cf. Heb. 11:35; 2 Macc. 7:29). Resurrection thus has a social dimension.[19] One of the great tragedies of death is that it separates us from our loved ones. Though our relationships are not merely bodily, the bodily dimension of our relationships is important.

Before turning to the NT, we should note that Harris's categories also illuminate the later, clearer OT expressions of hope for an eschatological

16. Harris, *Refiguring Resurrection*, 50n29, citing Theodoret of Cyrrhus, *Quaestiones in libros Regum* 777.

17. Harris, *Refiguring Resurrection*, 88–108. Harris bases his conclusion not only on these stories, but also on the accounts of Jesus raising the dead during his earthly ministry. For the sake of space, I have limited myself to the stories of Elijah and Elisha, because they illustrate the most salient points. For a briefer discussion of how Jesus's acts of raising the dead anticipate the general resurrection, see Matera, *Resurrection*, 22–28.

18. In addition to the references to "the living God" in 1–2 Kings, see, e.g., Deut. 5:26; Josh. 3:10; 1 Sam. 17:26, 36; Pss. 42:2; 84:2; Isa. 37:4, 17; Jer. 10:10; 23:36.

19. Levenson (*Resurrection and the Restoration of Israel*, 108–22) argues that the social character of ancient Israelite self-understanding played an important role in the development of resurrection hope.

resurrection.[20] Daniel 12 underscores God's power over life and death, as it looks forward to him awakening "many of those who sleep in the dust of the earth" (Dan. 12:2). Moreover, Daniel's vision implicitly expects some kind of bodily continuity, as it refers to the corpses of those in the earth who will one day arise. The story of the Maccabean martyrs reflects all three elements of the stories in the Elijah-Elisha cycle. God's power over life and death, as well as belief in bodily continuity, feature prominently throughout the passage (2 Macc. 7:9, 11, 14, 22–23, 27–29). Additionally, the mother's confidence in God's power of life over death goes hand in hand with her hope to be reunited with her sons: "Accept death, *so that in God's mercy I may get you back along with your brothers*" (7:29b). The social dimension of resurrection figures just as strongly in expressions of eschatological hope as it does in the temporary raisings of the dead in the Elijah-Elisha cycle.

Each of these three dimensions—God's victory over death, bodily continuity, and the restoration of relationships—also features in the NT interpretation of resurrection, both in the Gospel accounts of Christ's own resurrection and in Paul's discussions of the Christian hope. The resurrection of Jesus, however, also introduces elements of transformation and permanence, building on the hope implicit in the stories of Elijah and Elisha.

"Why Do You Seek the One Who Lives Among the Dead?"

At the heart of the NT lies the proclamation that Jesus Christ is risen from the dead, which stands as the basis of the Christian hope. Paul refers to the risen Christ as "the first fruits of those who have fallen asleep" (1 Cor. 15:20, NRSVue marginal note), and in 1 Peter we read, "By his great mercy he has given us a new birth into a living hope through the resurrection of Jesus Christ from the dead" (1 Pet. 1:3). Given the centrality of this event, it behooves us to consider the Gospel accounts of the events that followed Jesus's crucifixion. Much could be said about these passages. Harris's categories of victory over death, restoration of relationships, and bodily continuity provide a fruitful lens through which to interpret these texts and their implications for the Christian hope.[21]

None of the evangelists explicitly uses the language of "victory" in their accounts of the resurrection. Nevertheless, the notion of conquering death is

20. Strangely, Harris does not make this connection. Second Maccabees 7 does not even appear in any of the book's indices.

21. Although I have taken these categories from Harris, I articulate the way the Gospels exemplify them differently in a few ways. For his application of these (and other) categories to Jesus's resurrection, see *Refiguring Resurrection*, 88–108. For a brief interpretation of the resurrection narratives in each of the four Gospels, see Matera, *Resurrection*, 36–63. For a lengthier discussion in much more detail, see N. T. Wright, *The Resurrection of the Son of God*, 616–82.

implicit. For all the differences among the four Gospels regarding the events that followed Jesus's crucifixion, all agree that Jesus was no longer among the dead (Matt. 28:6–7; Mark 16:6; Luke 24:5–6; John 20:1–18). Additionally, although none of them explicitly says, as Paul writes in Romans, that "death no longer has dominion over him" (Rom. 6:9b), Matthew, Luke, and John all at least implicitly affirm that Christ's resurrection is more than temporary. In Matthew, Jesus tells the disciples, "I am with you always, to the end of the age" (Matt. 28:20). Luke recounts Jesus's bodily ascension into heaven (Luke 24:50–51; Acts 1:9) and affirms his ongoing activity through the church (Acts 1:1). In John, Jesus points forward to his ascension (John 20:17). The longer ending of Mark also refers to Jesus's continuing work in and through the disciples (Mark 16:20). Like the raisings in the Elijah-Elisha cycle, Jesus's resurrection is a victory over death; his resurrection, however, has a permanence that distinguishes it from the miracles of Elijah and Elisha.[22] For this reason the NT affirms that Christ's victory is definitive.

Christ's resurrection also entails a restoration of relationships. This can be seen in all four Gospel accounts. In both Matthew and Mark, the women at the tomb are instructed to tell the disciples that Jesus will meet them in Galilee (Matt. 28:7, 10; Mark 16:7), and Matthew describes this encounter (Matt. 28:16–20). The longer ending of Mark (Mark 16:9–20) includes a pastiche of meetings between the risen Jesus and the disciples, most of which have parallels in the other Gospels. Luke recounts meetings between the risen Lord and two disciples on the road to Emmaus (Luke 24:13–35), as well as an encounter with a larger group of disciples in Jerusalem (24:36–49). But the Gospel that most clearly illustrates the restoration of relationships is John. In the garden when Jesus addresses Mary by name, she recognizes him, addressing him as "Rabbouni" (John 20:16). The risen Jesus's first words to the disciples in the locked room are "Peace be with you" (20:19, 21; see also Luke 24:36). The final chapter of John depicts an even more poignant rapprochement in the famous interaction between Jesus and Peter. There Jesus offers Peter, who had denied him three times, an opportunity to reaffirm his love for Jesus three times (John 21:15–19).

This restoration of relationships does not mean that things simply continue as they were before, however. There are a few indications that these relationships have been transformed. First, as already noted, the references to the ascension in both Luke and John suggest that things will not simply return to the way they used to be. Jesus will ascend to the Father, putting an end to his ordinary, day-to-day interactions with the disciples. Second, there is the promise of the Spirit, anticipated in Luke (24:49) and proleptically

22. As Harris (*Refiguring Resurrection*, 107) puts it, "This is the *novum*, the difference so striking that all other resurrections pale in comparison and seem to require a different word to separate them from this lordly rising."

bestowed in John (20:22–23). Although Jesus will no longer be with them in the ordinary bodily mode of presence, he continues to be with them (Matt. 28:20) through the gift of the Spirit (John 14:26; 15:26).[23]

All four Gospels also imply bodily continuity in a number of ways. The affirmation of the empty tomb implies that the resurrection concerns Jesus's body.[24] This continuity appears most clearly in Luke and John, both of which refer to the marks of the crucifixion on Jesus's body as evidence that the disciples were encountering the same Lord in the flesh (Luke 24:40; John 20:27). The resurrection does not, however, mean a simple return to a mortal body, as in the case of the miracles worked by Elijah and Elisha. There remains a mystery surrounding the risen Christ: The disciples do not always recognize him immediately (Luke 24:16; John 20:14; 21:4).[25] Moreover, Jesus does astonishing things after the resurrection, simply appearing in the midst of the disciples (Luke 24:36), unhindered by locked doors (John 20:19), and disappearing at will (Luke 24:31).[26]

These developments in the expression of God's victory over death, the restoration of relationships, and bodily continuity in Jesus's resurrection show the fullness of the reality to which the resurrection stories of Elijah and Elisha point. They also carry over into many NT expressions of the Christian hope, especially the writings of Paul, to which we now turn.

"Conformed to His Glorious Body"

According to the Acts of the Apostles, when Paul visited Athens, some of the locals took him to be proclaiming foreign divinities "because he was preaching the good news about Jesus and the resurrection" (Acts 17:18).[27] Paul's letters confirm this picture—not that the apostle preached foreign divinities, but that he talked incessantly about the resurrection. Of the thirteen letters attributed

23. Harris (*Refiguring Resurrection*, 103–4) also rightly notes that these restored relationships are marked by Jesus's lordship.

24. Harris, *Refiguring Resurrection*, 94. Harris recognizes that the empty tomb is necessary but not sufficient to establish the resurrection. If Jesus's body remained in the tomb, then there would be no bodily continuity in the appearances to the disciples, but from the beginning there have been other explanations for the empty tomb (see, e.g., Matt. 28:11–15). For a thoughtful analysis of the emptiness of the tomb, taking into account the nature of tombs in first-century Jerusalem, see Goodacre, "How Empty Was the Tomb?"

25. It is worth noting, however, that Luke writes, "But their eyes were kept from recognizing him" (Luke 24:16). This lack of recognition may not stem solely from the transformation of the resurrected body.

26. Again, we should perhaps not press the point too much, as the Gospels also record Jesus doing astonishing things prior to his death and resurrection, such as walking on water (Matt. 14:22–33; Mark 6:45–52; John 6:16–21).

27. For the rest of this chapter, unless otherwise noted, translations of the NT are my own.

to Paul in the NT, only four lack resurrection terminology.[28] Most of them refer at least once to the resurrection. Like the Gospels, Paul's expressions of hope embody the themes we have seen in the OT accounts of raising the dead: He interprets resurrection as the victory of life over death (e.g., 1 Cor. 15:55–57); resurrection entails a restoration of relationships (e.g., 1 Thess. 4:17). The dominant note in Paul's thinking on the resurrection, however, is the transformation of the body, which entails bodily continuity, as well as discontinuity (e.g., Phil. 3:20–21). In this section and the next we will consider, first, the connection between Christ's resurrection and that of believers and, second, the characteristics of the resurrected body.

Throughout his letters Paul consistently associates Christ's resurrection with that of believers. Both the pattern and the form of the future resurrection imitate Christ's. Believers cannot simply bypass death—all must follow the pattern of death and resurrection.[29] With respect to form, the new body believers hope for will differ from the present body, though not in such a way as to remove all continuity.[30] In perhaps his earliest letter Paul comforts his audience by appealing to this hope in order to console the Christians at Thessalonica, who were grieving over the loss of loved ones. Toward the beginning of 1 Thessalonians 4, Paul points to Jesus's resurrection as the basis and the pattern of the Christian hope: "For if we believe that Jesus died and rose [*anestē*], so also, through Jesus, God will bring those who have fallen asleep together with him" (1 Thess. 4:14).[31] Paul uses the common euphemism "to fall asleep" for the dead and reminds the Thessalonians that those who sleep in Christ will one day awake.[32] Their having died will in no way put them at a disadvantage. On the contrary, Paul suggests that the dead will precede those who have not died when Christ returns. He further clarifies what it means for God to "bring those who have fallen asleep," using the same word that he uses to describe Christ's resurrection: "Because the Lord himself with a

28. None of the standard Greek "resurrection" words (*egeirō*, *anistēmi*, and *anastasis*) appear in 2 Thessalonians, Philemon, 1 Timothy, or Titus.

29. In both 1 Thess. 4 and 1 Cor. 15, Paul speaks as though he expects the Lord's return before he and at least some of his fellow believers taste death. This does not mean, however, that Christians can avoid death altogether, even if some may never experience the cessation of biological life. Every Christian participates in the dying and rising of Christ, first, through baptism (Rom. 6:1–11), and second, through a life that follows the pattern of Christ's death and resurrection (see, e.g., 2 Cor. 4).

30. See the following section.

31. Wanamaker (*The Epistles to the Thessalonians*, 168) suggests that this formulation may predate Paul, noting two unusual features of the verse. First, Paul's preferred word for resurrection is *egeirō*, appearing 37 times in his letters. Second, the lack of a title associated with the name "Jesus" is also unusual for Paul. See also Kim and Bruce, *1 & 2 Thessalonians*, 382.

32. Interestingly Paul never uses this euphemism with reference to Christ. See the discussion in Kim and Bruce, *1 & 2 Thessalonians*, 383. The expression likely has some connection to Dan. 12:2, which refers to "many of those who sleep in the dust of the earth."

shout of command, with the voice of the archangel and the trumpet of God, will descend from heaven and *the dead in Christ will rise* [*anastēsontai*] *first*" (4:16). As Christ rose from the dead, so the dead in Christ will one day rise in the same way. Again, this will result in restored relationships, both among the Thessalonians themselves and between them and the Lord. His return means that they will never again be separated from one another or from Christ (4:17).[33] The hope for the resurrection, then, is the ultimate consolation in the face of loss, in part because it includes reunion with those who have gone before us.

Although Paul exhorts the Thessalonians to persevere through their suffering, he does not explicitly connect the suffering of believers to Christ's passion, death, and resurrection as clearly as he does in other letters. This connection appears much more unambiguously in 2 Corinthians. One of the main themes of this letter is the paradoxical nature of glory. In 2 Corinthians 4, Paul develops the idea that believers follow the pattern of Christ's suffering in the hope of sharing in his glory. Paul's life is characterized by numerous trials, but those trials do not lead him to despair: "We are afflicted in every way but not crushed, perplexed but not driven to despair, persecuted but not forsaken, struck down but not destroyed" (2 Cor. 4:8–9 NRSVue).[34] Paul and his coworkers do not give in to despair because it is precisely through this suffering that they are united to Christ and the power of his resurrected life. He concludes this brief catalog of trials by summing up its significance, noting that he and his coworkers are "always carrying around in the body the dying of Jesus, so that the life of Jesus may also be made visible in our bodies" (4:10 NRSVue, modified).[35] Paul sees the sufferings of his life as paradoxical evidence that the life of Jesus is also at work in him. Thus, he goes on, "For while we live, we are always being given up to death for Jesus's sake, so that the life of Jesus may be made visible in our mortal flesh" (4:11). This dynamic has implications beyond the present life. As in 1 Thessalonians, Paul expresses the hope that one day he and his fellow believers will be raised from the dead: "knowing that the one who raised [*egeiras*] the Lord Jesus will also raise [*egerei*] us with Jesus and will present us with you" (4:14).[36] As God raised

33. Wanamaker (*The Epistles to the Thessalonians*, 176) suggests that one of Paul's primary goals "was to reassure the Thessalonians that their fellow Christians who had died would participate on equal terms with them in the salvation experience accompanying the parousia of the Lord." Cf. Kim and Bruce, *1 & 2 Thessalonians*, 409.

34. Barnett (*Second Corinthians*, 232–34) offers a good analysis of the increasing intensity of the sufferings Paul describes.

35. Barnett (*Second Corinthians*, 235) rightly interprets the "dying of Jesus" in v. 10 as a summary of the afflictions Paul lists in vv. 8–9.

36. This verse parallels 1 Cor. 6:14 and Rom. 8:11. N. T. Wright astutely notes (*The Resurrection of the Son of God*, 364), "The close parallel between [2 Cor. 4:14] and passages such as 1 Corinthians 6.14, not to mention 1 Corinthians 15 in its entirety and such other clear statements as Romans 8.11, should have given pause to those scholars who have tried to assert that

Jesus from the dead, so he will raise those united to him. This will involve both victory over death and restoration of relationships (God "will present us *with you*"). Once again, resurrection has a social dimension.

Paul appeals to the pattern of Christ's own death and resurrection once more in Romans 8. The chapter opens with a reminder of the freedom that believers have received: "For the law of the Spirit of life in Christ Jesus has freed you from the law of sin and death" (Rom. 8:2). Paul then returns to the conflict between the "flesh" and the Spirit (8:3–8).[37] By "flesh" Paul does not mean the physical component of the human being, at least not in every instance.[38] Rather, as is often the case in Paul's letters, "flesh" refers to the weakened human condition.[39] Those "in the flesh" set their minds on earthly things, which leads ultimately to death (8:5–6). "But," Paul reminds his audience, "you are not in the flesh but in the Spirit" (8:9a).[40] Being in the Spirit is another key component of the hope for the resurrection; because God raised Christ by the Spirit, those who are in the Spirit can expect a similar end: "Now if the Spirit of the one who raised Jesus from the dead dwells in you, the one who raised Christ from the dead will give life to your mortal bodies through his Spirit dwelling in you" (8:11).[41] Once again, there is a correspondence between Christ's resurrection and the future resurrection of those who have "the Spirit of Christ" (8:9).

A little later, Paul describes this hope using the language of "glory" and underscoring the need to suffer with Christ in order to attain eternal life. Expanding on the significance of having the Spirit, Paul notes that those who receive the Spirit have become children of God (Rom. 8:14), literally "sons" (*huioi*) in the Son (*huios*).[42] Just as the Son entered into glory by passing through

---

Paul here has left behind the Jewish doctrine of bodily resurrection and substituted something else instead." Space precludes a discussion of 2 Cor. 4:17–5:5, which some have interpreted as a move away from resurrection hope on Paul's part. For a refutation of such readings, see again Wright, *The Resurrection of the Son of God*, 362–69. For a good analysis of the word *egeirō* and its implications for understanding resurrection, see Ware, "The Resurrection of Jesus," 492–97. The idea that God will "present" believers is a little odd. Barnett (*Second Corinthians*, 243) argues that God will present the risen saints to Christ for judgment. Cf. 2 Cor. 11:2.

37. This conflict is hinted at earlier in Rom. 7:5–6.

38. In Rom. 8:3 he speaks of Christ coming "in the likeness of sinful flesh," which does seem to mean corporeal existence. Fitzmyer (*Romans*, 485) writes, "What is affirmed [in 8:3] is the soteriological assumption of the human condition by the Son."

39. Cf. Gal. 5:16–23.

40. This verse confirms that Paul does not intend the phrase "the flesh" to refer to bodily existence—he does not imagine his audience as disembodied spirits. On the importance of the Spirit throughout Rom. 8, see Gaventa, *Romans*, 218–19, 228–29. On 218n112 she notes that 21 of the 34 instances of the word *pneuma* in Romans occur in chap. 8.

41. The connection between the Spirit and life has roots in Ezek. 37:14. See Fitzmyer, *Romans*, 491.

42. See Fitzmyer, *Romans*, 499: "Into the hearts of such 'sons' God has sent the Spirit of *his* son (Gal 4:6) to establish that intimate relationship with himself" (emphasis original). See also Gaventa, *Romans*, 231.

suffering and death, so also God's adopted sons and daughters (8:15) must be conformed to the Son in both suffering and glory: "And if [we are] children, then also heirs, heirs of God and fellow heirs with Christ, provided we suffer with him so that we might also be glorified with him" (8:17). Christ's path is the path of all those who belong to him: Suffering with him leads to glory.[43]

The letter to the Philippians serves as a good transition to the next theme, because it brings together two aspects of Paul's understanding of the resurrection: the pattern of dying and rising and the expectation of a glorified body. In both these aspects, Christ is the paradigm. Participation in Christ's resurrection demands a share in his sufferings. Having cataloged the various things he has renounced or at least relativized for the sake of Christ, Paul gives the reason for his new priorities: "in order to know him [Christ], both the power of his resurrection and a participation in his sufferings, being conformed to his death, if somehow I might attain to the resurrection from the dead" (Phil. 3:10–11).[44] This resurrection reflects Christ's own not only in that it follows suffering and death, but also in that it will result in a new, transformed body upon Christ's return.[45] Toward the end of the chapter Paul writes, "For our citizenship is in heaven, from which we also eagerly await the savior, the Lord Jesus Christ, who will transform our lowly body to be conformed to his glorious body according to the power that enables him to subject all things to himself" (3:20–21). Resurrection hope does not mean returning to the weak, frail bodies of this life. It means being transformed into a glorious body.[46] Paul's most extensive discussion of this new body appears in 1 Corinthians 15.[47]

The "Spiritual" Body

For much of the Christian tradition, 1 Corinthians 15 has served as the basis for reflection on the characteristics of the glorified, resurrected body.[48] By

43. See the discussion in Fitzmyer, *Romans*, 502. As Gaventa (*Romans*, 233) notes, Rom. 8:17 sets up the discussion of suffering that follows in 8:18–30.

44. On the meaning of the phrase "the power of his resurrection," as well as the relationship between this power and Paul's share in Christ's suffering, see Bockmuehl, *Philippians*, 214–16. For the translation "both-and," see Fee, *Philippians*, 328–29.

45. Bockmuehl (*Philippians*, 216) suggests that being conformed to Christ's death should be interpreted in light of the obedience Christ displayed in "the form of a slave" (Phil. 2:7). See also Fee, *Philippians*, 334.

46. Bockmuehl (*Philippians*, 236) rightly notes, "The resurrection will not be a transition to a disembodied state, but a 'change' (1 Cor. 15.52), a 'transfiguring' of the whole person."

47. On the relationship between Phil. 3:21 and 1 Cor. 15, see Fee, *Philippians*, 381–84.

48. Augustine speaks of the resurrected body having beauty, incorruptibility, and ease of motion (*Civ*. 22.30). Thomas Aquinas ascribes to the resurrected body subtlety, agility, impassibility, and clarity (*Compendium* 1.168). The most recent and extensive treatments of 1 Cor. 15 as of this writing are Ware, *The Final Triumph of God*, and Cook, *The Enspirited Body in 1 Corinthians 15*. Both scholars conclude that the *sōma pneumatikon* refers to a transformed

contrast, many modern scholars have used this chapter to argue either that Paul denies a physical, bodily resurrection or that Paul envisions bodies made of spiritual stuff.[49] These interpreters typically point to two aspects of the chapter in support of such readings: Paul's language of a "spiritual body" (*sōma pneumatikon*, 1 Cor. 15:44) and his statement "Flesh and blood cannot inherit the kingdom of God" (15:50).[50] Taken in isolation, one can see how these phrases might lead to an understanding of the resurrection as something other than fleshly. Reading the phrases in context, however—both the context of the chapter and the context of the letter as a whole—warrants an interpretation of the resurrection as a fleshly reality.

The whole chapter merits a close reading, but I will focus on 1 Corinthians 15:35–55, which deals primarily with the nature of the resurrected body. Paul begins by posing two closely related questions, most likely questions the Corinthians had raised: "But someone will say, 'How are the dead raised? And with what sort of body do they come?'" (15:35). The bulk of Paul's response (vv. 36–49) addresses the second question, the nature of the resurrected body. It is easy to see how this question may have arisen. Although there are delightful aspects of bodily existence, bodies can also be burdensome (cf. 2 Cor. 5:4; Wis. 9:15).[51] If resurrection meant nothing more than a return to the corruptible existence that we presently experience, then escape from the body would be a better hope. One of the primary points of Paul's argument is to stress that the Christian hope involves a change that will somehow mysteriously render our weak, fleshly bodies glorious and incorruptible.

Paul begins his response by introducing an analogy that governs his explanation of the relationship between the present body and the resurrected body: "Fool! What you sow is not made alive unless it dies" (1 Cor. 15:36). Developing the image of sowing, Paul underscores that the present body is not identical *simpliciter* with the resurrected body for which Christians hope. Rather, the present body corresponds to a seed planted in the ground: "And as for what

---

and glorified body of flesh and blood. On the tradition of the *dotes* (i.e., the new characteristics) of the resurrected body, see Bynum, *The Resurrection of the Body in Western Christianity*, 131–32, 235–36.

49. In the modern period, such readings go at least as far back as Pfleiderer, *Paulinism*, 1:260–61 (though his interpretation also draws on 2 Cor. 5, recognizing that 1 Cor. 15 can be read in a way that involves some continuity between the present body and the resurrected body); among the many recent defenders of this position, see Fredriksen, "Vile Bodies"; D. Martin, *The Corinthian Body*, 108–32; Engberg-Pedersen, *Cosmology and Self in the Apostle Paul*, 8–38; Thiessen, *A Jewish Paul*, 139–47. For additional sources, see Ware, *The Final Triumph of God*, 5n14.

50. See D. Martin, *The Corinthian Body*, 126–28; Engberg-Pedersen, *Cosmology and Self in the Apostle Paul*, 27–28, 32–35; Fredriksen, "Vile Bodies." Fredriksen cites 1 Cor. 15:50 in the opening paragraph of her essay but offers no exegesis of the verse.

51. For a good description of the burden of the present body, alongside an expression of hope for a glorified body, see Augustine, *Enarrat. Ps.* 62.6, on which see pp. 186–88 below.

you sow, you do not sow the body that is to be but a bare seed, perhaps of wheat or of some other grain" (15:37 NRSVue).[52] With this introduction, Paul gives a negative answer to the second question raised in verse 35 ("With what kind of body do [the dead] come?"). The dead will not return to the same existence that we presently experience—the present body in all its frailty is "sown" in burial like a seed (15:42), but it will be raised in power, glory, and incorruptibility (15:42–43).[53] In the following verse, Paul offers an answer to the first question ("How are the dead raised?"): "But God gives it a body as he has chosen and to each kind of seed its own body" (15:38 NRSVue). Significantly, Paul follows this assertion that God gives each seed its own body with a discussion of different kinds of flesh. Whatever difficulties Paul's statement about "flesh and blood" not inheriting the kingdom in verse 50 may raise for a fleshly resurrection, here Paul closely associates resurrected bodies with flesh. Significantly, earlier he affirms that there is a certain kind of flesh for human beings (v. 39).[54] Flesh, it would seem, is a constitutive part of what it means to be human.[55] What, then, will the resurrected body look like?

Paul begins to speak of the transformation of the body in 15:42, returning to the image of sowing. In the first occurrences of this verb in the chapter (15:36–37), the implicit object of the sowing is the seed, an image for the present body. When Paul takes up this verb again, this time in the passive voice, it seems most natural to take the subject of the verb to be the present body.[56] As already noted, when he says that what is sown is not the body that is to come (v. 37), the image suggests that it is the present, corruptible body that is sown when buried in the ground after death. Here, then, the apostle begins to elaborate on the transformation that the body will experience at the resurrection, and he does so with four sets of contrasts: "So also the resurrection of the dead. It [i.e., the present body] is sown in corruption, it is raised in incorruptibility; it is sown in dishonor, it is raised in glory; it is sown in weakness, it is raised in power; it is sown a soulish body, it is raised a Spiritual body" (15:42–44).[57] The

52. For a similar use of this image in the Gospel tradition, see John 12:24.

53. As Ware (*The Final Triumph of God*, 283) puts it, "Like the seed, the present body will be resurrected to a radically new transformed existence."

54. For a technical discussion of flesh in Second Temple Jewish and Greco-Roman sources, see Cook, *The Enspirited Body in 1 Corinthians 15*, 30–36.

55. See also the discussion of Ware, *The Final Triumph of God*, 289–93, who argues that Paul's allusions to Gen. 1 and Ps. 8 imply both the goodness of human flesh (291) and that flesh is essential to human nature and will be constitutive of the resurrected body, albeit with important modifications (292–93): "This flesh of the risen saints will be the same substance as their present bodies but with new and different qualities. In the resurrection, the flesh of the faithful will be *glorified*" (emphasis original).

56. See Ware, *The Final Triumph of God*, 313.

57. The NRSVue and other translations obscure things without warrant, rendering the first set of contrasts, "What is sown is perishable, what is raised is imperishable" (1 Cor. 15:42b). This translation could imply that Paul is talking about two different things: One thing is sown

import of the first three pairs is fairly clear to see. Each points to an improvement to come with the resurrection. Whereas the present body is corruptible, dishonorable, and weak, the resurrected body will be incorruptible, glorious, and powerful.[58] The final pair, which I have rendered "soulish" and "Spiritual," has been the subject of much debate in modern scholarship.

Some have taken this reference to a "spiritual body" to suggest that Paul does not understand the resurrection as a physical phenomenon.[59] Others take Paul to be referring to a body that is made of spirit (as opposed to flesh).[60] There are at least three problems with these readings. First, if the adjective *pneumatikos* were meant to contrast a body made of spirit with a body made of flesh, then one would have expected Paul to use the adjective *sarkikos* ("fleshly" or "fleshy") in the first member of the pair.[61] He does not. Paul describes the first body as *psychikos* ("soulish"). There is no warrant for rendering the first phrase "a physical body," much less a "fleshly" body. Second, and relatedly, if Paul meant by *pneumatikos* a body composed of spirit, then the first half of the pair would have to refer to a body composed of soul.[62] This would mean that neither the body that is sown (that is, the present body) nor the body that is raised has flesh, which is absurd on the face of it, especially in light of Paul's discussion of the different kinds of flesh in verse 39.[63] Finally, both adjectives (*pneumatikos* and *psychikos*) appear elsewhere in 1 Corinthians, and in neither case do the adjectives mean, respectively, "spiritual" and "physical" as some modern interpreters take them in 1 Corinthians 15:44.[64]

---

perishable, a different thing is raised imperishable. The Greek, however, has no relative pronoun, but rather simply two finite verb forms. In this regard, the NABRE offers a better translation ("it is sown corruptible, it is raised incorruptible"). For a discussion of the grammar, see again Ware, "Paul's Understanding of the Resurrection," 822–24, and *The Final Triumph of God*, 310–14. I borrow the rendering of the adjective *pneumatikos* as "Spiritual" (with a capital *S*) from Michael Gorman for reasons that will become clear. See Gorman, *1 Corinthians*, 20n25.

58. Cook (*The Enspirited Body in 1 Corinthians 15*, 103–12) offers a detailed discussion of each of these characteristics.

59. Scroggs (*The Last Adam*, 66), for example, suggests that the term *sōma pneumatikon* "denotes a noncorporeal existence." D. Martin (*The Corinthian Body*, 128) rightly calls the notion of a nonbodily body an "impossibility." (I would call it nonsensical.) Some translations (e.g., NRSV, RSV) contribute to this confusion by rendering the first phrase "physical body."

60. D. Martin, *The Corinthian Body*, 125–28; Engberg-Pedersen, *Cosmology and Self in the Apostle Paul*, 27–28; Thiessen, *A Jewish Paul*, 146–47. These scholars interpret Paul's understanding of the resurrected body as consisting of matter, but of ethereal matter rather than fleshly matter. As Thiessen colloquially puts it (147), "The. Best. Matter. Ever." For a critique of this interpretation, see Ware, *The Final Triumph of God*, 324–26. See also the discussion of Augustine on pp. 193–98 below.

61. Ware, *The Final Triumph of God*, 324–25.

62. Ware, *The Final Triumph of God*, 325.

63. Ware, *The Final Triumph of God*, 325.

64. For much of what follows I draw on Ware, "Paul's Understanding of the Resurrection," 833. See also the detailed discussion in Cook, *The Enspirited Body in 1 Corinthians 15*, 183–242.

The two adjectives first appear together in 1 Corinthians 2, in the context of one of Paul's discussions of wisdom and the discernment of spiritual things. Here the adjective "Spiritual" (*pneumatikos*) is closely related to the noun "Spirit" (*pneuma*), which in context refers consistently to the Spirit of God (1 Cor. 2:11). Believers understand the things God reveals only because he has imparted to them the Spirit (2:10–13). Toward the end of the chapter, Paul introduces the contrast between the "soulish" (*psychikos*) human being and the "Spiritual" (*pneumatikos*) human being (2:14–16). In both cases (in contrast to 1 Cor. 15), Paul is speaking about people living in the present age. Those whose lives are governed only by the soul (the *psychikos* human being) can neither receive nor understand the things of the Spirit, because those things can be understood only by the same Spirit (2:14). By contrast, those who have received the Spirit of God (2:12) can be called "Spiritual" (*pneumatikos*) and understand the things of the Spirit.[65] This does not mean that they are made of spiritual matter, but rather that they are empowered by the Spirit of God.[66]

The word *psychikos* does not appear again in 1 Corinthians until chapter 15, but the word *pneumatikos* appears several times, and in none of those instances does it plausibly refer to something made of spiritual matter. In chapter 3, Paul contrasts "Spiritual" people with "fleshly" (*sarkinoi/sarkikoi*) people: "And so, brothers and sisters, I could not speak to you as Spiritual ones [*pneumatikois*], but rather as fleshly [*sarkinois*], as infants in Christ" (1 Cor. 3:1 NRSVue, modified). By "fleshly" Paul does not mean people made of flesh and bone. Rather, as is often the case in Paul's letters, to live "according to the flesh" means to live under the sinful human condition (see, e.g., Gal. 5:19–21). The Corinthians are not behaving as people guided and empowered by the Spirit, but rather as people whose minds are set on the flesh.

Toward the beginning of 1 Corinthians 10, Paul again uses the adjective *pneumatikos* three times in his retelling of a portion of the exodus story, referring to "spiritual food," "spiritual drink," and a "spiritual rock" (1 Cor. 10:3–4). It seems highly unlikely that Paul is reinterpreting these things as made of spiritual matter. Rather, he seems to suggest that earthly, material things were given power by the Spirit.[67] If anything, Paul's use of *pneumatikos*

65. The fact that Paul can speak of people in the present life as *pneumatikos* suggests that the Spirit does not replace the soul within the human person but rather supplements and strengthens the person. See Ware, *The Final Triumph of God*, 329–30.

66. As Ware (*The Final Triumph of God*, 328) puts it, "In this passage [2:11–16] the contrast is clearly not between a person composed of flesh and blood and a person composed of spirit matter or corporeal *pneuma*!"

67. Again, Ware ("Paul's Understanding of the Resurrection," 833) puts it well: Paul is speaking of "edible manna and water (10:3–4), and a very palpable rock (10:4)." Cf. Cook, *The Enspirited Body in 1 Corinthians 15*, 228–38, with comparisons to Philo.

to describe this food and drink suggests that he similarly understands the resurrection body in 15:44 as flesh empowered by the Spirit.[68]

Finally, in a few places, Paul uses the adjective *pneumatikos* to refer to spiritual gifts or benefits. In 1 Corinthians 9, as he explains the manner of his ministry and his rights as an apostle, he notes the fittingness of receiving material benefits from the Corinthians in exchange for the spiritual benefits he and his coworkers "sowed" among them (1 Cor. 9:11). A few chapters later, in 1 Corinthians 12, he discusses the Spiritual or charismatic gifts, such as prophecy, healing, and speaking in tongues. A similar dynamic is at work in this chapter to the one in 1 Corinthians 2. There Paul identifies the "Spiritual" person as the one who has received the Spirit (1 Cor. 2:12). Here the "Spiritual" gifts are those that are given *by the Spirit* (1 Cor. 12:7–11). Moreover, these gifts, though given by the Spirit, are actualized in the fleshy body (one of the gifts is healing!).[69]

Throughout 1 Corinthians, then, the adjective *pneumatikos* consistently refers to empowerment by the Spirit of God. Thus, when Paul speaks of the risen body as *pneumatikos*, he does not mean that it will be made of a different, spiritual substance. Rather, he means that the risen body will be empowered by the Spirit of God.[70] By this power, it will take on the other characteristics of the risen body: incorruptibility, glory, and power (1 Cor. 15:42–43).

One other difficulty must be addressed: Paul's statement that "flesh and blood cannot inherit the kingdom of God" (1 Cor. 15:50). On its surface, this clause would seem to undermine the traditional hope in the resurrection of the flesh. If, however, one reads the phrase in its historical and literary context, rather than in isolation, an explanation can be found. Historically, the phrase "flesh and blood [*sarx kai haima*]" typically indicates human mortality or perishability.[71] In its literary context, the whole verse reads, "This is what I am saying, brothers and sisters: flesh and blood cannot inherit the kingdom

68. Engberg-Pedersen (*John and Philosophy*, 165–69) seems to come to a similar conclusion with respect to the Eucharist in John, though it remains unclear to me how to reconcile his affirmation that Jesus speaks of giving his own flesh as food (166–67) with his later assertion (169, emphasis original) that Jesus speaks of "his flesh *as transformed* into *pneuma* at his resurrection into eternal life." I am also unpersuaded by Engberg-Pedersen's Stoic interpretation of *pneuma* language in the NT. For criticisms of a Stoic approach to *pneuma* in Judaism and the NT, see Rabens, *The Holy Spirit and Ethics in Paul*, 25–120.

69. I came to this reading independently of Cook (*The Enspirited Body in 1 Corinthians 15*, 226–28), who rightly notes on 227: "Although [the gifts] have a heavenly origin, they are physically present in the Corinthians' bodies."

70. The phrase is not, then, as Thiel suggests (*Icons of Hope*, 20), a "provocative oxymoron." Contrast, rightly, Matera (*Resurrection*, 95): "Both men, the first and the New Adam, are embodied beings; both have bodies. But whereas the body of the first was made alive by the ordinary life principle, the body of the second is animated by God's own Spirit. This is why Paul speaks of a 'spiritual body.'"

71. See, e.g., Sir. 14:18; 17:30–32; 1 En. 15:4, as well as the discussions of these and other texts in Ware, *The Final Triumph of God*, 374–77; Cook, *The Enspirited Body in 1 Corinthians 15*,

of God, nor does corruption inherit incorruptibility" (15:50). The parallelism between the two phrases "flesh and blood" and "corruption" suggests that the second half of the sentence clarifies the first half. By "flesh and blood" Paul does not mean bodies of flesh simply speaking, but rather bodies of *corruptible* flesh. On its own, as long as it remains (merely) *psychikos*, flesh and blood will not inherit the kingdom. If, however, it is empowered by the Spirit, becoming *pneumatikos*, then the body of flesh and blood will inherit the kingdom. Paul suggests as much a few verses later, writing, "For this corruptible [body] must put on incorruptibility, and this mortal [body] must put on immortality" (15:53).[72] The present, perishable and mortal body is not to be exchanged for an imperishable one.[73] Rather, the present, weak, dishonorable body (15:42–43) will be transformed by putting on immortality.[74]

Such a reading of the relationship between corruptibility and incorruptibility better explains the stirring climax of the chapter. Near the end of his argument, Paul writes, "When this corruptible [body] puts on incorruptibility, and this mortal [body] puts on immortality, then the saying that is written will be fulfilled: 'Death has been swallowed up in victory.' 'Where, O death, is your victory? Where, O death, is your sting?'" (1 Cor. 15:54–55). By definition, death turns bodies into corpses, corpses that lie lifeless in the grave. If that is the end, even if the human being continues in a "spiritual" existence, then death will have the last word. It is only if the present body is transformed and brought back to unending life that one can truly speak of death's defeat.[75]

"And I Will Raise Them Up on the Last Day"

Whereas Paul speaks of immortality and incorruptibility, John prefers the language of eternal life.[76] Despite this difference in language, both authors put the resurrection at the heart of the Christian hope. In John's Gospel the language of resurrection refers to numerous things: Jesus's own rising from

304–8. The most famous NT example is Matt. 16:17, where the phrase refers not to physical composition but rather to human beings in contrast to God.

72. On the chiastic structure of vv. 50 and 53, see Ware, *The Final Triumph of God*, 378.

73. Aquinas offers a similar reading of this passage. See *I Ad Cor*. 1013–17.

74. See also Rom. 8. A similar idea is at work in 2 Cor. 5. Again, Levenson's comments regarding Daniel (see n. 9 above) apply equally to Paul's understanding of resurrection. The resurrection does not mean for Paul, as Thiessen suggests (*A Jewish Paul*, 147), exchanging "inferior materials" for better material (as if the Creator of the universe initially furnished human beings with shoddy material). Rather, it means the perfection and glorification of the flesh, which, as 1 Cor. 15:39 seems to imply, is an intrinsic part of human nature.

75. So also Ware, *The Final Triumph of God*, 397: "Only a resurrection of the physical and fleshly body—the whole human being—makes sense of Paul's description of the resurrection here as the final destruction and defeat of death."

76. Feuillet, *Johannine Studies*, 68n31.

the dead (John 2:19–22; 20:9; 21:14); the general resurrection, when the dead will rise either to life or to condemnation (5:28–29); the raising of Lazarus, in which context Jesus identifies himself as "the resurrection and the life" (11:23–27); and, most importantly for the purposes of this study, in conjunction with the promise of eternal life on the last day (6:39–40, 44, 54). Space does not permit a full discussion of John's theology of resurrection. Instead, I would like to focus on the Bread of Life discourse and its surrounding context. Rather than offer a detailed analysis of John 6, I will highlight three aspects of this crucial section of John: the eucharistic imagery that pervades the chapter, the importance of faith in Christ, and the connection between both these themes and the resurrection.

John 6 begins with the only miracle story to appear in all four Gospels, the feeding of the five thousand. Each of the Synoptic Gospels draws connections between this story and the Last Supper, suggesting that the two events mutually illuminate each other. Although John's Gospel does not include the words of institution found in Matthew, Mark, and Luke, a few features of his account of the feeding also suggest eucharistic resonances.[77] Jesus's action of giving thanks and distributing the bread resembles the words of the Last Supper.[78] After the crowd has been fed, Jesus commands the disciples, "Gather up the fragments left over, so that nothing may be lost" (John 6:12 NRSVue). As some have noted, the Greek word for "fragments" (*klasmata*) is the same word used in the Didache with reference to the Eucharist (Did. 9.3–4).[79] When John later refers back to the feeding, he speaks of "the place where they ate bread after the Lord had given thanks [*eucharistēsantos*]" (John 6:23), epitomizing the miracle with the word at the heart of the church's liturgy.[80] The events also take place at the time of Passover, which the NT associates with the Eucharist, both its institution and its ongoing practice.[81] The feeding miracle thus sets a eucharistic tone for the chapter as a whole, a tone that is hinted at in the verses leading to the Bread of Life discourse, when the people appeal to the gift of manna in the wilderness, asking Jesus for a similar sign (6:30–31). Jesus eventually returns to the theme of the manna (6:48), but not before exhorting his audience to faith in him.

77. For a detailed discussion of the eucharistic themes in John's account of the feeding, see R. Brown, *The Gospel According to John*, 1:246–49.

78. Thompson, *John*, 141.

79. R. Brown, *The Gospel According to John*, 1:234.

80. See Hoskyns, *The Fourth Gospel*, 289: "The word 'Eucharist'—*when he had given thanks*—is repeated in the general reference to the miracle in *v*. 23. It belongs firmly to the synoptic tradition of the Feeding of the Four Thousand (Mark viii. 6; Matt. xv. 36) and of the Last Supper (Mark xiv. 23; Matt. xxvi. 27; Luke xxii. 19, cf. I Cor. xi. 24), and became almost a technical term in the letters of Ignatius."

81. In addition to Synoptics and John, see 1 Cor. 5.

This shift (if it is proper to call it a "shift") to an emphasis on faith has roots in the OT traditions surrounding the manna.[82] Already in the Pentateuch, Deuteronomy interprets the manna as a sign, pointing to the sustaining nourishment of God's word: "He humbled you by letting you hunger, then by feeding you with manna, with which neither you nor your ancestors were acquainted, in order to make you understand that one does not live by bread alone but by every word that comes from the mouth of the LORD" (Deut. 8:3). Jesus's emphasis on belief in his word in the first two parts of the discourse (John 6:35–40, 41–51) fits into this OT tradition of feeding on God's word.[83] On one level, Jesus is the Bread of Life because his words offer life, more specifically, hope for resurrection on the last day. All those who believe in him and his words will have eternal life (6:35, 47).

A clear shift takes place, however, somewhere around John 6:51, with some scholars suggesting that the last section of the discourse begins at 6:48.[84] Troels Engberg-Pedersen makes the excellent suggestion that the flow of this section becomes clear if one repunctuates 6:50.[85] Rather than putting a period at the end of the verse, he suggests a colon, such that the verses read as follows: "This is the bread that comes down from heaven, so that one may eat of it and not die: *I am* the living bread that came down from heaven. Whoever eats of this bread will live forever" (John 6:50–51a NRSVue, modified). The "this" of verse 50 thus points forward to Jesus as the one who comes down from heaven. This punctuation has the advantage of connecting verses 50 and 51 through the themes of "coming down" and of "eating,"[86] moving seamlessly into the eucharistic section of the discourse. Having spoken for several verses about his teaching as real food, Jesus now refers to his flesh in the same way: "And the bread that I will give is my flesh for the life of the world" (6:51b).

Several features of the last part of the discourse (6:51–59) point to a eucharistic meaning in Jesus's words. First, Jesus not only speaks of eating his flesh; he also introduces the idea of drinking his blood (6:53–54). Given the subtle allusions to the Last Supper throughout John 6, "flesh" and "blood"

82. Feuillet, *Johannine Studies*, 62–64.

83. For additional OT examples of this theme, see Amos 8:11; Jer. 15:16; Wis. 16:26. With respect to the division of the Bread of Life discourse, see Thompson, *John*, 149. She rightly notes, "In the first two parts of the discourse (6:35–40, 41–51), eating and drinking are metaphors for ingesting and imbibing God's word or instruction; hence, interwoven through these two parts one also finds the call to understand, to hear and learn from God, and to have faith in the one who instructs (6:36, 45–47)."

84. Schnackenburg, *The Gospel According to St. John*, 2:53–54. Moloney (*The Gospel of John*, 217–20) and Schneider (*Das Evangelium nach Johannes*, 150–52) include v. 51 as part of the second section of the discourse (6:41–51), implying a connection between vv. 48 and 51. Engberg-Pedersen (*John and Philosophy*, 165) argues that a new unit begins at v. 47, signaled by Jesus's double-amen introduction.

85. Engberg-Pedersen, *John and Philosophy*, 165–66.

86. Engberg-Pedersen, *John and Philosophy*, 166.

seem likely to be John's equivalent of the Synoptic Gospels' "body" and "blood."[87] Second, as is often noted, beginning in verse 54 Jesus uses much more graphic language (the Greek word *trōgō*, meaning to "munch" or to "gnaw") to speak of eating his flesh.[88] Third, although earlier in the discourse Jesus describes his teaching as food and drink, here he calls his *flesh* "real" or "true" (*alēthēs*) food and his blood "real" or "true" drink (6:55). Finally, in summing up his teaching, Jesus contrasts his flesh with the manna that the Israelites ate in the desert: "This is the bread that came down from heaven, not like that which the ancestors ate, and they died. But the one who eats this bread will live forever" (6:58 NRSVue). Jesus's offering of his flesh and blood as food and drink, like his teaching, has the same ultimate goal: eternal life on the last day. This is the thread that connects the whole Bread of Life discourse, the promise of resurrection (6:39–40, 44, 54).[89]

The last part of the Bread of Life discourse also connects the chapter to broader themes in the Gospel, specifically the incarnation and the passion. The language of "flesh" (rather than "body," found in the words of institution in the Synoptic Gospels and Paul) would naturally evoke the high point of John's prologue: "And the Word became flesh and tabernacled among us" (John 1:14).[90] John thus implicitly links the Eucharist with the incarnation.[91] One could even see the Eucharist as a kind of extension in time and space of the incarnation. At the same time, the language of "flesh and blood" also hints at Jesus's death, where blood flows from his side (19:34).[92] The Eucharist, then, is closely bound up with Jesus's fleshly existence and saving work, extending from the incarnation to his passion, death, and resurrection.[93] The fact that Jesus offers his *resurrected* flesh and blood as food is one of the things that distinguishes the Eucharist from cannibalism. Jesus's flesh and blood give

87. On the relationship between *sarx* and *sōma* in the eucharistic traditions, see Jeremias, *The Eucharistic Words of Jesus*, 140–41; Higgins, *The Lord's Supper in the New Testament*, 82–84. On the connections between John 6 and the institution narratives, see now Bukovec, *Die frühchristliche Eucharistie*, 106–10.

88. Feuillet, *Johannine Studies*, 55; Higgins, *The Lord's Supper in the New Testament*, 82.

89. N. T. Wright (*The Resurrection of the Son of God*, 441) notes the prominence of this theme throughout the Bread of Life discourse but makes no effort to interpret the promises of resurrection in light of the eucharistic themes in John 6.

90. Thompson, *John*, 154; Feuillet, *Johannine Studies*, 123.

91. Feuillet, *Johannine Studies*, 123.

92. Thompson, *John*, 154. John 19:34 is the only other place in John's Gospel, apart from the prologue (1:13), where the word "blood" appears.

93. John 6:62 may suggest that, for the evangelist, the Eucharist even encompasses the ascension. R. Brown (*The Gospel According to John*, 1:303) notes, "Some see in the theme of the ascension of the Son of Man in 62 an indication to the disciples that only after this ascension will they begin to receive the living bread of the Eucharist," though he does not affirm this position himself. Hoskyns (*The Fourth Gospel*, 301) suggests that "rightly understood, the Resurrection and the Ascension provide the solution to the riddle of the Eucharistic terminology." See also Higgins, *The Lord's Supper in the New Testament*, 83; Pitre, *Jesus and the Last Supper*, 215.

life because they have life, the life of the Word made flesh. The Eucharist and its connection to the resurrection hope underscores the importance of the flesh in God's saving plan. Christianity does not offer an escape from this created, fleshly reality. If it did, one would wonder what the whole point of the incarnation was.[94] The incarnation, the Eucharist, and the resurrection all point to the goodness of creation, a creation God has not abandoned but will one day make whole.

"I Look Forward to the Resurrection of the Dead"

Like the desire to see God, hope for the resurrection is deeply embedded in the Scriptures: foreshadowed and longed for in the Old Testament and fulfilled proleptically in the New. Numerous aspects of Christ's life and ministry underscore how important this hope is. His incarnation confirms the goodness of physical, embodied life. His passion, death, and resurrection form the pattern of the Christian hope. Just as Christ was raised from the dead, so, too, Christians hope one day to be raised from the dead. This resurrection does not mean, however, a simple return to our present mode of existence. Rather, we hope for "Spiritual" bodies, bodies that will be incorruptible, powerful, and glorious. Moreover, we hope to be reunited with our loved ones. In the meantime, as we continue this life, the Lord gives us a participation in his glorious, resurrected flesh under the humble appearance of bread and wine. Each of these themes has played an important part in the Christian tradition's reflection on its hope. In the following three chapters, I will explore how Irenaeus, Augustine, and Aquinas develop these biblical promises of resurrection, complementing each thinker's emphasis on the desire to see God and contributing to a robust account of the Christian hope.

94. As we will see in the next chapter, Irenaeus makes this same point.

NINE

Irenaean Anthropology and Resurrection Hope

In chapter 5 we explored the second half of Irenaeus's famous phrase, "For the glory of God is the living human being, and seeing God is the life of the human being."[1] There I argued that the great second-century bishop of Lyons understood the vision of God as essential to the Christian hope, for by this vision human beings receive immortality and incorruption. Toward the end of the chapter, I noted that this vision does not compete with the expectation of bodily resurrection but rather makes resurrection possible. Here I would like to consider why the resurrection plays such an important role in Irenaeus's presentation of the Christian hope. One can give the obvious answer that the Scriptures repeatedly promise a resurrection to come, but this raises the further question: Why do the Scriptures affirm such a hope? Why not suggest, as the Gnostics did, that salvation entails not the reunification of body and soul but rather an escape from the material world?

Confronting the Gnostic challenge, Irenaeus offers a rationale rooted in his anthropology and in his affirmation of the goodness of material creation. Bodies are an essential aspect of human nature (though he himself does not use the word "nature"). These bodies are good, created for glory—to deny this is to deny the faith. One can see the centrality of the resurrection for Irenaeus in that it touches on numerous aspects of the gospel: the miracles Jesus performed, the incarnation, anthropology, the sacraments (especially the Eucharist), God's power over sin and death, and the Christian hope to see God face to face.

1. Irenaeus, *Haer.* 4.20.7 (modified). Hereafter, parenthetical in-text citations come from *Against Heresies*.

Miracles, Creation, and Resurrection

According to Irenaeus, miracles, particularly healing miracles and even the raising of the dead, continued into his own day (2.32.4). Although they do not form a central part of his case for hope in the resurrection, he nevertheless does appeal to miracles a few times in order to explain the logic of the resurrection. For Irenaeus, the miracles recounted in the Scriptures attest to two things: the goodness of material creation in general and the capacity of the flesh to receive salvation and life.

In Book 3 of *Against Heresies*, Irenaeus appeals to the story of the wedding at Cana as a clear indication of the goodness of material creation. The wedding celebration began, he notes, with people (including the Lord himself) drinking wine "produced by God in a vineyard" (3.11.5). This wine was good, but, as the Gospel of John emphasizes, the quality of the wine Jesus produces from water far exceeds that of the ordinary wine. It is not the quality of the wine, however, that Irenaeus underscores, but rather the mode of its production. Jesus could have produced wine from nothing, eschewing the things of this creation. Instead, Jesus uses the good things of this creation, as he does again when multiplying loaves to feed the people. On the basis of this aspect of these miracles, Irenaeus underscores the continuity between the Old and the New Testaments. By using ordinary bread and wine, Jesus shows "that the God who made the earth, and commanded it to bring forth fruit, . . . was He who in these last times gave the human race, by His Son, the blessing of food and the favor of drink" (3.11.5, modified). The primary point regards the identity of the God of both Testaments, but implicit in Irenaeus's argument is an affirmation of the goodness of material creation. We will return to this point when we consider his teaching on the Eucharist.

Whereas the miracles involving bread and wine support belief in the resurrection indirectly, the healing miracles more clearly illustrate the logic of this hope. Irenaeus draws several lessons from the healing miracles. First, they indicate that the different parts of the body are capable of receiving salvation: "For what was His object in healing [different] members of the flesh [*carnis membra*], and restoring them to their original condition, if those parts which had been healed by Him were not in a position to obtain salvation [*non habebant salvari*]?" (5.12.6, modified). Restoring a withered man's hand or enabling a woman bent over for eighteen years to stand straight seems insignificant if these body parts will not one day partake of the salvation Christ offers.

Second, for this reason, Irenaeus also sees in these healings signs that point forward to the resurrection: "For if it was [merely] a temporary benefit which He conferred, He granted nothing of importance [*nihil grande praestitit*] to those who were healed by Him" (5.12.6, modified). The healings were, of course, "temporary benefits"—everyone who was healed or raised from the dead eventually died (or died again). Nevertheless, these "temporary benefits" point forward to the fullness of healing that is to come with the resurrection, which will extend not just to souls but to bodies.

Third, the healing miracles confirm that fleshly bodies are capable of receiving life: "Or how can they say that the flesh that received healing from Him is incapable of receiving the life which is from Him? For life is brought about through healing, and incorruption through life [*Vita enim per curationem, incorruptela autem per vitam efficitur*]" (5.12.6, modified). The miracles of raising the dead, a special subcategory of healings, point to the bodily continuity involved in the resurrection. Citing the raisings of Jairus's daughter, the widow of Nain's son, and Lazarus, Irenaeus asks his opponents, "In what bodies did they rise again? In those same [*in iisdem ipsis*], no doubt, in which they had also died. For if it were not in the very same, then certainly those same individuals who had died did not rise again" (5.13.1).[2] Bringing together the healings and the raisings, Irenaeus affirms continuity between Jesus's healing ministry as recounted in the Gospels and the hope for resurrection:

> As, therefore, those who were healed were healed in those members which had in times past been afflicted [*in his quae ante passa fuerant membra*]; and the dead rose in the identical bodies [*in iisdem surrexerunt corporibus*], their limbs and bodies receiving health, and that life which was granted by the Lord, who prefigures eternal things by temporal, and shows that it is He who is Himself able to extend both healing and life to His handiwork, that His words concerning its [future] resurrection may also be believed; so also at the end, when the Lord utters His voice "by the last trumpet," the dead shall be raised, as He Himself declares. (5.13.1, modified)

For Irenaeus, resurrection demands bodily continuity, based in part on the evidence of Jesus's healing miracles. The *vivens homo* lives with a resurrected, fleshly body.[3]

Incarnation and Resurrection

One of the clearest and most important elements of the gospel for Irenaeus's defense of the resurrection is the incarnation. For him, the incarnation seems to demand a resurrection: "For if the flesh were not in a position to be saved,

2. For a good discussion of the way Irenaeus draws on the raising of Lazarus to interpret the phrase "flesh and blood will not inherit the kingdom of God" in 1 Cor. 15:50, see Strawbridge, "How the Body of Lazarus Helps to Solve a Pauline Problem."

3. Irenaeus's argument from Jesus's healing ministry gains even more weight if, as Levenson suggests (*Resurrection and the Restoration of Israel*, 39), the ancient Israelites "saw illness as continuous with death and thought of the reversal of illness as so miraculous as to be in the nature of a resurrection." See the whole discussion on 38–39.

the Word of God would in no wise have become flesh" (5.14.1).[4] The logic is not hard to follow. The incarnation would seem superfluous if salvation meant escape from the body. Would it not have been easier for God simply to speak and to release us from our bodily prisons? Why should the Son bother taking on flesh and blood if his mission were to rescue human beings from fleshly existence? Irenaeus repeatedly appeals to the incarnation both to affirm the goodness of creation and to highlight the importance of hope in the resurrection.

We saw in chapter 5 that Irenaeus roots the promise of incorruptibility and immortality in the vision of God: "Seeing God is the life of the human being" (4.20.7, modified). As important as that vision is, it is only part of the story. Irenaeus also understands the incarnation as an important source of incorruptibility. In Book 3 of *Against Heresies*, he presents an account of the redemption that in some ways anticipates Anselm of Canterbury's much more detailed theory of the atonement. According to Irenaeus, the redeemer had to be human so that human beings could conquer the enemy; at the same time, he had to be God so that the redemption could not be taken away (3.18.7). In addition to securing a legitimate and lasting victory, the incarnation was essential to bring about the fruits of that victory—namely, an incorruptible life: "And unless the human being had been joined to God, he could not have become a partaker of incorruptibility [*incorruptibilitatis*]. For it was incumbent upon the Mediator between God and human beings, by His relationship to both, to bring both to friendship and concord, and that God would receive the human being and the human being would give himself to God" (3.18.7, modified). The Son's mission is not, as in the system(s) of the Gnostics, simply a matter of revealing knowledge (though it does include such revelation). Rather, through the incarnation the Son imparts to human nature the incorruptibility of God. Irenaeus emphasizes this point in the subsequent chapter:

> For *by no other means could we have attained to incorruptibility and immortality*, unless we had been united to incorruptibility and immortality. But *how could we be joined to incorruptibility and immortality, unless, first, incorruptibility and immortality had become that which we also are* [*nisi prius incorruptela et immortalitas facta fuisset id quod et nos*], so that what was corruptible might be swallowed up by incorruptibility, and what was mortal by immortality, that we might receive the adoption of sons? (3.19.1, modified and emphasis added)[5]

The union of divinity and humanity in Christ is not just important—it is essential. It is the only way human beings can achieve immortality. Although

4. *Si enim non haberet caro salvari, nequaquam Verbum Dei caro factum esset.*
5. Note the allusion to 1 Cor. 15:53–54.

he does not affirm this explicitly, the argument suggests that the life bestowed on human beings by the vision of God can be attained only if their bodies have been prepared for immortality by being joined to the Son.

Irenaeus's extended exposition and defense of the resurrection appears in Book 5, where the incarnation again plays a prominent role. He begins by pointing out the connection between the incarnation and Christ's role as revealer. In contrast to the Gnostics, for Irenaeus Jesus can reveal "the things of the Father" only because he became human (5.1.1). As in Book 3, however, Irenaeus speaks of revelation as only a part of Christ's mission, and only one of the goals of the incarnation. That further purpose, he suggests, shows the error of the Gnostics:

> Since the Lord thus has redeemed us through His own blood, giving His soul for our souls, and His flesh for our flesh, and has also poured out the Spirit of the Father for the union and communion of God and human beings, imparting indeed God to human beings through the Spirit, and, on the other hand, *attaching human beings to God by His own incarnation* [*per suam incarnationem*], *and bestowing upon us at His coming* [*in adventu*] *incorruptibility durably and truly*, through the communion that is with him, all the doctrines of the heretics fall to ruin. (5.1.1, modified and emphasis added)

Irenaeus suggests that God bestows immortality in stages, moving from the incarnation to the eschaton. By the incarnation, the Son joins the divine nature to human nature, making it fit for immortality. The fullness of that immortality, however, will be enjoyed "durably and truly [*firme et vere*]" only at his return.

In addressing the Ebionites, Irenaeus makes a subtle allusion to the Eucharist, thus connecting the incarnation, Christian sacramental practice, and resurrection hope.[6] The Ebionites reject Christ's divine nature and with it the incarnation, thereby obscuring the nature of the redemption: "Therefore do these men reject the commixture of the heavenly wine, and wish it to be water of the world only, not receiving God for commixture with Him [*ad commixtionem suam*], but they remain in that Adam who was conquered and was expelled from Paradise" (5.1.3, modified). The source of this error is that the Ebionites fail to see the analogy between the creation of human beings, when God breathed into Adam the breath of life, and the incarnation, when the Word united to himself Adam's flesh and blood. By this union, human beings are made alive again "spiritually" and, implicitly, prepared to receive the fullness of immortality when Christ returns (5.1.3).

Toward the middle of Book 5, Irenaeus presents a series of biblical texts highlighting the significance of blood. Each of these texts, he suggests, prefigures or points to Christ's own blood, by which the redemption is accomplished.

6. For more on the connection between the Eucharist and resurrection, see pp. 175–78 below.

The importance of blood connects to the importance of the incarnation and, by extension, to the nature of the resurrection: "Now this [blood] could not be required unless it also had the capability of being saved [*nisi et salvari haberet*]; nor would the Lord have summed up these things in Himself, unless He had Himself been made flesh and blood [*nisi et ipse caro et sanguis . . . factus fuisset*] after the way of the original formation [of the human being], saving in himself at the end that which had in the beginning perished in Adam" (5.14.1, modified).[7] Flesh and blood are essential to Christ's mission because flesh and blood are essential to what it means to be human.[8] This understanding of human nature underlies Irenaeus's understanding of the incarnation and the hope of the resurrection.

"A Due Mingling of Soul and Flesh"

In the preface to Book 4 of *Against Heresies*, Irenaeus offers a concise definition of human nature, describing human beings as "a due mingling of soul and flesh [*temperatio animae et carnis*]" (4, Pref.4, modified).[9] Although this definition does not have the rigor of the later anthropology of Aquinas (that was not, after all, Irenaeus's goal in writing), the composite nature of human beings plays an essential role in his exposition of the hope for the resurrection (5.6.1). Neither flesh nor soul independent of the other is a complete human being. God created human beings in his likeness as a body-soul unity, and the plan of salvation concerns the whole human being.[10]

Early in the treatise, Irenaeus appeals to the notion of judgment and reward to make a case for the resurrection. He does this to reveal a flaw in the Gnostic understanding of salvation. According to the Gnostics, only those souls that performed righteous deeds will attain salvation. If souls are to be rewarded on account of their righteous deeds, Irenaeus asks, then why should this reward not extend to the bodies that accomplished those deeds and made them possible? Righteousness must have the power not only to lead souls to salvation, but also to make bodies worthy of participation in incorruptibility and immortality (2.29.1–2).

The logic of Irenaeus's argument presupposes the complex unity of body and soul, an idea to which he appeals several times throughout *Against Heresies*.

7. For a discussion of various early interpretations of the phrase "flesh and blood cannot inherit the kingdom," see Lehtipuu, "'Flesh and Blood Cannot Inherit the Kingdom of God.'" The treatment of Irenaeus appears on 152–57.

8. Although Irenaeus does not cite Hebrews, the logic of his argument loosely resembles that of Heb. 2.

9. Cf. Irenaeus, *Epid*. 2.

10. As will become clear in the following two chapters, the composite nature of human existence unites Irenaeus, Augustine, and Aquinas, even as they articulate it in different ways.

In fact, later in the treatise, he seems to affirm a tripartite composition of the human being, made up of body, soul, and spirit, but several scholars rightly affirm that, regarding human nature, Irenaeus has a bipartite anthropology. Flesh/body and soul are parts of the human being, whereas the Spirit (by which he means the Holy Spirit) gives life to (at least some) human beings.[11] The important point is that no single part is a complete human being:

> For that flesh which has been molded is not a perfect human being in itself, but the body of a human being, and part of a human being [*pars hominis*]. Neither is the soul itself, considered apart by itself, the human being; but it is the soul of a human being, and part of a human being [*pars hominis*]. Neither is the spirit a human being, for it is called the spirit, and not a human being; but the commingling and union of all these [*commixtio autem et unitio horum*] constitutes a complete human being. (5.6.1, modified)[12]

Reflecting on this anthropology, Irenaeus appeals to Paul's prayer toward the end of 1 Thessalonians in which he asks for God to sanctify the Thessalonians spirit, soul, and body (1 Thess. 5:23). Paul's prayer, he suggests, implies that in the end the complete human being will be reintegrated by the Holy Spirit.[13] If not, the prayer would seem pointless, as would the healings Jesus performs in the Gospels.[14]

Within this anthropology, Irenaeus insists that only the physical body is mortal. The soul and the spirit, both being "incorporeal," cannot be called mortal (5.7.1). Thus, when Paul speaks of God giving life to "mortal bodies" (Rom. 8:11), he must be speaking of the physical component of the human

11. For a brief but helpful discussion of this question, see McGlothlin, *Resurrection as Salvation*, 59–60. For lengthier discussions, see Briggman, *Irenaeus of Lyons and the Theology of the Holy Spirit*, 157–61; Behr, *Asceticism and Anthropology in Irenaeus and Clement*, 99–105. McGlothlin and Briggman argue that, for Irenaeus, only Christians have the Holy Spirit (which is the "Spirit" of the threefold designation "body, soul, and Spirit") dwelling within them. Behr, by contrast, argues that all human beings have the Holy Spirit in some way, but that the Spirit dwells differently in Christians and in non-Christians. This does not mean, however, that Behr affirms a tripartite anthropology. He writes: "Yet, while the body, soul, and Spirit cannot individually be called a man, the body and soul can be called 'parts' of man in a way in which the Spirit cannot—for it is the Spirit, something other than man" (*Asceticism and Anthropology in Irenaeus and Clement*, 100). Steenberg (*Of God and Man*, 40) follows Behr, suggesting, "The human person is two 'parts' in composition (body and soul), yet three in actualization (body, soul and Spirit)."

12. As Behr notes (*Asceticism and Anthropology in Irenaeus and Clement*, 100), "Irenaeus's emphasis on this fact [the necessity of the flesh] is striking: what is important for him is not so much the presence of the Spirit in man, but the reality of the flesh."

13. Regardless of who is correct (Briggman or Behr) on the question of whether all human beings have the Holy Spirit in some way, here Irenaeus clearly has only believers in mind.

14. Irenaeus, *Haer.* 5.6.1. The latter connection with Jesus's healings is mine, not Irenaeus's. See the discussion on pp. 168–69 above on the connection between healing miracles and hope for the resurrection.

being: "What therefore is there left to which we may apply the term 'mortal body,' unless it be the thing that was molded, that is, the flesh [*caro*], of which it is also said that God will vivify it [*vivificabit eam*]? For this it is which dies and is decomposed, but not the soul or the spirit" (5.7.1, modified).[15] For Irenaeus, death primarily affects the body, depriving it of life and subjecting it to the forces of decomposition when it is separated from the soul. Paul calls those who have the Spirit dwelling within them "spiritual," not thereby suggesting that they do not have bodies, but rather that the Spirit is the source of their life and the promise of the future life, which will be a bodily existence: "Now, spiritual human beings shall not be incorporeal spirits [*incorporales enim spiritus non erunt homines spiritales*]; but our substance, that is, the union of soul and flesh [*animae et carnis adunatio*], receiving the Spirit of God, makes up the spiritual human being" (5.8.2, modified).[16] Only resurrection, understood as the reintegration of the soul and the body, can bring about the salvation of the complete human being.[17]

One of the difficulties for Irenaeus's view is the corruptible nature of material things. Toward the end of Book 4, he notes that, for the Gnostics, materiality is incompatible with immortality (4.37.6). Irenaeus addresses this problem directly in Book 5, arguing that the flesh is indeed capable of receiving incorruptibility. He begins with the obvious fact that the flesh currently participates in life: "But if [the Gnostics] are now alive, and if their whole body partakes of life, how can they venture the assertion that the flesh is not qualified to be a partaker of life [*non esse carnem participatricem vitae*], when they do confess that they have life at the present moment?" (5.3.3). Common human experience attests to the flesh's capacity for life, although the present life is weak because it cannot escape death. If even the weak present life can make material flesh live, Irenaeus continues, how much more so eternal life: "But if this which is temporal life, although it is much weaker than that eternal life, is nevertheless so powerful as to vivify our mortal members [*ut vivificet nostra membra mortalia*], why should not that which is eternal life vivify that flesh which is now practiced and accustomed to bearing life?" (5.3.3, modified). The present life and eternal life are not radically different, but rather seem to exist on a spectrum, or at least analogously to one another. Summing up his argument in the following chapter, Irenaeus writes, "Now that bodies

15. See also 5.7.2.

16. Irenaeus frequently alternates between speaking of human nature as flesh and soul (4, Pref.4), flesh and spirit (as in this text), and flesh, soul, and spirit (5.9.1). The important point is that, for him, human beings are composed of a physical part and a spiritual part, and the physical part is essential to human nature and to the scope of salvation.

17. See *Haer.* 5.20.1, where he speaks of "the same salvation of the complete human being, that is, of the soul and body." Jacobsen ("The Philosophical Argument in the Teaching of Irenaeus on the Resurrection of the Flesh," 256–57) helpfully notes that, for Irenaeus, salvation is a qualitative change rather than a substantial one. See also Andia, *Homo Vivens*, 245.

can receive life is to be seen by all. For they live to the extent that God pleases that they should live; and that being so, the [heretics] cannot say that [these bodies] are utterly incapable of receiving life [*quod minime valeant vitam capere*]" (5.4.2, modified). Human flesh, by its nature as part of a composite being, is necessarily capable of life. For this reason, he insists, flesh also has the capacity to receive eternal life together with the incorruptibility it imparts.

A Pledge of Future Glory

Irenaeus's affirmation of the goodness of the material world, the connection he draws between the incarnation and the resurrection, and his understanding of human nature come together in his teachings on the Eucharist. As it does for Ignatius of Antioch, the Eucharist serves as a refutation of the docetic denial of Christ's real flesh and blood and confirms the Christian hope for bodily resurrection.[18] The Eucharist makes the incarnate Christ available to believers in the here and now and prepares them to participate in his victory over death in the future.[19]

Irenaeus first briefly refers to the Eucharist in the context of discussing the nature and purpose of sacrifice. He insists that God does not demand sacrifice because he needs it. Rather, he does so for the benefit of human beings. Christ gave his disciples the Eucharist so that "they might be themselves neither unfruitful nor ungrateful" (4.17.5). The Eucharist, which assumes and transforms created things, constitutes "the new oblation of the new covenant" (4.17.5). Irenaeus thus connects the Eucharist with the Scriptures, seeing in it the fulfillment of the prophecy of Malachi 1:10–11, a text that points forward to a worldwide offering of sacrifice and praise to the Lord. In the church, a pure sacrifice is offered in every place, and the name of the Lord is glorified. The Eucharist thus brings together two important anti-Gnostic themes: the goodness of material creation, indicated by the use of bread and wine, and continuity with the OT, seen in the glorification of the name of the God of Israel.

In the following chapter, as Irenaeus continues his discussion of sacrifices, he contrasts the church's practice with that of the Jews and of the Gnostics: "And the Church alone offers this pure oblation to the Creator, offering to

18. See Ignatius, *Smyrn.* 7. In *The Resurrection of the Son of God*, N. T. Wright cites every passage regarding resurrection in *Against Heresies* except those passages that connect the resurrection to the Eucharist. One searches the index and body of Wright's book in vain for a single reference to *Haer.* 4.17–18 or 5.2. This omission is puzzling (one might even say glaring), given that these texts contain some of Irenaeus's strongest arguments for the goodness of the flesh against the Gnostics.

19. On the different contexts of Irenaeus's two treatments of the Eucharist, see Andia, *Homo Vivens*, 238.

Him, with giving of thanks, [the things taken] from his creation [*ex creatura eius*]" (4.18.4).[20] Throughout this discussion, Irenaeus makes two things clear. First, one of the chief characteristics of Christian worship is the giving of thanks, derived from the word "Eucharist," which literally means "thanksgiving." Second, even if the Gnostics go through similar motions and use similar language, their offerings are illegitimate. This is because some, by denying that the Father is the creator of the universe, offer to him things that do not (in their view) come ultimately from him (4.18.4). Moreover, they also deny that Christ is the Son of the Creator, thus rendering their sacrifice incoherent: "But how can they be consistent with themselves, [when they say] that the bread over which thanks have been given is the body of their Lord, and the cup His blood, if they do not call Him the Son of the Creator of the world [*Fabricatoris mundi*], that is, His Word, through whom the wood fructifies, and the fountains gush forth" (4.18.4, modified). More importantly, their denial of the resurrection renders their practice of offering the Eucharist unintelligible: "Then, again, how can they say that the flesh, which is nourished with the body of the Lord and with His blood [*quae a corpore Domini et sanguine alitur*], goes to corruption, and does not partake of life? Let them, therefore, either alter their opinion, or cease from offering the things just mentioned" (4.18.5). Again, as with the incarnation, there is an analogy to be drawn with Irenaeus's treatment of healings. The celebration of the Eucharist makes no sense if the flesh cannot participate in salvation.

The orthodox celebration of the Eucharist, by contrast, appropriately brings together practice and belief. Indeed, for Irenaeus, the Eucharist and orthodox belief support one another in that they bring together flesh and spirit: "For we offer to Him His own, announcing consistently the fellowship and union of the flesh and Spirit [*congruenter communicationem et unitatem praedicantes carnis et Spiritus*]" (4.18.5). This consistency has implications not only for the present life, but also for the future life. The Eucharist points forward to the hope of the resurrection: "For as the bread, which is from the earth, when it receives the invocation of God, is no longer common bread, but the Eucharist, consisting of two realities, earthly and heavenly; so also our bodies, when they receive the Eucharist, are no longer corruptible, having the hope of the resurrection [*iam non sunt corruptibilia, spem resurrectionis habentia*]" (4.18.5, modified). The Eucharist prepares believers to participate in the resurrection when Christ returns in glory.

Irenaeus discusses this idea at greater length in Book 5, once again connecting the incarnation, the Eucharist, and the hope of the resurrection. He counters the Gnostic denial that the flesh can attain salvation and incorruptibility by appealing to the Eucharist: "But if this [the flesh] indeed is not saved, then neither did the Lord redeem us with His blood, nor is the cup of

20. On the connection between the Eucharist and creation, see Kurz, "The Gifts of Creation."

the Eucharist the communion of His blood, nor the bread which we break the communion of His body" (5.2.2, modified). Drawing nourishment from Christ's body and blood serves as one of the clearest signs of the goodness of the body and of its fitness to participate in eternal life. Indeed, for Irenaeus the Eucharist makes those who partake of it members of Christ's body:

> When, therefore, the mingled cup and the manufactured bread receives the Word of God, and the Eucharist of the blood and the body of Christ is made, from which things the substance of our flesh [*carnis nostrae substantia*] is increased and supported, how can they deny that the flesh is capable of receiving the gift of God, which is life eternal, which [flesh] is nourished from the body and blood of the Lord [*quae sanguine et corpore Christi nutritur*], and is a member of Him? (5.2.3, modified)

The Eucharist, being the glorified body and blood of Christ, strengthens the flesh. In so doing, it prepares the flesh for the resurrection.[21] This strengthening does not, however, mean that our bodies will not one day die and decompose. Rather, to borrow a phrase from Aquinas, the Eucharist can be seen as "a pledge of future glory," a promise of the life to come. For Irenaeus, even the natural processes undergirding the Eucharist foreshadow the Christian hope:

> And just as a cutting from the vine planted in the ground fructifies in its season, or as a grain of wheat falling into the earth and becoming decomposed, rises with manifold increase by the Spirit of God, who contains all things, and then, through the wisdom of God, serves for the use of human beings, and having received the Word of God, becomes the Eucharist, which is the body and blood of Christ; so also our bodies, being nourished by it, and deposited in the earth, and suffering decomposition there, shall rise at their appointed time, the Word of God granting them resurrection to the glory of God the Father, who freely gives to this mortal immortality, and to this corruptible incorruption [*huic mortali immortalitatem circumdat et corruptibili incorruptelam gratuito donat*]. (5.2.3, modified)

Using language that appears in both the Gospel of John (John 12:24) and 1 Corinthians (1 Cor. 15:35–37), Irenaeus points out a symbolic fit between the Eucharist and the Christian hope. There are two levels of dying-and-rising imagery with respect to the Eucharist. First, the grain of wheat symbolically dies only to rise and multiply. Second, the Eucharist recalls Christ's own passion, death, and resurrection. Both images anticipate what Christians hope to experience: Their bodies will die and be buried in the ground, but having

21. As Bynum summarizes (*The Resurrection of the Body in Western Christianity*, 39, emphasis original): "The fact that we are what we eat—that we become Christ by consuming Christ, but Christ can never be consumed—guarantees that our consumption by beasts or fire or by the gaping maw of the grave is *not* destruction."

been strengthened and nourished by the Eucharist, one day they will be raised to immortality and incorruption.

Two final points regarding Irenaeus's treatment of the Eucharist deserve comment. The first is merely a puzzle. Although there are obvious affinities between his understanding of the Eucharist in its relationship to the resurrection and John 6, Irenaeus nowhere cites this passage. Given the Johannine character of much of his theology, it seems unlikely that he did not know the text.[22] Why he does not cite it is likely to remain a mystery, much like the fact that he never cites 1 John 3:2, despite clear continuity between that verse and his understanding of the vision of God. Second, and more importantly, even though Irenaeus discusses the Eucharist briefly compared to other topics, the Eucharist brings together many of the central themes of Irenaeus's thought: the continuity of the Old and the New Testaments; the goodness of material creation; the importance of the incarnation and its extension into the present; the composite nature of human beings and the ability of the flesh to receive immortality and incorruption; and the hope for the resurrection. We should not misinterpret the relative brevity of Irenaeus's appeals to the Eucharist as indicating its minor importance for his thought.

Resurrection and the Power of God

In addition to the various anthropological arguments Irenaeus makes in favor of the resurrection, he also appeals to the power of God. The resurrection demonstrates God's power over sin and death. If death were to have the last word over human beings, he argues, then God would have been conquered and his will thwarted (3.23.1). The resurrection shows forth God's power and his love for human beings: "But inasmuch as God is invincible and long-suffering, He did indeed show Himself to be long-suffering in the matter of the correction of man and the probation of all, as I have already observed; and by means of the second man did He bind the strong man, and spoiled his goods, and abolished death, vivifying that man who had been in a state of death" (3.23.1).[23] For Irenaeus it is crucial that Adam should partake in Christ's victory over death—otherwise, death would have the last word. By giving life to Adam, God confirms the defeat of death: "When therefore the Lord vivifies man, that is, Adam, death is destroyed [*evacuata est mors*]" (3.23.7, modified).

One of the primary errors of the heretics, according to Irenaeus, is their fixation on the weakness of the flesh. That weakness, he argues, serves to

22. See again Mutschler, "John and His Gospel in the Mirror of Irenaeus of Lyons" and *Irenäus als johanneischer Theologe*.

23. I retain the masculine "man" in this passage because it is difficult otherwise to convey the various parallels in Irenaeus's argument.

highlight God's power. It is not because of anything inherent in the flesh that human beings will one day partake of eternal life. Rather, it is God's power that will bring human beings back to life and bestow upon them incorruption: "They, therefore, reject the power of God [*potentiam Dei*] and do not consider what is true, who dwell upon the infirmity of the flesh [*infirmitatem carnis*], [and they] also do not consider the power [*virtutem*] of Him who raises it from the dead. For if He does not vivify what is mortal, and does not bring back the corruptible to incorruption, He is no longer a powerful God [*iam non potens Deus*]" (5.3.2, modified). Irenaeus associates God's power not only with resurrection, but also with creation. In fact, God's creation of human beings from the dust serves as an argument in favor of his power to raise the dead:

> But that He is powerful in all these respects, we ought to perceive from our origin, inasmuch as God took dust from the earth and formed the human being. And surely it is much more difficult and incredible, from non-existent bones, and nerves, and veins, and the rest of human arrangement, to bring it about that all this should be, and to make the human being an animated and rational creature, than to re-integrate again that which had been created and then afterwards decomposed into earth. (5.3.2, modified)

For Irenaeus, giving life to material that has died and decomposed is "easier" than creating something from nothing.[24] God's power overcomes the weakness of the flesh, making human beings capable of immortal life.

Flesh and Blood and the Kingdom

As we saw in the previous chapter, one of the challenges for early Christian understanding of the resurrection appears, ironically, in Paul's lengthy discussion of the resurrection in 1 Corinthians 15. Toward the end of the chapter, Paul writes, in part, "What I am saying, brothers and sisters, is this: flesh and blood cannot inherit the kingdom of God" (1 Cor. 15:50a). It is not hard to see how groups like the Gnostics would pounce on a statement like this to suggest that Paul denies a bodily resurrection. Irenaeus has ready answers for these objections, appealing both to 1 Corinthians itself and to passages from elsewhere in the Pauline epistles.

Within 1 Corinthians, Irenaeus reads the phrase "flesh and blood cannot inherit the kingdom of God" in its broader context. Immediately following this phrase, Paul writes, "For this corruptible must put on incorruption, and

24. In this, his argument reflects, whether intentionally or unintentionally, an early Jewish and Christian association between God's power to create and his power to raise the dead. See, e.g., 2 Macc. 7:28–29; Rom. 4:17.

this mortal must put on immortality" and goes on to speak of the defeat of death.[25] Death will be conquered, he argues, only if and when corruptible flesh is raised from the dead: "For then, indeed, shall death be truly vanquished, when that flesh which is held down by it shall go forth from under its dominion" (5.13.3). Other texts in the Pauline corpus further support the idea that it is the present, corruptible body that will be transformed into something incorruptible and immortal. Irenaeus quotes Philippians 3:21, which speaks of the transformation of this "body of humility" to be conformed to Christ's "body of glory." Here Irenaeus sees an analogy to the idea of the "corruptible" putting on the "incorruptible":

> What, then, is this "body of humiliation" which the Lord shall transfigure, [so as to be] conformed to "the body of His glory"? Plainly it is this body which is flesh [*corpus quod est caro*], which is indeed humbled when it falls into the earth. Now its transformation [takes place thus], that while it is mortal and corruptible [*cum sit mortalis et corruptibilis*], it becomes immortal and incorruptible, not after its own proper substance, but after the mighty working of the Lord, who is able to invest the mortal with immortality, and the corruptible with incorruption. (5.13.3, modified)

Once again, it is the power of God that grants to the lowly body, made that much lower by being buried in the earth, the power of immortality and incorruptibility. Again and again, Paul's letters suggest that God will transform and glorify the present, corruptible body. So, in 2 Corinthians, Paul speaks of mortality being swallowed up by life (2 Cor. 5:4), on which Irenaeus comments, "He uses these words most manifestly in reference to the flesh [*manifestissime hoc de carne dicens*]; for the soul is not mortal, neither is the spirit. Now, what is mortal shall be swallowed up by life, when the flesh is dead no longer [*quando et caro iam non mortua*], but remains living and incorruptible, hymning the praises of God, who has perfected us for this very thing" (5.13.3, modified). In addition to the reaffirmation that the mortal flesh will be transformed, this passage mentions in passing what activity might occupy those who attain the resurrection: They will be "hymning the praises of God" for his generosity.

Support for the hope of the resurrection is to be seen not only in Paul's statements about the future, but also in the way he describes the present life. Quoting 2 Corinthians 4:10–11, Irenaeus notes that Paul speaks of the life of Jesus being made manifest "in our mortal flesh." Earlier in the same letter the apostle writes of the Spirit dwelling in fleshy hearts (2 Cor. 3:3). If the present, fleshy body can become a dwelling for the Spirit, Irenaeus argues,

25. Irenaeus, *Haer*. 5.13.3. We will see a similar argument in Aquinas. For other ways of interpreting the phrase in early Christianity, see Lehtipuu, "'Flesh and Blood Cannot Inherit the Kingdom of God.'"

then it stands to reason that in the resurrection these bodies will partake of the life given by the Spirit (5.13.4).

Rising to See and Worship God

Given all these arguments in favor of the resurrection of this mortal flesh, one may rightly ask how Irenaeus understands the goal of the resurrection. To put it bluntly, what will those who attain to the resurrection *do*? He seems to offer a twofold answer to this question. First, as already suggested in an earlier chapter, for Irenaeus the resurrection of the body and the vision of God are intertwined. At times he speaks of this vision explicitly as seeing God; at other times he speaks of entering into the presence of God. To take an example of the latter description, Irenaeus even refers in passing to an intermediate state between death and resurrection, basing this idea on Christ's own experience:

> For as the Lord "went away in the midst of the shadow of death," where the souls of the dead were, yet afterwards arose in the body, and after the resurrection was taken up [into heaven], it is manifest that the souls of His disciples also, upon whose account the Lord underwent these things, shall go away into the invisible place allotted to them by God, and there remain until the resurrection, awaiting that event; then receiving their bodies, and rising in their entirety, that is bodily, just as the Lord arose, they shall come thus into the contemplation of God [*conspectum Dei*]. (5.31.2, modified)[26]

For Irenaeus, following Paul, Christ sets the pattern for the Christian hope.[27] Following death, the souls of Christ's disciples will wait in "the invisible place allotted to them by God" until the time of the resurrection. When they are raised in the same manner as Christ rose from the dead, they will enter into the presence of God with their resurrected bodies. The analogy with Christ might lead one to conclude that Irenaeus expects those risen to ascend into heaven as Christ did, but it is important to read this passage in its larger context. In the very next paragraph of the work, Irenaeus shifts to the language of seeing God and combines this with that of "new creation," noting that those who rise will "behold God in this creation which is renewed."[28] The resurrection of the body and the vision of God are complementary aspects of the Christian hope.

26. This passage and the following one appear in Irenaeus's account of the millennium. The complementarity between resurrection and seeing God, however, do not depend on accepting his millenarianism. On this topic see the excursus below.

27. On the various ways that Paul influences Irenaeus's theology of resurrection, see McGlothlin, *Resurrection as Salvation*, 48–95.

28. Irenaeus, *Haer.* 5.32.1. See the discussion of this passage on pp. 101–2 above.

The second, related, goal of the resurrection according to Irenaeus is that this vision of God leads human beings to worship him. In Book 3 of *Against Heresies*, he appeals to the story of Jonah as a figure for the whole human race.[29] As God allowed Jonah to be swallowed by the whale and eventually cast out back onto the shore, so he allowed the human race to be swallowed up by "the great whale" (Satan) so that human beings might praise God continually:

> [This was done] that man, receiving an unhoped-for salvation from God, might rise from the dead, and glorify God [*clarificet Deo*], and repeat that word which was uttered in prophecy by Jonah: "I cried to the Lord my God in my affliction, and He heard me out of the belly of hell;" and that he might always continue glorifying God [*glorificans Deum*], and giving thanks without ceasing [*sine intermissione gratias referens*], for that salvation which he has derived from Him, "that no flesh should glory in the Lord's presence;" and that man should never adopt an opposite opinion with regard to God, supposing that the incorruptibility which belongs to them is their own naturally, and by thus not holding the truth, should boast with empty superciliousness, as if they were naturally like to God. (3.20.1)

A superficial reading of this text might render God as an insecure figure who allows human beings to undergo horrible suffering just so that they might express their gratitude to him. Three aspects of Irenaeus's thought speak against such a reading. First, in a later passage (discussed in chap. 5, above), Irenaeus describes the glorification of God as a spontaneous act of joy and gratitude in response to the experience of the resurrection and the vision of God: "If therefore, at the present time, having the pledge, we do cry, 'Abba, Father,' what shall it be when, on rising again, we behold Him face to face; when all the members shall burst out into a continuous hymn of triumph, glorifying Him who raised them from the dead, and gave the gift of eternal life?" (5.8.1, modified). Second, throughout *Against Heresies*, Irenaeus emphasizes that God needs nothing from human beings.[30] Everything he does for the human race he does out of love. Finally, and relatedly, the goal of eliciting praise from human beings is so that they might grow in love: "This, therefore, was the [object of the] long-suffering of God, that humanity, passing through all things, and acquiring the knowledge of death, then attaining to the resurrection from the dead, and learning by experience from where he was liberated, may always live in a state of gratitude to the Lord, having obtained from Him the gift of incorruptibility, that he might love Him the more [*ut plus diligeret*

29. For a discussion of the way Irenaeus uses Jonah as an image of the human race and its atonement, see Behr, "Irenaeus of Lyons," 570–71.

30. See, e.g., *Haer*. 2.2.5; 2.5.4; 3.12.9 (loosely citing Acts 17); 4.13.4; 4.14.1–2; 4.16.3–4; 4.18.6.

eum]" (3.20.2, modified).[31] According to Irenaeus, the purpose of both the resurrection and the vision of God is, in a word, love. This love (that is, the love of human beings for God) is an essential feature of the vision of God, in which human beings find their fulfillment.[32]

Excursus: Irenaeus's Millenarianism

One aspect of Irenaeus's eschatological schema gradually fell out of favor in the early Christian tradition—namely, his millenarianism or chiliasm.[33] In *Against Heresies* 5.31–36, Irenaeus describes a literal one-thousand-year period in which the just will be raised from the dead prior to entering into the fullness of eschatological joy. His description of this period, an idea derived from Revelation 20:4, also draws extensively on the major prophets. On the basis of these and other texts, Irenaeus envisions an earthly kingdom in which the just will reign (5.33.3) and the saints will cultivate the earth and govern the animals (5.33.3–4). For Irenaeus, the millennium serves the purpose of preparing the saints for the vision of God (5.35.1–2). It is thus, in a sense, of a piece with his understanding of the divine pedagogy.

Several scholars have argued that Irenaeus's adoption of chiliasm stems from his polemical purposes.[34] His teaching regarding an earthly reign affirms the goodness of material creation against the Gnostics, and his reliance on OT texts opposes the Marcionite rejection of Israel's God. Charles Hill makes a strong case that chiliasm is a late development in Irenaeus's writing of *Against Heresies*.[35] Earlier in the work he speaks of only one resurrection (1.10.1; 2.33.5; 3.23.7), and even though the idea of the millennium fits his pedagogical schema, the schema does not demand a millennium. As Hill notes, preparation for the vision of God already takes place in this world (4.38.3; 5.8.1), and one could "multiply future ages *ad infinitum* as intermediate, gradational steps towards a clearer vision of God."[36] For these

31. On the importance of love in Irenaeus's thought, see Slusser, "The Heart of Irenaeus's Theology."

32. Irenaeus, *Haer*. 4.20.5. I owe this point to Slusser, "The Heart of Irenaeus's Theology," 138.

33. For a discussion of this early Christian phenomenon, see Charles Hill's classic study *Regnum Caelorum*.

34. For different accounts of the polemical background of this Irenaean doctrine, see Hill, *Regnum Caelorum*, 254–59; O'Rourke Boyle, "Irenaeus' Millennial Hope," 9–13; Nielsen, *Adam and Christ in the Theology of Irenaeus of Lyons*, 93. Although Hill rejects Irenaeus's chiliasm, he nevertheless writes regarding the end of *Against Heresies*, "Indeed, the last five chapters in *Adversus Haereses* do, in a way, form a fitting capstone to his whole 'promaterialist' polemic against heresy" (258–59).

35. For the following, see Hill, *Regnum Caelorum*, 254–56.

36. Hill, *Regnum Caelorum*, 256.

and other reasons, Hill argues that chiliasm is not essential to Irenaeus's theology of creation.[37]

Resurrected for the Sake of Love

Irenaeus offers a robust and coherent account of resurrection hope, one that integrates the goodness of creation, the significance of the incarnation, Christ's healing ministry, a composite anthropology, the Christian practice of the Eucharist, and the power of God. Prompted by the errors of the Gnostics, he upholds the goodness of material creation in general and of human flesh in particular, pointing to the goodness of God both in creating the world and in coming close to the human race through the incarnation. He also insists on the power of God to give life and incorruptibility to weak human flesh. God already gives natural life to the flesh in the present; how much more does he have the power to give eternal life to bodies in which the Spirit already dwells and in which the dying of Jesus plays out in this life! We receive a foretaste of that power in the Eucharist, another indication of the goodness of the flesh. The connection Irenaeus draws between the Eucharist and the resurrection points to another important dimension of the next life: It will be characterized by worship. In Book 3 he describes the resurrected life of the saints with the language of gratitude, noting that God grants the saints resurrection so that they might "always live in a state of gratitude to the Lord" (3.20.2). In the end, the Lord will give these bodies the power of eternal life and grant them to see him at last, evoking from them the love by which they come to be like him.

As beautiful as Irenaeus's account of the resurrection is, it might unwittingly give the impression that there will be little difference between the flesh as we now experience it and the flesh as it will be in the resurrection. The trials of bodily existence, both the insignificant and the profound, make the Gnostic temptation understandable, even if it is ultimately misguided. In the writings of Augustine we will see an account of the resurrection hope that addresses these trials, highlighting both the continuity and the discontinuity with the present life that form an essential part of this hope.

37. Hill, *Regnum Caelorum*, 256.

TEN

Augustine, the "Soulish" Body, and the "Spiritual" Body

Augustine has sometimes been accused of allowing his Platonic (or, perhaps more accurately, Neoplatonic) philosophical presuppositions to unduly influence basic Christian beliefs.[1] One area in which this is said to be the case concerns the resurrection. A cursory reading of the bishop of Hippo's works would seem to support such an interpretation. In the early years after his conversion and baptism, he continued to have reservations about the flesh and sensible things.[2] In the *Soliloquies*, for example, he seems to suggest that sensible things must be abandoned in order to ascend to the heights of happiness.[3] Over the course of his post-conversion life, however, Augustine gradually came to a much more integrated understanding of resurrection.[4] In this

1. Middleton, *A New Heaven and a New Earth*, 293.

2. By the end of his life, Augustine strongly condemned some aspects of Platonic philosophy: "Likewise, the praise with which I greatly extolled Plato and the Platonists (or the Academic philosophers) was most inappropriate for these impious persons and rightly displeases me; it is especially in the face of their great errors the Christian teaching must be defended" (*Retract.* 1.1.4). See the discussion in Van Fleteren, "Augustine and *Corpus Spirituale*," 333–34.

3. *Solil.* 1.14.24. As Van Fleteren ("Augustine and *Corpus Spirituale*," 336) notes, Augustine later regretted this formulation, which resembles Porphyry's dictum *omne corpus fugiendum* ("every kind of body is to be shunned"). For a forceful rejection of this position, see *Serm.* 241.7, where Augustine says philosophers holding to this position "are raving [*delirant*]."

4. On this development, see the two articles by Van Fleteren ("Augustine and *Corpus Spirituale*"; "Augustine and the Resurrection"). Rákos-Zichy rightly notes ("The Resurrection Body in Augustine," 375), "It is unclear at which point Augustine began to imagine resurrected bodies in material form." As I suggest below, in *Serm.* 362, commonly dated to 411, Augustine still entertains a distinction between flesh and body. By the time of his writing Book 13 of *City of God*, he has settled on a position that affirms flesh as the matter of the resurrected and glorified body.

chapter I will explore a few key features of Augustine's mature understanding of the resurrection hope.[5] First, Augustine frequently meditates on the continuity and discontinuity between the present body and the resurrected body, emphasizing that the defects and hardships of this present life will not affect the future resurrected body. Second, he offers replies to the objections of the cultured despisers of his day, addressing many of the challenges to the resurrection. Finally, he also offers an insightful interpretation of Paul's description of the present body and the future "spiritual" body in 1 Corinthians 15. Rather than treat these themes in the order just given, we will consider Augustine's thoughts on the resurrection by focusing primarily on three texts. By way of introduction, we will begin with a brief passage from his exposition of Psalm 63 (62 LXX) in which he expounds on the flesh's desire for God. We will then consider the closely related *Sermons* 361 and 362.[6] We will conclude with his mature reflections on the subject in Books 13 and 22 of *City of God*. As with his exposition of the vision of God, we will again see continuity as well as development in Augustine's understanding of the resurrection. Early in his musings on the question, he suggests that the resurrected body will be a body, but (perhaps) not flesh, on the basis of Paul's statement "Flesh and blood cannot inherit the kingdom of God" (1 Cor. 15:50). Toward the end of his life, however, he comes to an interpretation of this phrase similar to that of Irenaeus, affirming that the resurrected body will be made of flesh, albeit transformed flesh. Guided by Scripture, especially the example of Christ's resurrection, and by his understanding of human nature as a complex unity of body and soul, Augustine consistently maintains that resurrection does not mean the transformation of the body into spirit, but rather the glorification of the body. The power of the life-giving Spirit makes that body incorruptible, such that, even though composed of flesh, it will no longer experience the various sufferings and trials that characterize the present life.

"For You My Flesh Thirsts, Too, in Manifold Ways!"

Psalm 63 begins with an expression of the soul's thirst for God, which resonates with Augustine's insatiable desire for the living God.[7] He does not, however, limit this desire to the soul. Rather, following the lead of the psalmist,

5. For a full, recent study of this topic in Augustine, including his understanding of a spiritual resurrection in the present and its relation to the future bodily resurrection, see Reisenauer, *Augustine's Theology of the Resurrection*.

6. Because they were preached so close together, and because *Serm.* 362 takes up questions left unanswered by the end of *Serm.* 361, I am treating them effectively as one composite text, though I acknowledge that this is an imposition Augustine did not intend. McGlothlin ("Augustine's Resurrection Framework," 210) suggests that *Serm.* 362 "offers the first full, integrated articulation of Augustine's mature resurrection framework."

7. For one of the most beautiful and ardent expressions of this desire, see *Conf.* 10.27.38.

he notes that the body, too, thirsts for God. The soul's thirst is not hard to understand: Our intellect and our will long for knowledge and for love. But why does the psalmist insist that the body also longs for God? Augustine answers the question by appealing to the resurrection: "Why is our flesh [*caro nostra*] thirsting, and this in manifold ways? 'For you my flesh thirsts, too, in manifold ways!' it says. Because resurrection is promised even to our flesh [*et carni nostrae promittitur resurrectio*]. As beatitude is promised to our soul, even so is resurrection promised to our flesh."[8] So important is the resurrection for Augustine that he digresses for a bit to remind his audience of the centrality of the resurrection and to address, briefly, some common objections to this belief. Christians, he notes, do not hope for this-worldly prosperity, such as what "even robbers and other criminals often enjoy."[9] Christians await a better hope, an indestructible life, as the author of Hebrews puts it (Heb. 7:16): "The resurrection even of our flesh is promised to us, such that this very flesh we carry now shall rise again in the end."[10] This hope rests on the power of the God who creates the universe out of nothing: "If when we did not exist God made us, is it any great task for him to remake us who formerly did exist?"[11] Because of this creative power, the common objections to faith in the resurrection—the decomposition of bodies, their destruction by burning, their consumption by animals—pose no real obstacles. If God can call human beings out of nonexistence into being, then he can certainly raise the dead.[12]

Next, Augustine discusses the differences between the present body and the resurrected body. Our present bodies are marked by two kinds of instability. First, our bodies are frail:

> So frail, so corruptible are we now that if we do not eat, we grow faint and hungry; if we do not drink, we faint with thirst; if we keep vigil for a long time, we faint with weariness and fall asleep; if we sleep too long, we weaken, and need to be energetic again; if we spend too much time eating and drinking, then even though our intention was to refresh ourselves with food and drink, we shall scarcely survive what was meant to revive us; if we stand for a long time, we get tired, and have to sit down; but if we sit for a long time, we find that tiring as well, and have to stand up.[13]

8. Augustine, *Enarrat. Ps.* 62.6 (modified).

9. Augustine, *Enarrat. Ps.* 62.6.

10. Augustine, *Enarrat. Ps.* 62.6.

11. Augustine, *Enarrat. Ps.* 62.6. As I note in chap. 8, this connection between resurrection and creation goes back to the earliest Jewish expressions of hope for the resurrection. Irenaeus similarly appeals to God's creative power in responding to objections against the resurrection. See pp. 146–47 and 178–79 above.

12. Augustine, *Enarrat. Ps.* 62.6.

13. Augustine, *Enarrat. Ps.* 62.6. Cf. *Serm.* 305A.8. It is not hard to see how these kinds of burdens, to say nothing of the harsher sufferings many people experience, contribute to the constant temptation to dualism and the rejection of the body.

Such corruptibility, Augustine suggests, will not characterize life in our resurrected bodies. We will receive new flesh that participates in God's immortality.

The second instability concerns the natural growth of the human being. We pass from infancy to childhood and on through the various stages of life (for those who reach old age) until death. Each stage of life passes on, such that we cannot recover it in this life: "No age, no stage of our life stands still; everywhere there is fatigue, weariness, and corruption."[14] These two kinds of instability, Augustine suggests, explain the flesh's thirst for God expressed in the psalm: "When we reflect on what kind of hope of resurrection God promises us, and on what manner of hope it instills in us, then in the midst of all our manifold weaknesses we thirst for that incorruption, and so our flesh thirsts for God in manifold ways."[15] In the resurrection, the toil, the frailty, the pain, the sorrow of this life will not affect us, not because we will be freed from bodily life, but because we will receive an incorruptible body.[16] For this reason, Augustine exhorts his audience to desire God with both soul and flesh: "God who created your soul created your flesh too; and he who made both, himself nourishes both. Let each of the components in us thirst for God, and after our manifold labor may our thirst be quenched in utter simplicity."[17]

"The Resurrection of the Dead, You See, Is Our Hope"

Sometime in the year 411, Augustine devoted two sermons to various questions regarding the resurrection. The way he speaks about the nature of the resurrected body makes it seem likely that these sermons preceded his exposition of Psalm 63.[18] Whereas in that exposition Augustine happily affirms that the resurrected body will be made of flesh, albeit incorruptible flesh, in *Sermons* 361 and 362 he speaks of a "body" that is not composed of flesh, properly speaking.[19] This rejection of a fleshly understanding of the resurrection does not, however, mean that he expects only a spiritual postmortem existence. On the contrary, he is adamant that the Christian hope consists in resurrection, and that to deny the resurrection (both Christ's own and the future

14. Augustine, *Enarrat. Ps.* 62.6 (modified).

15. Augustine, *Enarrat. Ps.* 62.6 (modified).

16. There is certainly some discontinuity between the present body and the resurrected body. Nevertheless, in light of Augustine's affirmation of bodily, fleshly existence, it seems to me that G. Boersma ("Augustine on the Beatific Vision," 17) overemphasizes the discontinuity at the expense of Augustine's sense of continuity. In context the sentence Boersma cites in support of his point (*Ep.* 148.1.3) is part of a counterfactual that Augustine ends up rejecting in the letter.

17. Augustine, *Enarrat. Ps.* 62.7 (modified).

18. On the difficulty of dating the various sermons that make up the *Expositions of the Psalms*, see *Expositions of the Psalms 1–32*, 15–16.

19. See Augustine, *Serm.* 362.17, 21, and the discussion of these texts below.

resurrection) is to deny the Christian faith. In *Sermon* 361 Augustine addresses common objections to the resurrection at greater length; in *Sermon* 362 he discusses "what sort of life" the saints will enjoy.[20]

In *Sermon* 361 Augustine expresses in no uncertain terms the centrality of the resurrection, closely associating it with the three theological virtues:

> The resurrection of the dead, you see, is our hope [*spes enim nostra est resurrectio mortuorum*]; the resurrection of the dead is our faith. It is also our charity, which blazes up at the proclamation of things that cannot yet be seen, and grows hot with a desire so huge that it gives our hearts the capacity to receive the bliss which is promised us for the future, enlarging them as long they believe what they cannot yet see. (361.2)

It may seem odd to equate the resurrection with charity, but the connection is rooted in the centrality of desire for Augustine. The resurrection is not simply an object of intellectual belief (faith) or even of expectation (hope), but also of charity, set ablaze by this expectation of a future, incorruptible life. So important is the resurrection for Augustine that, without it, Christianity becomes meaningless: "And so take away faith in the resurrection of the dead, and the whole of Christian doctrine collapses [*omnis intercidit doctrina christiana*]" (361.2).[21] Augustine happily accepts the resurrection on faith. It is not, after all, something that can be established by reason. Nevertheless, his approach is not anti-intellectual. On the contrary, he devotes this sermon to offering answers to objections to the resurrection.

When it comes to the arguments of skeptics, "there is nothing new under the sun" (Eccles. 1:9b). The obvious objection to the resurrection is that, in most people's experience, the dead tend to remain dead.[22] Augustine addresses the issue, first, by acknowledging that, for the most part, dead people do not return from the grave, but, second, by pointing to Christ's resurrection as the exception (361.8). Even if our loved ones have not come back from the dead, Christ has, and his disciples encountered him, feeling "the solidity of his body [*soliditas corporis*]" (361.8). Christ's resurrection was not merely a spiritual vision of the heart, but something physical, seen with the eyes, and the testimony of the disciples confirms its reality.

20. Augustine, *Serm.* 361.2. Hereafter, parenthetical in-text citations are from this sermon.

21. Cf. 1 Cor. 15:19. In the subsequent paragraph (361.3), Augustine bluntly states, "So those who say the dead do not rise again are not Christians [*qui ergo dicunt mortuos non resurgere, christiani non sunt*]."

22. Augustine (*Serm.* 361.6) formulates this objection in the voice of a skeptic: "Who has ever risen again from [the grave]? Who has ever indicated what goes on among those in the netherworld?" The ancients understood the finality of death no less than we do, our chronological snobbery notwithstanding.

Augustine next appeals to agricultural analogies to illustrate the logic of the resurrection.[23] Likely inspired by Paul's words in 1 Corinthians 15, he compares the burial of corpses to the burial of seed. Just as seed does not spring up immediately into a full-grown plant, so also the corpses of loved ones lie in the ground awaiting the harvest of the resurrection (361.9). All analogies limp, and Augustine acknowledges important differences between the sowing of seed and the resurrection. Planting and harvesting occur every year, whereas Christians expect one resurrection at the end of time. Nevertheless, Christ, as "the one principal grain," serves as a pledge of future glory for those who believe in him (361.10). Moreover, Augustine continues, creation itself abounds with images that reflect the Christian hope: Sleeping and waking, the waning and the waxing of the moon, the death of leaves in the fall and their return in the spring—all these natural phenomena offer imperfect illustrations of what Christians hope for (361.10).

We have already seen the second objection Augustine addresses—namely, the corruption of corpses.[24] This natural process does not faze him, and he deals with it swiftly. As in his exposition of Psalm 63, Augustine appeals again to God's power to call things out of nonexistence into being (361.12).

Finally, some of Augustine's pagan contemporaries willingly acknowledged Christ's own resurrection but denied the Christian hope for a future resurrection (361.14). In answer to this objection, he appeals to the unity between the head (Christ) and the body (the church), drawing on Paul's encounter with Christ (Acts 9:4) as well as his theology of the body of Christ (1 Cor. 12).[25] Christ's connection to his church is so intimate that his victory over death will one day extend to all those joined to him. Indeed, this is why Christ took "the form of a servant," so that he might undergo death and resurrection on our behalf (361.16). As "the form of God," Christ has the power both to raise himself and to raise those united to him (361.16).

Sermon 362, which one translator has described as "monstrously long," takes up the second of the two questions raised in *Sermon* 361: What sort of life will the saints enjoy in their resurrected bodies (362.1)?[26] Augustine further subdivides this question into two: What kind of body will the saints have? And

23. Augustine's use of seed imagery in this sermon challenges Bynum's claim (*The Resurrection of the Body in Western Christianity*, 95–96) that "Augustine rejects the Pauline seed metaphor with its attendant implication that body is fluid, dynamic, potential, open to infinite development." It may be true that he favors other metaphors for resurrection, but he does not absolutely reject the imagery of planting and harvesting.

24. Augustine refers to this as "the objection you usually raise [*quod soles opponere*]" (361.12), indicating how common it was.

25. For a similar explication of this connection between the head and the members, see *Enarrat. Ps.* 26.2.4.

26. The description of the sermon as "monstrously long" is Edmund Hill's. See Augustine, *Sermons 341–400*, 267n1. Hereafter, parenthetical in-text citations are from this sermon.

what activities will they perform (362.6–7)? In this chapter we will explore Augustine's answer to the first question, reserving the second for chapter 12.

Early in the sermon Augustine acknowledges the speculative nature of this meditation. He speaks not of what he knows, but rather of what he believes, of what he confesses by faith (362.5).[27] Reiterating his rejection of the idea that the resurrection involves only the soul and not the body (362.6–7), Augustine spends most of the sermon considering the nature of the resurrected body. The bodies of the saints will be suited to the activity of the life of the world to come, which will differ from the present life in that the saints will not perform "perishable and passing deeds" (362.7).

With respect to the characteristics of the resurrected body, Christ serves as the exemplar. As Christ rose in his own body, so, too, Christians hope to rise in their own bodies (362.10). Christ ate with his disciples between the resurrection and the ascension, and so, at the very least, the resurrected bodies of the saints, too, will have the capacity to eat. The saints, however, will not *need* to eat. In the present state eating is bound up with maintaining life—if we do not eat, we eventually die (362.11). By contrast, in the world to come, Augustine suggests, our life will not be sustained by food.

From there Augustine turns to the phrase that has puzzled interpreters from the earliest days of Christianity, "Flesh and blood cannot inherit the kingdom of God" (1 Cor. 15:50). Approaching the phrase from several angles, he affirms, first, the importance of the flesh because of the incarnation. Christ accomplished the work of redemption in the real flesh that he received from his mother (362.13). In light of the incarnation, as well as the resurrection appearances, Augustine maintains both Paul's statement about "flesh and blood" and Jesus's affirmation in Luke that the risen Christ has "flesh and bone" (362.14, citing Luke 24:39).[28] One answer Augustine gives is that the flesh technically does not inherit or possess anything—it is the soul that possesses things through the body, and so "flesh and blood" will not inherit the kingdom (362.14). Augustine then reads the phrase in light of Paul's contrast between the "earthly one" and the "heavenly one" in 1 Corinthians 15:47–50. Read in context, "flesh and blood" may also refer to the "earthly one"—that is, all those who are going to die. "Flesh and blood" thus seems to refer to our present earthly existence. Christ, risen and ascended into heaven, is now the "heavenly one," and those united to him

27. In addition to our lack of experience with respect to the next life, the present condition of our corruptible bodies means we are unsuited to have full knowledge about their future, glorious condition. See Reisenauer, *Augustine's Theology of the Resurrection*, 216. With this distinction between knowledge and belief Augustine indicates not relative certainty or uncertainty but rather two different modes of knowing.

28. On the importance of Luke 24:39 for Augustine's mature understanding of resurrection, see Alfeche, "The Basis of Hope in the Resurrection of the Body," 263–80. For a similar argument in Irenaeus, see pp. 169–72 above.

are slowly being conformed to his image in anticipation of experiencing a resurrection like his (362.15).

Finally, Augustine entertains the possibility of distinguishing between "body" and "flesh." Read in this light, the phrase "flesh and blood" points to the possibility of decay. By contrast, the resurrected body will be incorruptible, and for that reason, he suggests, it should not be called "flesh and blood," properly speaking: "The body, you see, that is not subject to decay is not properly called flesh and blood, but simply body [*corpus enim sine corruptione, non proprie dicitur caro et sanguis, sed corpus*]. If it's flesh, I mean, it's subject to decay and mortal; but if it now dies no more, it is now no more subject to decay" (362.17).[29] There is a similarity between the resurrected body and the flesh, and for that reason it might be called "flesh," but a Christian must maintain that the resurrected body is not corruptible like our ordinary flesh. Thus, he adds, "while retaining its own specific nature without being subject to decay, it is not now called flesh, but body [*et ideo sine corruptione manente specie, non iam caro, sed corpus dicitur*]" (362.17). Augustine rounds out this section of the sermon with an interpretive move we have seen in Irenaeus and that we will see again in Aquinas: Paul's reference to "flesh and blood" in 1 Corinthians 15:50 must be understood in light of the parallel reference to "the perishable" in the same verse.[30] It is not flesh according to its specific nature that will not participate in the resurrection, but rather the corruptible flesh (362.17). A little later in the sermon, returning to Paul's remark about "flesh and blood," Augustine argues that the apostle wrote that verse "to show that by the expression 'flesh and blood' he wished us to understand the tendency to decay of a mortal and merely soul-animated body [*mortalis animalisque corporis*]" (362.19). Although he does not draw attention to it, here Augustine draws on Paul's reference to the "soulish [*psychikos*]" body in 1 Corinthians 15:44.[31] As we will see in the next section, this text strongly influences Augustine's understanding of the resurrection, although there one sees a subtle shift in his understanding of flesh. In this

29. As Rákos-Zichy ("The Resurrection Body in Augustine," 376) notes, "Augustine, however, underlines that these heavenly bodies will have a different flesh; not *caro*, but *corpus*."

30. In a later letter, Augustine offers a more subtle interpretation of the phrase "flesh and blood will not inherit the kingdom":

> In the same way, when we say, "Flesh will possess the kingdom of God," and, "Flesh will not possess the kingdom of God," the meaning of this term is also distinguished, and the matter is resolved. For "flesh" in the sense of its substance [*quoniam caro secundum substantiam*], in accordance with the words, "A spirit does not have flesh and blood, as you see that I have," will possess the kingdom of God, but "flesh" when understood in the sense of its corruption [*caro autem cum secundum corruptionem intellegitur*] will not possess it. For this was explained when, after it said, "Flesh and blood will not possess the kingdom of God," there was immediately added, "Nor will corruption possess incorruptibility." (*Ep*. 205.2.16)

31. See the discussion of this verse on pp. 158–61 above, as well as Augustine's discussion of the "soulish body" in the following section.

sermon, he continues to maintain a distinction between the flesh and the body: "The body, though, which is no longer mortal, cannot properly be called flesh and blood [*corpus autem quod iam mortale non est, non proprie dicitur caro et sanguis*], which are earthly bodies; but it is called body, because it can now be called a heavenly one" (362.21).[32] In *City of God*, by contrast, he strongly affirms the resurrection of the flesh.

Despite Augustine's caution regarding "flesh and blood" and his reference to a "heavenly body," he nevertheless strongly rejects the idea that the future resurrection will be merely spiritual (362.22). Appealing to 1 Corinthians 15 and 2 Corinthians 5, Augustine insists that the NT speaks not of a spiritual resurrection, but rather of the defeat of death and mortality, at least with respect to the ultimate Christian hope. He does not deny the reality of a spiritual resurrection, which plays an important role in his theology.[33] Rather, he denies that Christ came to give us *only* a spiritual resurrection. The people Paul critiques are wrong not in what they affirm, but in what they deny: a future bodily resurrection (362.22).

Toward the end of the sermon, Augustine returns to the tentativeness that should characterize speculation about the future life. He urges his audience not to worry too much about what the resurrected body will look like. Instead, he points them to Christ: "It's enough for you to know that your flesh will rise in the same form [*resurgit caro tua in ea specie*] as that in which the Lord appeared, in the form, of course, of a human being [*in hominis utique specie*]" (362.27). The risen flesh will no longer be subject to decay but will still maintain the specific nature of a human being. In the last few paragraphs of the sermon Augustine considers what the resurrected saints will be doing. We will return to this matter in the final chapter of this study. Now, however, we turn to one of his last works, where he once again addresses many of the questions regarding the resurrection hope.

"Soulish" Bodies and "Spiritual" Bodies

Whereas in *Sermon* 362 Augustine discourages his audience from speculating too much about what the resurrected life will be like, in *City of God* he devotes two major sections (Books 13 and 22) to questions about the resurrection.[34]

32. Augustine reiterates this point toward the end of the same paragraph. As Van Fleteren ("Augustine and *Corpus Spirituale*," 333) notes, Augustine died before finishing the *Retractationes* and never had the opportunity to review his sermons. One suspects that, had he done so, he would have clarified his understanding of the fleshly nature of the resurrected body.

33. He briefly discusses this spiritual resurrection and its relation to the future hope in 362.23–25. For a fuller treatment of this theme in Augustine, see Reisenauer, *Augustine's Theology of the Resurrection*, 119–72.

34. Although these two sections are the most extended discussions of resurrection, the topic appears several times throughout the work. References to the general resurrection occur at

How are we to explain this apparent inconsistency? The most obvious answer is that, at this point in his life, the bishop saw a pressing need to address the challenges of critics. Christians who accept Christ's resurrection and the hope of the future resurrection on faith can remain satisfied with the expectation that their bodies will one day become like Christ's. When outsiders ridicule this central Christian belief, however, he deems it necessary to offer a reasoned response (cf. 1 Pet. 3:15).[35] In this section we will examine Augustine's discussion of the resurrection in Book 13, highlighting his interpretation of what he calls the "soulish body" and the "spiritual body," reflecting the Latin translation of 1 Corinthians 15. In the following section, we will consider his additional replies in Book 22 to those who mock the Christian hope for the resurrection.

In the first two-thirds of Book 13 of *City of God*, Augustine discusses death, which assumes various forms. In response to the question "what sort of death God threatened to the first human beings" in Genesis, he enumerates at least four possibilities: "Was it the death of the soul? Or of the body? Or of the whole person? Or was it what is called the second death?" (13.12). Although all four kinds of death are interesting and worthy of consideration, with respect to the present question (i.e., the resurrection of the body), it is the second kind—the death of the body—that most concerns us. One of Augustine's central convictions is that death is evil. With respect to biological death, he writes:

> For this reason, the death of the body, *the separation of the soul from the body* [*separationem animae a corpore*], is not good for anyone, as it is experienced by those who are, as we say, dying. This violent sundering of the two elements, which are conjoined and interwoven in a living being, is bound to be *a harsh and unnatural experience* as long as it lasts, until the departure of all feeling, which depended on this interconnection of soul and body. (13.6, emphasis added)

As Paul had put it a few centuries before Augustine's day, death is an "enemy"—indeed, it is "the last enemy to be destroyed" (1 Cor. 15:26).

Given Augustine's description of death as "the separation of the soul from the body," as well as his understanding of resurrection as Christ's victory over death, resurrection cannot simply mean an ongoing postmortem existence for the soul.[36] The ultimate hope in the resurrection must include the ongoing

Civ. 1.11–13; 9.23; 10.29–30, 32; 11.10; 12.14; 20.7, 10; and to Christ's resurrection at 7.33; 10.29. Hereafter, parenthetical in-text citations are from *City of God*.

35. On the centrality of the resurrection, see *Serm.* 361.2 and the discussion of that text above.

36. For Augustine's denial of this understanding of resurrection, see again *Serm.* 362.6–7. As Toom ("*Totus Homo*," 59) puts it, "For Augustine, resurrection means nothing less than the resurrection of *totus homo*, the resurrection of the whole human being, body and soul." In *Civ.*

immortality of the body, reunited with the soul. In the last third of Book 13, Augustine addresses various philosophical objections to the possibility of the body attaining immortality, as well as the nature of the resurrected body.

Many of the arguments Augustine engages are bound up with a cosmology most people would no longer affirm, as well as with a pagan theology he obviously rejects. Nevertheless, it is worth examining his rebuttals to some of these arguments in order to see the logic of his position. Some philosophers deny the possibility of immortality for the earthly body, while at the same time maintaining that the world itself is a component of one of their gods, rendering it immortal (13.17).[37] Such a position, Augustine argues, is inconsistent. If the world, which is material, can exist eternally as part of a god, then there is no reason human bodies cannot become immortal if God so wills it. These same philosophers also argue that earthly bodies must return to the earth from which they came. By this logic, however, the bodies of the heavenly beings, made of the heavenly element fire, must also eventually return to the element from which they came.

Two aspects of Augustine's present argument are significant for this study. First, Augustine eventually names Plato and the Platonists as his target. He critiques their positions in light of Christian faith in the resurrection. As already noted above in chapter 6, for all the influence Plato had over Augustine, he is not an unreconstructed Platonist.[38] His first commitment is to the gospel, including its hope in the resurrection. When necessary, he criticizes elements of Platonic philosophy; at other times he synthesizes aspects of Plato with his vision of the Christian hope. Second, there are indications of development in his thought from *Sermons* 361 and 362. Whereas he seems to deny that a fleshly body can attain immortality in the sermons,[39] in *City of God* he affirms that God, if he so wills, can make an earthly, fleshly body immortal.

A few chapters later Augustine once again addresses the possibility of a bodiless immortal existence for the soul, taking on the arguments of Plato and Porphyry.[40] With respect to Plato, he notes that, while the soul is occasionally "set free" from the body, according to the *Phaedrus* it continually returns to a body. For Plato, human life is characterized by a "ceaseless alternation" of living with and without a body (13.19). On Augustine's reading, Plato deals

1.13 Augustine denies that the body is "mere adornment [*ornamentum*]" or "external convenience [*adiutorium*]." Rather, it belongs to human nature as such.

37. Throughout this section, Augustine is engaging Plato's *Timaeus*.

38. As Reisenauer (*Augustine's Theology of the Resurrection*, 181) puts it, "[Augustine] has come to grasp how much the resurrected and ascended Christ has shaken the foundations and shattered the ceilings of even the best of philosophical worldviews."

39. See *Serm.* 362.18: "The body, you see, that is not subject to decay is not properly called flesh and blood, but simply body. If it's flesh, I mean, it's subject to decay and mortal; but if it now dies no more, it is now no more subject to decay; and therefore, while retaining its own specific nature without being subject to decay, it is not now called flesh, but body."

40. For an earlier engagement with Plato and Porphyry on these questions, see *Serm.* 241.5–8.

even to wise souls a cruel fate, making them return again and again to different bodies and never giving them an immortal, incorruptible body.[41] Porphyry, by contrast, affirms an everlasting bodiless existence for virtuous souls. At the same time, he understands the gods as embodied deities. By Porphyry's logic, then, virtuous souls are in a better position than the gods (13.19), since these souls remain unencumbered by a body.[42]

In the last few chapters of Book 13 Augustine offers a positive exposition of the Christian hope for an immortal body. In the present life, he notes, the saints at times "hated" their flesh when it resisted their attempts to lead a life of virtue (13.20). In the resurrection, the saints will love their bodies all the more when those bodies become "spiritual." By "spiritual" Augustine means, among other things, that the flesh will obey the spirit: "For just as the spirit is quite appropriately called carnal when it is the servant of the flesh, the flesh will with equal propriety be called spiritual, when it serves the spirit [*caro spiritui serviens recte appellabitur spiritalis*]" (13.20). Note that, in contrast to *Sermon* 362, Augustine freely refers to the resurrected body as "flesh [*caro*]."[43] Moreover, he quickly clarifies that the phrase "spiritual body" does not refer to an immaterial existence:[44]

> This is not because the flesh will be converted into spirit [*non quia in spiritum convertetur*] (a notion which some people derive from the scriptural text: "It is sown as a soulish body: it will arise as a spiritual body") but because it will submit to the spirit with a ready obedience, an obedience so wonderfully complete that the body will fulfill the will of the spirit in such a way as to bring perfect assurance of indissoluble immortality, free from any feeling of distress, and relieved of any possibility of corruption, any trace of reluctance. (13.20, modified)

In stark contrast to some modern readings of 1 Corinthians 15, Augustine rejects the interpretation of the word "spiritual" as referring to the substance of which the resurrected body will be made.[45] The resurrected body will be fleshly, but it will be freed from the burdens and pains of the present life, as well as from slavery to sin.

41. Plato's affirmation of reincarnation leaves the soul in a constant state of instability. Only resurrection to an incorruptible life can result in stable happiness for the whole human being. See Reisenauer, *Augustine's Theology of the Resurrection*, 183.

42. Augustine makes a similar argument earlier in *Civ*. 10.29.

43. Significantly, Augustine speaks of the flesh resting "in hope." Alfeche ("Augustine's Discussions with Philosophers on the Resurrection of the Body," 134–35) notes that this implies an ongoing connection between the flesh and the soul. With one stroke Augustine challenges two Platonic notions: Plato's negative view of the flesh and his theory of forgetfulness.

44. As noted above, in *Serm*. 362 Augustine already denied that the body would be transformed into spirit.

45. For a discussion of modern readings of the "soulish" body and the "spiritual" body, see pp. 158–61 above.

Augustine makes this argument on the basis of the nature of Christ's resurrected body. Jesus appears to the disciples "in spiritual, though still real, flesh [*in spiritali carne, sed tamen vera*]" (13.22). He eats not because he needs to, but in order to show the reality of his flesh. So, too, the resurrected saints will not need to eat, even as they will retain the ability to eat.

In the second to last chapter of Book 13 Augustine discusses at greater length the meaning of the "soulish" body and the "spiritual" body of 1 Corinthians 15:44. According to him the adjectives "soulish [*animale*]" and "spiritual [*spiritale*]" refer not to the substance of which the bodies are composed, but rather to their animating principles:

> Bodies which have a living soul, but not yet a life-giving spirit, are called "soulish" bodies [*animalia dicuntur corpora*] (yet they are not souls, but bodies). In the same way, those other bodies are called "spiritual" [*ita illa spiritalia vocantur corpora*]. Yet we must not allow ourselves to believe that they will be spirits; we must think of them as *bodies having the substance of flesh* [*corpora carnis habitura substantiam*], though never having to experience corruption or lethargy, being preserved from such a fate by the life-giving spirit. (13.23, modified and emphasis added)

Much could be said about this rich passage, but I will limit myself to three points. First, although Augustine is working with a Latin text rather than Greek, the adjectives *animale* and *spiritale* closely resemble the Greek adjectives *psychikos* and *pneumatikos*.[46] Augustine rightly interprets them not in terms of substance, but rather in terms of animating principle.[47] Second, here again he affirms the *fleshly* substance of the resurrected body.[48] Indeed, he

46. Like their Greek equivalents, the Latin adjectives also pose difficulties for translators. I have chosen to render *animale* with the somewhat clunky "soulish" to underscore the importance of the soul (*anima*) for Augustine's understanding of the term.

47. Here one sees a classic case of Dale Allison's delightful phrase "exegetical amnesia." Many of the modern arguments for such a reading of 1 Cor. 15:44 seem oblivious to Augustine's interpretation in *City of God*. For the term "exegetical amnesia," see Allison, *Resurrecting Jesus*, 9.

48. Augustine offers a similar interpretation, though without any reference to the "flesh," in an earlier epistle:

> But we must reflect so that we do not venture too far by saying that the body will lose not only corruptibility and mortality but also its very nature as a body and become a spirit through the glory of the resurrection [*etiam hoc ipsum, quod corpus est, per gloriam resurrectionis amittere et spiritum fieri*]. In that way, of course, the substance of spirit will become twofold if the body will also be a spirit. Or if there will be only one spirit in a human being so that, after the body has been changed and transformed into a spirit, the spirit is not doubled either by receiving a twin or by increase or in any way enlarged by some addition in quantity, we would have to fear that it would seem that we were saying nothing else but that those bodies would not only not remain immortal but would not exist at all and would utterly perish [*videatur quam corpora*

goes on to suggest that the resurrected body will be "heavenly" not because it is no longer made of its natural substance, but because it will receive a heavenly gift (13.23).[49] Finally, the key for Augustine is the lack of "corruption or lethargy." Although the resurrection entails a return to fleshly existence, that existence will include new qualities, the most important of which is incorruptibility.[50]

A little later in the chapter, Augustine reiterates the point that the quality of a body derives from its relation to either the soul or the spirit. The source of the resurrected body's incorruptibility will be this life-giving spirit (13.23).[51] In the present, however, the apostle can describe the body as "dead" (Rom. 8:10) because it is mortal and susceptible to corruption. The "soulish" body, as Paul refers to it in 1 Corinthians 15, is characterized by corruption, humiliation, and weakness.[52] Christ took on such a body "not of necessity, but as an act of power," and passed through death into new life. He did so as "our head," making it possible for "members of Christ" to receive the same kind of body at the final resurrection.

In the final chapter of Book 13, Augustine once more underscores the importance of flesh for the bodily resurrection, noting how resurrection life both resembles and differs from that of the angels: "The immortality with which [the saints] are clothed will be like that of the angels, an immortality which cannot be taken away by sin; and though the natural substance of flesh will continue [*natura quidem manente carnis*], no slightest trace of carnal corruption or lethargy will remain" (13.24).[53] By this point in Augustine's life, fleshly existence is an essential part of human nature, something that the saints will resume after the resurrection. As has been noted practically from the first days of Christianity, the nature of the corruption that affects corpses poses certain challenges to the resurrection hope. Augustine addresses these difficulties in the final book of *City of God*.

> *non illa mutatione inmortalia mansura, sed nulla potius futura et omnino peritura*]. (*Ep*. 147.22.51)

See also *Serm*. 242.11.

49. Cf. *Ep*. 205.2.9: "But a body is called spiritual because it is now immortal with its spirit [*quod iam cum spiritu inmortale est*]."

50. For a discussion of some of the qualities of the resurrected body, see also *Serm*. 277.7–8, 12.

51. Augustine makes this point in several places. See *Serm*. 256.3; 277.15; *Gen. Litt*. 11.18.24.

52. For a further elaboration of the burdens of the present body, see *Serm*. 277.4–6 and *Enarrat. Ps*. 62.6.

53. For a similar point, see *Civ*. 22.17. Although Augustine does not cite Hebrews, his understanding resembles the way that text contrasts angelic existence with the flesh and blood that the Son takes on in the incarnation (Heb. 2:14–16) and brings into the heavenly tabernacle (Heb. 9:11–12). On the importance of the resurrection for Hebrews, see Moffitt, *Atonement and the Logic of Resurrection*.

"Not a Hair of Your Head Will Perish"

The importance of the resurrection for Augustine is especially evident at the conclusion of *City of God*, which culminates in another defense of the resurrection and a discussion of the embodied nature of the future life.[54] Here he reprises certain objections to the resurrection hope, the first of which he also treats in Book 13. One difficulty stems from the NT belief in Christ's bodily ascension into heaven.[55] The philosophical objection stems from the notion that each of the elements has its proper place. On the basis of ancient cosmology and the four elements, certain pagan philosophers argue that an earthly body cannot inhabit a heavenly realm. Earthly bodies belong to earth, whereas heavenly bodies belong in the heavens (22.11).

According to this cosmology, the cosmos is made up, in ascending order, of earth, then water, then air, and finally the sky or the heavens (22.11). Augustine's philosophical opponents argue that bodies belong to the realm of the material of which they are composed, the absurdities of which Augustine easily points out. Birds, which are made of earthly stuff, nevertheless fly through the air. Moreover, if earthly beings are supposed to inhabit the earthly realm, then human beings should live under the earth, as fish live under the water. Augustine adds that some philosophers describe the soul as a "fifth substance," whether material (so Aristotle) or immaterial (so Plato). This substance, he suggests, is superior to the other four, and yet in human beings it mingles with the lowest. If the soul can inhabit the lowest region, he continues, then there is no reason why it should not be able to elevate the body to the highest region at the resurrection.[56] The notion that every element must remain in its own realm simply cannot be an absolute rule.

In addition to these arguments based on nature, Augustine points to stories in the pagan tradition in which the ordinary course of nature is suspended.[57] Once when a Vestal Virgin was suspected of unchastity, she proved her innocence to the judges by carrying water from the Tiber to them in a sieve

54. Cavadini ("Ideology and Solidarity in Augustine's *City of God*," 97) aptly characterizes this last part of *City of God* as "a book of wonders and miracles, all centered on the body and the renewal of the body."

55. In 13.18 Augustine refers to both Christ's ascension and the resurrected bodies of the saints, suggesting that in some sense the saints will inhabit a heavenly realm. Nevertheless, as with the bodies of the saints, to affirm that the new creation will be "heavenly" need not imply that it is immaterial.

56. There seems to be a bit of an inconsistency with Augustine's discussion of the soulish and spiritual bodies here. This part of his argument presumes that the soul is a constitutive part of the human being. Perhaps it would have been better to say that the life-giving spirit can elevate the body to the heavenly regions. This section also seems to imply that this spirit will be given in addition to the soul, thus making the entire body-soul composite spiritual and incorruptible.

57. In a letter written a few years earlier to a fellow Christian, Augustine makes a similar argument in favor of Christ's bodily, fleshly ascension into heaven, though there he appeals to miracles of the OT. See *Ep*. 205.1.2.

without spilling a drop. If the pagan gods can perform such a miracle, what is to prevent God from making it possible for earthly bodies to inhabit the heavenly realm?

Augustine also addresses difficulties with the resurrection that persist to this day.[58] Augustine's contemporaries raise questions regarding abortions, the death of infants, and the nature of the resurrected body, both with respect to its conformity to Christ and with respect to parts of the body that disappear, such as hair and nails (22.12–21). Augustine acknowledges both the force of these challenges and the speculative nature of the answers offered to them. Although he holds firmly to hope in the resurrection, he openly admits that we do not know what it will be like: "But what will be the grace of that spiritual body, and the extent of that grace, is something of which we have had as yet no experience; and I am afraid that it would be rash to offer any description of it" (22.21).[59] Nevertheless, he offers tentative answers to the challenges of the skeptics.

One set of difficulties stems from the Christian understanding of Christ as the paradigm for the resurrection. Does this mean that all the saints will conform to the same stature as Christ's resurrected body (22.15)? For people taller than Christ, this would seem to entail the loss of some measure, which Augustine sees as contradicting Christ's promise that "not a hair of your head will perish" (Luke 21:18). For this reason, he interprets the language of "the full stature of Christ" (Eph. 4:13) as referring either to the full number of the saints or to the fullness that each individual will attain at the resurrection (22.15). With respect to Paul's language of being "conformed to the image of [God's] Son" (Rom. 8:29), Augustine takes the phrase to refer either to the inner human being or to the immortality that the saints will enjoy in conformity to Christ's immortality (22.16). Based on these principles, it should come as no surprise that Augustine also denies that women will become men at the resurrection. He reasons that "a woman's sex is not a defect; it is natural [*non est autem vitium sexus femineus, sed natura*]" (22.17).[60] Thus, the conformity of women to Christ in the resurrection means immortality, not becoming male.[61]

Finally, Augustine considers what will happen with parts of the body that are lost, particularly in light of the promise of Luke 21:18. One of his guiding principles is that there will be no deformity or ugliness in the resurrection.

58. For an honest contemporary account of these difficulties, see Allison, *Night Comes*, 19–25.

59. For a similar caution, see *Serm.* 277.13.

60. As Toom ("*Totus Homo*," 61–62) notes, Augustine also bases his argument on Jesus's statement that "in the resurrection they neither marry nor are given in marriage" (Matt. 22:30). This denial presumes that both men and women will attain to the resurrection in their sexed existence.

61. Contrast Gospel of Thomas 114.

Thus, "if the restoration of what has been cut would disfigure the body, then it will not be restored" (22.19). Drawing on an analogy of the way a potter molds clay, using the same material but reshaping it in such a way as to remove any disfigurement, he suggests that God can similarly restore all the parts of the body in such a way that will not result in ugliness caused by disharmony.[62] One of his most intriguing speculative proposals in this section regards the martyrs. Noting that their testimony to Christ unto death is their glory, Augustine suggests that perhaps their scars will remain visible on their resurrected bodies (presumably on analogy to Christ's wounds), but in such a way that "there will be no deformity, but only dignity, and the beauty of their valour will shine out, a beauty in the body and yet not of the body" (22.19). In line with the tradition that goes back to Irenaeus as well as to some of the earliest Jewish expressions of hope for resurrection, Augustine again bases his arguments on the omnipotence of God the Creator (22.20). Even if we do not understand how God can accomplish such a feat, Augustine suggests that we must affirm a belief in the power of God to fulfill the statement that "not a hair of your head will perish."[63] The almighty Creator will re-create the saints, giving them new spiritual bodies that are incorruptible and immortal, while retaining the nature God gave them (22.21).

Continuity and Discontinuity

As with his account of the vision of God, there is both continuity and development, even in Augustine's mature understanding of the resurrection. The continuity lies in his resolute faith in the bodily resurrection. Even if at times he entertains a distinction between body and flesh, he nevertheless denies that resurrection means the transformation of body into spirit. Whether he speaks of flesh or of body, however, he insists that there will be both continuity and discontinuity in the resurrection. As Christ rose in the same body, so also the saints will rise in their own bodies. Like Christ, however, their risen bodies will be incorruptible and immortal. Conformed to the image of Christ, those who are faithful to him will participate in his victory over the painful separation of body and soul that is death, receiving a body that no longer suffers the trials of embodied existence as we now experience it. Augustine thus addresses one of the most common objections to hope in the resurrection of the body: Resurrection does not mean simply returning to our present

62. For a discussion of why the saints will recover organs whose function will no longer be necessary, see *Serm.* 243.3–4, 6–7, as well as the brief treatment in Bynum, *The Resurrection of the Body in Western Christianity*, 100.

63. Reisenauer (*Augustine's Theology of the Resurrection*, 179) puts it well: "Regardless of the posthumous condition of the body, whether intact or decomposed, God's omnipotence is the necessary and sufficient condition for its resurrection."

condition. Rather, to borrow language more frequently used in discussions of the relationship between nature and grace, the resurrection will heal, perfect, and elevate the flesh. Augustine also serves as a model for responding to philosophical challenges to the resurrection. Rather than simply appealing to a kind of fideism, he offers reasoned responses to these critiques, taking seriously the difficulties involved in affirming the resurrection. At the same time, he recognizes the speculative nature of his responses and so holds them tentatively, appealing ultimately to the omnipotence of God, an idea that harkens back to some of the earliest expressions of hope for the resurrection (see, e.g., 2 Macc. 7:28–29).

Like Augustine, Aquinas bases the hope for the resurrection in the testimony of Scripture and supports it with appeal to philosophical principles. But whereas Augustine's treatment in *City of God* is primarily apologetic, Aquinas offers a positive philosophical account of the reasonableness of the resurrection, appealing to the composite nature of human beings as well as their inherently social character in a way that complements and elucidates the testimony of Scripture. To that account we now turn.

ELEVEN

Thomistic Anthropology and Resurrection Hope

How important was the body for Aquinas's understanding of the Christian hope? At first glance, one might be tempted to say, very little. A superficial reading of his interpretation of the beatific vision might suggest that the resurrection is unnecessary, a superfluous add-on to the immaterial, intellectual experience that alone can satisfy all human longing. In the *Summa Theologiae* Aquinas even argues that, strictly speaking, the body is not necessary for human happiness, precisely because this happiness consists in an activity of the soul.[1]

Although Thomas does affirm that the soul can enjoy happiness apart from the body, it is only by reading these statements out of context—both the immediate context of the article and the broader context of his entire corpus—that one would mistakenly conclude that he considered the resurrection superfluous. Even within the article discussing whether the body is necessary for happiness, Thomas argues that, in order to attain happiness "in every way [*omnimodae*]," the soul must be reunited to the body, because only so can it act in full accord with its nature: "For since operation depends on a thing's nature, the more perfect is the soul in its nature, the more perfectly it has its proper operation, wherein its happiness consists."[2] For Aquinas, the "proper operation" of the soul is to animate the body. So, a disembodied soul is inherently incomplete. This argument from the nature of the soul is one of

1. *ST* I-II, q. 4, a. 5.
2. *ST* I-II, q. 4, a. 5.

at least four reasons Aquinas gives throughout his corpus for the necessity of the resurrection.[3]

In this chapter we will consider each of these four arguments.[4] First, without the resurrection Christ's act of redemption would be incomplete. Christ came to conquer sin *and death*. If salvation were to consist simply in souls floating off to heaven detached from their bodies, then Christ's saving action would be deficient. Second, Thomas argues that the resurrection is necessary because Christ's passion, death, and resurrection is the pattern of *our* redemption. Without the general resurrection, we would not be perfectly conformed to Christ. Third, Thomas develops an anthropological argument for the resurrection: Human beings are not, by nature, disembodied souls, but rather a complex unity of body and soul. If human beings are to be saved *as human beings* (and not, say, as quasi-angelic creatures), their bodies and their souls must be reunited. Whereas the first two arguments depend on the scriptural testimony, this third argument is a philosophical one. Finally, in scattered places throughout his corpus, Aquinas points to another aspect of human nature to argue for the necessity of the resurrection. Human beings are social animals, and human society is necessarily an embodied phenomenon. Without the resurrection, this social aspect of human existence would be left out of Christ's act of redemption. The resurrection, then, is essential to Thomas's understanding of redemption, stemming from foundational philosophical and theological principles.

Victory over Sin and Death

In the *Summa Contra Gentiles*, Aquinas appeals to the completeness of Christ's redemption to argue for the necessity of the resurrection. Christ came to liberate human beings not only from sin itself, but also from the effects of sin, especially death. This liberation from sin comes about not only by

3. Aquinas distinguishes between two kinds of necessity. Some things are necessary strictly speaking, as human beings need food, air, and water to survive. Other things are "necessary" in the sense that they are more fitting, as taking a horse (or, in our day, a car) is "necessary" for a long journey. Throughout this chapter, with respect to the resurrection Aquinas uses the language of "necessity" with the sense of fittingness. For a concise discussion of this distinction, see *ST* III, q. 1, a. 2.

4. In addition to these arguments, Aquinas, much like Irenaeus, argues for the resurrection of the body in part so that the whole human being can receive recompense, whether reward or punishment, in the body by which a person performed meritorious or blameworthy acts in this life. On Aquinas, see the discussion in Gaine, "Resurrection and Eschatology," 364–73; on Irenaeus, see p. 172 above. For the moment, I will refrain from discussing one of the most famous aspects of Aquinas's understanding of the resurrection—namely, the marks of the resurrected body (subtlety, agility, clarity, and impassibility). We will consider these attributes in the following chapter. In this chapter, I am more interested in explaining why the resurrection is important for Thomas rather than in his account of the nature of the resurrected body.

forgiveness, but also by the healing of our wounded nature, one of the punishments for sin: "It has been proved that Christ has delivered us from those things we have incurred through the sin of the first man, from whom we have contracted not only sin, but also death, which [is] the punishment of sin."[5] Christ, then, frees human beings both from the guilt of sin and from death (4.79.1). Without the resurrection, then, redemption would be incomplete. On the basis of texts like Romans 5 and 1 Corinthians 15, Aquinas concludes that the resurrection of the dead at the end of the world is a "necessity of the faith [*necessitate fidei*]." At that time, "we shall all rise again by the power of Christ" (4.79.4).

As the evidence of the NT shows, however, the language of resurrection is not without ambiguity. A few NT texts imply that some Christians wrongly interpreted the resurrection as only a spiritual phenomenon, not a bodily one. Thomas, aware of this issue, addresses the question directly. He describes those who interpret the resurrection in only a spiritual fashion as "perverse in their understanding [*perverse intelligentes*]" (4.79.5). Paul encountered this error and warned his coworker Timothy against Hymenaeus and Philetus, who seem to have held that the (general) resurrection had already taken place. As Aquinas notes, such a teaching is tenable only if one understands the resurrection spiritually, since the bodies of the dead remain in the ground. In light of Paul's warning, then, Thomas concludes, "It is, therefore, contrary to the truth of the faith to accept a spiritual resurrection and deny a bodily one [*contra veritatem fidei ponere resurrectionem spiritualem, et negare corporalem*]."[6] Aquinas sees further support for this interpretation in 1 Corinthians, where Paul speaks specifically of a bodily resurrection:

> It is clear from what the Apostle says to the Corinthians that the words cited [from 2 Tim. 2 in the preceding paragraph] are to be understood of a bodily resurrection. For, after a bit, he adds: "It is sown a natural body, it shall rise a spiritual body," wherein, manifestly, the body's resurrection is touched on; and a little later he adds, "This corruptible must put on incorruption; and this mortal must put on immortality."[7]

Although some have taken the phrase "spiritual body" to imply something other than a physical resurrection, Thomas makes the same move we have seen in Irenaeus and Augustine. By speaking of the corruptible putting on

5. Aquinas, *SCG* 4.79.1; Aquinas appeals to Rom. 5:12 to establish the connection between sin and death. Hereafter, parenthetical in-text citations are from *SCG*.

6. *SCG* 4.79.6 (O'Neil, *On the Truth of the Catholic Faith*, 298), referring earlier in the same paragraph to 2 Tim. 2:16–18.

7. *SCG* 4.79.7 (O'Neil, *On the Truth of the Catholic Faith*, 298), citing 1 Cor. 15:44, 53. As in chap. 7 above, unless otherwise noted, I cite the biblical text as it appears in Aquinas's works, which at times differs from modern translations.

incorruption, and the mortal immortality, Paul suggests that it is precisely the body, which is mortal and corruptible, that will be raised and transformed.[8]

A few chapters later in *SCG*, Aquinas turns to the question of the nature of the resurrected body, once again touching on the nature of Christ's victory over death. Specifically, he argues that the dead will be raised to life immortal, rather than to a life that will once again end in death. Thomas begins by reiterating the connection between sin and death, the latter being the punishment for the former: "Now the necessity of dying is a defect in human nature stemming from sin [*defectus in naturam humanam ex peccato proveniens*]."[9] It is this defect that Christ conquers through the merits of his passion, removing not only the guilt of sin but also the punishment of mortality (4.82.2). Moreover, Thomas continues, Paul describes the gift of salvation in Romans 5 as far surpassing the tragic consequences of Adam's offense. In light of this superabundance, the dead will rise never to die again: "From this we gather that Christ's merit is more efficacious in destroying death than Adam's sin in causing it. Therefore, those who rise again, being delivered from death by the merits of Christ, will not die again" (4.82.2). If the general resurrection were only temporary and were to end once again in death, then Christ would not have actually conquered death, a point Thomas underscores in the next paragraph. If human beings are to rise only to die again, then death will not have been destroyed: "Therefore, if after rising from the dead [human beings] are to die again, so that death will go on forever, death was in no sense [*nullo modo*] destroyed by the death of Christ" (4.82.3, modified). Scripture, however, attests to the destruction of death in both the Old and the New Testaments. For Christ's victory to be complete, then, the dead must rise one day, never to die again (4.82.3).[10]

Thomas's insistence on the bodily nature of the general resurrection does not exclude a spiritual resurrection in the present life. He knows that the NT refers to both kinds of resurrection (4.79.8). In the Gospel of John, for example, Christ promises both a spiritual and a bodily resurrection: "Amen, amen, I say unto you that the hour comes and now is when the dead shall hear the voice of the Son of God and they that hear shall live" (John 5:25). The adverb "now" indicates that this rising from the dead is not bodily, but rather spiritual (4.79.8).[11] A few verses later in John, however, Christ also promises a

8. *SCG* 4.79.7 (O'Neil, *On the Truth of the Catholic Faith*, 298): "But the corruptible and the mortal mean the body. Therefore, it is the body that will rise."

9. *SCG* 4.82.2 (my translation). See also the discussion in Gaine, "Resurrection and Eschatology," 371–72.

10. Regarding the destruction of death, Aquinas cites Hosea 13:14 ("I will be your death, O death") and 1 Cor. 15:26 ("The last enemy to be destroyed is death").

11. Aquinas comments: "And this seems to pertain to the spiritual resurrection of souls, which even then was beginning to be completed, when some were cleaving to Christ in faith" (O'Neil, *On the Truth of the Catholic Faith*, 298).

bodily resurrection: "The hour is coming, when all who are in the graves shall hear the voice of the Son of God" (John 5:28). Noting that corpses rather than souls lie in graves, Thomas concludes that this second resurrection is a bodily one: "Therefore, the resurrection of bodies is foretold here [*Praedicitur ergo hic corporum resurrection*]" (4.79.8). Although he does not comment on this aspect of the passage, the absence of the adverb "now" also points to a future resurrection in contrast to the one described in John 5:25, and so one might expect it to be of a different nature. As we will see, though, there is a close connection for Aquinas between the spiritual resurrection in the present life and the bodily resurrection in the next life.

Without the defeat of death brought about by the actual raising and transformation of the body, then, Christ's victory over sin would be incomplete. The connection between sin and death, which appears numerous times in the NT, thus serves as an important basis for Thomas's affirmation of the resurrection of the body.

The Exemplarity of Christ's Resurrection

Aquinas offers a second argument in *SCG* to support the bodily resurrection—namely, the paradigmatic role that Christ's own resurrection plays in several NT passages. In characteristic fashion, he often interprets this pattern through the notion of causality, pointing out the correspondence between the cause and the effect. For example, in discussing the immortality of the resurrected bodies, he argues that their properties must resemble the cause of their resurrection, Christ's own resurrected body: "An effect, moreover, is likened to its cause. But the resurrection of Christ is the cause of the future resurrection [*causa est futurae resurrectionis*], as was said. But Christ so rose from the dead as to die no longer. . . . Therefore, human beings will so rise as to die no longer [*Homines igitur sic resurgent ut ulterius non moriantur*]" (4.82.4).[12] This kind of reasoning reappears in several of Thomas's biblical commentaries, as we will see, but first let us consider one other passage in *SCG*.

In addition to considering whether the resurrection will be bodily, Aquinas also inquires into the nature of the resurrected body—that is, whether the resurrected body will be of the same kind as our mortal bodies (that is, consisting of flesh and blood). The question arises because some had argued that the resurrection would be spiritual rather than bodily: "Of these [people who say that bodies are necessarily subject to corruption] some held that our bodies will not rise again with a corporeal nature, but will be transformed into

12. O'Neil, *On the Truth of the Catholic Faith*, 309 (modified). With respect to Christ's immortality, Aquinas cites Rom. 6:9.

spirits" (4.84.2).[13] Those who take this position, Thomas notes, misinterpret 1 Corinthians 15 with its reference to a "spiritual body" (4.84.2). Others read it as suggesting that the risen body will be something like air, taking the adjective "spiritual" to be related to the word for "spiration," which refers to air (4.84.2). Still others affirm that the risen saints will have bodies, but heavenly rather than earthly bodies. This position, Thomas suggests, stems from combining Paul's distinction between celestial bodies and earthly bodies in 1 Corinthians 15:40 with his assertion that "flesh and blood cannot inherit the kingdom" (1 Cor. 15:50).[14]

Aquinas argues against all three of these positions by interpreting Paul's understanding of the resurrection in light of Luke's description of the risen Jesus. In the letter to the Philippians, Paul describes the resurrection of believers as a conformity to Christ's own resurrection: "He will change our lowly body to be like his glorious body."[15] Thomas understands this statement to suggest that the risen bodies of the saints will be like that of the risen Christ described in the Gospels. Christ's body, particularly as presented in Luke, maintains several characteristics of our earthly bodies—it is able to touch and to feel. Moreover, Christ tells the disciples that, unlike a spirit, his body is made of flesh and bone. In light of this description, the risen bodies of the saints will not be pure spirit, nor will they be made of air. Rather, "other [human beings], when they rise again, will likewise have palpable bodies, consisting of flesh and bone [*ex carnibus et ossibus composita*]" (4.84.3).[16] This is not, of course, to say that the resurrected bodies will differ in no way from our present bodies. The most important and obvious difference, one that also stems from the paradigmatic nature of Christ's resurrection, is that these bodies will be incorruptible.[17] Thomas gives several reasons for this incorruptibility, but the most important is the cause of the resurrection, God himself, who will preserve forever the new life given to the body (4.85.6). The key point is that the risen body will be of the same nature as the body in this present life.

The idea that Christ's resurrection serves as the exemplar for the general resurrection appears at several points in the Pauline corpus.[18] In order to flesh out Thomas's interpretation of this paradigmatic character, it is worth considering a few of his commentaries on the Pauline epistles.

13. For a brief discussion of Aquinas's arguments in favor of a flesh-and-blood resurrected body, see Gaine, "Resurrection and Eschatology," 366–67.

14. *SCG* 4.84.2. There is nothing new under the sun. This (mis)reading of 1 Cor. 15:50, it seems, will be with us always.

15. Phil. 3:21 (as cited in *SCG* 4.84.3).

16. The same argument appears in Aquinas's lectures on 1 Corinthians. See *I Ad Cor.* 984. For a similar move in Augustine, see chap. 10 above.

17. See again, briefly, Gaine, "Resurrection and Eschatology," 371–72.

18. See the discussion of some of these texts on pp. 152–56 above.

In his lectures on 1 Thessalonians, Aquinas develops the connection between Christ's resurrection and the general resurrection, presenting the former not only as the model but also as the efficient cause of the latter. Commenting on 1 Thessalonians 4:14, he points out the structure of Paul's argument regarding our resurrection: "It should be realized that the Apostle constructs the case for our resurrection on the basis of the resurrection of Christ, for Christ's resurrection is the cause of our resurrection."[19] The power of Christ's resurrection thus provides a basis for the hope with which Paul encourages the Thessalonians. But, Thomas adds, Christ's resurrection also is the model of our resurrection: "Christ's resurrection is not only the cause but also the pattern of our resurrection [*non est causa solum, sed etiam exemplar*]."[20] More specifically, the effects of Christ's resurrection on his flesh point to the nature of the Christian hope: "Christ is the pattern [*exemplar*] of our resurrection in that Christ assumed flesh, and also rose embodied in flesh."[21] As in *SCG*, Aquinas here insists on the fleshly nature of the resurrection.

Thomas expands on the exemplary nature of Christ's resurrection in his lectures on 1 Corinthians, drawing a close connection between conformity to Christ in the present through the life of grace and conformity to Christ in the life of glory. Thomas bases this understanding on the parallels Paul draws between Adam and Christ in 1 Corinthians 15:48–49. Because Adam was mortal and corruptible, so also are all his descendants. But by the same logic, "Because the second man was from heaven, i.e., spiritual and immortal, so we all will be both immortal and spiritual: 'for if we have been united with him in a death like his, we shall certainly be united with him in a resurrection like his.'"[22] This conformity to Christ takes two forms. In the present life, we must be like him by pursuing the life of grace. It is only on this basis that one can subsequently be conformed to him in glory.[23]

Earlier in these lectures Thomas argues for the resurrection on the basis of efficient causality. On his reading, Paul's argument presupposes a connection between Christ's resurrection and the future resurrection of believers, an assumption the apostle makes explicit elsewhere in his letters. Commenting on Paul's question, "How can some of you say there is no resurrection of the dead?" (1 Cor. 15:12), Aquinas paraphrases: "As if to say: if Christ rose from the dead, as we preach: 'since we believe that Christ died and rose again,' no one should doubt the future resurrection of the dead. Hence: 'he who raised

19. *I Ad Thess.* 95.
20. *I Ad Thess.* 95.
21. *I Ad Thess.* 95. *Etenim eo quod Christus accepit carnem, et in ea resurrexit, est exemplar nostrae resurrectionis.*
22. *I Ad Cor.* 997.
23. *I Ad Cor.* 998.

Christ Jesus from the dead will give life to our mortal bodies.'"[24] Thomas suggests that the underlying logic of Paul's argument depends on the causal nature of Christ's resurrection, which is twofold. First, following the *Glossa Ordinaria* (a medieval collection of biblical interpretations drawn primarily from the early church), Christ is the efficient cause of the resurrection: "according to a Gloss it should be said: 'if Christ,' who is the efficient cause of our resurrection [*qui est causa effeciens nostrae resurrectionis*], 'arose, how do some in you say that there is no resurrection of the dead?'"[25] Christ is the efficient cause through his humanity, which acts as "an instrument of his divinity [*instrumentum divinitatis suae*]."[26] As noted above, the resurrection of Christ's human body also serves as an exemplar cause, providing the pattern by which all believers will one day rise.[27]

Paul's statement that "flesh and blood cannot possess the kingdom of God" leads Aquinas to address the nature of the resurrection. In defense of the bodily nature of this event, he repeats an argument seen in *SCG*. To say that the body will become a spirit or air or some other substance is an error. Rather, Christ's resurrection serves as the paradigm for the general resurrection: "For the Apostle says that our body will be conformed to his body of radiance. Therefore, since Christ after his resurrection has flesh and blood [*carnem et sanguinem*], . . . it is certain that we too will have flesh and blood [*carnem et sanguinem*] in the resurrection."[28] The phrase "flesh and blood" should not be taken to refer to what makes up the substance of our body per se, then, but rather to the corruption of our mortal flesh.[29] This is why Paul follows up the statement about "flesh and blood" with the assertion "Neither shall corruption possess incorruption." In the kingdom the saints will rise in glory, freed from corruption.[30]

At a few points in his commentary on Romans, Thomas again draws a close connection between spiritual resurrection in the present life through

24. *I Ad Cor.* 912. On the origins of this commentary, see 130n50 above. Bynum (*The Resurrection of the Body in Western Christianity*, 233) notes with respect to his exposition of 1 Cor. 15, "[Aquinas's] clear but conventional readings can serve to introduce the issues and images characteristic of scholastic discussion in the 1250s and 1260s."

25. *I Ad Cor.* 913.

26. *I Ad Cor.* 914. By describing Christ's humanity as an "instrument of his divinity," Aquinas is affirming at least two things. First, Christ's humanity does not have power in its own nature to bring about resurrection—only God can raise the dead. Second, though, in Christ God brings about resurrection *through* Christ's humanity, not apart from it.

27. *I Ad Cor.* 914.

28. *I Ad Cor.* 999 (modified). The ellipses replace Luke 24:39, which Thomas frequently cites in defense of the bodily nature of the resurrection.

29. *I Ad Cor.* 1000: "That is, after the resurrection, the body will not be subject to the corruption of flesh and blood." Aquinas also suggests that "flesh and blood" might refer to "those devoting themselves to flesh and blood, namely, human beings given to vices and lusts" or to "the works of flesh and blood."

30. *I Ad Cor.* 1000.

the power of grace and the future bodily resurrection. These two different aspects of resurrection are linked by the way they conform us to Christ. In the present life, Christians are to conform their spiritual lives to the example of Christ. Only by doing so will they attain to a glorious resurrection at Christ's return. For the sake of brevity, I will limit myself to Thomas's discussion of one passage from Romans 8.

Romans 8:9–11 ties together the indwelling of Christ in believers with the Spirit's action both in raising Christ from the dead and in raising believers. Aquinas interprets this indwelling as being conformed to Christ, once again implying Christ's paradigmatic role for the Christian life in the present and for the resurrection: "'But if Christ is' thus 'in you,' you should be conformed to Christ."[31] Before explicitly drawing out the implications for the Christian life, Thomas notes the transformation that the Spirit will bring about through the resurrection: "He does not say 'dead,' but 'mortal,' because in the resurrection there will be taken away from our bodies not only that they are dead, i.e., having the necessity of death [*necessitatem mortis habentia*], but also that they are mortal, i.e., capable of dying [*potentia mori*], as was Adam's body before sin. For after the resurrection our bodies will be wholly immortal [*penitus immortalia*]."[32] Just as Christ was raised immortal, so, too, those in Christ will receive bodies that are indestructible. But the proper preparation for such a reward is putting sin to death in the present: "'But if by the spirit,' i.e., through the spirit, 'you mortify the deeds of the flesh,' i.e., deeds which flow from the desires of the flesh, 'you will live,' namely, the life of grace in the present and the life of glory in the future."[33] Thomas again presents the life of grace as leading to the life of glory, which takes the shape of an immortal, bodily life, free from corruption.

"More Pleasing in Being More Complete"

The first two arguments Aquinas gives for the necessity of the resurrection apply only to the redeemed. In addition to these, he offers an argument for the bodily nature of the resurrection based on his anthropology. This third argument extends not only to the saints, but also to the damned. In keeping with several biblical texts, Thomas believes that all human beings will rise at the end of time, either to glory or to condemnation.[34] This argument stems from two crucial aspects of Thomas's anthropology: The soul is immortal,

31. *Ad Rom.* 629.
32. *Ad Rom.* 630.
33. *Ad Rom.* 633.
34. Aquinas notes, for example, Christ's statement that "*all* in the tombs will hear [the Son of God's] voice" (John 5:28). See, e.g., *I Ad Cor.* 932.

and the soul is not the entire human being.[35] A full account of Thomas's understanding of human beings as composed of matter (the body) and form (the soul) lies beyond the scope of the present study.[36] For my purposes, a brief discussion of the immortality of the soul, body-soul unity, and death as both natural and unnatural will have to suffice.

Aquinas bases his argument for the immortality of the soul on two fundamental principles.[37] First, the soul is subsistent, as it can exist and act (perform intellectual operations) independently of the body. He grounds the first principle in the nature of human knowledge. Because the human being can have a knowledge of all corporeal things by means of the intellect, the intellect cannot be corporeal. If it were corporeal, there would be a limit to what the intellect could know, both with respect to amount and with respect to the kinds of things known. But since the intellect has the potency to know anything in the universe, it must be incorporeal. Moreover, it must have its own operation distinct from the body, and so must be something that subsists per se.[38]

Second, because the soul is the form of the body, it is not composed of matter and, as such, is incorruptible. Aquinas defends this point in articles 5 and 6 of question 75 of the *Prima pars*. In article 5, he asks whether the soul is composed of matter and form, and answers in the negative for two reasons. First, because the soul is the form of the body, by definition it cannot be composite, since the form is what gives act to matter. To illustrate Aquinas's point with a simpler example, the shape of a coffee mug makes the material into a mug. The shape inheres in the matter but does not have any matter of its own. Similarly, the soul makes the body a body rather than a corpse, but it does not have matter separate from that which makes up the body.[39] Second, the argument given in article 2 regarding the soul's intellectual nature also shows that the soul cannot be composed of matter and form. If the soul were composed of matter, it would not be capable of knowing all things.[40] This is because matter is limited—a coffee mug can hold only so much coffee. If the soul were material, it would be limited in the number of things it could learn, but, for Thomas, the intellect is potentially capable of knowing all things.

35. See M. Brown, "Aquinas on the Resurrection of the Body," 172. Aquinas adumbrates this argument in *SCG* 4.79.10.

36. For a good recent account of Thomas's view, see M. Brown, "Aquinas on the Resurrection of the Body," 172–78. One of Aquinas's fullest discussions of the question appears in *SCG* 2.46–94. See also Conn, "Aquinas on Human Nature and the Possibility of Bodiless Existence," 325–28.

37. Here I will be following the arguments laid out in *ST* I, q. 75. See also the discussion in McCord Adams, "Why Bodies as Well as Souls in the Life to Come?," 271–77.

38. *ST* I, q. 75, a. 2.

39. *ST* I, q. 75, a. 5.

40. *ST* I, q. 75, a. 5.

For Aquinas, the nature of the soul as a form also explains why it is incorruptible. Again, on Aristotelian terms, a form is in act, not in potency. Were it otherwise, the form could not give act to matter. The shape of a mug does not depend on the matter but rather makes that matter into a mug. Conversely, matter is corrupted when it is separated from its form, but nothing happens to the form.[41] A form, Thomas argues, cannot be separated from itself and, therefore, is incorruptible. Because the soul is the form of the body, it, too, is incorruptible.[42]

The incorruptible nature of the soul puts the human being in an unusual situation. As a composite creature, the human being is both corruptible (the body, composed of matter) and incorruptible (the soul), the two parts forming an integrated whole. As Thomas argues in question 76 of the *Prima pars*, the soul is united to the body as its form, being that whereby the body lives and performs all its doings from simple metabolic activity to the higher intellectual functions.[43] Moreover, this union between body and soul is a fitting one, because the soul by its nature depends on the body for the sense data it needs for reasoning.[44] But, since the human being is a unified whole of body and soul, the separation of the two at death results in God sustaining the soul in an unnatural existence. This unnatural existence explains why Thomas sees the resurrection as in a certain sense "necessary"—that is, fitting. Before we consider his arguments for this position, it would be worth considering in what sense he sees death as both natural and unnatural.

This dual aspect of death is treated in the *Compendium*. On the one hand, death flows naturally from the material nature of the body. The body is composed of material elements, and so it is subject to change and corruption. Since the soul is not made of matter, however, it is not subject to corruption and continues to exist even after the dissolution of the body. Thus, the separation of the soul from the body appears to be something natural. On the other hand, the continued existence of the soul apart from the body is, in another sense, unnatural, because the soul is by its very nature the form of the body. Without the body, it lacks one of its perfections. For that reason, Thomas argues, in the beginning God gave the body supernatural help to resist corruption, so that the soul would not be separated from matter. With the sin of Adam, however, human beings forfeited this grace, and so the body became corruptible, subject to its nature as a material thing. From the former perspective, then, death is natural. But from the perspective of the union of body and soul, death is unnatural, "since

41. This is why corpses decay. They no longer have the soul making them into a body rather than a corpse.

42. *ST* I, q. 75, a. 6.

43. *ST* I, q. 76, a. 1.

44. *ST* I, q. 76, a. 5.

it is natural for the soul to be united to the body [*cum naturale sit animae corpori esse unitam*]."[45]

Based on this natural union of body and soul, Aquinas argues for the necessity of the resurrection in a qualified sense, and not only for the just.[46] His argument proceeds along three interrelated lines. First, the resurrection is necessary because the separation of body and soul is unnatural. Second, it completes human happiness. Finally, it ensures that salvation does not bring about a change in the species of the one saved.

The first argument stems from Thomas's analysis of human nature and from the principle that nothing contrary to nature can exist in perpetuity.[47] This argument is not demonstrative, but rather an argument from fittingness. Although the soul persists after death because of its immaterial nature, it nevertheless lacks an important aspect of its essence—namely, animating the body. If the soul continued in such an existence, it would exist contrary to its own nature. Such an unnatural existence cannot go on indefinitely, thus at some point the soul must no longer exist without a body. Aquinas concludes, "Since, then, [the soul] persists perpetually, it must once again be united to the body; and this is to rise again. Therefore, the immortality of souls seems to demand [*exigere videtur*] a future resurrection of bodies."[48] It is worth noting that this line of reasoning follows several arguments based on the authority of Scripture in the same chapter of *SCG*. Thus, it serves not as the basis of belief in the resurrection, but rather as a supporting argument for its fittingness.[49]

Just as death is both natural and unnatural, Thomas suggests that the resurrection is also both natural and unnatural in different senses.[50] If one considers the resurrection from the perspective of its end, then it is "natural," since it aims at the union of body and soul. Considered from the perspective of its cause, however, the resurrection is not natural—that is, it does not

45. *Compendium* 1.152.

46. For a good treatment of this issue, see again M. Brown, "Aquinas on the Resurrection of the Body." On 178–79 Brown writes, "It is the nature of the human soul to be at once rational (and hence immortal) *and* the form of this particular individual. Although the doctrine of the resurrection may seem surprising, Aquinas would say that it is more reasonable than any other alternative." Similarly, Hütter notes (*Bound for Beatitude*, 426), "The beatitude of the blessed in its full integrity does not simply pertain to the blessed *qua* separated souls but to the blessed *qua* human beings. Embodiment is natural to human beings; hence, also in resurrection life, the human soul remains ordered to inform and enliven a body; for the human being is essentially an embodied being." A little later (427) he adds, "The resurrection of the body belongs to the full integrity of the beatitude of the blessed *qua* human beings."

47. *SCG* 4.79.10.

48. *SCG* 4.79.10 (O'Neil, *On the Truth of the Catholic Faith*, 299). Strictly speaking, the resurrection is not necessary.

49. Thomas is happy to bring in these philosophical arguments in support of the authority of Scripture. He thus offers a similar version of the argument in his lectures on 1 Corinthians. See *I Ad Cor*. 924.

50. *SCG* 4.81.14.

happen by human power, but through divine power. Because the resurrection conforms with nature by reuniting body and soul, Aquinas argues that both the just and the unjust will rise: "For the Son of God assumed human nature to restore it. Therefore, *what is a defect of nature* [*defectus naturae*] *will be restored in all, and so all will return from death to life* [*a morte redibunt ad vitam*]."[51] Again, this argument from reason serves to support a position held on the authority of Scripture.

Aquinas also offers an argument for the necessity of the resurrection on the basis of human happiness. Happiness, he notes, signifies the perfection of a being: "Ultimate happiness is the perfection of the happy one."[52] Without its natural perfection, then, a creature cannot truly enjoy happiness in every way. It belongs to the essence of the soul to inform the body, such that a separated soul lacks perfection: "The soul separated from the body is in a way imperfect [*aliquo modo imperfecta*], as is every part existing outside of its whole, for the soul is naturally a part of human nature [*anima enim naturaliter est pars humanae naturae*]."[53] Without a resurrection of the body, then, the human desire for happiness would be frustrated.[54] A lovely poetic depiction of this argument appears in the fourteenth canto of Dante's *Paradiso*. There the souls affirm: "When our flesh, made glorious at the Judgment Seat, / dresses us once again, then shall our persons / become more pleasing in being more complete."[55] The person cannot experience beatitude in every way as long as the soul does not perform its function of animating the body.

A third argument offers not so much a defense of the necessity of the resurrection as a specification of its nature. Later in Book 4 of *SCG*, Thomas returns to the question of the nature of the resurrection.[56] Some interpreters, he notes once more, suggest that the resurrection entails the transformation of the body into a spirit or air. In response to such interpretations, Thomas again points to the paradigmatic nature of Christ's resurrection. As Christ rose with a (glorified) body of flesh and bone, so, too, human beings will rise

51. *SCG* 4.81.15 (O'Neil, *On the Truth of the Catholic Faith*, 308, emphasis added). McCord Adams puts it well ("Why Bodies as Well as Souls in the Life to Come?," 296): "Because soul-body composites are what we *are* metaphysically, the intellectual soul is only a metaphysical fragment of a human being. Resurrection and reunion make the human individual a better being because metaphysically perfect and complete."

52. *SCG* 4.79.11.

53. *SCG* 4.79.11 (O'Neil, *On the Truth of the Catholic Faith*, 299).

54. *SCG* 4.79.11. Again, Thomas offers a similar argument in his lectures on 1 Corinthians: "It is clear that the human being naturally desires his own salvation; but the soul, since it is part of the human being's body, is not an entire human being, and my soul is not I; hence, although the soul obtains salvation in another life, nevertheless, not I or any human being" (*I Ad Cor.* 924, modified). See also Leget, *Living with God*, 226: "Thus the essence of beatitude is reached [before the resurrection]; its ultimate perfection, however, is delayed until corporal resurrection."

55. Dante, *Paradiso* 14.43–45.

56. *SCG* 4.84.1–17.

one day with bodies of flesh and bone.[57] Aquinas then supplements this argument from authority with another anthropological point. Relying once again on the nature of the human being as a body-soul composite, he notes that, because the soul retains its species when separated from the body, when the two are reunited, the body, too, must retain its species in order for the risen human being to remain a human being.[58] Moreover, since the matter of the human body belongs to the essence of the species, if the soul were united to an altogether different kind of matter, the one "raised" would be a human being "only equivocally [*tantum aequivoce*]."[59]

The intrinsically composite nature of human beings, then, serves as a supporting argument for Thomas regarding both the necessity and the nature of the resurrection. In addition to this anthropological argument, he offers a fourth reason for the resurrection, one also based on an important aspect of anthropology. This argument does not appear in any one place in his writings, but rather must be gleaned from a variety of texts. The argument concerns the social nature of human beings.[60]

"A Human Being Rejoices More with Many Rejoicing"

When Aquinas discusses anthropology explicitly, he tends to focus on the individual, treating the nature of the soul, its powers, and its union with the body. Neither in the *Summa Theologiae* nor in *SCG* does he address the nature of the human being as a social animal.[61] The reason may lie in the aim of those two works, where he focuses with precision on the substance of human nature. Since sociality falls under Aristotle's category of "relation," it is an "accident" and therefore not a part of the substance of being human.[62] This does not, however, mean that Thomas ignores the social

57. *SCG* 4.84.3.

58. *SCG* 4.84.4; see also *Compendium* 1.153: "And since the soul is united to the body as its form, and proper matter corresponds to each form, the body to which the soul will be reunited needs to belong to the same nature and kind as the body that death put an end to. Therefore, the soul in the resurrection regains a human body composed of flesh and bones, with the same organs of which it now consists, not a celestial or brazen body, or the body of another animal, as some have fantasized."

59. *SCG* 4.84.5. The question of bodily continuity between death and resurrection is a complicated one. For a few recent attempts to address the question, see M. Brown, "Aquinas on the Resurrection of the Body"; Van Dyke, "Human Identity, Imminent Causal Relations, and the Principle of Non-Repeatability"; Gaine, "Resurrection and Eschatology," 366–70.

60. For a brief modern perspective on the social nature of the resurrection, see Ratzinger, *Eschatology*, 159–60, 234–38. On 160, Ratzinger writes, "Eternal life does not isolate a person, but leads him out of isolation into true unity with his brothers and sisters and the whole of God's creation."

61. See *ST* I, qq. 75–102; *SCG* 2.46–90.

62. I am grateful to my colleague Travis Lacy for suggesting this explanation to me.

dimension of human nature or thinks it unimportant. Scattered throughout his writings there emerges an important role for the sociability of the human race, more specifically with respect to the resurrection.[63] This communal element of human existence helps Thomas explain both the fittingness of the resurrection and its timing.[64] In this section I will focus solely on how the social nature of human beings serves as an additional argument for bodily resurrection.[65]

Although not the most prominent theme in his eschatology, Aquinas does speak occasionally of the social dimensions of beatitude.[66] In his commentary on the Psalms, for example, he expounds on the importance of friendship, even in the next life. Commenting on Psalm 5, he notes that heaven will have the character of a society: "[The joy of the saints is derived] from society. For, a human being alone cannot rejoice well over anything, but only when he has friends with him sharing in his good."[67] Thomas then suggests that such society perfects those who dwell there "because it is appropriate for friends to rejoice in the good of a friend."[68] As Ray Petry notes, Thomas frequently speaks of ultimate beatitude in social terms, referring especially to the redeemed as a "company of those mutualized by their love of God."[69] In the *Tertia pars*, for example, Aquinas notes the continuity between the church on earth and the church in heaven: "The Church, on earth, is the congregation of the faithful; but, in heaven, it is the congregation of the comprehensors."[70] The character of the church as a community on earth, then, extends into the next world.

These and other texts underscore the communal nature of salvation as Aquinas understands it, but what of the resurrection? In at least two texts, he draws a connection between the communal nature of salvation and the

63. In this section, I depend heavily on Kromholtz, *On the Last Day*, 337–53, 423–34. In addition to the examples given here, Gaine ("Resurrection and Eschatology," 363–64) suggests that Aquinas's understanding of the last judgment also underscores the social character of human nature.

64. Kromholtz, *On the Last Day*, 338–41, 423–34.

65. As noted in chap. 8, according to Jon Levenson, the social character of ancient Israelite self-understanding played an important role in the development of hope in the resurrection. See Levenson, *Resurrection and the Restoration of Israel*, 108–22.

66. For an older essay on this question, see Petry, "The Social Character of Heavenly Beatitude." For a more recent defense of Aquinas's understanding of the social dimension of beatitude, see Hütter, *Bound for Beatitude*, 437–45. Thiel (*Icons of Hope*, 36–37) is simply incorrect when he implies that there is no social dimension to Thomas's eschatology.

67. *Sup. Ps.* 5.8. Translations are mine from the text found at http://www.corpusthomisticum.org/iopera.html. The Latin reads *Tertio ex societate: quia solus homo non potest bene gaudere aliquo, sed quando amicos habet secum participes illius boni.*

68. *Sup. Ps.* 5.8: *Hoc enim proprium est amicorum gaudere de bono amici.*

69. Petry, "The Social Character of Heavenly Beatitude," 72–75; the quoted phrase appears on 72.

70. *ST* III, q. 8, a. 4, ad 2.

necessity of the resurrection. In the *Sentences* commentary, he suggests that the resurrection will add to the joy of the just in two ways. Speaking of the general judgment, he writes, "For the good will also be further rewarded after the judgment, both by the addition of the body's glory and *by the number of the saints being complete* [*ex numero sanctorum completo*]."[71] The resurrection thus has a twofold significance: It contributes to the perfection of the human being both individually through the reunion of body and soul and corporately, thus fulfilling the social dimension of human nature. Thomas returns to this notion in his lectures on Hebrews. Commenting on Hebrews 11:39–40, he again describes the joy of the resurrection in communal terms as something shared with others: "As a Gloss says, the joy of each will become greater in the common joy of all. Hence, God provides for us in this matter. Therefore, he says, 'God providing some better thing for us': 'Behold how good and how pleasant it is for brethren to dwell together in unity.' *For a human being rejoices more with many rejoicing* [*Magis enim gaudet homo cum pluribus gaudentibus*]."[72] The social nature of human beings illuminates an additional purpose for the resurrection: The resurrection perfects not only the composite unity of body and soul, but also the communal dimension of human existence, and extends the joy of the redeemed both personally and communally. Once again, Dante offers a beautiful poetic depiction of this teaching in the *Paradiso*. Following a description of the glory of the resurrection, the saints cry out with longing to experience this transformation:

> And "Amen!" cried the souls of either chain
> with such prompt zeal as to make evident
> how much they yearned to wear their flesh again;
>
> *perhaps less for themselves than for the love*
> *of mothers, fathers, and those each soul held dear*
> before it became an eternal flame above.[73]

71. *Scriptum* 4.47.1.1.1 ad 2 (emphasis added). For a brief discussion of this text, see Kromholtz, *On the Last Day*, 376–77.

72. *Ad Heb.* 655 (modified and emphasis added). Part of the English translation of this passage is missing in the hard copy of the Aquinas Institute's edition of the Hebrews commentary. I have taken the missing portion from https://aquinas.cc/la/en/~Heb.C11.L8.n655. For a fuller discussion of this text see Kromholtz, *On the Last Day*, 428–33.

73. Dante, *Paradiso* 14.61–66 (emphasis added). For a good recent discussion of the nature of the soul's desire for the body from Thomas's perspective, see Dillard, "Keeping the Vision," 408–11. Dillard offers a plausible account of how the soul's desire for reunion with the body need not imply a lack in the soul's enjoyment of the beatific vision. See also, more recently, Hütter, *Bound for Beatitude*, 433–36, who speaks of the soul's "ontological" desire for the body in such a way that does not compromise the soul's enjoyment of the vision of God during the interim state.

The souls in this canto reflect Thomas's observation that "a human being rejoices more with many rejoicing."[74] Implicit in Thomas's teaching and the cry of the saints in the *Paradiso* is an understanding of human interaction that demands bodily presence. To be reunited with loved ones, human beings must once again be embodied souls.[75] Without the resurrection, then, the perfection of the redeemed, and thus the extension of their joy, would remain incomplete.

Resurrection and Beatific Vision

I noted toward the end of part 2 that certain elements in Aquinas's account of the beatific vision might imply that the resurrection of the body is unnecessary. At times Thomas even says, incautiously, that the body hinders the soul from seeing God.[76] Moreover, given that he interprets this vision as an act of the soul that satisfies the deepest human desires, the resurrection would seem to be superfluous. The burden of this chapter has been to show that the resurrection plays no less important a role in Thomas's understanding of the Christian hope than the vision of God. Depending on the writings of St. Paul, he argues that the resurrection is a nonnegotiable aspect of salvation, because only if the saints are raised does Christ's victory extend over *both* sin and death. Aquinas also adopts Paul's idea that Christ's resurrection is the pattern of our own future resurrection. Perhaps Thomas's greatest contribution, though, is his anthropological argument for the fittingness of the resurrection, with respect to both the composite nature of human beings and the social character of human life. If we do not receive our bodies back through resurrection, then it is not the whole human person who is saved, because a soul is not a complete human being. And even if the corporate nature of the resurrection does not increase the intensity of the joy of seeing God, it nevertheless extends that joy in a more fitting way.

Like the vision of God, the resurrection features prominently both in the biblical witness and in the Christian tradition. The Scriptures hold out the promise of a bodily resurrection that involves both a definitive victory over death and the restoration of relationships. Christ's resurrection represents

74. See also Levering, *Jesus and the Demise of Death*, 112: "The blessed enjoy God together rather than solely individually, because sharing happiness with friends belongs to the *bene esse* of happiness."

75. The unified chorus of the saints in the quotation above might seem to contradict this point, but Dante can be forgiven for taking poetic license. We have no way of describing the status of the disembodied soul other than through the language and images of ordinary interaction that we experience daily, since a completely immaterial existence is, by definition, beyond the sense and imaginative powers. This desire need not imply any lack of enjoyment in the beatific vision. See again Dillard, "Keeping the Vision," 408–11.

76. See *Sup. Io.* 213 and the discussion of this text on pp. 128–30 above.

the fullness of these promises and serves as the pattern for the hope of Christians; it is also made present in the Eucharist, a foretaste of the glory to come. Each of the three thinkers we have considered highlights important elements of the resurrection, either by connecting this hope to other biblical themes or by articulating it philosophically. In the writings of Irenaeus, we see a synthesis of the biblical material underscoring the goodness of creation and the flesh. Jesus's incarnation, his healing activity, his institution of the Eucharist, and his resurrection all point to the capacity of the flesh one day to receive eternal life. In Augustine, we have found replies to some of the most common existential objections to the hope of the resurrection—namely, the various kinds of suffering that attend embodied life as we currently experience it. Reading 1 Corinthians 15 closely, he insists that the resurrected body will consist of flesh, but of a flesh transformed by and obedient to the Spirit, no longer capable of suffering. Aquinas supplements these arguments with a robust anthropological defense of the resurrection, incorporating the nature of human beings as a complex unity of body and soul and our inherently social orientation. Moreover, he roots the significance of the resurrection in Christ's victory, which must conquer both sin and death.

Having explored the nature of the beatific vision and the resurrection as aspects of the Christian hope, it remains to bring the two together into a synthesis. In the final part of this study, I will propose an integrated picture of this hope, considering the question in light of the biblical categories of worship, dominion, and rest surveyed in the first part of this study as well as the understanding of vision and resurrection that has emerged in parts 2 and 3.

PART 4

"WITH MY BODY I THEE WORSHIP"

The Life of the World to Come

TWELVE

Worship, Dominion, and Rest in the New Creation

Thus far, we have considered the threefold human vocation in light of our ultimate end, as well as the hope for the vision of God and the bodily resurrection as articulated in Scripture and three major Christian thinkers. But the question remains: What is the relationship between the general resurrection and the beatific vision? What does each of these two aspects of Christian eschatology contribute to human happiness, and how might they be integrated? To address these questions, I will return to the threefold human vocation of Genesis, though I will discuss these three themes in a different order. I will begin with worship, which serves as the governing theme in the closing chapters of the book of Revelation. Dominion, which also plays a prominent role in NT eschatology, will then follow. Finally, I will conclude with rest, with which Augustine's *City of God* culminates. Each of these three dimensions of the human vocation contributes to an integral understanding of our end. The vision of God and the resurrection of the body come together in the fully human (i.e., body and soul) response of praise and thanksgiving to God for his acts of creation and redemption, as well as for his own goodness.

"With My Body I Thee Worship"

In his *Reflections on the Psalms*, C. S. Lewis devotes a chapter to discussing why the psalms so frequently encourage the people to praise the Lord.[1] A superficial reading of the Psalter might interpret these exhortations as an

1. Lewis, *Reflections on the Psalms*, 90–98.

imposition, or worse, as a sign of neurosis on the part of God. As Lewis notes, "We all despise the man who demands continued assurance of his own virtue, intelligence or delightfulness; we despise still more the crowd of people round every dictator, every millionaire, every celebrity, who gratify that demand."[2] What, Lewis asks, distinguishes the biblical summons to offer praise to the Lord from the petty demands to flatter an insecure tyrant or the sycophantic adulation of his unquestioning followers? The key distinction, he suggests, lies in the wonder that motivates the calls to praise. Whereas the tyrant's demand stems from raw power and self-promotion, the worship of God is something appropriate to the nature of the one praised. We call objects "admirable" not in an arbitrary manner, but because there is something in them worthy of admiration.[3] Similarly, though on a much grander scale—indeed, on an infinitely grander one—God is the one most worthy of praise. The purpose of praise, however, is not to offer God something he lacks. As Lewis notes, the Scriptures make it quite clear that God has no need of our praise.[4] Rather, the purpose of worship is to enter into communion with God, the ultimate Good: "It is in the process of being worshipped that God communicates His presence to men."[5] Lewis's observation finds considerable biblical support, in that the language commonly used to describe God's presence among his people has cultic overtones. As we saw in chapter 3, in Revelation 21 John writes, "See, the home [lit., "tabernacle," *skēnē*] of God is among mortals. He will dwell [*skēnōsei*] with them" (Rev. 21:3a). This language reflects God's presence in the tabernacle following the exodus and, later, in Solomon's temple.

The connection between worship and presence, however, does not constitute the most important aspect of praise for Lewis. Reflecting on the instinctive human inclination to praise people or things, he suggests that praise is not simply a superfluous addition to an already complete experience. Rather, in a real sense praise brings an enjoyable experience, whether of a person or of a thing, to its completion: "I think we delight to praise what we enjoy because the praise *not merely expresses but completes the enjoyment*; *it is its appointed consummation*. It is not out of compliment that lovers keep on telling one another how beautiful they are; the delight is incomplete till it is expressed."[6] When people encounter something wondrous, praise comes naturally to their lips. Moreover, Lewis continues, a penchant for praise—genuine praise, rather than obsequiousness—is a good indicator of a healthy mind: "The humblest, and at the same time most balanced and capacious,

2. Lewis, *Reflections on the Psalms*, 90.

3. Lewis, *Reflections on the Psalms*, 90.

4. Lewis, *Reflections on the Psalms*, 93. Lewis cites Ps. 50:12 ("If I were hungry, I would not tell you") to make the point.

5. Lewis, *Reflections on the Psalms*, 93.

6. Lewis, *Reflections on the Psalms*, 95 (emphasis added).

minds, praised most, while the cranks, misfits and malcontents praised least. The good critics found something to praise in many imperfect works; the bad ones continually narrowed the list of books we might be allowed to read."[7] Perhaps more important for the present study, however, is Lewis's reflection on the social dimension of praise. Rarely, if ever, does a person struck by beauty keep the praise to herself: "Just as men spontaneously praise whatever they value, so they spontaneously urge us to join them in praising it: 'Isn't she lovely? Wasn't it glorious? Don't you think that magnificent?' The Psalmists in telling everyone to praise God are doing what all men do when they speak of what they care about."[8] By its very nature, praise seems incomplete until one shares it with another person.

Lewis's meditation on the nature of praise has significant implications for the primary question of this study. If the simple natural delights of this world evoke praise within us, then how much more will the beatific vision—which Aquinas describes as the fulfillment of all human desires and Augustine equates with perfect Goodness, perfect Beauty, perfect Love—draw out a perfect act of worship. Lewis himself draws this conclusion:

> If it were possible for a created soul fully (I mean, up to the full measure conceivable in a finite being) to "appreciate," that is to love and delight in, the worthiest object of all, and simultaneously at every moment to give this delight perfect expression, then that soul would be in supreme beatitude. It is along these lines that I find it easiest to understand the Christian doctrine that "Heaven" is a state in which angels now, and men hereafter, are perpetually employed in praising God.[9]

Worship and delight go hand in hand. For that reason, in the next life to glorify God and to enjoy him amount to the same thing.[10]

If we combine this insight regarding the nature of praise with the classical Christian anthropology we have seen expressed in different ways in Irenaeus, Augustine, and Aquinas, we can see a further reason for the resurrection, as well as how it is ordered to the beatific vision. Human beings are by nature both embodied souls and social animals. For them to express their praise in a fully human manner—that is, to respond fittingly to the glory of the beatific vision—they will need a reunification of body and soul. Dante poetically depicts this aspect of the human end in the fourteenth canto of the *Paradiso*, in a passage we encountered in the previous chapter. Responding to the promise of the resurrection for which the souls in heaven await, they

7. Lewis, *Reflections on the Psalms*, 94.
8. Lewis, *Reflections on the Psalms*, 94–95.
9. Lewis, *Reflections on the Psalms*, 96.
10. Lewis, *Reflections on the Psalms*, 97.

cry out with longing for the resurrection.[11] Dante's description suggests that, even though the saints in heaven seem to sing in chorus, their reunion with loved ones remains incomplete until they receive back their flesh and bones, granting them full, genuine human interaction with one another. Only when they are once again fully human will beatitude be complete.[12]

The notion that the life of the resurrected saints will consist in worship has an ancient pedigree. The idea appears in each of the three figures considered in parts 2 and 3 above. Irenaeus describes the spontaneous praise that will erupt from the saints when they are raised from the dead: "If therefore, at the present time, having the pledge, we do cry, 'Abba, Father,' what shall it be when, on rising again, we behold Him face to face; when all the members shall burst out into a continuous hymn of triumph, glorifying Him who raised them from the dead, and gave the gift of eternal life?"[13] Irenaeus brings together the resurrection, the immediate vision of God, and worship as the consummation of human redemption. Similarly, Aquinas mentions in passing that the saints will need their resurrected tongues back so that they can praise God with them.[14]

This emphasis on worship comes through most clearly, however—and perhaps most often—in the writings of Augustine. In the famous Easter sermon discussed above (*Serm.* 362), he describes the activity of the saints as continually singing "Amen" and "Alleluia."[15] Fully aware of the response such a description might evoke in his listeners, he immediately reassures them that such activity will not result in boredom:

> But don't let yourselves again be depressed by the flesh-bound thought that if any of you were to stand and say Amen and Alleluia all day long, you would droop with fatigue and boredom; and you will drop off to sleep in the middle of your words, and long to keep quiet; and for that reason you might suppose it is a life you can well do without, not at all desirable, and might say to yourselves, "Amen and Alleluia, we're going to say that forever and ever? Who will be able to endure it?"[16]

11. Dante, *Paradiso* 14.61–66. Dante's language of the saints' yearning for the flesh might seem to contradict the notion that the beatific vision fulfills all human desires, but the context suggests that it refers primarily to the importance of psychosomatic wholeness for salvation.

12. See Levering, *Jesus and the Demise of Death*, 114: "Indeed, no human intimacy with God can be fully human when it lacks bodily expression. . . . The body will be fully 'for the Lord' in the resurrection."

13. Irenaeus, *Haer.* 5.8.1 (modified).

14. Thomas Aquinas, *I Ad Cor.* 789. He bases the expectation of praise as the activity of the saints on Ps. 149:6.

15. Augustine, *Serm.* 362. See the fuller discussion of this text on pp. 190–93 above.

16. Augustine, *Serm.* 362.29.

Augustine goes on to note that the "Amen" and "Alleluia" will be an activity of the mind and the heart motivated by the deep love evoked by the greatness of God and what he has done for us. Moreover, this continual praise will at once satisfy our longings and at the same time keep us longing for more: "And when we say this, we shall of course be saying Amen, but with a different kind of never satisfied satisfaction [*insatiabili satietate*]. Because there will be nothing lacking, you see, that's why complete satisfaction; but because what is not lacking will always be giving delight, that's why, if one can so put it, it will be an unsatisfied satisfaction [*insatiabilis satietas*]."[17] Perhaps most importantly, this activity will not be individualistic, but rather the common worship of the heavenly city:

> And so because we shall see the truth without any distaste and with perpetual delight, and gaze upon it with the most evident certainty, we shall be fired with love of this truth and cling to it with a sweet and chaste embrace—a non-bodily one, of course; and so we shall also praise him with the same kind of voice, and say, Alleluia. *All the citizens of that city, you see, will be urging each other to equal heights of praise with the most ardent charity toward one another and toward God*, and so they will be saying, Alleluia, because they will be saying, Amen.[18]

Augustine's vision of the heavenly city thus brings together love of God and love of neighbor in one chorus of praise. His reference to a "non-bodily" embrace must not mislead one to think that he has a disembodied understanding of the life of the world to come. The entire sermon focuses on the bodily resurrection. The embrace is "non-bodily" because it is an embrace of truth, which is immaterial. Nevertheless, the saints will require their bodies to praise together the glory and love of God.

The connection between love and the praise that will characterize the life of the saints is not limited to this famous Easter sermon. Augustine frequently returns to this idea in his *Expositions of the Psalms*. In a sermon on Psalm 27 (26 LXX), he once again describes the activity of the saints as involving praise, inflecting it through the lens of love:

> If you wonder what we may be doing in that house, you find another psalm expressing it clearly: "Blessed are they who dwell in your house; they will praise you for ever and ever." The psalmist here is aflame with greed [*cupiditate ardens*], one might almost say. Burning with love [*amore aestuans*], he longs to live all the days of his life in the house of the Lord, to spend all those days in the Lord's house not as days which must come to an end, but as eternal days.[19]

17. Augustine, *Serm*. 362.29.
18. Augustine, *Serm*. 362.29 (emphasis added).
19. *Enarrat. Ps*. 26.2.7.

Long before Lewis reflected on the nature of praise, Augustine saw clearly how it springs forth from love. In fact, it is a recurring theme in the *Expositions*.[20] Commenting on Psalm 84 (83 LXX), he writes, "The psalmist has given voice to our desire and our longings, telling us what we are to have in that homeland for which we long, by his words, 'blessed are they who dwell in your house'; let him also tell us what we are to do. 'They will praise you for ever and ever.' This will be the work that occupies us totally, an 'Alleluia' that never fades away."[21] Once again anticipating the fear of boredom, Augustine reassures his audience, "Brothers and sisters, do not imagine that there will be weariness in that. If you go on saying it for a long time now, you flag, but only because your needs distract you from the joy."[22] Boredom and weariness, in other words, are a result of the fall. When we rise again incorruptible, we will no longer tire of praising God without end. The only way a person could weary of such activity is if one grew tired of love: "Let us be secure, then, brothers and sisters. Praising God, loving God, will not glut us [*non nos satiabit*]. If you weary of love, you will weary of praise; but if love is everlasting, because that beauty can never sicken, have no fear that you will not be able to praise forever him whom you will be able to love forever."[23] Because God is perfect, infinite beauty, we can never tire of him once we see him face to face.

Augustine once more brings together praise, love, and the notion of never-satisfied satisfaction in his comments on Psalm 86 (85 LXX), again emphasizing that the only way one will tire of praising in the world to come is if one tires of loving: "This will be our activity: praising God. If you love him, you also praise him. You will break off your praise only if you stop loving. But you will not stop loving because it is characteristic of the One you see that he cannot cause the slightest weariness in you: he satisfies you, yet he leaves you unsatisfied [*et satiat te, et non te satiat*]."[24] Augustine explains the importance of this tension in light of common human experience. If he were to say simply that God will satisfy us, this might give the impression of boredom. When we are satisfied with our food, we (usually) stop eating. If, on the other hand, he were to say that we will not be satisfied with praising God, then we might despair.[25] This tension plays a key role in Augustine's argument that human beings will never grow weary of praising God in the world to come. Equally essential, though, are the incorruptible bodies we hope to receive, which will make it possible for us to praise without growing weary physically.[26]

20. I owe the following two citations to Pierce, "Augustine's Eschatological Vision," 229–30.

21. *Enarrat. Ps.* 83.8.

22. *Enarrat. Ps.* 83.8.

23. *Enarrat. Ps.* 83.8 (modified). I have translated *satiabit* as "glut" here because it seems to connote more than mere satisfaction.

24. *Enarrat. Ps.* 85.23.

25. *Enarrat. Ps.* 85.23.

26. Cf. *Enarrat. Ps.* 62.6–7.

Augustine's vision is also a social one. He speaks of the saints encouraging one another, spurring each other on to praise God more and more. As I argued in the previous chapter, a similar idea appears in the writings of Aquinas, for whom beatitude is both bodily and social. In at least two of his biblical commentaries, Thomas underscores the communal nature of worship as a part of human happiness. Commenting on Psalm 5, he notes that the joy of the saints will come, in part, from human society.[27] Similarly, and even more explicitly, in his lectures on Hebrews, Aquinas connects the resurrection of the body to communal joy.[28] Despite Thomas's primarily intellectual description of the beatific vision, he also recognizes the social dimension of redemption.[29]

Given the significance of worship for the Christian hope, one can also see the importance of worship in the present as a preparation for the life of the world to come. Much could be said about this, but I would like to highlight just two points. First, as Irenaeus argues, the Eucharist underscores the goodness of the flesh and prepares our human flesh to be made incorruptible.[30] Second, Christian worship has a social dimension, and in this way, too, it anticipates the activity of the saints. Although in the present we often tire of the activity of praising God, in the next life we will be strengthened, both physically and spiritually, to delight in the Lord and to exult in that joy with all the saints, as Augustine suggests.[31]

This traditional emphasis on worship as our final end, present in all three of the figures we have considered, flows logically from the book of Revelation. As I noted in chapter 3, the culmination of Revelation, and therefore of the Bible as a whole, abounds with liturgical imagery. Moreover, the description of the saints suggests that their role will be a priestly one. John writes in Revelation 22:3–4, "Nothing accursed will be found there any more. But the throne of God and of the Lamb will be in [the city], and his servants will worship him; they will see his face, and his name will be on their foreheads." The removal of every curse leads the saints to exult in their worship of God and of the Lamb. But this is not just any worship. The imagery John uses points to a priestly role. The writing of God's name on the forehead not only fulfills a promise made earlier in the book (Rev. 3:12); it also alludes to the description of the priest's vestments in the book of Exodus, which included a

27. *Sup. Ps.* 5.8.

28. *Ad Heb.* 655.

29. Although this social dimension does not feature as prominently in Irenaeus, he, too, occasionally speaks of it, suggesting that the saints will have "intercourse and communion with the holy angels, and union with spiritual beings" (*Haer.* 5.35.1).

30. See *Haer.* 5.2.2–3 and the discussion of this text on pp. 176–78 above.

31. Augustine, *Serm.* 362.29. Augustine also comments on the importance of worship in the present life in his exposition of Ps. 148: "Our thoughts in this present life ought to be centered on the praise of God, because to praise God will be our everlasting joy in the life to come, and no one will be fit for that future life unless he or she is well practiced in the art of praising God now" (*Enarrat. Ps.* 148.1).

signet bearing the phrase "sacred to the Lord" worn by the high priest on his forehead.[32] Additionally, although Augustine probably draws the imagery of the heavenly society as a city from a broader biblical tradition, it is significant that Revelation culminates with the descent of a city from heaven in which the redeemed worship God and the Lamb. Finally, Augustine's emphasis on praise springing forth from love also fits Revelation's description of the end as the worship elements of these last few chapters appear in the context of the "marriage supper of the Lamb" (Rev. 19:9; cf. 21:2, 9; 22:17).[33] Thus, the social and liturgical dimensions of redemption, rooted in the joy that is the fruit of love, feature prominently in the final vision of the Bible.

Worship, then, provides a fruitful category for understanding the relationship between the beatific vision and the resurrection of the body. It has a solid basis in both Scripture and tradition, and it helps explain the necessity of the reunion of body and soul in a way that suits the composite character of human nature but also incorporates the social dimension of human existence. What, then, of the other two biblical categories considered in part 1 of this study, dominion and rest?

"God Will Be All in All"

Although worship enjoys pride of place in Augustine's vision of the end, it is by no means the only activity he anticipates for the redeemed. In *City of God* he considers precisely the question we have been exploring. Augustine's robust understanding of the resurrection leads him to ask what the just will do in their resurrected bodies: "Now let us see, as far as the Lord deigns to help us to see, what the saints will be doing in their immortal and spiritual bodies, when the flesh will no longer be living 'according to the flesh' but 'according to the spirit.'"[34] Readily acknowledging that he cannot give a definitive answer to the question, having not yet seen the new heaven and the new earth, he nevertheless proceeds to speculate regarding the nature of the life of the world to come. Despite his characterization of this life in *Sermon* 362 as nothing but singing "Amen" and "Alleluia," Augustine offers a fuller picture of the activity of the saints in the closing chapters of *City of God*.

In line with the tradition that preceded him and the tradition that would follow him, Augustine emphasizes the importance of vision, asking about

32. Williamson, *Revelation*, 360, citing Exod. 28:36–38; cf. Beale, *Revelation*, 1116: "It is not coincidental that Rev. 22:4 has also applied the divine name on Aaron's forehead to all of God's people, as his priests. The 'agelong benediction' of Numbers 6 reaches its fullest possible application in the new world."

33. For a detailed treatment of this motif, see Zimmermann, "Nuptial Imagery in the Revelation of John."

34. *Civ.* 22.29.

the nature of the beatific vision. In light of his insistence on the necessity of the resurrection of the body, he brings out an important distinction. The redeemed will see God "in the body [*in ipso corpore*]," but, he adds, it is hard to say whether they will be able to see him "through the body [*per ipsum*]."[35] Regardless of whether the saints will be able to see God with their resurrected eyes, this vision will not depend on whether the eyes of the resurrected body are open or shut. Comparing the vision of God with Elisha's awareness of Gehazi's duplicity without being present for that deed (2 Kings 5:19–27), Augustine insists, "How much more then in that spiritual body will the saints see everything, not only if they close their eyes, but even when they are not present in the body!"[36] As Elisha saw Gehazi's misdeed without the mediation of bodily organs, so the saints will see God by intuition regardless of the activity of their bodily eyes. This implies that the language of face-to-face vision in the writings of Paul (1 Cor. 13:12) and other texts must not be taken in an overly literal way. Rather, this phrase refers to an immediate, intuitive vision of the divine nature: "We shall see God by the spirit without any interruption."[37]

Even if it does somehow become possible for the saints to see God with their bodily eyes—a position Augustine considers "credible [*credibile*]"—such a vision will not exclude the use of those resurrected eyes to see other things, as well. One of his proposals for how such a vision might work even suggests an overlap between the vision of God and the vision of the new heavens and the new earth:

> Perhaps God will be known to us and visible to us in the sense that he will be spiritually perceived *by* each one of us *in* each one of us, *perceived in one another, perceived by each in himself*; he will be seen in the new heaven and the new earth, in the whole creation as it then will be; he will be seen in every body by means of bodies, wherever the eyes of the spiritual body are directed with their penetrating gaze.[38]

In other words, the presence of God, so mysterious and elusive in this life, will come to pervade everything in an easily perceptible fashion. One could take this description of the bodily awareness of God in the next life as Augustine's interpretation of 1 Corinthians 15:28 ("God will be all in all"), a verse that features in the final chapter of *City of God*.[39] Significantly, this vision of God will not compete with, nor will it exclude, vision of and interaction with other human beings, or with enjoying the new heaven and the new earth. God will be "spiritually perceived by each one of us in each one of us, perceived in one

35. *Civ*. 22.29. For this and what follows, see the fuller discussion of this text on pp. 113–15.
36. *Civ*. 22.29.
37. *Civ*. 22.29.
38. *Civ*. 22.29 (emphasis added). Cf. Aquinas, *Sup. Mt*. 434, relying on Augustine.
39. *Civ*. 22.30.

another." The entire new creation, then—both living and inanimate—will shine forth with the light of God's glory.

Imagining such a noncompetitive perception of both created things and God himself is difficult, but we can perhaps get a hint of what it might look like by considering the life of a great mystic like St. Catherine of Siena.[40] Catherine speaks of how those who advance in the spiritual life eventually come to experience a complete immersion in God, such that "the soul is in God and God in the soul, just as the fish is in the sea and the sea in the fish."[41] This all-pervasive awareness of God's presence, however, does not detract from the activities of the present life, as Catherine's own life demonstrates. In the early part of her life, Catherine made a cell for herself in her family's home, dedicating herself to prayer. But after a time, the Lord ordered her to leave her physical cell and engage in numerous activities in the world. Obedient to her Lord, Catherine set out, engaging in ecclesiastical and political affairs while maintaining the interior cell within her soul, constantly aware of God's presence within her even as she fulfilled the various tasks he appointed for her. This close communion that Catherine sustained in the midst of an active season of her life may serve as an image for how the beatific vision would be compatible with activity on the part of the resurrected saints. The saints will have an uninterrupted vision of the divine essence; this vision will not, however, exclude other activities. On the contrary, the promise of a new heaven and a new earth suggests that the human task of participating in God's governance of creation will come to its fulfillment in the world to come. The saints will be able to fulfill this aspect of the human vocation (Gen. 1:26–28) while at the same time remaining fully aware of God's presence.

Another aspect of traditional eschatology suggests that it is reasonable to expect some kind of activity in the resurrection. Both Aquinas and Augustine, interpreting Paul's description of the resurrected body in 1 Corinthians 15:42–44, ascribe various qualities to the risen bodies of the saints. Aquinas suggests that the body will be characterized by subtlety, agility, impassability, and clarity.[42] Augustine describes the risen body as having beauty, incorruptibility, and ease of motion.[43] While it is true that liturgy as we know it involves various movements, it is difficult to imagine a liturgical regimen so rigorous as to require ease of motion or agility in addition to incorruptibility or impassability. The mark of agility suggests that the risen saints, in addition

40. Cf. the eschatological interpretation of Ratzinger, *Eschatology*, 235: "This [ecclesial aspect of eschatology] is not by way of competition with the perfect disclosure of God's Face, but, on the contrary, is its very consequence."

41. Saint Catherine of Siena, *The Dialogue* 2 (p. 27).

42. Aquinas, *Compendium* 1.168; *I Ad Cor.* 980–88. See also *SCG* 4.86.1–6 and the discussion in Gaine, "Resurrection and Eschatology," 370–74. On the background of these characteristics, see Bynum, *The Resurrection of the Body in Western Christianity*, 131–32.

43. *Civ.* 22.30.

to enjoying the presence and direct vision of God, will be doing something with their bodies.[44]

Even apart from any exercise of these characteristics of the risen body, though, by their very nature these qualities may point to another way the royal vocation of the human being will be fulfilled in the new heaven and the new earth. This becomes particularly clear if we consider the way Paul describes these qualities. The risen bodies of the saints will be incorruptible, glorious, powerful, and Spiritual (1 Cor. 15:42–44). Each of these characteristics reflects the ways Paul describes God. In Romans he speaks of "the glory of the incorruptible [*aphthartou*] God" (Rom. 1:23, my translation; cf. 3:23; 5:2; 2 Cor. 3:18; 4:6; Eph. 1:17; 1 Tim. 1:17); God is the one who has power (1 Cor. 2:5; 6:14); and the quality of being "Spiritual" relates directly to having the Spirit of God (1 Cor. 2:10–16). In other words, in the resurrection the bodies of the saints will become like God, who rules over all (1 Cor. 15:27–28). The image of the King will be perfected in those who attain to the resurrection, giving them a share in his royal status.[45]

The biblical vision of a new heaven and a new earth, which Augustine develops in the last book of *City of God*, also suggests activity of some sort on the part of the redeemed. After all, if the life of the world to come were to consist only in worship analogous to worship as we know it in the here and now, then a temple would suffice. But Scripture also speaks of a new heaven and a new earth (e.g., Isa. 65:17; 66:22), as well as of a hope for the redemption of all creation (Rom. 8:19–23).[46] Moreover, in addition to priestly activity, Revelation speaks of the blessed reigning (Rev. 22:5), although it is worth noting that every expression of the saints reigning in Revelation is closely associated with priestly ministry, whether explicitly (5:10; 20:4–6) or implicitly (22:4–5). Those who conquer will sit on the throne with God and the Lamb, participating in the divine glory and rule (Rev. 3:21). This sharing in the reign of God and the Lamb fulfills the human vocation to participate in God's reign over creation so prominent in Genesis 1:26–28.[47] In light of the connection the NT frequently draws between resurrection and reign, it seems reasonable that governance of the new creation should constitute an important part of humanity's final end, though not the whole of it. This reign

44. In this regard, I find some aspects of N. T. Wright's description of the resurrection appealing: "All the skills and talents we have put to God's service in this present life—and perhaps too the interests and likings we gave up because they conflicted with our vocation—will be enhanced and ennobled and given back to us to be exercised to his glory." See Wright, *Surprised by Hope*, 161. For reasons that will become clear, however, I have my doubts about whether one should describe this activity as "work," as Wright does earlier on the same page, at least not in the sense of something toilsome.

45. See chap. 1.

46. See Schmaus, *Dogma 6: Justification and the Last Things*, 210–14; Ratzinger, *Eschatology*, 237; Caird, "The Christological Basis of Christian Hope," 21–24.

47. See the discussion on pp. 19–21 above.

would in no way detract from or compete with the vision of God or with the worship that will flow from that vision. Rather, it would fulfill the vocation God gave human beings from the beginning.[48]

"It Will Be a Perpetual Sabbath"

To return to *Sermon* 362, Augustine describes another characteristic of eternal life, indicating that certain activities will come to an end, because the new heaven and the new earth will also be a place of rest.[49] He first notes ordinary biological activities that will cease due to the implications of immortality: marrying, the conception of children, growth, and nourishment, for example.[50] But, he adds, even certain virtuous acts will not continue: "There won't even be any of those praiseworthy works of innocent people, which the poverty and the necessities of this life oblige them to engage in."[51] Not only sins like theft but also acts of mercy will cease, because the latter are prompted by the needs of human beings in a fallen world.[52] The new creation, on the contrary, will be a place of rest: "It will be a perpetual sabbath, which is celebrated by the Jews in a temporal sense, but is understood by us to be eternal. There will be inexpressible peace and quiet, quite impossible to describe."[53] Augustine roots this vision in Christ's promise of rest (Matt. 11:28). Misery will have ended, and so the task of relieving misery—the works of mercy—will no longer be necessary, or even possible.[54]

The nature of this rest is described with three characteristics in the final chapter of *City of God*. Rest will consist in genuine freedom, in right knowledge of our past, and in a praise that bursts forth from this proper understanding of the past. The freedom of the next life will be a participation in God's own freedom—that is, a freedom from the compulsion to sin. In the heavenly city, Augustine notes, there will be no jealousy or envy—all will be content with their proper place. But, he continues, this inability to sin does not mean a curtailment of freedom. On the contrary, "the will will be the freer in that it is freed from a delight in sin and immovably fixed in a delight in

48. It is also worth noting that in Rev. 19–22 the accent falls much more heavily on worship and liturgy than on reign. This is not to deny that human beings have a royal vocation, but rather to note that worship seems to hold pride of place in Scripture's presentation of the end.

49. Interpreters have at times emphasized Augustine's notion of rest in an imbalanced way, suggesting that it rules out activity on the part of the saints. For a helpful corrective, see Pierce, "Augustine's Eschatological Vision."

50. Augustine, *Serm.* 362.28.

51. *Serm.* 362.28.

52. *Serm.* 362.28; see also *Ennarat. Ps.* 83.8.

53. *Serm.* 362.28. For a good, brief discussion of the relation between peace and rest in Augustine, see Pierce, "Augustine's Eschatological Vision," 221–25.

54. *Serm.* 362.28.

not sinning."[55] This freedom stems not from human nature, but from the gift of participating in God's own freedom. Moreover, by virtue of this freedom, past sins will no longer have a grip on us: "[The will] will be freed from all evil and filled with all good, enjoying unfailingly the delight of eternal joys, forgetting all offences, forgetting all punishments."[56] Not only, then, will the miseries of this present life cease to exist; the memory of them will cease to bring us sadness.

This "beatific forgetfulness" does not mean, however, that we will have no knowledge of our past sins and sorrows. Rather, Augustine distinguishes between two types of knowledge and two types of forgetfulness. With regard to misery and sorrow, a person can have experiential knowledge, by which he suffers under the painful condition, or a person can have intellectual knowledge of the pain, as a medical doctor has theoretical knowledge of numerous diseases without experiencing them herself. There are two corresponding ways of forgetting sorrow, one theoretical and the other experiential. In the new heaven and the new earth, the redeemed will no longer experience their sorrows viscerally, but they will remember them in their intellects: "The saints will have no sensible recollection of past evils; theirs will be the second kind of forgetfulness by which they will be set free from them all, and they will be completely erased from their feelings."[57] Nevertheless, the saints will retain cognitive knowledge of their sins and sorrows.

Before continuing to explore Augustine's interpretation of rest, it is worth considering a second-century precursor to his emphasis on memory. Khaled Anatolios has recently argued that memory plays a similar role in Irenaeus's eschatological vision.[58] According to Anatolios, for Irenaeus it is not just our bodies that will become incorruptible—so, too, will our memories.[59] In Book 3 of *Against Heresies*, asking why God allowed death and the various sufferings of history, Irenaeus compares the human race to Jonah. God allowed Jonah to be swallowed by the whale not for his destruction, but so that the prophet would learn obedience and would praise God for his rescue from the grave.[60] Similarly, God allowed human beings to fall into transgression for two reasons. First, their experience of death and of redemption through

55. *Civ.* 22.30.

56. *Civ.* 22.30.

57. *Civ.* 22.30.

58. Anatolios, "Historical Memory and the Eschatological Vision of God's Glory in Irenaeus." On the similarities between Irenaeus and Augustine, see 115–17.

59. Anatolios, "Historical Memory and the Eschatological Vision of God's Glory in Irenaeus," 102: "Irenaeus here [in *Haer.* 3.20.1] describes the condition of deified incorruptibility as a particular condition of consciousness, of which a significant element is humanity's memory of its own historical experience." This aspect of incorruptibility is in addition to physical incorruptibility, not an alternative to it.

60. The latter point is seen most clearly in Jonah's prayer from the belly of the fish (Jon. 2:1–9), even if he does not maintain this posture of submission throughout the rest of the book.

resurrection would lead them to praise God: "[This was done] that man, receiving an unhoped-for salvation from God, might rise from the dead, and glorify God . . . and that he might always continue glorifying God, and giving thanks without ceasing, for that salvation which he has derived from Him."[61] Second, this experience was also intended to remind human beings of their creaturely status: "and that man should never adopt an opposite opinion with regard to God, supposing that the incorruptibility which belongs to him is his own naturally, and by thus not holding the truth, should boast with empty superciliousness, as if he were naturally like to God."[62] This understanding of memory gives the events of history an ongoing significance even in the eschaton, an idea Augustine explores in a little more depth.

Anatolios acknowledges that Irenaeus nowhere works out these ideas systematically.[63] Nevertheless, he shows how this understanding of memory as continuing into the eschaton supports three fundamental Irenaean ideas, though I will focus only on two. First, the persistence of memory serves as a reminder to the redeemed of their creaturely status, maintaining a clear line between the creature and the Creator.[64] For Irenaeus, the latter term can be applied to the Word because he existed from before all time with the Father, but it cannot be applied to creatures: "But the things which have been made cannot have this term ["God" and "Lord"] applied to them, neither should they justly assume that appellation which belongs to the Creator."[65] Second, Irenaeus's emphasis on memory fits with his understanding of "the knowability of God in history."[66] For Irenaeus, God makes himself known in and through Christ. This is why the Father sends the Son: "And for this purpose did the Father reveal the Son, that through His instrumentality He might be manifested to all, and might receive those who believe in Him rightly into incorruption and everlasting rest."[67] The Christian belief in the resurrection and ascension of Christ's body indicates that this body was not something to be discarded. Rather, it plays an ongoing role in the memory of believers, which leads them to praise God not only for who he is, but also for what he has done.

Returning to Augustine, ongoing cognitive memory in the eschaton plays a similar role for him—namely, to lead the redeemed to praise God. According to him, recalling the sorrows of the past will spur the just to worship: "If

61. *Haer*. 3.20.1.

62. *Haer*. 3.20.1.

63. Anatolios, "Historical Memory and the Eschatological Vision of God's Glory in Irenaeus," 103.

64. Anatolios, "Historical Memory and the Eschatological Vision of God's Glory in Irenaeus," 103–6.

65. *Haer*. 3.8.3.

66. Anatolios, "Historical Memory and the Eschatological Vision of God's Glory in Irenaeus," 106–11.

67. Irenaeus, *Haer*. 4.6.5 (modified). On this and other texts, see chap. 5 above. Note how Irenaeus connects incorruption and rest.

[the saints] were to lose the knowledge of their past misery how will they, as the psalm says, 'sing the mercies of the Lord for all eternity'? Nothing will give more joy to that City than this song to the glory of the grace of Christ by whose blood we have been set free."[68] Augustine's vision of the end thus safeguards the significance of the present life. It is not something to be left completely in the past and forgotten. Rather, even the sorrows of this life have a purpose—namely, moving the saints to give thanks to the Lord, whose mercy endures forever. Reflecting on this mercy will constitute the rest that characterizes that life:

> That will truly be the greatest of Sabbaths; a Sabbath that has no evening, the Sabbath that the Lord approved at the beginning of creation. . . . We ourselves shall become that seventh day, when we have been replenished and restored by his blessing and sanctification. There we shall have leisure to be still, and we shall see that he is God, whereas we wished to be that ourselves when we fell away from him, after listening to the Seducer saying, "You will be like gods."[69]

In worship the saints will find true freedom and genuine rest. Moreover, they will participate in the kingdom, fulfilling the vocation God gave to human beings in the beginning. Nevertheless, this reign will in no way detract from the rest that the vision of God offers. The whole human person, Augustine suggests, will experience the rest for which God created us:

> The important thing is that [the age to come] will be our Sabbath, whose end will not be an evening, but the Lord's Day, an eighth day, as it were, which is to last forever, a day consecrated by the resurrection of Christ, foreshadowing the eternal rest not only of the spirit but of the body also. There we shall be still and see; we shall see and we shall love; we shall love and we shall praise. Behold what will be, in the end, without end! For what is our end but to reach that kingdom which has no end?[70]

Once again, this vision of the end in terms of memory and praise captures something of the picture in Revelation. In the two famous throne room scenes toward the beginning of the book, the heavenly assembly worships God and the Lamb, first, for the act of creation (Rev. 4:11), and second, for the act of redemption (Rev. 5:9–14). Anatolios rightly characterizes the life of the saints as "forever Eucharistic, containing an eternal thankful anamnesis of God's salvific activity within human history."[71] The saints must never forget the

68. *Civ*. 22.30.

69. *Civ*. 22.30. Cf. N. T. Wright, *History and Eschatology*, 167: "The world to come will be a kind of perpetual Sabbath."

70. *Civ*. 22.30.

71. Anatolios, "Historical Memory and the Eschatological Vision of God's Glory in Irenaeus," 103.

awful deeds that won for them so great a savior, even as they will no longer experience the pain of such memories.[72] Perhaps no text expresses this connection between praise and rest more eloquently than one of the most famous lines from Augustine's *Confessions*, which speaks of present human experience in a way that anticipates its eschatological fulfillment: "Yet these humans, due part of your creation as they are, still do long to praise you. You stir us so that praising you may bring us joy, because you have made us and drawn us to yourself, and our heart is restless until it rests in you."[73] In addition to the overt language of praise, there is also a subtle affirmation of the importance of worship in this famous line. As some have noted, the singular "our heart" reflects the form of the *sursum corda* in the North African liturgy of Augustine's day. It is one of his favorite prayers to cite and a theme to which he turns frequently in his sermons.[74] For Augustine, then, the rest we long for is anticipated in the liturgy and will find its fulfillment when our hearts are lifted up in eternal praise of God. True to the biblical vision, rest and praise go hand in hand.

Entering into God's Rest

As I note in the introduction, we cannot know with any certainty (this side of the eschaton) exactly how the biblical images of the end will actually unfold.[75] The language of worship, dominion, and rest gives a good indication of what human beings were created for, but how this vocation will be fulfilled in the next life must remain a mystery until we actually experience it. Nevertheless, there is good reason to see rest as the primary category, particularly as Augustine interprets it.[76] Rest indicates the peace and stillness that the

72. Thus, while I agree with Rowe ("Becoming Human," 44) that we will not suffer "eschatological contrition," I cannot agree with him that all memory of sin will be wiped away (46). Without at least some knowledge of why Christ gave himself for us, eternal gratitude for the redemption would become incomprehensible. Rowe further suggests (46n15) that Augustine's understanding of evil as a privation makes it difficult to maintain the ongoing memory of sin. As I have tried to show, Augustine sees no difficulty here; rather, he affirms the importance of memory as one element of the rest for which we hope. Whether this position is consistent with his understanding of evil as parasitic and privative is a conversation worth having, but it lies beyond the scope of this study.

73. *Conf.* 1.1.1 (modified).

74. See, e.g., Augustine, *Serm.* 52.15; 68.6; 86.14; *Ennarat. Ps.* 90.14–16. Augustine alludes to this liturgical phrase two other times in the *Confessions*, at 12.16.23 and 13.7.8. I owe this point and these citations to Liz Klein. See also Ortiz, "*You Made Us for Yourself*," 123–25.

75. In this regard I agree with N. T. Wright, *Surprised by Hope*, 107: "All our language about the future, as I have said, is like a set of signposts pointing into a bright mist."

76. Augustine's notion of "rest" is frequently contrasted with Eastern articulations of *epektasis*, the idea that the eschaton will be characterized by ongoing progress. This contrast strikes me as exaggerated, as is so often the case with hackneyed theological dichotomies that pit the East against the West. Augustine's notion of "never satisfied satisfaction" seems to imply ongoing

redeemed will enjoy, freed from the toil and pain that attend our fallen condition. To reign with God in the kingdom of heaven will not be burdensome, but rather filled with the joy that comes from the face-to-face vision of God, a joy that erupts in praise. This vision, however, will not compete with other activities, but rather will somehow be experienced in and through them, thus maintaining other important, albeit lesser, aspects of human nature in the new heaven and the new earth.

exploration of the goodness and beauty of God. The theme of "rest" simply complements this striving with a sense of stillness and peace. For a fuller discussion of the question with respect to Augustine, see again Pierce, "Augustine's Eschatological Vision." For a treatment of a similar attempt to balance rest and *epektasis* in Maximus the Confessor, see Blowers, "Maximus the Confessor, Gregory of Nyssa, and the Concept of 'Perpetual Progress.'"

Epilogue

The Christian Hope

In Marilynne Robinson's Pulitzer Prize–winning novel, *Gilead*, John Ames, a Congregationalist pastor suffering from a terminal heart condition, reflects on what repercussions the events of this world might have in the next. Unwilling and unable to imagine that all that happens in this life will simply pass away into oblivion, he proposes a vision that resembles the closing chapter of Augustine's *City of God*:

> I can't believe that, when we have all been changed and put on incorruptibility, we will forget our fantastic condition of mortality and impermanence, the great bright dream of procreating and perishing that meant the whole world to us. In eternity this world will be Troy, I believe, and all that has passed here will be the epic of the universe, the ballad they sing in the streets. Because I don't imagine any reality putting this one in the shade entirely, and I think piety forbids me to try.[1]

This picture of the age to come captures what seem to be essential features of that world, at least on Augustine's reading. The central hope of the NT, made sure by Christ's victory over the grave, is that we will all be "changed and put on incorruptibility." Our nature as embodied creatures would seem to demand such a transformation, one that makes the reunion of body and soul permanent. Moreover, the saints will remember the great acts of God, seeing his providential hand guiding all human history. This clear vision of God's care for the world will fittingly erupt into praise, a praise made possible by the resurrection of the body—the events of this life will be "the epic of

1. M. Robinson, *Gilead*, 57.

the universe, the ballad they sing in the streets." It is significant that, in the book of Revelation, the twenty-four elders worship God both for his act of creation (Rev. 4:11) and for the redemption wrought by the Lamb (5:9–10).

In addition to praising God for what he has done, though, there can be little doubt that the saints will also praise him for who he is. The longing frequently expressed in the OT to see God's face—"to behold the beauty of the Lord, and to inquire in his temple" (Ps. 27:4)—will finally come to pass in its fullness. The pure in heart will see God (Matt. 5:8) face to face (Rev. 22:4), knowing him as they themselves are fully known (1 Cor. 13:12), and in this manner they will come to be like him (1 John 3:2). Contemplating God, like the memory of the sufferings endured in this life, will lead the saints to burst forth into praise. If the glory of mundane events like a symphony or a sunset evokes praise and admiration, how much more so the vision of the One who is Goodness itself, Beauty itself! Only this vision can fully satisfy the deepest human longing, but it need not compete with the biblical hope of the resurrection and the new creation.

Seeing God will also ensure that the future life is not toilsome, nor characterized by the restlessness that plagues us in this life. While it is reasonable to expect that our resurrected bodies will have some kind of activity, this activity must be balanced with the promised rest for which God made us, as the letter to the Hebrews reminds us (Heb. 3:1–4:13). This rest does not mean that our bodies will be idle. Rather, as Augustine suggests, it will mean stillness, peace, and joy in the loving presence of God.[2] This stillness, peace, and joy will come to fruition when our souls and our bodies are reunited, transformed, and glorified, such that we worship God in and through the new creation. This will be the crowning beatitude of the life of the world to come.

2. *Civ*. 22.30.

Bibliography

Ancient and Medieval Sources

Augustine of Hippo

The City of God. Translated by Henry Bettenson. Penguin Books, 1972.

The Confessions. Translated by Maria Boulding. WSA I/1. New City Press, 1997.

Expositions of the Psalms 1–32. Translated by Maria Boulding. WSA III/15. New City Press, 2000.

Expositions of the Psalms 33–50. Translated by Maria Boulding. WSA III/16. New City Press, 2000.

Expositions of the Psalms 51–72. Translated by Maria Boulding. WSA III/17. New City Press, 2001.

Expositions of the Psalms 73–98. Translated by Maria Boulding. WSA III/18. New City Press, 2002.

Letters 1–99. Translated by Roland Teske. WSA II/1. New City Press, 2001.

Letters 100–155. Translated by Roland Teske. WSA II/2. New City Press, 2003.

Letters 156–210. Translated by Roland Teske. WSA II/3. New City Press, 2004.

On Genesis. Translated by Edmund Hill. WSA I/13. New City Press, 2002.

Revisions. Translated by Boniface Ramsey. WSA I/2. New City Press, 2010.

Sermons (51–94) on the New Testament. Translated by Edmund Hill. WSA III/3. New City Press, 2009.

Sermons (230–272B) on Liturgical Seasons. Translated by Edmund Hill. WSA III/7. New City Press, 1993.

Sermons (273–305A) on the Saints. Translated by Edmund Hill. WSA III/8. New City Press, 1994.

Sermons (341–400) on Various Subjects. Translated by Edmund Hill. WSA III/10. New City Press, 1995.

Teaching Christianity: De Doctrina Christiana. Translated by Edmund Hill. WSA I/11. New City Press, 1996.

The Trinity. Translated by Edmund Hill. 2nd ed. WSA I/5. New City Press, 2017.

Catherine of Siena

The Dialogue. Translated by Suzanne Noffke. Classics of Western Spirituality. Paulist Press, 1980.

Dante Alighieri

The Divine Comedy: The Inferno, The Purgatorio, and The Paradiso. Translated by John Ciardi. New American Library, 2003.

Gregory of Nyssa

On the Making of Man. *NPNF*^{2} 5:387–427.

Irenaeus of Lyons

Against Heresies. *ANF* 1:309–567.

Against the Heresies. In A. Rousseau and L. Doutreleau, SC 210–11 (Book 3); A. Rousseau, B. Hemmerdinger, L. Doutreleau, and C. Mercier, SC 100 (Book 4); A. Rousseau, L. Doutreleau, and C. Mercier, SC 152–53 (Book 5). Éditions du Cerf, 1974, 1979, 1982.

John Chrysostom

Homilies on Genesis 1–17. Translated by Robert C. Hill. FC 74. Catholic University of America Press, 1986.

Thomas Aquinas

Commentary on the Gospel of John. Translated by Fabian R. Larcher. WSTA 35–36. Aquinas Institute for the Study of Sacred Doctrine, 2013.

Commentary on the Gospel of Matthew, Chapters 1–12. Translated by Jeremy Holmes and Beth Mortensen. WSTA 33. Aquinas Institute for the Study of Sacred Doctrine, 2013.

Commentary on the Letter of Saint Paul to the Hebrews. Translated by Fabian R. Larcher. WSTA 41. Aquinas Institute for the Study of Sacred Doctrine, 2012.

Commentary on the Letter of Saint Paul to the Romans. Translated by Fabian R. Larcher. WSTA 37. Aquinas Institute for the Study of Sacred Doctrine, 2012.

Commentary on the Letters of Saint Paul to the Corinthians. Translated by Fabian R. Larcher, B. Mortensen, and D. Keating. WSTA 38. Aquinas Institute for the Study of Sacred Doctrine, 2012.

Commentary on the Letters of Saint Paul to the Philippians, Colossians, Thessalonians, Timothy, Titus, and Philemon. Translated by Fabian R. Larcher. WSTA 40. Aquinas Institute for the Study of Sacred Doctrine, 2012.

Commentary on the Sentences Book IV, Distinctions 43–50. Translated by Beth Mortensen, Peter Kwasniewski, and Dylan Schrader. WSTA 10. Aquinas Institute for the Study of Sacred Doctrine, 2018.

Compendium of Theology. Translated by Richard J. Regan. Oxford University Press, 2009.

On the Truth of the Catholic Faith. Book 3, *Providence, Part I*. Translated by Vernon J. Bourke. Image Books, 1956.

On the Truth of the Catholic Faith. Book 4, *Salvation*. Translated by Charles J. O'Neil. Image Books, 1957.

Summa Contra Gentiles Books III–IV. Translated by Laurence Shapcote. WSTA 12. Aquinas Institute, 2018.

Summa Theologiae Prima Pars, 1–49. Translated by Laurence Shapcote. WSTA 13. Aquinas Institute for the Study of Sacred Doctrine, 2012.

Summa Theologiae Prima Pars, 50–119. Translated by Laurence Shapcote. WSTA 14. Aquinas Institute for the Study of Sacred Doctrine, 2012.

Summa Theologiae Prima Secundae, 1–70. Translated by Laurence Shapcote. WSTA 15. Aquinas Institute for the Study of Sacred Doctrine, 2012.

Summa Theologiae Tertia Pars, 1–59. Translated by Laurence Shapcote. WSTA 19. Aquinas Institute for the Study of Sacred Doctrine, 2012.

Secondary and Modern Sources

Alexander, Philip S. "Targum, Targumim." *ABD* 6:320–31.

Alfeche, Mamerto. "Augustine's Discussions with Philosophers on the Resurrection of the Body." *Augustiniana* 45 (1995): 95–140.

Alfeche, Mamerto. "The Basis of Hope in the Resurrection of the Body." *Augustiniana* 36 (1986): 240–96.

Allison, Dale C., Jr. *Night Comes: Death, Imagination, and the Last Things*. Eerdmans, 2016.

Allison, Dale C., Jr. *Resurrecting Jesus: The Earliest Christian Tradition and Its Interpreters*. T&T Clark, 2005.

Allison, Dale C., Jr. *Studies in Matthew: Interpretation Past and Present*. Baker Academic, 2005.

Anatolios, Khaled. "Historical Memory and the Eschatological Vision of God's Glory in Irenaeus." In *Jewish Roots of Eastern Christian Mysticism: Studies in Honor of Alexander Golitzin*, edited by Andrei A. Orlov, 99–117. VCSupp 160. Brill, 2020.

Anderson, Gary A. *The Genesis of Perfection: Adam and Eve in Jewish and Christian Imagination*. Westminster John Knox, 2001.

Anderson, Gary A. *That I May Dwell Among Them: Incarnation and Atonement in the Tabernacle Narrative*. Eerdmans, 2024.

Anderson, Gary A. "To See Where God Dwells: The Tabernacle, the Temple, and the Origins of the Christian Mystical Tradition." *Letter & Spirit* 4 (2008): 13–45.

Anderson, Gary A. "Towards a Theology of the Tabernacle and Its Furniture." In *Text, Thought, and Practice in Qumran and Early Christianity*, edited by Ruth A. Clements and Daniel R. Schwartz, 161–94. STDJ 84. Brill, 2009.

Andia, Ysabel de. *Homo Vivens: Incorruptibilité et divinisation de l'homme selon Irénée de Lyon*. Études Augustiniennes, 1986.

Arnold, Brian J. "'To Behold Its Own Delight': The Beatific Vision in Irenaeus of Lyons." *Perichoresis* 17 (2019): 27–40.

Aune, David E. *Revelation 1–5*. WBC 52A. Thomas Nelson, 1997.

Aune, David E. *Revelation 17–22*. WBC 52C. Thomas Nelson, 1998.

Balentine, Samuel E. *The Hidden God: The Hiding of the Face of God in the Old Testament*. Oxford University Press, 2010.

Barber, Michael Patrick. *The Historical Jesus and the Temple: Memory, Methodology, and the Gospel of Matthew*. Cambridge University Press, 2023.

Barnes, Michel René. "Irenaeus's Trinitarian Theology." *Nova et Vetera* 7 (2009): 67–106.

Barnes, Michel René. "The Visible Christ and the Invisible Trinity: Mt. 5:8 in Augustine's Trinitarian Theology of 400." *Modern Theology* 19 (2003): 329–55.

Barnett, Paul. *The Second Epistle to the Corinthians*. NICNT. Eerdmans, 1997.

Barrett, C. K. *The Gospel According to St John: An Introduction with Commentary and Notes on the Greek Text*. 2nd ed. Westminster, 1978.

Beale, G. K. *The Book of Revelation: A Commentary on the Greek Text*. NIGTC. Eerdmans, 2008.

Beale, G. K. *The Temple and the Church's Mission: A Biblical Theology of the Dwelling Place of God*. NSBT. InterVarsity, 2004.

Behr, John. *Asceticism and Anthropology in Irenaeus and Clement*. OECS. Oxford University Press, 2000.

Behr, John. "Flesh Invested with Paternal Light: St Irenaeus on the Transfiguration of the Body." In *Jewish Roots of Eastern Christian Mysticism: Studies in Honor of Alexander Golitzin*, edited by Andrei A. Orlov, 118–27. VCSupp 160. Brill, 2020.

Behr, John. "Irenaeus of Lyons." In *T&T Clark Companion to Atonement*, edited by Adam J. Johnson, 569–75. Bloomsbury, 2017.

Benin, Stephen D. *The Footprints of God: Divine Accommodation in Jewish and Christian Thought*. State University of New York Press, 1993.

Blenkinsopp, Joseph. *Ezekiel*. Interpretation. Westminster John Knox, 1990.

Blenkinsopp, Joseph. *Isaiah 1–39: A New Translation with Introduction and Commentary*. AB 19. Doubleday, 2000.

Blenkinsopp, Joseph. *Isaiah 56–66: A New Translation with Introduction and Commentary*. AB 19B. Doubleday, 2003.

Blond, Phillip. "The Beatific Vision of St Thomas Aquinas." In *Encounter Between Eastern Orthodoxy and Radical Orthodoxy: Transfiguring the World Through the Word*, edited by Adrian Pabst and Christoph Schneider, 185–212. Ashgate, 2009.

Blowers, Paul M. "Maximus the Confessor, Gregory of Nyssa, and the Concept of 'Perpetual Progress.'" *VC* 46 (1992): 151–71.

Bockmuehl, Markus. *A Commentary on the Epistle to the Philippians*. BNTC. A&C Black, 1997.

Boersma, Gerald. "Augustine on the Beatific Vision as *ubique totus*." *SJT* 71 (2018): 16–32.

Boersma, Hans. "The 'Grand Medium': An Edwardsean Modification of Thomas Aquinas on the Beatific Vision." *Modern Theology* 33 (2017): 187–212.

Boersma, Hans. *Seeing God: The Beatific Vision in Christian Tradition*. Eerdmans, 2018.

Boersma, Hans. "Thomas Aquinas on the Beatific Vision: A Christological Deficit." *TheoLogica* 2 (2018): 129–47.

Brakke, David. *The Gnostics: Myth, Ritual, and Diversity in Early Christianity*. Harvard University Press, 2010.

Braun, Roddy. "Solomon, the Chosen Temple Builder: The Significance of 1 Chronicles 22, 28, and 29 for the Theology of Chronicles." *JBL* 95 (1976): 581–90.

Briggman, Anthony. *Irenaeus of Lyons and the Theology of the Holy Spirit*. OECS. Oxford University Press, 2012.

Brown, Montague. "Aquinas on the Resurrection of the Body." *The Thomist* 56 (1992): 165–207.

Brown, Raymond E. *The Epistles of John: Translated, with Introduction, Notes, and Commentary*. AB 30. Doubleday, 1982.

Brown, Raymond E. *The Gospel According to John*. 2 vols. AB 29–29A. Doubleday, 1966–70.

Brueggemann, Walter. *Isaiah 1–39*. Westminster Bible Companion. Westminster John Knox, 1998.

Brueggemann, Walter. "Weariness, Exile, and Chaos (A Motif in Royal Theology)." *CBQ* 34 (1972): 19–38.

Bucur, Bogdan. "Christological Exegesis of Theophanies and the Making of Early Christian Theology." *CTQ* 86 (2022): 97–124.

Bucur, Bogdan. "Theophanies and Vision of God in Augustine's *De Trinitate*: An Eastern Orthodox Perspective." *SVTQ* 52 (2008): 67–93.

Bukovec, Predrag. *Die frühchristliche Eucharistie*. WUNT 499. Mohr Siebeck, 2023.

Bynum, Caroline Walker. *The Resurrection of the Body in Western Christianity, 200–1336*. Columbia University Press, 1995.

Caird, G. B. "The Christological Basis of Christian Hope." In *The Christian Hope*, edited by G. B. Caird et al., 9–24. SPCK, 1970.

Caird, G. B. *A Commentary on the Revelation of St. John the Divine*. Adam & Charles Black, 1966.

Cassuto, Umberto. *A Commentary on the Book of Genesis: Part I: From Adam to Noah*. Magnes Press, 1961.

Cathcart, Kevin J. "The Idea of 'Rest' in the Old Testament: Reflections on a Neglected Theme in Biblical Studies." *PIBA* 40 (2017): 1–22.

Cathcart, Kevin, Michael Maher, and Martin McNamara, eds. *The Aramaic Bible: The Targum of Psalms*. Translated by David M. Stec. Liturgical Press, 2004.

Cavadini, John C. "Ideology and Solidarity in Augustine's *City of God*." In *Augustine's "City of God": A Critical Guide*, edited by James Wetzel, 93–110. Cambridge University Press, 2012.

Chavel, Simeon. "The Face of God and the Etiquette of Eye-Contact: Visitation, Pilgrimage, and Prophetic Vision in Ancient Israelite and Early Jewish Imagination." *JSQ* 19 (2012): 1–55.

Childs, Brevard S. *Biblical Theology of the Old and New Testaments: Theological Reflection on the Christian Bible*. Fortress, 1993.

Childs, Brevard S. *Exodus: A Critical, Theological Commentary*. OTL. Westminster, 1974.

Childs, Brevard S. *Isaiah: A Commentary*. OTL. Westminster John Knox, 2001.

Ciampa, Roy E., and Brian S. Rosner. *The First Letter to the Corinthians*. PNTC. Eerdmans, 2010.

Clines, D. J. A. "The Image of God in Man." *TynBul* 19 (1968): 53–103.

Collins, Raymond F. *First Corinthians*. SP 7. Liturgical Press, 1999.

Coloe, Mary L. *Dwelling in the Household of God: Johannine Ecclesiology and Spirituality*. Liturgical Press, 2007.

Coloe, Mary L. *God Dwells with Us: Temple Symbolism in the Fourth Gospel*. Liturgical Press, 2001.

Conn, Christopher. "Aquinas on Human Nature and the Possibility of Bodiless Existence." *NBf* 93 (2012): 324–38.

Cook, John Granger. *The Enspirited Body in 1 Corinthians 15*. WUNT 530. Mohr Siebeck, 2025.

Crouch, C. L. "Genesis 1:26–7 as a Statement of Humanity's Divine Parentage." *JTS* 61 (2010): 1–15.

Curtis, Edward Mason. "Man as the Image of God in Genesis in the Light of Ancient Near Eastern Parallels." PhD diss., University of Pennsylvania, 1984.

Daley, Brian E. "A Hope for Worms: Early Christian Hope." In *Resurrection: Theological and Scientific Assessments*, edited by Ted Peters et al., 136–64. Eerdmans, 2002.

Daley, Brian E. *The Hope of the Early Church: A Handbook of Patristic Eschatology*. Baker Academic, 2010.

Davies, W. D., and Dale C. Allison Jr. *A Critical and Exegetical Commentary on the Gospel According to Saint Matthew*. Vol. 1. ICC. T&T Clark, 1988.

Davison, Andrew. *Astrobiology and Christian Doctrine: Exploring the Implications of Life in the Universe*. Cambridge University Press, 2023.

Dillard, Peter. "Keeping the Vision: Aquinas and the Problem of Disembodied Beatitude." *NBf* 93 (2012): 397–411.

Doering, Lutz. "*Urzeit-Endzeit* in the Dead Sea Scrolls and Pseudepigrapha." In *Eschatologie—Eschatology: The Sixth Durham-Tübingen Research Symposium; Eschatology in Old Testament, Ancient Judaism and Early Christianity*, edited by Hans-Joachim Eckstein, Christof Landmesser, and Hermann Lichtenberger, 19–58. Mohr Siebeck, 2011.

Donovan, Mary Ann. "Alive to the Glory of God: A Key Insight in St. Irenaeus." *TS* 49 (1988): 283–97.

Eichrodt, Walther. *Ezekiel: A Commentary*. OTL. Westminster, 1970.

Engberg-Pedersen, Troels. *Cosmology and Self in the Apostle Paul: The Material Spirit*. Oxford University Press, 2010.

Engberg-Pedersen, Troels. *John and Philosophy: A New Reading of the Fourth Gospel*. Oxford University Press, 2017.

Enns, Peter E. "Creation and Re-Creation: Psalm 95 and Its Interpretation in Hebrews 3:1–4:13." *WTJ* 55 (1993): 255–80.

Farris, Joshua R. "An Immaterial Substance View: *Imago Dei* in Creation and Redemption." *Heythrop Journal* 58, no. 1 (2017): 108–23.

Fee, Gordon D. *The First Epistle to the Corinthians*. NICNT. Eerdmans, 1987.

Fee, Gordon D. *Paul's Letter to the Philippians*. NICNT. Eerdmans, 1995.

Feuillet, André. *Johannine Studies*. Translated by Thomas E. Crane. Alba House, 1965.

Filtvedt, Ole Jakob. "The Transcendence and Visibility of the Father in the Gospel of John." *ZNW* 108 (2017): 90–118.

Firmage, Edwin. "Genesis 1 and the Priestly Agenda." *JSOT* 24 (1999): 97–114.

Fitzmyer, Joseph A. *Romans: A New Translation with Introduction and Commentary*. AB 33. Doubleday, 1993.

Fletcher-Louis, Crispin. "God's Image, His Cosmic Temple, and the High Priest: Towards an Historical and Theological Account of the Incarnation." In *Heaven on Earth: The Temple in Biblical Theology*, edited by T. Desmond Alexander and Simon Gathercole, 81–99. Paternoster, 2004.

France, R. T. *The Gospel of Matthew*. NICNT. Eerdmans, 2007.

France, R. T. "The Writer of Hebrews as a Biblical Expositor." *TynBul* 47 (1996): 245–76.

Fredriksen, Paula. "Vile Bodies: Paul and Augustine on the Resurrection of the Flesh." In *Biblical Hermeneutics in Historical Perspective: Studies in Honor of Karlfried Froehlich on His Sixtieth Birthday*, edited by Mark S. Burrows and Paul Rorem, 75–87. Eerdmans, 1991.

Gaine, Simon Francis. "The Beatific Vision and the Heavenly Mediation of Christ." *TheoLogica* 2 (2018): 1–13.

Gaine, Simon Francis. *Did the Saviour See the Father? Christ, Salvation, and the Vision of God*. Bloomsbury, 2015.

Gaine, Simon Francis. "Resurrection and Eschatology." In *The New Cambridge Companion to Aquinas*, edited by Eleonore Stump and Thomas Joseph White, 361–80. Cambridge University Press, 2022.

Gaine, Simon Francis. "Thomas Aquinas, the Beatific Vision, and the Role of Christ: A Reply to Hans Boersma." *TheoLogica* 2 (2018): 148–67.

Gaine, Simon Francis. "Thomas Aquinas and John Owen on the Beatific Vision: A Reply to Suzanne McDonald." *NBf* 97 (2016): 432–46.

Gaventa, Beverly Roberts. *Romans: A Commentary*. NTL. Westminster John Knox, 2024.

Gendle, Nicholas. "St. Irenaeus as Mystical Theologian." *The Thomist* 39 (1975): 185–97.

Gieschen, Charles A. "The Divine Name as a Characteristic of Divine Identity in Second-Temple Judaism and Early Christianity." In *Monotheism and Christology in Greco-Roman Antiquity*, edited by Matthew V. Novenson, 61–84. Brill, 2020.

Goldingay, John. *Psalms 42–89*. BCOTWP. Baker Academic, 2007.

Goodacre, Mark. "How Empty Was the Tomb?" *JSNT* 44 (2021): 134–48.

Gorman, Michael J. *1 Corinthians: A Theological, Pastoral, and Missional Commentary*. Eerdmans, 2025.

Gorman, Michael J. *Paul and John in Harmony: A Theological and Historical Exploration*. Baker Academic, 2026.

Gray, Timothy C. *The Temple in the Gospel of Mark: A Study in Its Narrative Role*. WUNT 2.242. Mohr Siebeck, 2008.

Griffiths, Paul J. *Decreation: The Last Things of All Creatures*. Baylor University Press, 2014.

Gunkel, Hermann. *Schöpfung und Chaos in Endzeit und Urzeit: Eine Religionsgeschichtliche Untersuchung über Gen 1 und Ap Joh 12*. Vandenhoeck & Ruprecht, 1895.

Hanson, Anthony T. "The Treatment in the LXX of the Theme of Seeing God." In *Septuagint, Scrolls and Cognate Writings: Papers Presented to the International Symposium on the Septuagint and Its Relation to the Dead Sea Scrolls and Other Writings*, edited by George J. Brooke and Barnabas Lindars, 557–68. Scholars Press, 1992.

Harris, Steven Edward. *Refiguring Resurrection: A Biblical and Systematic Eschatology*. Baylor University Press, 2023.

Hart, Ian. "Genesis 1:1–2:3 as Prologue to the Book of Genesis." *TynBul* 46 (1995): 315–36.

Haydock, Nicholas. *Old Testament Theology and the Rest of God*. Wipf & Stock, 2016.

Heschel, Abraham Joshua. *The Sabbath: Its Meaning for Modern Man*. Farrar, Straus and Giroux, 2005.

Higgins, A. J. B. *The Lord's Supper in the New Testament*. SCM, 1952.

Hill, Charles E. *Regnum Caelorum: Patterns of Millennial Thought in Early Christianity*. 2nd ed. Eerdmans, 2001.

Hollander, Harm W. "Seeing God 'in a Riddle' or 'Face to Face': An Analysis of 1 Corinthians 13:12." *JSNT* 32 (2010): 395–403.

Hoskyns, Edwyn Clement. *The Fourth Gospel*. Edited by Francis Noel Davey. Faber and Faber, 1947.

Humbert, Paul. *Études sur le récit du paradis et de la chute dans la Genèse*. Secréteriat de L'Université, 1940.

Hütter, Reinhard. *Bound for Beatitude: A Thomistic Study in Eschatology and Ethics*. Catholic University of America Press, 2019.

Irwin, Luke. "Divine Visibility in the Gospel of John." *HTR* 117 (2024): 417–35.

Jacobsen, Anders-Chr. Lund. "The Philosophical Argument in the Teaching of Irenaeus on the Resurrection of the Flesh." In *Papers Presented at the Thirteenth International Conference on Patristic Studies Held in Oxford, 1999*, edited by Maurice Wiles et al., 256–61. Peeters, 2001.

Jeremias, Joachim. *The Eucharistic Words of Jesus*. Translated by Norman Perrin. SCM, 1966.

Jipp, Joshua W. *The Messianic Theology of the New Testament*. Eerdmans, 2020.

Johns, Laurentia. "Seeing Salvation: The Vision of St Irenaeus of Lyons." *DRev* 126 (2008): 263–84.

Kaiser, Walter C., Jr. "The Promise Theme and the Theology of Rest." *BSac* 130 (1973): 135–47.

Kearney, Peter J. "Creation and Liturgy: The P Redaction of Ex 25–40." *ZAW* 89 (1977): 375–87.

Kim, Daniel E. "Jewish and Christian Theology from the Hebrew Bible: The Concept of Rest and Temple in the Targumim, Hebrews, and the Old Testament." In *Hebrews in Contexts*, edited by Gabriella Gelardini and Harold W. Attridge, 31–46. Brill, 2016.

Kim, Seyoon, and F. F. Bruce. *1 & 2 Thessalonians*. 2nd ed. WBC 45. Zondervan, 2023.

Kloos, Kari. *Christ, Creation, and the Vision of God: Augustine's Transformation of Early Christian Theophany Interpretation*. BAC 7. Brill, 2011.

Kloos, Kari. "Seeing the Invisible God: Augustine's Reconfiguration of Theophany Narrative Exegesis." *AugStud* 36 (2005): 397–420.

Koester, Craig R. *Hebrews: A New Translation with Introduction and Commentary*. AB 36. Doubleday, 2001.

Koester, Craig R. *Revelation: A New Translation with Introduction and Commentary*. AB 38A. Yale University Press, 2014.

Krause, Katja. *Thomas Aquinas on Seeing God: The Beatific Vision in His "Commentary on Peter Lombard's Sentences" IV.49.2*. Marquette University Press, 2020.

Kromholtz, Bryan. *On the Last Day: The Time of the Resurrection of the Dead According to Thomas Aquinas*. Studia Friburgensia 110. Academic Press, 2010.

Kruse, Colin G. *The Letters of John*. PNTC. Apollos, 2000.

Kurz, Joel R. "The Gifts of Creation and the Consummation of Humanity: Irenaeus of Lyons' Recapitulatory Theology of the Eucharist." *Worship* 83 (2009): 112–32.

Kutsko, John F. *Between Heaven and Earth: Divine Presence and Absence in the Book of Ezekiel*. Eisenbrauns, 2000.

Kysar, Robert. "'As You Sent Me': Identity and Mission in the Fourth Gospel." *Word & World* 21 (2001): 370–76.

Laansma, Jon. *"I Will Give You Rest": The "Rest" Motif in the New Testament with Special Reference to Mt 11 and Heb 3–4*. WUNT 2.98. Mohr Siebeck, 1997.

Lagrange, Marie-Joseph. *The Meaning of Christianity According to Luther and His Followers in Germany*. Translated by W. S. Reilly. Longmans, Green, 1920.

Lanne, D. E. "La vision de Dieu dans l'oeuvre de saint Irénée." *Irenikon* 33 (1960): 311–20.

Lee, Chee-Chiew. "Rest and Victory in Revelation 14.13." *JSNT* 41 (2019): 344–62.

Leget, Carlo. *Living with God: Thomas Aquinas on the Relation Between Life on Earth and "Life" After Death*. Peeters, 1997.

Lehtipuu, Outi. "'Flesh and Blood Cannot Inherit the Kingdom of God': The Transformation of the Flesh in the Early Christian Debates Concerning Resurrection." In *Metamorphoses: Resurrection, Body and Transformative Practices in Early Christianity*, edited by Turid Karlsen Seim and Jorunn Økland, 147–68. De Gruyter, 2009.

Leim, Joshua E. *Matthew's Theological Grammar: The Father and the Son*. WUNT 2.402. Mohr Siebeck, 2015.

Leim, Joshua E. "Worshiping the Father, Worshiping the Son: Cultic Language and the Identity of God in the Gospel of Matthew." *JTI* 9 (2015): 65–84.

Leithart, Peter J. *The Priesthood of the Plebs: A Theology of Baptism*. Wipf & Stock, 2003.

Levenson, Jon D. *Creation and the Persistence of Evil: The Jewish Drama of Divine Omnipotence*. Princeton University Press, 1994.

Levenson, Jon D. *Israel's Day of Light and Joy: The Origin, Development, and Enduring Meaning of the Jewish Sabbath*. Eisenbrauns, 2024.

Levenson, Jon D. *Resurrection and the Restoration of Israel: The Ultimate Victory of the God of Life*. Yale University Press, 2006.

Levenson, Jon D. *Sinai and Zion: An Entry into the Jewish Bible*. Harper & Row, 1987.

Levenson, Jon D. *Theology of the Program of Restoration of Ezekiel 40–48*. Scholars Press, 1976.

Levering, Matthew. *Jesus and the Demise of Death: Resurrection, Afterlife, and the Fate of the Christian*. Baylor University Press, 2012.

Lewis, C. S. *Reflections on the Psalms*. Harcourt, Brace & World, 1958.

Lootens, Matthew R. "Augustine." In *The Spiritual Senses: Perceiving God in Western Christianity*, edited by Paul L. Gavrilyuk and Sarah Coakley, 56–70. Cambridge University Press, 2011.

Lossky, Vladimir. *The Vision of God*. Translated by Asheleigh Moorhouse. St. Vladimir's Seminary Press, 1983.

Macaskill, Grant. *Union with Christ in the New Testament*. Oxford University Press, 2013.

Mare, W. Harold. "Zion." *ABD* 6:1096–98.

Marshall, I. Howard. *The Epistles of John*. NICNT. Eerdmans, 1984.

Martin, Dale B. *The Corinthian Body*. Yale University Press, 1995.

Martin, Francis, and William M. Wright IV. *The Gospel of John*. CCSS. Baker Academic, 2015.

Mason, Eric F. *"You Are a Priest Forever": Second Temple Jewish Messianism and the Priestly Christology of the Epistle to the Hebrews*. STDJ 74. Brill, 2008.

Matera, Frank J. *Resurrection: The Origin and Goal of the Christian Life*. Liturgical Press, 2015.

Mauser, Ulrich. "God in Human Form." *ExAud* 16 (2000): 81–100.

McCord Adams, Marilyn. "Why Bodies as Well as Souls in the Life to Come?" In *The Science of Being as Being: Metaphysical Investigations*, edited by Gregory T. Doolan, 264–97. Studies in Philosophy and the History of Philosophy 55. Catholic University of America Press, 2012.

McDonald, Suzanne. "Beholding the Glory of God in the Face of Jesus Christ: John Owen and the 'Reforming' of the Beatific Vision." In *The Ashgate Research Companion to John Owen's Theology*, edited by Kelly M. Kapic and Mark Jones, 141–58. Ashgate, 2012.

McDowell, Catherine L. *The Image of God in the Garden of Eden: The Creation of Humankind in Genesis 2:5–3:24 in Light of the mīs pî pīt pî and wpt-r Rituals of Mesopotamia and Ancient Egypt*. Eisenbrauns, 2015.

McDowell, Catherine L. "'In the Image of God He Created Them': How Genesis 1:26–27 Defines the Divine-Human Relationship and Why It Matters." In *The Image of God in an Image Driven Age: Explorations in Theological Anthropology*, edited by Beth Felker Jones and Jeffrey W. Barbeau, 29–46. IVP Academic, 2016.

McGinn, Bernard. "Visions and Visualizations in the Here and Hereafter." *HTR* 98 (2005): 227–46.

McGlothlin, Thomas D. "Augustine's Resurrection Framework: Clarifying and Connecting Senses of 'Resurrection.'" *AugStud* 55 (2024): 25–42.

McGlothlin, Thomas D. *Resurrection as Salvation: Development and Conflict in Pre-Nicene Paulinism*. Cambridge University Press, 2018.

Meyendorff, John. *Byzantine Theology: Historical Trends and Doctrinal Themes*. Fordham University Press, 1987.

Middleton, J. Richard. "Image of God." In *The Oxford Encyclopedia of the Bible and Theology*, edited by Samuel E. Balentine et al., 2:516–23. Oxford University Press, 2015.

Middleton, J. Richard. *The Liberating Image: The Imago Dei in Genesis 1*. Brazos, 2005.

Middleton, J. Richard. "A New Earth Perspective." In *Four Views on Heaven*, edited by Michael Wittmer, 65–94. Zondervan, 2022.

Middleton, J. Richard. *A New Heaven and a New Earth: Reclaiming Biblical Eschatology*. Baker Academic, 2014.

Miles, Margaret. "Vision: The Eye of the Body and the Eye of the Mind in Saint Augustine's *De trinitate* and *Confessions*." *JR* 63 (1983): 125–42.

Moberly, R. W. L. "Anatomizing God?" *JTS* 75 (2024): 273–90.

Moffitt, David M. *Atonement and the Logic of Resurrection in the Epistle to the Hebrews*. Brill, 2011.

Moffitt, David M. "God Attested by Men: Echoes of Jonah and the Identification of Jesus with Israel's God in the Storm-Stilling Stories of Matthew's Gospel." In *A Scribe Trained for the Kingdom of Heaven: Essays on Christology and Ethics in Honor of Richard B. Hays*, edited by David M. Moffitt and Isaac Augustine Morales, 25–45. Lexington Books/Fortress Academic, 2021.

Moffitt, David M. *Rethinking the Atonement: New Perspectives on Jesus's Death, Resurrection, and Ascension*. Baker Academic, 2022.

Mollat, Donatien. *Études johanniques*. Éditions du Seuil, 1979.

Moloney, Francis J. *The Gospel of John*. Sacra Pagina. Liturgical Press, 1998.

Morales, Isaac Augustine. *The Bible and Baptism: The Fountain of Salvation*. CBTS. Baker Academic, 2022.

Morales, Isaac Augustine. "Genesis, the Threefold End of Human Beings, and Biblical Eschatology." *JTI* 13 (2019): 200–218.

Morales, Isaac Augustine. "Père Lagrange and the Criticism of Criticism: The Philosophical Underpinnings of Modern Biblical Scholarship." In *The Future of Catholic Biblical Interpretation: Marie-Joseph Lagrange and Beyond*, edited by James B. Prothro and Isaac Augustine Morales, 60–78. Eerdmans, 2024.

Morales, Isaac Augustine. "Washed, Sanctified, Justified: 1 Corinthians 6 and Baptismal Participation in Christ." In *A Scribe Trained for the Kingdom of Heaven:*

Essays on Christology and Ethics in Honor of Richard B. Hays, edited by David M. Moffitt and Isaac Augustine Morales, 91–108. Lexington Books/Fortress Academic, 2021.

Morales, Isaac Augustine. "'With My Body I Thee Worship': New Creation, Beatific Vision, and the Liturgical Consummation of All Things." *ProEccl* 25 (2016): 337–56.

Morales, L. Michael. *The Tabernacle Prefigured: Cosmic Mountain Ideology in Genesis and Exodus*. BTS 15. Peeters, 2012.

Morenz, Siegfried. *Egyptian Religion*. Translated by Ann E. Keep. Routledge, 2004.

Morrow, Jeffrey L. "Creation as Temple-Building and Work as Liturgy in Genesis 1–3." *Journal of the Orthodox Center for the Advancement of Biblical Studies* 2 (2009): 1–13.

Mowinckel, Sigmund. *Psalms Studies*. Vol. 1. Translated by Mark E. Biddle. SBL Press, 2014.

Mutschler, Bernhard. *Irenäus als johanneischer Theologe: Studien zur Schriftauslegung bei Irenäus von Lyon*. STAC 21. Mohr Siebeck, 2004.

Mutschler, Bernhard. "John and His Gospel in the Mirror of Irenaeus of Lyons: Perspectives of Recent Research." In *The Legacy of John: Second-Century Reception of the Fourth Gospel*, edited by Tuoma Rasimus, 319–43. Brill, 2010.

Mzebetshana, Mzayifani, and Annang Asumang. "Temple Christology in the Gospel According to John: A Survey of Scholarship in the Last Twenty Years (1996–2016)." *Conspectus* 24 (2017): 133–63.

Newsom, Carol A. "Angels (Old Testament)." *ABD* 1:248–53.

Nielsen, J. T. *Adam and Christ in the Theology of Irenaeus of Lyons: An Examination of the Function of the Adam-Christ Typology in the "Adversus Haereses" of Irenaeus, Against the Background of the Gnosticism of His Time*. Van Gorcum, 1968.

O'Callaghan, Paul. *Christ Our Hope: An Introduction to Eschatology*. Catholic University of America Press, 2011.

Orbe, Antonio. "Visión del Padre e incorruptela según san Ireneo." *Gregorianum* 64 (1983): 199–241.

O'Regan, Cyril. *Gnostic Return in Modernity*. State University of New York Press, 2001.

Ormerod, Neil. "'And We Shall See Him Face to Face': A Trinitarian Analysis of the Beatific Vision." *TS* 82 (2021): 646–62.

O'Rourke Boyle, Marjorie. "Irenaeus' Millennial Hope: A Polemical Weapon." *RTAM* 36 (1969): 5–16.

Ortiz, Jared. *"You Made Us for Yourself": Creation in St. Augustine's "Confessions."* Fortress, 2016.

Ortlund, Gavin. "Image of Adam, Son of God: Genesis 5:3 and Luke 3:38 in Intercanonical Dialogue." *JETS* 57 (2014): 673–88.

Osborn, Eric Francis. *Irenaeus of Lyons*. Cambridge University Press, 2001.

Painter, John. *1, 2, and 3 John*. SP 18. Liturgical Press, 2002.

Parkison, Samuel G. *To Gaze upon God: The Beatific Vision in Doctrine, Tradition, and Practice*. IVP Academic, 2024.

Parpola, Simo. *Letters from Assyrian and Babylonian Scholars*. Helsinki University Press, 1993.

Peppiatt, Lucy. *The Imago Dei: Humanity Made in the Image of God*. Cascade Books, 2022.

Peterson, Ryan S. *The Imago Dei as Human Identity: A Theological Interpretation*. JTISupp 14. Eisenbrauns, 2016.

Petry, Ray C. "The Social Character of Heavenly Beatitude According to the Thought of St. Thomas Aquinas." *The Thomist* 7 (1944): 65–79.

Pfleiderer, Otto. *Paulinism: A Contribution to the History of Primitive Christian Theology*. Vol. 1, *Exposition of Paul's Doctrine*. Translated by E. Peters. London: Williams & Norgate, 1877.

Pierce, Alexander H. "Augustine's Eschatological Vision: The Dynamism of Seeing and Seeking God in Heaven." *ProEccl* 29 (2020): 217–38.

Pinckaers, Servais. *The Sources of Christian Ethics*. Translated by Sr. Mary Thomas Noble. Catholic University of America Press, 1995.

Pitre, Brant. *Jesus and the Last Supper*. Eerdmans, 2015.

Proctor, John. "Fire in God's House: Influence of Malachi 3 in the NT." *JETS* 36 (1993): 9–14.

Provan, Iain W. "To Highlight All Our Idols: Worshipping God in Nietzsche's World." *ExAud* 15 (1999): 19–38.

Rabens, Volker. *The Holy Spirit and Ethics in Paul: Transformation and Empowering for Religious-Ethical Life*. 2nd rev. ed. Fortress, 2014.

Rákos-Zichy, Johanna. "The Resurrection Body in Augustine." In *Papers Presented at the Seventeenth International Conference on Patristic Studies Held in Oxford 2015*, edited by Markus Vinzent, 373–84. Studia Patristica 98. Peeters, 2017.

Ratzinger, Joseph. "Biblical Interpretation in Crisis: On the Question of the Foundations and Approaches of Exegesis Today." In *Biblical Interpretation in Crisis: The Ratzinger Conference on Bible and Church*, edited by Richard John Neuhaus, 1–23. Eerdmans, 1989.

Ratzinger, Joseph. *Eschatology: Death and Eternal Life*. Translated by Michael Waldstein. 2nd ed. Dogmatic Theology 9. Catholic University of America Press, 2007.

Ratzinger, Joseph. *The Spirit of the Liturgy*. Translated by John Saward. Ignatius, 2000.

Reisenauer, Augustine M. *Augustine's Theology of the Resurrection*. Cambridge University Press, 2023.

Robinson, Gnana. "The Idea of Rest in the Old Testament and the Search for the Basic Character of the Sabbath." *ZAW* 92 (1980): 32–42.

Robinson, Marilynne. *Gilead*. Farrar, Straus and Giroux, 2004.

Root, Michael. "The Christological Character of the Beatific Vision: Hans Boersma's *Seeing God*." *The Thomist* 84 (2020): 127–51.

Roth, Wolfgang. "The Deuteronomic Rest Theology: A Redaction-Critical Study." *BR* 21 (1976): 5–14.

Rowe, C. Kavin. "Becoming Human: Deification in the Image of Christ." *IJST* 25 (2023): 39–46.

Sankamo, Juho. "Rival Visions of the Eschatological Temple of Jerusalem." In *Understanding the Spiritual Meaning of Jerusalem in Three Abrahamic Religions*, edited by Antti Laato, 85–100. SCA 6. Brill, 2019.

Sawyer, J. F. A. "The Image of God, the Wisdom of Serpents, and the Knowledge of Good and Evil." In *A Walk in the Garden: Biblical, Iconographical and Literary Images of Eden*, edited by Paul Morris and Deborah Sawyer, 64–73. LHBOTS. JSOT Press, 1993.

Schmaus, Michael. *Dogma 6: Justification and the Last Things*. Sheed & Ward, 1977.

Schnackenburg, Rudolf. *The Gospel According to St. John*. Translated by Kevin Smyth. 3 vols. Burns & Oates, 1968–82.

Schneider, Johannes. *Das Evangelium nach Johannes*. THKNT. Evangelische Verlagsanstalt, 1976.

Schneiders, Sandra M. *Jesus Risen in Our Midst: Essays on the Resurrection of Jesus in the Fourth Gospel*. Liturgical Press, 2013.

Schrage, Wolfgang. *Der erste Brief an die Korinther*. 4 vols. EKKNT. Benziger, 1991–2001.

Scroggs, Robin. *The Last Adam: A Study in Pauline Anthropology*. Blackwell, 1966.

Selman, Martin J. "The Kingdom of God in the Old Testament." *TynBul* 40 (1989): 161–83.

Slusser, Michael. "The Heart of Irenaeus's Theology." In *Irenaeus: Life, Scripture, and Legacy*, edited by Sara Parvis and Paul Foster, 133–39. Fortress, 2012.

Smith, Dain Alexander. "Reflecting Ancient Ethics: Reconsidering the Mirror Metaphor in 1 Cor 13:12." *NovT* 64 (2022): 291–317.

Smith, Gary V. "The Concept of God/the Gods as King in the Ancient Near East and the Bible." *TJ* 3 (1982): 18–38.

Smith, Mark S. *The Priestly Vision of Genesis 1*. Augsburg Fortress, 2009.

Smith, Mark S. "'Seeing God' in the Psalms: The Background to the Beatific Vision in the Hebrew Bible." *CBQ* 50 (1988): 171–83.

Steenberg, Matthew C. *Irenaeus on Creation: The Cosmic Christ and the Saga of Redemption*. VCSupp 91. Brill, 2008.

Steenberg, Matthew C. *Of God and Man: Theology as Anthropology from Irenaeus to Athanasius*. T&T Clark, 2009.

Strand, Vincent L. "Seeing Christ, Seeing the Trinity: Beyond Boersma's Trinitarian Deficit." *IJST* 26 (2024): 409–28.

Strawbridge, Jennifer R. "How the Body of Lazarus Helps to Solve a Pauline Problem." *NTS* 63 (2017): 588–603.

Strecker, Georg. *The Johannine Letters: A Commentary on 1, 2, and 3 John*. Translated by Linda M. Maloney. Hermeneia. Fortress, 1996.

ten Klooster, Anton. *Thomas Aquinas on the Beatitudes: Reading Matthew, Disputing Grace and Virtue, Preaching Happiness*. Peeters, 2018.

Teresa of Ávila. *The Collected Works of St. Teresa of Avila*. Vol. 3. Translated by Kieran Kavanaugh and Otilio Rodriguez. ICS Publications, 1985.

Teske, Roland J. "St. Augustine and the Vision of God." In *Augustine of Hippo: Philosopher, Exegete, and Theologian*, 145–66. Marquette University Press, 2009.

Thiel, John E. *Icons of Hope: The "Last Things" in Catholic Imagination*. University of Notre Dame Press, 2013.

Thiessen, Matthew. "Hebrews and the End of the Exodus." *NovT* 49 (2007): 353–69.

Thiessen, Matthew. *A Jewish Paul: The Messiah's Herald to the Gentiles*. Baker Academic, 2023.

Thompson, Marianne Meye. *John: A Commentary*. NTL. Westminster John Knox, 2015.

Toom, Tarmo. "*Totus Homo*: Augustine on Resurrection." In *Resurrection and Responsibility: Essays on Theology, Scripture, and Ethics in Honor of Thorwald Lorenzen*, edited by Keith D. Dyer and David J. Neville, 59–75. Pickwick, 2009.

Tournay, Raymond Jacques. *Seeing and Hearing God with the Psalms: The Prophetic Liturgy of the Second Temple in Jerusalem*. JSOT Press, 1991.

Van Dyke, Christina. "Human Identity, Imminent Causal Relations, and the Principle of Non-Repeatability: Thomas Aquinas on the Bodily Resurrection." *RelS* 43 (2007): 373–94.

Van Fleteren, Frederick. "Augustine and *Corpus Spirituale*." *AugStud* 38 (2007): 333–52.

Van Fleteren, Frederick. "Augustine and the Resurrection." *SMC* 12 (1978): 9–15.

von Rad, Gerhard. "There Remains Still a Rest for the People of God: An Investigation of a Biblical Conception." In *The Problem of the Hexateuch and Other Essays*, translated by E. W. Trueman Dicken, 94–102. Oliver & Boyd, 1965.

Waddell, Michael M. "Aquinas on the Light of Glory." *Tópicos* 40 (2011): 105–32.

Walton, John H. "Genesis 1:1–2:3 and the Ancient Near East: Order out of Disorder After *Chaoskampf*." *CTJ* 43 (2008): 48–63.

Wanamaker, Charles A. *The Epistles to the Thessalonians: A Commentary on the Greek Text*. NIGTC. Eerdmans, 1990.

Ware, James P. *The Final Triumph of God: Jesus, the Eyewitnesses, and the Resurrection of the Body in 1 Corinthians 15*. Eerdmans, 2025.

Ware, James P. "Paul's Understanding of the Resurrection in 1 Corinthians 15:36–54." *JBL* 133 (2014): 809–35.

Ware, James P. "The Resurrection of Jesus in the Pre-Pauline Formula of 1 Cor 15.3–5." *NTS* 60 (2014): 475–98.

Weinfeld, Moshe. "Sabbath, Temple, and the Enthronement of the Lord—The Problem of the Sitz im Leben of Genesis 1:1–2:3." In *Mélanges bibliques et orientaux en l'honneur de M. Henri Cazelles*, edited by A. Caquot and M. Delcor, 501–12. Neukirchener, 1981.

Wenham, Gordon J. "Sanctuary Symbolism in the Garden of Eden Story." In *I Studied Inscriptions from Before the Flood: Ancient Near Eastern, Literary, and Linguistic Approaches to Genesis 1–11*, edited by Richard S. Hess and David Toshio Tsumura, 399–404. Eisenbrauns, 1994.

Wessner, Mark D. "Toward a Literary Understanding of 'Face to Face' (פָּנִים אֶל־פָּנִים) in Genesis 32:23–32." *ResQ* 42 (2000): 169–77.

Wessner, Mark D. "Toward a Literary Understanding of Moses and the Lord 'Face to Face' (פָּנִים אֶל־פָּנִים) in Exodus 33:7–11." *ResQ* 44 (2002): 109–16.

Westermann, Claus. *Genesis 1–11: A Continental Commentary*. Translated by John J. Scullion. Fortress, 1994.

Westermann, Claus. *Genesis 12–36: A Commentary*. Translated by John J. Scullion. Augsburg, 1985.

Wildberger, Hans. "Das Abbild Gottes: Gen 1:26–30." *TZ* 21 (1965): 245–59.

Wildberger, Hans. *Isaiah 1–12: A Continental Commentary*. Translated by Thomas H. Trapp. Fortress, 1991.

Wildberger, Hans. *Isaiah 13–27: A Continental Commentary*. Translated by Thomas H. Trapp. Fortress, 1997.

Wilken, Robert Louis. *The Spirit of Early Christian Thought: Seeking the Face of God*. Yale University Press, 2003.

Williams, Michael Allen. *Rethinking "Gnosticism": An Argument for Dismantling a Dubious Category*. Princeton University Press, 2001.

Williamson, Peter S. *Revelation*. CCSS. Baker Academic, 2015.

Wilson, Ian. "'Face to Face' with God: Another Look." *ResQ* 51 (2009): 107–14.

Wolfe, Judith. *The Theological Imagination: Perception and Interpretation in Life, Art, and Faith*. Cambridge University Press, 2024.

Wright, N. T. *God's Homecoming: The Forgotten Promise of Future Renewal*. HarperOne, 2026.

Wright, N. T. *History and Eschatology: Jesus and the Promise of Natural Theology*. Baylor University, 2019.

Wright, N. T. *The Resurrection of the Son of God*. Fortress, 2003.

Wright, N. T. *Surprised by Hope: Rethinking Heaven, the Resurrection, and the Mission of the Church*. HarperOne, 2008.

Wright, William. *The Lord's Prayer: Matthew 6 and Luke 11 for the Life of the Church*. Touchstone Texts. Baker Academic, 2023.

Zacharias, H. Daniel. *Matthew's Presentation of the Son of David*. Bloomsbury T&T Clark, 2017.

Zimmerli, Walther. *Ezekiel: A Commentary on the Book of the Prophet Ezekiel*. Vol. 2. Translated by James D. Martin. Hermeneia. Fortress, 1983.

Zimmermann, Ruben. "Nuptial Imagery in the Revelation of John." *Biblica* 84 (2003): 153–83.

Subject Index

Author Index

Scripture and Other Ancient Sources Index

Old Testament

Genesis

Exodus

2 Chronicles

Psalms

Proverbs

Ecclesiastes

Isaiah